BAD
BOY

BAD BOY

THE LIFE AND POLITICS OF LEE ATWATER

John Brady

The things we admire in men, kindness and generosity,
openness, honesty, understanding and feeling are the
concomitants of failure in our system. And those traits
we detest — sharpness, greed, acquisitiveness, meanness,
egotism and self-interest — are the traits of success. And
while men admire the quality of the first, they love the
produce of the second.
— John Steinbeck, *Cannery Row*

ADDISON WESLEY PUBLISHING COMPANY, INC.
Reading, Massachusetts Menlo Park, California New York
Don Mills, Ontario Harlow, England Amsterdam Bonn
Sydney Singapore Tokyo Madrid San Juan
Paris Seoul Milan Mexico City Taipei

Many of the designations used by manufacturers and sellers to distinguish their products are claimed as trademarks. Where those designations appear in this book and Addison-Wesley was aware of a trademark claim, the designations have been printed in initial capital letters (e.g., Tabasco).

Library of Congress Cataloging-in-Publication Data

Brady, John Joseph, 1942–
    Bad boy : the life & politics of Lee Atwater / John Brady.
        p.   cm.
    Includes index.
    ISBN 0-201-62733-7
    1. Atwater, Lee.   2. Political consultants—United States—
Biography.   3. Republican Party (U.S. : 1854–)—Biography.
4. United States—Politics and government—1981–1989.   5. United
States—Politics and government—1989–1993.   I. Title.
E840.8.A89B73   1996
324.2734′092—dc20   96-42205
[B]   CIP

Unless otherwise noted, the photographs in this book are reprinted from the Atwater family archives. The author has identified and contacted the photographers wherever possible, and extends thanks to those whom he could not locate.

Jacket photograph by Lou Salvatori
Jacket design by Suzanne Heiser
Author's photograph by Steve Marsel
Set in 11-point Electra by Pagesetters

1 2 3 4 5 6 7 8 9-MA-99989796
First printing, December 1996

For Linde

See what you started?

Contents

Preface

This book began in August of 1992 when my teenage daughter Linde and I were driving from Boston to Freeport, Maine, to do some shopping at L.L. Bean. It was a summer of presidential politics, and we were listening to radio talk shows discuss the fitful campaign of George Bush, whose summer home we passed that afternoon as we drove along the coast. "Where is Lee Atwater now that George *really* needs him?" asked one radio commentator.

My daughter turned to me. "Who *was* Lee Atwater?" she asked.

I told her what I could remember, which wasn't much. The next day I looked for a book about him in our town library. There was none. I began to read about the man, and make phone calls to people in his life. What began as a simple inquiry soon turned into a book of my own. Although Lee Atwater is mentioned in numerous books about southern politics and the Reagan and Bush years, there is much that the press missed or got wrong. The man was always spinning, ever the maelstrom of conservatism and controversy.

He was a man of many passions. He loved dry rib barbecue and junk food, he was obsessed with women, he played the guitar with a vengeance, he thrived on Tabasco sauce and had an unquenchable curiosity about how beat the heart of the boomer generation. But the one thing he loved more than anything else was politics.

"Lee Atwater did not invent the campaign consultancy business," the *New York Times* reported in a 1989 profile of the chairman of the Republican National Committee, "but he may be the person most responsible for the way it's practiced today." Atwater didn't mind winning ugly, even if it meant using the politics of division. Even before the '88 presidential campaign — during which he vowed to turn an escaped murderer named Willie Horton into Michael Dukakis's running mate — Lee Atwater had established himself as the master of negative campaigning, of winning by attacking opponents on such "wedge" or "values" issues as crime, gun control, taxes, national defense, abortion, and school prayer.

Lee brought an intensity to his task as campaign manager that had never been seen before. "The contest, the winning and losing thing is big for me," said Atwater, sounding a bit like his client George Bush. Neither was above stooping to conquer. "I can't stand to lose," Atwater confessed. "I lost a congressional race in Texas, and, man, I had the dry heaves for two days. I'm not ashamed of it. It's right healthy to be a poor loser in this business."

Lee Atwater was more than a successful political operative: He was a celebrity. He made it cool to be a Republican. The first baby-boom politician who was really *of* the baby boom, he was idolized and vilified. He was called mischievous, fiercely competitive, driven, focused, combustible, spontaneous, instinctive, smart, simple, complicated, both generous and ruthless to a fault. He ran fifty miles a week, no matter what the weather, no matter what the distractions. He was a partner in a Washington barbecue restaurant. He turned down a role in a Chuck Norris film. He owned a dozen guitars, including a beloved Stratocaster presented to him by Ron Wood of the Stones. He recorded a blues album with B. B. King that received a Grammy nomination, featuring a signature song called — what else? — "Bad Boy." A record was cut *about* him — a blues salute called *Black Like Lee*. As Republican National Committee chairman he posed for an *Esquire* portrait with his running pants down at his ankles.

In his last dark year, battling a brain tumor, Atwater lost his strength, his power — but not the desire to control his image, even while dying. He declared that he had found Jesus, and he used a personal testament in *Life* magazine to become a political Scrooge, renouncing the decade he had helped make possible. "My illness helped me to see that what was missing in society is what was missing in me: a little heart, a lot of brotherhood," he said. "The '80s were about acquiring — acquiring wealth, power, prestige. I know I acquired more wealth, power, and prestige than most. But you can acquire all you want and still feel empty. What power wouldn't I trade for a little more time with my family? What price wouldn't I pay for an evening with friends? It took a deadly illness to put me eye to eye with that truth, but it is a truth that the country, caught up in its ruthless ambitions and moral decay, can learn on my dime. I don't know who will lead us through the '90s, but they must be made to speak to this spiritual vacuum at the heart of American society, this tumor of the soul."

Lee Atwater died early on the Friday morning of March 29, 1991, as rain began to fall on the city of Washington. "My campaign-honed strategies of political warfare were simply no match for this dogged opponent," he had reflected in *Life* magazine. "Cancer is no Democrat."

Beyond my daughter's inquiry — who *was* Lee Atwater? — I have tried to come to terms with a more critical question: What did Lee Atwater *mean*? He is remembered mostly for the rise of mean politics. But he was also an early force in the rise of media politics, the conflation of politics and pop culture, and the use of shock TV techniques. He was pivotal in the repositioning of the Republican Party in the South, the first step in the process of building a national Republican majority, which he predicted would be accomplished by the year 2000. How right he was.

Although this is not a treatise of political science, I hope this book belongs on the shelf with other biographies of the political age, for Lee Atwater was like a reverse mirror to Mark Rudd, Bernadine Dohrn, and others from the student rebellions of the '60s and early '70s. He was about the same age, but southern, not northern; conservative, not liberal; low white collar, not high white cravat; and he was modestly educated by Ivy League standards. Yet he shaped the politics of his age as much as any of his counterparts did. To follow his meteoric career is to chart the rise and fall of the Republican Party over the past twenty years.

As Emerson put it, a biographer writes "to tell the truth truly." The risk in doing a biography of Lee Atwater is succumbing to his own hype. Nothing pleases a political operative more than manipulating the media and distorting the perceptions of history's first draft. How does one separate Lee's real self from the version he spun for media consumption? In doing research for *Bad Boy*, I found that numerous newspaper and magazine clips, even some books chronicling political campaigns, were often unreliable.

Lee Atwater was neither devil nor angel. My job as biographer meant protecting the reader from not only the barbs of Lee's enemies, but also from the adoration of his friends. Lee was surrounded by many people, yet he compartmentalized nearly everyone. Very few of his confidants crossed from one compartment to another. "I don't think anybody knew the whole of Lee," said Mary Matalin, herself a master of spincraft, "and I doubt that even he knew the whole of himself." The reporting in this book is based for the most part on interviews with those who knew Lee best when he wasn't "on": members of his family, schoolmates, colleagues at work and after hours, lovers, enemies, and, yes, members of the media who were willing to discuss Lee in full candor, looking back in tranquility on his busy life. Ultimately I spoke with over two hundred sources.

Though I had the cooperation of Lee's family, Toddy and Sally Atwater imposed no limitations on me; occasionally, they opened doors or pointed me in other directions when they were unable to answer all of my questions. I spoke with numerous sources several times, often months or years apart, visiting and revisiting the past for all the particulars. Some sources had letters, journals, notebooks, memos, pictures, videotapes. I was given access to Lee's schedule books for most of his Washington years; unlike most operatives, Lee kept meticulous records of his crowded schedule, usually done in pencil and updated at the end of each day by a series of secretaries who saved Lee from his own bad habits. I also obtained copies of Lee's unfinished doctoral dissertation and his master's degree "work project" at the University of South Carolina.

To document the last months of Lee's life, I was given access to his medical records at George Washington University Medical Center. I also discovered transcript versions of memoirs that Lee dictated in those months, largely unreliable for their rambling nature, high spin quotient, and cosmetic touches by colleagues to whom Lee entrusted them for editing.

I have endeavored to give credit where credit is due to print sources within the text. Quotations and dialogue come from either

participants in or witnesses to conversations; or from tape recordings, notes, memos, or diaries written after the conversations
occurred. I have also used quotes from press coverage of public events, along with videotapes and audio recordings of private
events. Quotes from press conferences and public events were
taken from multiple sources, often blended together, to avoid
depending on a single reporter's point of view.

There were a number of sources — not listed with the
"Sources and Acknowledgments" at the back of this book — who
spoke to me on the condition of confidentiality. Insofar as was possible, I verified such information using other sources; thus I was
able to arrive at accuracy by consensus.

On his deathbed, Lee made tape recordings to explore the
midnight of his mind with personal observations, prayers, political business, and commentary on people and events of the day. A
number of these tapes were made available to me by sources to
whom Lee entrusted them. "I hope I'm not going to be out of work
after this book is in print," one source told me.

"I'm just trying to tell the true story of Lee Atwater," I
explained.

"It's that true part that worries me," the source replied.

• • •

This is the story of what made Lee Atwater run.

John Brady

Prologue

Columbia, South Carolina
April 1, 1991

The godfather of politics was dead. His funeral was supposed to be as private as such affairs can be. No press. Only Lee Bandy of *The State*. They wanted Strom, of course. Then someone said Jim Baker was going to have a plane. The cabinet secretaries wanted to come. Bob Mosbacher was in Japan, but his wife would be able to attend. It grew. Sally felt they couldn't say no to anyone. Vice President Dan Quayle would attend, so the Marriott became a planning area, and the funeral became a national political event, complete with Secret Service. Mary Matalin made sure that anybody who was somebody got VIP seating. Many came with their contingents. Dick Cheney, back from the Gulf War, had a military escort. Limos had to be brought in from Tennessee so that there would be enough vehicles for some of the most powerful people in the world, all coming at four o'clock on this particular day to Trinity Cathedral, across from the state capitol in the heart of Columbia, South Carolina, to pay respect to the memory of Lee Atwater.

"Politics wasn't Lee Atwater's career," said Dan Quayle in his eulogy. "It was his calling." The consummate political handler was doubtless in heaven now, "where I'm sure Lee has already launched an absentee voter–registration drive."

Atwater, the world's leading stand-up Republican, would

have liked the light touch. And the timing: death on Good Friday, the day that Christ died, with burial on April Fool's Day. An exquisite contrast. "He came to Washington as a young punk and died a respected legend," said Ron Kaufman, Lee's co-conspirator in political mischief during the '88 presidential campaign. "A huge growth spurt there."

By the time Lee Atwater expired, his last year had become a grotesque tale of death in Washington, inspiring more disbelief than pity, closely followed by a swirl of delicious rumors. Rumors of a conversion to Catholicism. Rumors of an attempt to divorce Sally. Rumors of letters written to Mike Dukakis, apologies all around.

Harry Dent, one of Lee's earliest political mentors who had since become a preacher, said that Lee didn't apologize; he repented. And although he had climbed the political heights, sitting at the right hand of the president in Washington D.C., Lee had never really left Columbia. "A lot of Washington types live in the Beltway and become lost in that little reality up there," said Richard Quinn, who worked with Lee on some of his early campaigns. "Lee never did that. He always came back to South Carolina and jogged these streets, hung out in bars here, Waffle Houses, American Legion posts. Lee never lost the common touch, the gift for figuring out — maybe just a few weeks or months before others — what was on people's minds, what they would respond to, and translating that into a campaign strategy, coming up with a kind of simple theme that would really catch fire."

To create rapport, Lee gave jobs to thousands over the years. He saw rewarding loyalty as an obligation, and he pursued it over building intimacy. He populated his life with many people who became useful to him . . . and vice versa. "He probably didn't have five friends in Washington," said Charlie Black, a senior partner at the consulting firm where Lee once had an office, Black Manifort Stone. Charlie was like a big brother, someone Lee went to for counsel. When finances crunched, or when Sally panicked, Lee called Charlie, who would resolve the crunch or talk to Sally and calm her down. Charlie was damage control.

Friends could be two-way streets, useful give-and-get relationships. Roger Stone, another partner at the firm, was fun, Lee's cohort in crime. Roger was not Columbia: He liked expensive suits, palled around with Donald Trump and the jet set. But he whiled away many comfortable hours with Lee, watching movies, helping him unwind. Friends could be acolytes, upcoming politicos like Mary Matalin, who studied Lee, read whatever he read, intent on becoming the next Lee Atwater.

Or friends could be just facts of life — people who were *there*. Jim Pinkerton was there for mental stimulation. Lee liked commentary on news, culture, anything. Pink was his resident commentator, extremely well read — "six foot nine, with a thirty-pound brain," Lee liked to say. Working with Pink was like having a human encyclopedia at his fingertips. Ed Rogers was the younger brother to whom Lee handed off all the mechanical follow-through that was so crucial to establishing credibility. Pinkerton and Rogers were allies, and served as pallbearers, along with Jim McCabe, Warren Tompkins, Mike Ussery, Ned Tupper, David Yon, and Steve Chase — all school and fraternity buddies Lee never forgot as he became one of Washington's brightest political stars.

James Brown was there — Lee's idol — walking down the center aisle, wearing a light striped suit with a black shirt and a white tie. "Of all the people here, Lee would be proudest to see *you*," Lee's sister Anne told the godfather of soul.

Strom Thurmond was a mentor who remembered Atwater in glory: "He had been such a vibrant, wide-awake, alert man. And then to see him almost helpless, that was very pitiful. It really stirred my heart. On the other hand, he knew his condition, he realized what was going to happen, and he stood it like a man and fought to the last."

Governor Carroll Campbell was another mentor. On this particular morning, he arose early to rewrite the eulogy, then practiced reading it to a staffer, and choked up. "During the years I watched Lee grow as a person as well as a politician," he said. "Over the last year, during the most important campaign he ever ran, Lee may have grown the most. He won that campaign. Lee won peace with himself, peace with his fellow man, and peace with his God. He was a winner." Lee would have loved that one, too.

Lee was not star husband material. He wasn't there to help with the kids. Still, life in Sally Atwater's eyes had been just fine. She didn't complain. Lee would talk about how tough she was, wearing a combination of armor and moral courage. He had seen her cry but once — when her father died. Long ago Sally had developed her own methods for rearing a family in the hard-nosed world of politics. Beneath her calm exterior was a pragmatism not unlike Lee's. She too had learned to play dumb and just keep movin'. Lee ran around, did what he wanted to do, and when something visible was required — a White House dinner, a political trip — she was front and center. He liked the behind-the-scenes sense of power; she liked the political see-and-be-seen glitter and glamour. The past year had changed all of that. One day at a time became her philosophy. She now saw politics and the drive for power as frivolous gestures.

In the front row of the church, Toddy Atwater felt a strange mixture of grief and emotional fatigue. Thirty-five years earlier she and Harvey had buried their other son, Joe, but that ordeal had not prepared them for Lee's brain tumor. Lee's enemies could not have wished a worse death on him, thought Toddy. Over the last thirteen months she had seen a grotesque distortion of the son she thought she knew better than anyone in the world. Her husband, Harvey, in the final round of his own battle with cancer, would die six weeks later.

Friends, mentors, wife, mother: All here. Everyone but the president. The man Atwater had put in the White House. Where was George Bush?

Well, everyone would have had to be metal-detectored. And he had visited Lee both at the hospital and at home. His office said he would attend a memorial service in D.C. later that week, though he wouldn't speak at it. For George Bush, Lee had been the young shining star, the best political operative out there. After meeting with all of their advisers when planning for the '88 campaign, George and Bar had decided this was the guy to go with. It was an intense few years. But it was just a few years. After the victory they rewarded Lee, gave him the job he wanted. Bush jogged with him, grew fond of him. But Bush's world was huge — his personal address book included binders full of single-spaced, typed addresses maintained by two staffers — and was Lee among the inner Bush circle? No.

Ironic. Lee had gone to work for Bush because it seemed like the right career move, but he became devoted to the man. The month that Lee died, Bush was 91 percent in the polls and was no longer listening to his dying political adviser. If there had been another Lee, he would have told the president, "You need to be seen at this funeral. Everyone else is going to be there." But Bush lacked good political advisers at this juncture. He was off in the Florida Keys angling for bonefish. Not prudent. Thereafter, an amazingly swift fall.

The guys in South Carolina had handled all funeral details but two. Sally had decided where the plot would be and what clothing Lee would wear. The Atwaters had never really discussed funeral particulars. With his blues album clutched to his chest, the bad boy of American politics was buried wearing a blue jogging suit and gray running shoes. In the casket, Sally put a picture of the girls — a Christmas card photo from the previous year — but no picture of herself.

In Washington, Brooke Vosburgh, Lee's personal assistant during the Republican National Committee years, went to Lee's favorite spot along the Tow Path, where he liked to run and think through problems in the glory days, and where he'd go and sit in his wheelchair in his final months of pain. She sat there alone now, at the moment he was being buried, feeling closer to Lee than she would have had she attended the funeral with all of Lee's allies. They could banish her, she thought, but they could never change reality.

From the church, police cars blocked off side streets for two or three miles along the route to the cemetery. A city mourned. Black limousines, snaking through downtrodden neighborhoods. Blacks came out of shops, stood along the streets, hats off and arms across the heart. Lee loved a crowd, especially one that thought he was great. He loved entering a room and having people come up, want to talk with him, sit next to him. He loved attention.

After the graveside ceremony, Sally changed into sweats and went to party at Bullwinkle's, where Lee's gang of political cronies and down-home good ol' boys were drinking longneck Buds. Ed Rollins was in the midst of it all. "No one would have been prouder of his funeral than Lee," he would later reflect. "It was a great staged show. I just hope in the end he found the real peace that he was searching for. I'm not sure he did."

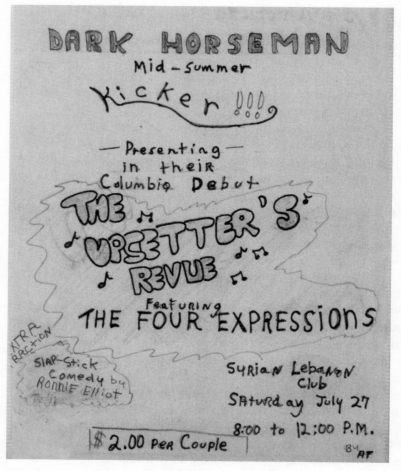

This handwritten poster announced the first gig of Lee Atwater's first band, sponsored by the Dark Horseman, his high-school fraternity. Lee kept this page in a scrapbook he titled "Lee Atwater's Public Life Through Age 20."

1

DEFINING EVENTS

Knowledge of human nature is the beginning and end
of political education.
— Henry Adams, *The Education of Henry Adams*

If Lee Atwater learned one thing during his brief but crowded lifetime, it was how to handle the media. He used the same manipulative skills to orchestrate press coverage as he had applied to developing as a musician over the years. The spin doctor was always in. Even when a reporter had done a little homework, which was surprisingly rare, and tried to get "up close and personal," Atwater knew how to change the topic or cut things short. Magazine writers could be a problem, of course. They usually wanted to hang out for a day or two, and it could be tough to avoid the personal stuff. Even then, if his brother Joe ever came up, Lee made light of the accident that had happened when he was a youngster, as though he barely remembered it. Hardly meant a thing at all. Then he'd put on that tough, bad-boy demeanor that the press gobbled up. "I think I learned pretty early that in the end it's only you," he once reflected stoically. "To an extent, you're all alone." But Joe never left Lee alone for long.

Lee liked to say that a winning campaign was marked by a series of defining events along the path to victory. Events that define *who we are*. If life is like a campaign, the defining event for Lee Atwater occurred in the kitchen of a little house in Aiken, South Carolina, on the Tuesday afternoon of October 5, 1956. Toddy Atwater had been struggling all week with a sinus infection, and that day she had inhaled a bunch of fumes as she stripped paint from an old iron bed. A splitting headache — and where was Harvey? In eight years of marriage, he had never been late for dinner. Not once. And now the kids were starting to bounce, especially Lee, so wiry and impatient. "Where's Daddy?" he asked.

Harvey Atwater, known for his punctuality, was listening to a late-arriving client drone on. Normally, Harvey left his office at the insurance company by five-thirty, and he'd be walking through the door to Toddy and the boys by now. But he didn't know the man well enough to cut him short, so he decided to wait him out. It was nearly six o'clock. A half hour late.

Toddy thought Harvey might have had trouble with his car, another in a line of junk heaps. "Let's make some donuts while we're waiting for Daddy," she said to the boys. Lee drifted into the living room to watch TV. Joe began to snoop around the stove.

How different the boys were, thought Toddy. Even though she often dressed them alike, they differed both physically and temperamentally. Lee, who would be six in February, was blond with a crewcut, all hard and wiry, tightly wound, impatience on wheels. Joe, at three, was more soft and cuddly, with brown curly hair, rounded cheeks, and a gentle disposition. The only thing the two had in common was striking blue eyes, and a brotherly bond that was starting to surface. "I've got me a playmate for the rest of my life!" Lee had announced to his parents a few weeks earlier. Lee worshipped his little brother. But Joe was star-crossed. Harvey and Toddy had already had a premonition that something was going to happen to the child. In the spring of that year he had nearly died after an awful bout with the measles. Then, during a spring storm, Joe had been sitting in front of a window fan that was struck by lightning. When that occurred, they were relieved.

"If the Lord were going to take him," Toddy told her husband, "he'd have let that lightning strike him today. I don't guess anything's going to happen now."

She found the deep-fat fryer that her father had given her the previous year. She set it atop the stove, filled it with oil, plugged in the cord, and waited for it to reach 340 degrees. Joe climbed up on the trash can to get a closer look. "Joe, get down!" said Toddy. "That grease is hot!"

As Joe started to get down, the trash can toppled. Instinctively, his hand reached out and grasped the cord. The fryer tipped.

The boiling oil came down over Joe on the floor. In one horrifying instant, Toddy Atwater knew that her son was going to die. The screaming began.

Harvey Atwater came through the door. In a panic, he reached for a jar of rice and started throwing it wildly in the air. Lee ran into the kitchen and saw Joe lying there, his skin starting to peel. Toddy was hysterical. They wrapped Joe in sheets and got him to the hospital. Joe's burns covered 90 percent of his body, and he had lost his right eye to the scalding liquid. Toddy stayed that night and into the morning. "Mama, please don't cry," Joe kept saying. "Please don't cry."

Three days later, as Joe was being buried, a neighbor went into the house on Wildwood Road and removed his clothing, shifted some furniture around. Toddy wanted to move to another house, but Harvey insisted, "No, we've got to face it." But they didn't.

Silence fell on the family like an admission of careless neglect and complicity. Lee clung to his mother. "Repression is a terrible thing," their minister told Toddy one day. "Remember, you and Harvey can express your grief, but Lee can't." But there was no room for religious consolation now, or for a long time. If there was a God, how could he let that happen to a little kid? That was the reasoning. That was the anger. Neither Toddy nor Harvey could mention Joe without breaking into tears.

Lee would hear Joe's little voice lifted in pain for the rest of his life.

• • •

Toddy had wanted a baby, but Harvey was in no rush. In fact, even the notion of marriage caught him by surprise. After serving in World War II he went to see his best friend, Cliff Page, and here was this kid sister, six years younger, now all grown up. And quite lovely. He and Toddy went out on New Year's Eve, kissed at midnight in Spartanburg, and were married on Thanksgiving day, 1947. The next year they moved to Atlanta, where Harvey attended Emory Law School for two years — a false start — and Toddy taught high school Spanish. They were living in university apartments when Toddy became pregnant with their first child. Harvey was so absorbed across town in the business of selling his car — he was almost always selling a car — that when Lee was born, on Tuesday, February 27, 1951, neighbors had to take Toddy to Emory Hospital. Of course, Lee was three weeks early — a lifetime trait, his parents would later conclude. He weighed in at seven pounds, three ounces, at 1:05 in the morning, and Harvey was enormously proud. "Ain't he the prettiest thing?" he said.

They named him Harvey LeRoy Atwater after his dad and his mother's father, LeRoy Randolph Page. To trace the Page family tree, which several of Toddy's forebears have done, is to go back to the Presbyterian minister Alexander Craighead, a Revolutionary War patriot who lived in Cumberland County, Pennsylvania. The Craigheads married into the Carruths of North Carolina, who migrated to the town of Landrum, South Carolina, in the early nineteenth century, where the Pages of Charlotte County, Virginia, had also established residence. On November 2, 1882, Nannie Elizabeth Carruth married Gabriel Cannon Page, postmaster and prominent area Republican, and LeRoy Randolph Page was born on January 1, 1891.

In his early teens, Lee Page fell beneath a horse-drawn wagon, which broke his left leg. When a country doctor set the leg improperly, Lee was left with a severe limp that made farming an ordeal, but he refused to let the disability get in his way. During this period, he met Alma Irene Foster, whose family had just moved to Landrum from Polk County, North Carolina. Lee enrolled in Wofford College, and Irene attended high school in Landrum, but not for long, for they soon eloped and were married on February 23, 1911, in Campobello, South Carolina. Lee was twenty, Irene sixteen. Using family and political connections, Lee applied for a rural mail route and began delivering mail via horse and buggy in Landrum, later becoming a railroad mail clerk on train runs from Asheville in the mountains to Columbia, South Carolina. Eventually, he took the post as transfer clerk in the Spartanburg office so that his family could get better education at city schools.

They lived on Dallas Place in a working-class Spartanburg neighborhood, raising five children during the dark days of the Depression and the anxious World War II years. Sarah Alma Page — called Toddy because as a baby she toddled around — was born on July 20, 1924. The Pages considered themselves lucky because Lee had a job. Others in the family did not (one of his brothers, two of Irene's), so Lee's salary had to go a long way. "If we ever

did ask for anything, we knew the answer was 'No!' immediately,"
recalled Toddy's sister Mickey. One of their father's favorite expressions was, "We will have to eat dirt and go naked!" Their mother
sewed dresses for the girls (Irene could even make skirts out of
men's worn-out pants), kept a garden, baked bread, and prepared
three hot meals daily. She also struggled with bouts of depression,
since life for Lee Page "was serious business, a work or die affair."
After all, Lee was accustomed to being the wage earner, the leader
of the flock.

His crippled condition had two noticeable side effects. On
the up side, it encouraged the development of his engaging storytelling skills — Lee could swap stories with anyone, recapturing
his youth with tales that he eventually published in a slender volume called *Memories of My Childhood*. On the down side, it also
left him with a crusty demeanor and impatience with anyone who
didn't share his view of the world. That included his politics, of
course. The Pages were Republicans in an era when there was no
Republican Party in South Carolina. In 1932, when the framed
portrait of FDR replaced the picture of Herbert Hoover in the
classrooms of Spartanburg, there was enthusiastic applause from
all but the Page children, who sat on their hands.

Both parents were avid readers, insisting that the children
have library cards. The library was on the other side of town — a
long walk that the Page children made regularly. They also visited
a music teacher for piano lessons. At night the children studied at
the dining table under the overhead light while Lee and Irene sat
by the coal heater reading, always ready to check homework, call
out multiplication tables, or coach with spelling. The radio was
not turned on until all homework was completed.

On August 17, 1947, shortly after her fifty-third birthday,
Irene Foster Page died of cancer. After working forty-one years
for the mail service, Lee Page died on August 7, 1982, at the age
of ninety-two. Because her grandmother had lived until the age
of ninety-three, and her aunt had lived to the age of ninety-four,
Toddy would later recall thinking that the Page progeny had two
things in common: longevity and the Republican Party.

Harvey Dillard Atwater was born on June 18, 1919, in
Winston-Salem, North Carolina. He was one of three boys born
to Charles Bynum Atwater and his wife Sally Belle Dillard. When
Harvey was four, his parents separated. Sally Belle came home to

Spartanburg with the boys, where she worked for the telephone company and lived with her sister Bessie Dillard, who worked for the Southern Railway and never married. All the boys went on to graduate college, a testament to their mother's hard work and belief in the importance of education. Harvey weighed 210 in high school and played football. In 1938 he started at Wofford College in Spartanburg on a football scholarship. His schooling was interrupted in 1941 when he went into the service, but he later graduated college in '48.

Like all Atwaters in this country, Harvey could trace his lineage to David Atwater of Royton in Lenham in Kent, England, who, according to a family historian, "came across in the good ship *Hector* [to New Haven] in 1637. He and his good wife Demaris, and their six sons and four daughters and their children and grandchildren endured as many hardships, felled as many trees, fought as many Indians, burned as many witches and tossed over as much tea, and were as good all 'round pilgrim fathers and mothers as if Grandfather David had arrived in the Mayflower in 1620." David Atwater was characterized as a tough-minded soul. He later became one of the founding fathers of Yale.

By the time of the Revolution, David's great-grandson Enos Atwater was continuing the hard-charging family tradition. During the plundering of New Haven by the British in 1779, he held his daughter Mary up inside one of the open chimneys to hide the silver communion service of the First Church of New Haven, according to family lore. During the same invasion, brother Russell Atwater was wounded and left for dead, but he recovered and was later employed by the Emperor Napoleon after the battle of Waterloo to purchase a tract of land in New York State as a refuge, should he escape his imprisonment on the isle of Elba. And William Cutler Atwater, another brother, carried dispatches from New Haven to the army at New London and back on horseback.

According to Francis Atwater's *Atwater History & Genealogy*, from Enos Atwater, apparently the first North Carolinian Atwater, born in 1748, there sprang subsequent generations: Titus, his son, born in 1775; and Jehiel, his son, born in 1817. "His prominent trait was devotion to principle, judicial trend of mind, and fearlessness in doing what he considered to be right," observed Jehiel's son Edmund Warren Atwater, born in 1842. The descendants of the original North Carolina Atwater settlers, he added, "carry the same characteristics. They occupy socially the very best places, not society people, but for pure thoughts and character, and safe morals, none excel them. . . . They have been and will continue to be Puritans; free from intolerance, indeed I might say the spirit of intolerance has no foothold in them."

Edmund Warren Atwater was a brother of John N. Atwater (1858–1930), of Chapel Hill, the progenitor of Lee's line. And then there was Francis Atwater, a cousin whose chief characteristic seemed to be a faculty for starting things. "Indeed, his capacity for nosing around, prying into, putting out, stirring up family affairs, tampering with county and state records, scraping up old wills and mortgages, disclosing graveyard secrets, and making the *other* fellow *do* is unparalleled in the annals of Atwater history," reported family historian Lillie Gannon Atwater Parker at the annual family picnic in Chapel Hill in 1919. "I doubt if there is a state in the Union, or an Atwater in the state who has escaped this man. When he makes up his mind to do a thing, it is done. He suggested a reunion. . . . He told all of you to come to Chapel Hill and I see you are all here. If this man should ask any of you confidentially to take a trip to the moon to see if any of the Atwaters have escaped up there, my advice to you is to start."

Harvey LeRoy Atwater seems to have sprung from this mold — the pusher, the delegator, the manipulator, *the doer.*

● ● ●

Lee was a difficult child. Toddy couldn't get a baby-sitter. No one wanted to deal with the crying. His legs jerked, his chin quivered, his arms shook. Doctors said his nervous system was not entirely developed owing to the premature birth. "It'll go away," they said. But it never did. Toddy tried to nurse him. He cried. She put him on a bottle. He cried. He didn't like being alone. She held him, rocked him. He cried, hardly slept at all. When he did fall asleep, it was almost by default, only after rocking himself to sleep by knocking his head repeatedly against the headboard of the crib, creating a bald spot with a callus on his head. One evening Toddy heard a crash. Lee had rocked some screws loose, and the crib had fallen apart. He cried.

For two and a half years Lee was Toddy's entire life. She idol-

ized him. Lee walked at one year . . . but then he *ran*. He talked
early — and often. By two, onlookers thought he could read, but
he had memorized books his mother read to him in her lap. At
age two and a half he could recite the Pledge of Allegiance at
the Charleston commencement program in nursery school. Proud
Toddy made him say it for company.

But Lee seemed to be lacking in coordination. He had
the worst handwriting his mother had ever seen in a youngster, and it never got much better. Even as an adult, he held
a pen as you would hold a piece of chalk. Toddy was worried about Lee's nervousness, his quivering mouth, his legs that
shook all the time. She asked a doctor whether it was something to worry about and was told that it was just high energy.
It never changed. Lee just discovered outlets. At three Lee took
an interest in Indian lore. He carried a tomahawk and wore a
feather hat and blanket that hot summer. Toddy always read to
him, always nourished his sense of curiosity, taking him to mu-
seums. By the time he went to school, he had developed a remarkable memory (he knew all the presidents) and a fondness for
history.

Toddy worshipped Lee, but he was exasperating. After Joe
was born on November 18, 1953, Lee wanted even more attention.
When Toddy fed or bathed Joe, Lee would jerk down curtains,
pull off bedspreads, do anything to get his mother's attention. Only
when Joe could play and interact with Lee was there any time for
Toddy to fuss over Harvey.

After quitting law school, Harvey had joined an insurance
company, and the family had moved to Charleston in April 1951
when Lee was six weeks old. For six months they rented an un-
heated house with no closets on Lightwood Lane from the Porcher
(pronounced por-*chay*) family for $55 a month. Locals referred to
them as "the Porcher tenants," never the Atwaters, there being a
line between bluebloods and commoners in Charleston. In 1956
Harvey was transferred, and the family moved to the rental home
on Wildwood Road in Aiken, where Joe's death would bring such
pain to their lives.

The trauma occurred precisely when Lee should have become an independent little boy. "Get me another baby!" he
moaned. It was the last thing Toddy wanted, but "guilt is a great
motivator," she said, so Anne was born August 19, 1957. Lee didn't

really want another baby, either, but she was so adorable — now he found himself competing with her as well as with his dead brother for the attention that he craved.

The move would have other implications as well: Strom Thurmond, who was born near Aiken, lived but a few doors from the house on Wildwood Road. Young Lee's first encounter with the senator occurred during a trick-or-treat stop at the Thurmond home that first Halloween in Aiken. "He came out and gave me a Snickers candy bar," Lee would later recall. "That was the best thing I got that year. So I liked Senator Thurmond, but I didn't know anything about politics."

Aiken is a small city in the third congressional district, which runs along the Georgia border and up to North Carolina. In 1948, nearly four years before Lee Atwater was born, Thurmond — then South Carolina's Democratic governor — ran as a Dixiecrat for president. In 1952 Aiken supported Eisenhower in the presidential election. It was the beginning of a rising Republican tide in the South. By 1964, Thurmond, by then a senator, would become a Republican as South Carolina supported Goldwater.

In 1957, at the age of six, Lee started school and appeared in his first stage production, called "Wedding of the Flowers." He was a dandelion. The Atwaters had eventually bought a home at 1428 Parsons Lane, but in 1961, when Harvey was promoted to manager, the family moved to Columbia. The move disturbed Lee. At nine, he was starting to feel he wanted to *be* from somewhere. "Will y'all promise me one thing?" he inquired when they arrived in Columbia. "Never to move again. I don't want to change schools anymore." They didn't. Harvey and Toddy bought a ranch-style house at 4720 Norwood Road (for $18,300) that would be their home for the next twenty-nine years. With three bedrooms, plus a garage for Harvey's auto workshop and boat (another major vice was fishing), the Atwaters lived in what Lee would refer to as "the middle of the middle class."

Politics, like real estate, is often a matter of location. In Columbia, the state capital and hotbed of political activity, Lee would later find his niche. "It was very good for me politically," he explained. "We moved to the key, critical political points of the state: Charleston, Aiken, Columbia, and Spartanburg. So I had a good understanding of the state because of the places I'd lived."

Although never diagnosed as being hyperactive, Lee had

nearly all of the classic symptoms. In grammar school he couldn't sit still, had a short attention span, was impulsive, and had an insatiable need for attention. "Lee was a poor student," recalled classmate and lifelong pal David Yon. "Bright, but unable to stay focused; he was always switching channels." Lee learned early how to have his way with other kids — not physically, but through other means of manipulation and control that left him clearly in charge of relationships. Lee became a prankster, sending birthday invitations to all of the girls in class from David Yon, who was too shy to throw a party, even if it was his birthday. (It wasn't.)

Another classmate was Warren Tompkins, who would go on to achieve fame as a political consultant and chief of staff to South Carolina governor Carroll A. Campbell Jr. "The rest of us would all sit around and talk about baseball, football, hunting, and fishing. With Lee, it was always oddball things: music, books," he recalled. "He was always sort of a leader, always the person who could organize people. He would get people to go to all-star pro wrestling — in the sixth grade."

Lee's home life was a mystery to his school pals. Lee's need for attention was compounded by his parents' devastation after the death of Joe. Hearing his father cry cut deeply into Lee. He could never think of his dad as a rock, and he leaned increasingly on his mother, the nurturer. Indeed, if Lee's life was defined by any one person, it was Toddy. At some point she had decided she just had to go on and *be there* for her children, and that she was just going to enjoy Lee. If laughter is the stepchild of tears, it became an unspoken bond between mother and surviving son. Not only were the kids at school laughing, but there was laughter at home again. "They were always yucking it up," recalled a visitor. "You never got a sense of what the *real* mother-child relationship was."

David Yon once commented on a tender yet haunting portrait of Lee and Joe, hung over the living-room sofa, done by Toddy's artist sister Mickey just before Joe's death. "Oh, that's my little brother," said Lee. "He died."

Money was tight. When Lee and Anne were old enough, Toddy went back to teaching. With Harvey on a salary (no commission or bonus), they needed her income to save for education, a priority they both shared — along with a sense of thrift — having grown up during the Depression. Toddy clipped grocery store coupons, budgeted one dollar a day for meat at supper, and reared her family on southern fried chicken, pork chops, biscuits, rice and beans. No liver, no squash, and no leftovers. In fifth grade Lee became a Laddy Boy, wearing a plaid tie and selling eggs door to door for sixty cents a dozen. He made a nickel on each sale and was soon appointed sales manager in charge of getting "starts." Although Lee loved to sell, he was indifferent to money, or to the lack of it. Once he lost a dollar in the family yard and quickly gave up the search. Toddy looked and looked. "That's your profit for a week!" she said. Toddy found the dollar, of course, just as Lee knew she would.

In eighth grade, Lee's class went to Washington, D.C., where he saw politics in action for the first time. Most of his classmates had $10 to spend, but Toddy had given Lee $5 as an exercise in resourcefulness. Miss Speigner, the teacher/chaperone, had feared that Lee would be trouble. His reputation in the classroom preceded him. But on this trip Lee seemed to blossom. He thrived on the excitement of politics in action. Miss Speigner told Toddy that Lee asked the most intelligent questions, and when the class posed for a photo in front of the Capitol after a visit to Strom Thurmond, there was Lee, sitting right in front of the senator. He spent most of the $5 on a little black bear souvenir for his sister Anne.

One afternoon, as Harvey was test-driving one of his cars, Lee sat on the automobile's floor fiddling with the radio dial. A song came on with a cadence, a beat, a spirit that seemed to transfix the youngster. It was James Brown singing "Please, Please, Please." Harvey turned the dial, but that night Lee found the same station on the radio in his room — WLAC in Nashville, Tennessee — and he was hooked on rhythm and blues. At five he had seen Elvis Presley on TV, after which he began to do gyrations in the living room, pleading for a guitar for his birthday. But his parents wanted him to learn the piano. Soon James Brown pirouettes were part of Lee's repertoire.

OK, here's the deal with the music, Toddy told him. If you will take piano lessons for three years, we will get you a guitar for your eleventh birthday. Agreed. Lee never missed a piano lesson, but when Toddy purchased a guitar for $14 on February 27, 1962, they never heard the piano again. Though its wire strings made Lee's fingers bleed, he was consumed by the instrument. On weekends he rose early and practiced until seven in the evening. The first song he learned was a piano tune, Ray Charles's "What'd I

Say?" (To appease his father, he also learned the theme from *Bonanza*.) Once, when he wanted to practice but had to entertain sleepover guests Charles Strickland and David Yon, Lee made a fifty-cent wager that he could make them say uncle by playing the same five notes over and over. For six hours he played those notes, until, at three o'clock in the morning, they didn't say uncle; they *moaned* it. In June 1963, Lee sang heartfelt renditions of "This Land Is Your Land" and "If I Had a Hammer" at his grammar school graduation. His voice already had a bit of gravel in it, and teachers who were there still recall how Lee sang with a wrinkled boyish nose, a touch of impishness at the attention he was receiving, and penetrating beautiful blue eyes that were impossible to forget.

● ● ●

At W. J. Keenan Junior High School, Lee quickly developed a reputation as a hellion. Lee's own copy of *The Rebel*, the school's first yearbook, is covered with seventh-grade sentiments and references to his passions for wrestling, singing, playing the guitar, and cracking up most of his classmates most of the time. "Our class might have been very dull without you," wrote social studies teacher Mrs. Edith Joy on the autographs page at the end of the book. "I have enjoyed teaching you."

On the cover of the yearbook, Lee's English teacher, Mrs. Marigene Loving, was more to the point: "To my first nightmare every morning!"

As puberty settled in, Lee realized that there was only one sure way to get the attention of girls: football. On the up side for Lee, he could do a James Brown slide in cleats. The downside was he was scrawny, pigeon-toed, ran funny, and his left leg twitched all the time. In ninth grade, he tried out for the B team. "Mrs. Atwater, Lee will never be a football player," the coach told Toddy. "You have to be aggressive to play football, and that's just not in Lee. He's not mean enough."

Lee didn't play a minute. He spent the season entertaining his fellow benchmates as team mascot. After the team banquet, he threw his letter on the kitchen table and announced to his parents: "That's the end of my football career!"

So how to impress girls? If he couldn't play football, he would play rock 'n' roll. At twelve he started smoking cigarettes, trying to act older. He talked his way into the Green Door, a black club near Shakespeare Road where he caught the band and ended up onstage doing James Brown–style splits for the crowd.

At home he held his mother's hairbrush the way Elvis cradled a mike, singing the songs he heard on the radio. Yes, that's what he wanted to be. A rocker. The next year he formed a band and spent weekends playing gigs where he could find them. No job was too small. Classmates recall seeing Lee strumming away on the back of a flatbed truck for the grand opening of a grocery store in the Forest Lake shopping center. He had unusual stamina, high energy, and a devilish mind. But still no girls.

In ninth grade, Lee seemed naive in the ways of women. "There was a latent sexual drive — you had the feeling that there was this really tightly bound drive within him — but it did not come out as pressure to be sexually active with him," recalled one of his dates. "I really don't think he was very experienced at that point. He bluffed a lot and told a lot of jokes, but I don't think he knew as much as he acted like he knew. From the questions he asked, I just think he was largely ignorant of a lot of things related to females in particular, life in general, in terms of human behavior."

Once Lee established conversational rapport with a girl, he'd ask lots of questions. He was very curious about people, about motivations, even biological particulars. He asked questions that he didn't feel comfortable asking at home. "I can remember telling him about girls and what a menstrual cycle was like," recalled one girlfriend. "He would ask, 'What do you do? What do you use? Do you have cramps?' He was just eternally curious. It was as though he wanted to vacuum my brain. He plied me with questions all the time, and I think his curiosity was genuine. I don't think he had any bad motives. He would just ask me any question that came to his mind."

Insofar as girls were concerned, the big problem with Lee was trust. Even guys who enjoyed being with Lee could never be sure that he wouldn't do something for a laugh at their expense. Some girls enjoyed Lee's wild streak, but most wouldn't settle for being one member of his audience, someone he would return to after he had performed. Then, in ninth grade, Lee had his first serious flirtation. Her name was Debbie Carson, and, in addition to

being cute, Debbie was a member of the National Junior Honor
Society, a class officer who had been voted most likely to succeed
as well as "best all 'round" in the class. Well, now. Here he was,
class clown, and his girl is an honor roll student, a student body
officer! It validated his sense of worth. It was too good to last. And
it didn't.

Lee's addictive personality pulled him back into the spotlight, where he basked in crowd approval. He loved being the center of attention and could always devise a way of putting himself
there. At school dances, he would get onstage and dance around,
playing air guitar, mugging with his "blues face," upstaging acts,
creating dance contests in the area right in front of the stage. Afterward he would apologize to Debbie for behavior that must have
struck her as being compulsive. "I know I acted badly," he would
say on the phone the next day. "I hope you'll still go out with
me."

When Debbie began to draw away, Lee asked her why. She
explained that girls like sincerity, that they want to feel that somebody is genuinely interested in them. "I'm just tired of being the
second half of the show," she said. "I feel like I've got to be part of
a stunt routine."

"There were sides of Lee that I certainly adored," she
recalled. "But the opportunist in him — the person seeking popularity and a stage — would almost always overrule the nice guy, the
more genuine part of him. I don't think he could stop it."

Toddy was then teaching Spanish at Keenan part-time, and
she was weary of fellow teachers telling her what Lee had done
in class day after outrageous day. Lee didn't even care enough to
cheat. His grades were Ds and Fs. He thought it was cool to be
dumb. One day, when Lee's teacher had left the classroom to go
to the lounge, Lee stood atop an overturned waste basket, playing
air guitar and starring in his own rhythm and blues show, when his
mother walked by. "He decided that since he wasn't the smartest
in the room, he would be the dumbest," she said. "He had to
be different." By the time Lee graduated junior high in June of
1966, his parents thought that he had to be different, too. Military
school.

"Too bad you won't be at Flora next year!" wrote one schoolmate in Lee's yearbook, which was filled with notations from
classmates attesting to Lee's reputation as a schoolyard wrestler, a

guitarist, the leader of a band, a teller of jokes, a pursuer of girls, and resident class clown. Lee thumbed through the yearbook and added some gag captions to photos of faculty and friends. On page 35 there was the Keenan Concert Band, with Lee looking positively wholesome in jacket and tie, with a sax in hand. No guitar playing 'round here! "You are the greatest, you are the strongest, you are the biggest," Lee scrawled in his wobbly script above his picture. "You are the star."

• • •

At Fork Union Military Academy in Virginia, most of the students were discipline problems, though none of them knew it until they showed up. A cadet could pull guard duty just for having a bad haircut. He could complain, but not between seven and ten P.M. That period was for Closed Quarters — CQ to the embittered — when there was only silence and studying. It was lights out with taps at ten-thirty.

Some cadets ran off from FU, refusing to return. Those who stuck it out attended classes taught one topic at a time in six-week segments. If they didn't make a 75, they failed the course and had to repeat it. Outside the classroom, they could look forward to inspections and drills. "Four boys got into serious trouble last week for buying this lemon extract, which is 80 percent alcohol, and getting drunk," Lee wrote in an early letter home. "They didn't get kicked out but they were all sergeants or above, and now they're reduced to the rank of private and have no more leaves and have to march tours every day till the end of the year."

Wow, thought Harvey and Toddy. Just what Lee needs!

Lee knew what he needed, too — and generally got it. "He was a manipulator," recalled a roommate. "He could talk you into agreeing to anything." Their room, on the second floor of the barracks, didn't have to be as clean as the others, because Lee was in with the upperclassmen. If a room up the hall had anything amiss, "You're on report!" As for the Atwater abode — A company, second platoon — a scuff on the floor would simply elicit an upperclassman's compassion. "They'd actually help us with a rag to buff the floor."

When the upperclassmen were out of sight, Lee reverted to his former life as Dennis the Menace. He had arrived with a guitar, a saxophone, and a moniker: "Little LeRoy." He dubbed his roommate Benny Ferrell "B.B. Bluesboy." Lee sold memberships in a record club to his classmates and thereby enriched his own blues collection. "For every new member you get, you get a free album," he wrote home. "So far I've got four new members — that's four free albums right there!"

There were quicker routes to collecting glory. One night, Lee bet Benny a handful of record albums that he could jump out a second-story window in the barracks and return to their room undetected. He won that bet, so he offered another. After lights out, he bet that Benny couldn't even go down the hall to get a magazine and return undetected. As Benny returned triumphantly to his room he found that Lee had placed a locker behind the door, leaving Benny stranded in the hall where he was sure to be caught.

Lee was addicted to the showy gamble. In the mess hall he bet an upperclassman $3 that he could drink an entire bottle of Tabasco sauce, which he did. After collecting the money, Lee laughed all the way to the barracks head. "You could hear him laughing and barfing at the same time," recalled a classmate. "He never made a wager for the money. It was just to show he could do it."

Lee's extracurricular pursuits included signing out for visits to a roommate's home and going instead to a couple of rented hotel rooms in Georgetown for a weekend of hard partying. When Lee did go home with another classmate, it was to party with the roomie that he called a hillbilly — Benny, from Tazewell, Virginia, population 4,700. On weekend leaves, they took the family car (driving age was fifteen) and motored to Bluefield, West Virginia. Lee, wearing his academy uniform to look older, purchased six-packs of Pabst Blue Ribbon at a grocery store that didn't check IDs. In the car, he changed back into civvies and chugged beers in long extended gulps like a sword swallower. He could consume a six-pack in ten miles, tossing cans out the car window, then arriving at a rock or soul dance thoroughly blitzed. On the dance floor, he did James Brown splits and pirouettes. He picked up girls who were impressed at first by his wildness and wit, but who slowly froze on the unbearable ride home.

And then it was back to good ol' FU. "Life up here is routine," Lee sighed in a letter home. He wrote home weekly, because he had to. That was another thing about Fork Union: rules, rules, rules. "I'm beginning to get fed up with this place," said

Lee after two months. "I don't really miss anything in Columbia except my family and a home environment." Toddy and Harvey did not relent. After all, Lee's grades were better. He averaged 87 now.

Lee wanted to enroll with his friends at J. C. Flora High, a campus-style school, complete with social clubs, in Columbia. So he devised a campaign (not his last). It began with letters that told his parents what they wanted to hear. "This school is doing wonders for me and I'm really maturing a lot up here," he wrote in December. "I have been thinking a lot about the future and I think the best thing for me to do is come home this summer and take an advanced subject in summer school." As his parents began to yield to the promise of a new maturity, Lee's countdown began.

"I don't think I could stand another year of this place," he wrote in March.

"In only twelve days I'll be out of here for good," he wrote in May. "I know this place has done a lot of good for me but I still will be glad as heck to get out of here."

Harvey and Toddy caved in. Lee would enroll at Flora for eleventh grade. He promised to do better. He had even devised a career strategy in a letter from Fork Union that winter, hadn't he? "I think that at the beginning of 12th grade I will apply at South Carolina, the Citadel, N.C. State, and Wofford," he said, tossing in Harvey's alma mater. "I would especially like to go to Wofford. I think I would like to be a lawyer and maybe someday go into politics."

Well, now. A career in politics. Harvey and Toddy were skeptical as ever.

• • •

Columbia in the late 1960s was a small segregated city, struggling like so many other southern communities as the Old South was on the verge of becoming the New South. Pols met then, as now, at the Capitol Restaurant, where legislators enjoyed a weekly hoedown with banjos and guitars. Columbia was not a particularly rich or moneyed town, but the economy was strong because of the diversity that had built up over the years — state government, city and county government, the University of South Carolina, local businesses, and the big army base, Fort Jackson, nearby. It all kept the economy steady, with no rocking up or down in boom-and-bust cycles. The first mall in the state had just opened opposite Flora High, but downtown was still the hub of commerce and where everyone went on Saturday morning. There were numerous department stores and eight movie houses downtown — bottom floor and balcony for whites; back balcony for blacks, with separate water fountains. At that time Forest Acres, where the Atwaters lived, was a middle- and occasionally upwardly middle-class suburb, somewhat rural and uncluttered by commerce. Now it's all part of a city that has doubled in size and sprawl.

In the pivotal summer of '67, Lee — free at last from the rigors of Fork Union — hooked up with his old junior high classmate Steve Sisk, whose father was director of state parks in South Carolina. Lee and "Sisko" made an odd pair. Steve had spent most of his boyhood doing the things that Lee could barely tolerate — fishing, swimming, and camping out in the woods. With chiseled features and a winning smile, he was a boisterous, mischievous tease, whose heart was as big as his size — at graduation from Flora, he was six two and 235 pounds. Steve was sincere, a bit innocent, even shy. He could stumble when trying to give voice to a serious thought. He loved watching cartoons, playing sports, and writing. He kept a journal, and several of his writings appeared in the Flora literary yearbook. "He lived 120 minutes of every hour," said a friend. At Flora, he broke the school shot-put record in his junior year. He played varsity football for three years, leading the Flora Falcons to a season record of 9-1-1. Once, when the team lost a tough game, Sisko visited each teammate at home and urged him to snap back. The Falcons didn't lose another game that season.

Lee respected Steve because they could go toe-to-toe — not in fisticuffs (Steve could kill him) but in humor. Steve could muscle his way through a prank, whereas Lee could only talk his way out. That summer of '67 Steve and Lee became lifeguards at Kings Mountain State Park near the North Carolina line. No fishing or camping out required, and girls aplenty at the lake — Lee's kind of job. One night Steve fell out of a boat and feigned drowning. He swam ashore underwater then watched as Lee paddled around in the moonlight, calling for his buddy. The next morning, when Steve showed up at camp, he expected to walk in and see Lee's jaw drop. Not exactly. Lee, smelling a watery rat, had not even reported his buddy absent. "I just couldn't decide whether to report you as missing," said Lee, "or dead."

Lee had been chasing the ladies since age fourteen. He once crawled under the tent at the annual Newberry County Fair to watch a dancer take the glasses off a nosy male viewer, insert them between her legs, then return the smudged optics to the transfigured patron. You could look, but you couldn't touch, that was the rule. Lee touched and was thrown out. He snuck back in and was about to touch again when two bouncers escorted him to the exit, this time with a terminal oof.

From watching the barkers at carnivals, Lee learned how to hype, how to promote. He especially loved pro wrestling shows, where he learned the importance of bombast, and how to immobilize a larger opponent. The Grapevine, the Figure Eight, the Boston Crab — these holds required more ingenuity than brawn; with these moves a shrimp of a wrestler could control a whale. Lee, who had strong hands from years of guitar calisthenics, devised a sport. Two opponents stood a few feet apart, facing each other. They extended their hands and interlocked their fingers. The goal was to push your opponent's hands backward without moving your legs. Lee "lost" only to the oversized Rex Brown, who had threatened to beat him up after the humiliation of an earlier, very public defeat.

• • •

"My childhood, adolescence and high school days are unusually important," Lee reflected near the end of his life. "If there has ever been a time that I developed a uniqueness and sense of humor and the ability to organize, it was then. In those early days I developed the skills that gave me a certain degree of success in American politics."

Lee honed his skills in the class of '69 with 250 students at Flora High — elitist, suburban, and white. There were some 1500 students in the school, but in this era before busing, Flora's "freedom of choice" program drew about 50 black students, mainly from professional families with cars. The school had cliques but no drugs. Just pranks and fooling around. The Selma March and Vietnam had passed Flora by.

After a few months of good behavior at Flora, Lee returned to his old ways. He joined the Dark Horseman, a fraternity that threw the school's best parties. "If you dated someone, you would never tell your mother he was a Dark Horseman," recalled Emily Grice Lumpkin. On weekends the group would rent the Knights of Columbus hall or the Syrian Lebanon Club — a warehouselike building with a stage and a dance floor — for $100. Once Lee led partygoers in a search for leftover booze tossed in the weeds along Ivy Hall, off Covenant Road, a popular parking spot for young lovers. They found enough discards to mix up lethal amounts of "P.J.," or Purple Jesus, a home-brewed concoction made with purple juice and alcohol.

Dark Horseman hazing was brutal. Heating liniment was rubbed on the genitals of pledges. Initiation left Lee's backside purple and black for weeks. The point was to show that you could take pain. In the slap fight, pledges stood toe-to-toe and exchanged slaps to the face while brothers urged them on: "Harder! Harder!" One afternoon at Flora, Lee was pitted against Doug Seigler, a Cavaliers fraternity pledge and neighborhood pal, who was small and wiry like himself. They slapped the hell out of each other in a lose-lose standoff. That night Lee called Seigler, saying he was sorry that they had had to fight each other, and it was nothing personal. "We're still friends, right?" Absolutely, said Seigler. Fight hard, forgive readily was the rule. They became friends for life.

Lee Atwater was, by consensus, the biggest hell-raiser in his class. "He was a terrible student, terrible," remembered his mother, who taught Spanish at Flora High. Once, after giving him an F on his report card, Toddy Atwater wrote a note: "This student needs stronger parental guidance at home." Lee roared at that one.

He later remembered that two Cs were the highlights of his academic career. His grades, he claimed, were "carefully contrived to increase my popularity and make sure that everyone knew that I was cool." Lee thought of himself as self-educated. "I would read a book or two a week, and the only thing that would keep me from reading a book was if it was assigned reading."

For an English course where the theme for the semester was character development, Lee did a book report on the Columbia telephone directory. "He said it jumped around too much from character to character without sustaining any of them," recalled Robert C. Ellenburg, Atwater's eleventh-grade English teacher. "He predicted it would have to be revised next year." Lee got a D for content, an A for originality. On another occasion, he gave an oral report on *The Hunchback of Notre Dame* — as a football saga.

Lives, not ideas, intrigued him. He read every biography he could get his hands on: Thomas on Lincoln, Flexner on Washington, Coit on Calhoun. He read, and if what he read intrigued him, he remembered it. Dinosaurs were a passion. Bugs were not. When students had to gather a bug collection for biology class, Lee's was an assortment of plastic creepy crawlers — all displayed on cardboard with proper names: Plastico Bugaremus, et alia. During a lecture one day, Lee was talking with Steve Chase at the back of the room. The teacher stopped. "Lee, what are you talking about back there that's so interesting?" she said.

"Dinosaurs!" he replied.

"Well, if it's that interesting, why don't you come up and tell the rest of the class about it."

Lee walked up and went into a half-hour discourse on the topic. He was factual, accurate, and anecdotal. The teacher could not shut him up.

Lee's hunt for the limelight seemed compulsive. He organized students to follow prearranged commands during assemblies. Once the program featured a champion glassblower, and when he was earnestly leaning into his task, all the students in the front row crossed their legs in unison. "This guy almost died," Lee remembered. "You could see him almost inhale the glass." Another time, during Vocational Week, he arranged for everyone to give a speaker a standing ovation at the end of every sentence.

After spending his lunch money on blues music, one day Lee broke into the cafeteria line past the cashier for a free meal. He was expelled from school for three days. Lee's version: "I did go to the detention center a few times, but I did that intentionally because it's a different crowd in there. There's two groups. There's people like us, the hell-raisers. But every now and then it's good to just go with the hoods, the assholes in detention center, the ones who have knives and shit. I just wanted to see those guys; it's fun to study those guys." In later years, Lee would call such gatherings the swing vote.

The pranks continued outside school. Once Lee took a black snake and put it in an old pocketbook he had found in lost and found at a pool hall. He placed the purse in the middle of the road on a quiet Sunday and waited until a '59 Chevy, packed full of kids, roared past the purse, then stopped and backed up slowly. An oversized black woman in a red dress got out, looked around, picked up the purse, and got back in the car. The Chevy started down the road again but came to a sudden stop after fifty yards. The doors flew open and everyone began jumping out, led by the heavyset woman, who leaped over a wire fence to escape.

Despite his constant clowning, Lee wanted to be taken seriously — at certain times and by certain girls. "He may have felt ambivalent about the two roles," recalled Debbie Carson. "He was always trying to understand the female perspective. 'What do girls think? How would you . . . ? How does a girl see such and such?' He seemed to think there were huge differences between girls and boys — out of scale to the obvious ones. Maybe that reveals how mystified he was. That's how he struck me: baffled. I think he was frustrated. He never was probably as desirable to girls as he wished to be, and he was trying to understand that — because if he knew why, he could fix it. That's sort of the way he worked. If you don't know what makes somebody tick, then you find out."

He still seemed hyperactive. "Lee's leg was like his personality — ever moving," Toddy said. When they were seated she would reach over and gently tap the jiggling left leg to stop it. Then the right would start.

"Was he compulsive? I think so," one girlfriend said. "Lots of little nervous habits and twitches and taps. Could just about drive you crazy. He acted almost hunted at times, constantly alert, ever watchful. Always tuned in. On edge. Very tuned into people around him, but in a guarded sense."

He had trouble dialing a phone, using a typewriter, tying a tie. His mother had always read to him, and he would later learn primarily by ear and by query. If he were a student today, he would be considered learning disabled and given extra help. In the '60s he was on his own, and he had to find his own mountain road to success — which he did, as a performer.

Eugene Gatlin, English teacher and chair of the drama department, had seen the Broadway production of *Bye Bye Birdie*. He was casting a high-energy version of it at Flora, something that would compete for the downtown crowd, but he needed a Conrad Birdie. The word on Lee in the teachers' lounge was not good. A discipline problem, a troublemaker who would let you down. When Lee showed up at tryouts, though, Gatlin saw a guy with stage presence who could sing with feeling. So Gatlin built the show around Lee, changing the locale from Sweet Apple, Ohio, to

Sweet Apple, Georgia, to account for Lee's drawl. Rehearsal was from seven to midnight, and Lee was there every night. When the play called for a slight burp, Lee gave forth a belch that could be heard in the back row.

"That's fantastic," said Gatlin. "I wish you could do it all the time."

"I can," said Lee. And he did, at every show for a week.

"Never dropped a line," his director said.

After the curtain fell on the night of the final performance, Gatlin praised the cast but — fearing to omit someone — singled out no one. Lee was crushed. He didn't like being part of the crowd. Though he had received kudos aplenty from local critics and viewers, "All the compliments don't mean a thing," Lee told his mother, "because Dr. Gatlin didn't tell me I did a good job." The following year when Gatlin held tryouts for *Oklahoma!*, Lee wasn't around.

From the stage it was but a short step to politics. Lee made his debut as a political consultant in the eleventh grade when he convinced his longtime pal and fellow Horseman David Yon to run for student body president as Dewey P. Yon. The Yon campaign showed Lee's early genius for two key campaign consultant qualities — identifying hot issues and making over a weak candidate.

Lee made up a list of issues to run on: no homework, free beer on tap in the cafeteria, hot dates, unlimited cuts, no grades less than Bs. He also created credentials for Dewey: among them, Yon had led an Arctic expedition and was winner of the International Hairy Legs Contest.

When an informal poll showed that Yon wasn't well known outside the Dark Horseman, Lee created his own medium to publicize his candidate: *Big At's Comedy Ratings*, a flier printed on the school mimeograph machine when no one was looking and distributed around campus. The first issue featured listings of the funniest guys in school. Number one, of course, was Dewey P. Yon. There was also a girls' top ten list, and tag-team listings. When Dewey won big in the election, the school principal called for another election.

Though his candidate was tossed out of the winner's circle, Lee got an early education in politics — and in how to manipulate people through the power of the press. Lee noticed that after

his broadside appeared, students he didn't know were telling him
jokes and literally doing somersaults to get his attention. One student wore an oversized plastic display bottle of liquid Ivory soap
around Flora for a day. "It took me about an hour to realize that
they all wanted to get into the *Comedy Ratings*."

Lee expanded the handout, adding funny stories, a Bad
Breath of the Week award, a "Dial-a-Slut" service run by one Suzy
B. Cloksmeyer. Circulation increased, along with Lee's promi-
nence among his peers. Lee was the emcee, the impresario, the
delegator of wit and awards. Lee was in the spotlight, though
slightly in the shadows. "Nothing ever taught me more cleanly
and clearly that people like to see their names in the paper," he
said. "And people like to be number one at something. I always
remembered that lesson." Another thing that Atwater learned was
detachment. Lee's own name never appeared on any of the top
ten lists. "By not being involved, I could have a lot more fun with
it," he said. "I learned back then that I was just going to cool it and
stay out of the scene."

While many of his classmates were enthralled by the Beatles,
Lee admired James Brown, Sam and Dave, Wilson Pickett, and
Otis Redding, backed by the Memphis Horns, featuring the in-
comparable Wayne Jackson on that ballsy trumpet of the '60s. In
sixth grade, he had sat in the balcony, with the few other white
folks, to watch James Brown — and he used binoculars so that he
could learn the guitar parts. Now he listened to soul music on
WOIC, a black station that featured Big Sol, a deejay who also had
a record shop on Jervais Street. "Here we are sitting on the banks
of the Congaree," was Sol's signature line, "sipping our Kool-Aid
and doolin' on down the line."

Lee saw to it that black bands were well received at white
Flora High. "He showed sensitivity toward blacks that he didn't
always show to his good friends," recalled Debbie Carson.

One December morning in 1967, when an assembly was
ending, Lee ran up to the stage, distraught. He stood before the
entire student body and faculty, raising his hands like a preacher,
his body like a wound-up, frenzied doll. "Otis Redding has just
died!" he shouted. "I think we should have a silent prayer." He
bowed his head, and the congregation did likewise.

Lee's next starring role was as leader of Upsetter's Revue.
"Most of the time I was in grammar school through high school,

I was in some kind of rock 'n' roll band," he said. "I would say that at least 80 percent of my energy was involved with whatever band I was involved in. The other 20 percent of course was involved in trying to get drunk and get laid. Just like any other normal guy." Lee's band was a boy's club in revue, with fifteen members at one time — including a horn section and four singers, "the Four Expressions," who wore electric green pants, tux shirts, and bow ties. With songs like "Watermelon Man" and "Spanish Harlem," they quickly graduated from malls to club gigs in Alabama and Mississippi. They practiced incessantly in Lee's two-car garage. On hot summer nights crowds would gather in the driveway, listening to the electric wail. Once, the parents of band member J. B. Nelson asked Lee if he would let their son attend a film with them the next night. "He can go if he wants to," said Lee, who was beginning to develop a skill for inflicting discipline on others. "But he's not in the band anymore if he doesn't attend practice."

• • •

Discipline was a trait that Harvey Atwater also admired. But father and son didn't act like they had anything in common. Lee had already realized early in life that it was futile to try to please his father, who expected Lee to learn practical things, evidently by osmosis. Their biggest divergence occurred over Harvey's passion in life, cars. In most aspects of his life, Harvey Atwater was a controlled man; his life was molded by clients who demanded his full attention while chatting on about their own lives and the details of their insurance destinies. Behind the wheel of a car, though, Harvey was in control. A car depended on him for repair and maintenance, for leadership even. Harvey performed mechanical tasks with ease, and when a car grew old, began to waver, no longer had the feel, the noises, the smells that told Harvey things — then that car was gone, replaced by another, and another. Anne Atwater once estimated that her father had given care and shelter to forty cars over the years. Harvey had an inordinate capacity for clunkers, such as the jalopy that Lee drove, a $150 pea green '52 Plymouth. Lee was absolutely indifferent to the vehicle. When it began belching black smoke, Harvey told him to go check the oil.

Lee went out, came back. "I don't know where you check the oil," he said.

Harvey was enraged. Toddy asked him how Lee should know

what to do if Harvey didn't show him first. "He's just supposed to know!" said Harvey. "I knew that when I was a kid."

Lee watched in wonder one day as his father dismantled an entire toilet to locate a face towel that had been flushed, accidentally to be sure, by Some Culprit in a hurry. Had Lee been in charge, he would have located a plumber instead.

It was the same with fishing. Lee would tangle the line, lose the lure, break the pole. Harvey even fussed after Lee for not doing better in school, though he had failed eighth grade himself — a lifelong secret he kept from Lee.

But the Atwater men finally bonded over women on the night that Lee literally lost his date. At the Twilight Drive-in, a young couple could park in the back row, facing backward, and get down to business, all for $1. After the movie that night, Lee drove to a lover's lane for even more serious endeavors. That night, while Lee was parked with a date in his backseat, a cop shone a light on them through the steamy windows and told them to move along. The girl panicked and scrammed. Lee went home and told his father what had happened, certain that he would be grounded for life. Instead, Harvey phoned the police department to say it was outrageous for a public servant to poke his nose in the business of young lovers. What a dad, thought Lee.

Bright, brooding, dryly witty, Harvey was a point of reference for Lee, but Toddy was the moral compass. "He always acted like he knew he was letting his mother down," said a Flora classmate.

Up to the last day of his senior year, Lee's graduation was a cliffhanger, because he had to pass psychology. Teacher John Ellsworth called his colleague, Toddy. "It's doubtful about Lee passing," he said. "I'm gonna do what I think is best for Lee."

"Do what you've got to do," said Toddy. By now she was hoping that Lee would keep his job as a stock boy at Winn Dixie. Maybe something full-time would eventually open up there.

Lee passed. Later Ellsworth explained that Lee had contributed more to the class than any other student. "Lee just wouldn't take the time to study for a test."

After graduation, Lee had wanted to accept an offer to tour the South with Lee Dorsey, who had recorded the hits "Ya Ya" and "Working in a Coal Mine." It would have been forty bucks a night. Instead, at the insistence of Toddy, he was off to a Lutheran college: Newberry, forty miles north of Columbia. Toddy arranged a personal interview with the dean of admissions, who struck Lee as being all business. "I can make it, if you'll just give me the chance," Lee told him. The dean was just skeptical enough to bring out Lee's competitive underside. They struck a deal. If Lee passed two summer-school sessions with a C average, he would be accepted in the fall. Lee made As.

That September, as Lee readied for Newberry, Steve Sisk was preparing for the football season at the University of South Carolina. He could have gone to Alabama, but he wanted to stay close to home. He had been staying up nights, unable to sleep. "I know I'm different," he had written in his diary. "There are great things for me in life. All I have to do is reach and pluck the apple of good fortune. I only hope it will be ripe!" He shaved his head, like all the freshmen on the squad. Coach Paul Dietzel wanted to turn the fullback into a lineman, perhaps a center, and Sisk was working at it on September 3 — not a scorcher of a day, but humid nonetheless. Steve had a history of allergies; as a youngster he had had night sweats and fever rages. On the practice field that day he collapsed from heat exhaustion, complicated by a viral infection that was making the rounds on campus. In minutes his temperature rose from 104 to 109 degrees. By the time the he arrived by ambulance at the Charleston hospital, he was comatose. His organs were burned, his brain was gone — only the strong athlete's heart pounded on. He lingered for five days. On September 8 he died.

Steve's funeral was one of the largest that Columbia had seen, drawing hundreds of young mourners, including his fellow frosh "baldies" from the USC squad and the boys of autumn from Flora. Steve had been the toughest guy in the Flora '69 class. The look on the young mourners' faces went beyond puzzlement. It was the look of fear. A few days after the funeral, Lee and Joe Sligh, a fellow soul singer in Upsetter's Revue, went out to Steve's grave. They drank beer and left an empty can atop the grave with a single artificial flower, borrowed from a nearby grave, pointing up at the Carolina sky.

CHAPTER

2

LIFE OF THE PARTY

Flower child, hip chick, sweet smelling love girl. I love
girls, Jack, because I am young and I am a man. Wild
lights, wild night, sweet girls and the night is young.
Lean back and smile awhile. Ain't we lucky, Jack?
— Steve Sisk, "A Friend and Me"

Newberry was a small Lutheran school, and a freshman quickly
got to know everybody, usually at a party. The four fraternity and
two sorority houses were located on a cul-de-sac called Carol
Courts; each frat also had a party house — off campus, of course.
Lee joined Alpha Tau Omega, the fraternity that dominated all
the others. While its hard-drinking parties were no *more* ruly than
those of Flora's Horseman, its live-in arrangement invited more
camaraderie and team pranks.

At "white liquor" nights, everyone brought vodka to pour into
a bowl of mystery juices and Kool-Aid flavorings. At annual parties
such as German's Weekend, most of the guys had dates that were
sleepovers; the frat would rent a place in Lake Lure, North Carolina, for "three days of banging away." At the Boxers Party, the formal attire consisted of colorful boxer shorts. Topping it all off, just
before graduation, was the BIOYA Party (Blow It Out Your Ass),
where the guys would ritually chug boilermakers of bourbon and
beer out in the boondocks. (One year, a local bubba — stung by the
drunken teasing at the party — pulled an enormous Western-style
pistol. He was persuaded to put it away.)

Lee became social chairman at ATO. He was also impresario at the Gas House — the off-campus frat house, two blocks from

the campus residence. It was a converted old-style gas station, with a large room for dancing, a bar, and a smaller room for watching TV or movies on old-style reels. Lee started X-rated film festivals, charging admission to old porn movies featuring models wearing fake noses, masks, socks. He considered himself a connoisseur of porn flicks — appreciating both their production values and their content. "Lee would watch these things in a very detached way, as though we were at a serious movie festival," recalled one of the brothers.

On dates, too, Lee had a one-track mind. He was an old-fashioned southerner: to him, there were the nice girls you took home to Mama, and the naughty ones you took on dates. "If a date didn't end up in sex, it wasn't a very productive evening for Lee," said a brother. "It wasn't a good use of his time."

In the cafeteria one day, Lee and some of the brothers were deep in a discussion of what makes a woman hot. Back in his days of hot pursuit at Flora, Lee had driven an unsuspecting date down a lover's lane one evening — with a fellow Horseman stashed in the trunk. The plan called for Lee to loosen up the date with alcohol and foreplay, then to excuse himself for nature's call. He would unlock the trunk and the brother would move in on the mam'selle unawares. A good time would be had by all, at least in theory. In fact, Lee got swept up in his own backseat adventure, and the brother in the trunk got his own call from nature. When he started pounding on the wall behind the backseat, Lee's date bolted. So Lee's plan was never fully executed. Now he saw opportunity knocking again.

"I think it's the girl who wants to do a bunch of guys at the same time," Lee told his frat brothers, fueling their fantasies. A plot was soon underway. Lee called a coed he had been eyeing. "I'm Brother of the Month," he explained. "That means all the brothers have to wait on me hand and foot. Would you like to be my date?" Wellll, OK. Lee arranged everything. If all the guys did their part, there would be a sexually ravenous babe in his room — and everyone would get a turn.

One brother, who worked at a funeral home, borrowed the limo and picked up the girl at her house. Once at the frat house, she was escorted into the sitting room by another brother serving as butler, wearing a vest and serving "rum a dums," a mixture of light rum and 7 Up. The girl was served doubles. "We're gonna drink hard tonight, honey," said Lee, whose 7 Up had no rum in it but was dressed up to look official. After a few rounds, Lee and his date headed upstairs to his room. On the way they passed a room with the door open. Two brothers (one of them wearing a wig) were in bed simulating lovemaking. This was Lee's idea of a mood stimulator. When the date looked at him, he shrugged indifferently. Didn't *everyone* do this sort of thing at seven-thirty in the evening?

Lee and his date spent an hour behind closed doors while the other brothers gathered outside in the hall, awaiting a signal to disrobe. Finally, Lee stepped out of the room in his undershorts. "Sorry, guys," he said. "Man, she was even upset for me to *ask* her if she would do anyone else. We're just gonna have to take her on back." The limo took the Brother of the Month's date back to her quarters with suitable formality.

• • •

Back at Flora, Lee had done a landmark term paper for drama class on "The Effects of W. C. Fields's Childhood on His Four Greatest Films." Lee analyzed *The Bank Dick, My Little Chickadee, Never Give a Sucker an Even Break,* and *You Can't Cheat an Honest Man,* pointing out how Fields used pain from his childhood to create a character that his audience found entertaining because there were touches of humanity in his defining events on-screen. "Young Fields and his father hated each other from the very beginning," reported Lee. "The elder Dukinfield [Fields's real name] thought nothing of whacking his young son with his fist or anything else he could lay his hands on." The parallels between Atwater's youth — being at odds with his father (albeit without fisticuffs), determined to become an entertainer, and always having the raspiest voice, the shrewdest mind in the room — and the childhood of Fields are striking. Fields and his mother, however, "seemed to get along all right," said Lee. "She was hardworking and extremely funny. From her, Fields borrowed much of his vigilance as well as the muttered asides that were later to convulse audiences." Fields took up juggling with a passion, became a pool shark and schemer. "His trick of chattering on and on while a faraway look came on his face, he ascribed to the fact that when he was a youngster, as he chatted with his friends he was busy thinking of schemes to cheat them."

Not unlike Lee's lottery at ATO, for instance. You would

draw a number, one to one hundred. If you drew, say, seventy-five, then you had to put seventy-five cents into the pot. Frat and friends might run up the pot to $50 or $60. The secret drawing was usually "won" by one of Lee's friends or Lee's roommate, Jim McCabe, and they would split the pot three ways. Ah, yes.

By the end of his freshman year at Newberry, Lee Atwater had mediocre grades and a beer body — his five-nine frame was carrying 200 pounds. That summer of 1970 he worked in a rock quarry, drank tons of beer, and earned the nickname Fat At. History does not record which made him bristle more, the stinging nickname or the physical labor. He cut back on his drinking gradually, imbibing mostly on weekends. And he began to realize the importance of a college degree. "You know that black man who worked beside me — he'd been on the job for twenty-five years, and I could shovel the gravel just as good as he could from the first day," he told his mother. "I'm not spending the rest of my life shoveling gravel."

When Lee's close friend David Yon got a summer job with Senator Ernest "Fritz" Hollings in '71, Lee told his mother, "Gosh, I'd give my right arm if I could do that." Toddy couldn't help with Hollings, a Democrat. But she had gone to school in Spartanburg with Warren Abernathy, who now ran Strom Thurmond's state office. She called him.

"Send him on up," said Abernathy. "We've got some intern spots open in August."

No wonder: August was dead time in D.C. — the rich and infamous were all on vacation — and internships paid poorly anyway. But Lee didn't much care. In D.C. he got the political bug. "I'll never forget the look on Lee's face when he saw the Senate floor. It was vibrant," recalled Linda Catoe Guell, the aide who introduced Lee to Thurmond that summer.

Part of the charm was Senator Thurmond himself. Lee Atwater adored him as the master politician, believing that Thurmond's feisty write-in victory in 1954, which made him a senator, was "the eighth wonder of the world." One afternoon the senator asked for volunteers to help him move some furniture into a new home, and Lee jumped at the chance. Atwater was on the premises for only one month, but the senator took a liking to him, teaching him "the game, the competition, the show" of politics.

Lee was special, like a son. Soon Lee was driving him, albeit pre-
cariously, to events all over the state just for the chance to spend
those hours learning in the car.

When Lee Atwater was embarking on white southern man-
hood in the '60s, most of the nationally prominent southern white
men were known for their toughness. Lester Maddox of Georgia
and Ross Barnett of Mississippi and George Wallace of Alabama
all stood firm against integration. Bull Connor of Alabama sicced
the dogs on peaceful civil rights demonstrators. The world had not
yet encountered the likes of Georgia's Jimmy Carter, or the sac-
charine cinematic niceness of Alabama's Forrest Gump. Although
Strom had previously been a Dixiecrat and prominent segregationist, he wasn't a segregationist when Lee came under his influence in 1971. Lee admired the senator's passion for individualism
and freedom. "When I was working with him," Lee recalled, "he
told me that when he was a kid he decided he didn't want to be a
common man; he wanted to be an *un*common man. He told me
how he had used self-discipline to get to where he was in life."

Inspired, Lee began to read Plato, Bentham, Locke — and
the two thinkers who most influenced him, the Virginians Madison and Jefferson. "Not only did I want to read, but I learned to
read the things that counted," Lee recalled later. "What we are
looking for in life is wisdom. If you understand what wisdom is,
you can pick up any book in any bookstore and within two minutes
figure out whether the book you are holding contains any wisdom.
Wisdom as opposed to knowledge and facts." In college he was
a history major, and he read ravenously. He looked on history as
"merely a storehouse" of examples and tools on which to draw for
political decisions, he later told Columbia journalist Jan Stucker.
"And in the middle of a campaign, I have to make decisions so fast
that it's only afterwards that I realize the historical basis on which
those decisions are made."

At age twenty, Lee decided that someday he would become
a teacher. His mother would like that. For now, though, he would
teach the art of the political hustle. When he returned to school
in the fall, he launched little Newberry into the heart of Carolina Republican politics. Clemson and the University of South
Carolina had traditionally controlled the state's College Republicans, but when Atwater asked for a constitutional convention, they
smugly agreed — much to his delight. Within months, Newberry

had taken control of the College Republicans, and Atwater, after drawing all the small constituencies under one tent, was state chairman. He became a record-setting recruiter for the group.

First, he persuaded his best-looking fraternity brothers to drive to women's colleges to recruit new members. Atwater equipped the recruiters with three pens — red, blue, and black — and asked them to rate the girls as date material, for the benefit of the brothers. "The red were the best-looking girls, the blue were the mediocre, and the black were 'Don't call,' " recalled one recruiter. "That was 90 percent of the incentive." Lee would then enlist the best-looking females to recruit new members at all-male schools. He used his office to establish college outposts for Thurmond's reelection campaign in 1972. He did the same for Nixon's reelection in five southern states. Nothing motivated Lee more than self-interest.

It was an early political pyramid scheme that created an army of volunteers Lee could call on — to plant questions at rallies, for example. During the Thurmond race, when the senator's opponent appeared on campus, Lee had his pals stand up and read prepared questions from index cards. Often they read in a monotone, which Lee imitated and laughed at afterward. Later he got better actors, people who didn't have to look at their cards. The effect was the same either way: Lee made the opponents squirm.

Struck by Thurmond's physical vigor at his age, Lee started jogging. As a runner, Lee was not fast, but he was relentless: the race went not always to the swiftest, but to the one who just kept movin'. "I'll never put that weight on again," he vowed. His new fighting weight was 155, and that was that. Lee had "a quality of physical toughness that you couldn't take for granted," said Mike Ussery, a fraternity brother. Were someone to try to hurt Lee in a real street fight, "I think Lee would throw the first one and try to make it lethal. . . . One of his pet sayings was 'Don't ever give a rattlesnake the chance to strike twice.' "

For Lee Atwater, politics became a way for him to express his spirit. He took to it like someone born again to religion. "It was part rebellion," he later explained to journalist David Remnick. "When I got into politics, the establishment was all Democrats, and I was antiestablishment. The young Democrats were all the guys running around in three-piece suits, smoking cigars and cutting deals, so I said, 'Hell, I'm a Republican.' But much more of it was a response to what was going on in the early '70s. I resented the way the left wing claimed to have captured the hearts and minds of American youth. They certainly hadn't captured mine. I knew whom I wanted to be fighting for, and it wasn't George McGovern."

In college Lee informally managed Ron Hightower, a lawyer and adviser to ATO, who was running for state office. In one instance Lee enlisted fellow ATO brothers and placed them strategically in a crowd that was gathering to hear Hightower speak. Lee called it "the diamond trick," placing three or four brothers down front in the center of a row. Then, with this as "home base," he put similar groups at first, second, and third base — second base being near the middle of the room. Not unlike the standing ovations Lee had staged during Vocational Week back at Flora High, whenever Hightower made a point in his speech, the triangle of brothers would all arise and applaud vigorously. Their placement and enthusiasm were intoxicating. Others in the crowd followed suit. Hightower was getting standing ovations for making routine observations.

During his junior year, Atwater managed his first real campaign, for Bill Edens, who had served as a part-time advance man ("expenses only") for Richard Nixon in 1968. Edens, who owned a GM truck dealership, decided to run for mayor in Forest Acres, the bedroom community where the Atwaters resided and where Al Burks, a Democrat and well-known hardware dealer, had been mayor for sixteen years. Lee signed on with the understanding that he would be paid $150. He was in charge of mailings, as well as covering the community in one of Eden's pickup trucks filled with posters and yard signs.

Yard signs were allowed "with the stipulation that they had to be removed within twenty-four hours after the election," recalled Edens. If there was one thing that disturbed the Forest Acres community, it was clutter. Thus cleanliness and orderliness became two of the big issues that Lee helped develop during the campaign. Edens called for keeping the streets clean with a better trash pickup system, adding more police to the department, and improving police response time. He also vowed not to increase taxes — and won the election, in which fewer than three thousand votes were cast, by a margin of nearly three to one. "The polls closed at seven that night, and Lee had all the signs down by seven the next morning," recalled Edens. "He was a hustler."

All along the way, his parents tried to discourage Lee. "What mother wants her son to become a politician?" said Toddy. "A doctor, a lawyer, an Indian chief — *anything* but a politician." Still Lee hogged the phone — calls came throughout the night from campuses in other time zones — and bummed travel expenses off his family so he could attend Republican functions around the state. He also wrecked two family cars.

"Lee, those grown men are just using you as a kid to do what they want," said Toddy one exasperating afternoon.

"Well, Mama," said Lee, "I may be using them, too."

The academic year at Newberry featured a month break between semesters. In January of 1972 Lee used the time for another internship in the office of Strom Thurmond. He and high school pal David Yon rented a room at the old Capitol Hotel, where they kept a loaf of bread, mayo, mustard, and baloney in a cooler, replenished regularly with free ice from the hotel. They survived on it — and on politics. A little sacrifice in order to wander around the Capitol unsupervised, "acting and feeling like big shots," said Yon.

The swagger began here, as did a certain political awakening. Yon recalled how astonished Lee was to find that Strom's staff used autowriters to sign all those personal letters, that politics ultimately must be mass-produced to affect the masses. "It was Lee's first wake-up call to the fact that there was a lot of bullshit in the business." They watched Ed Muskie and Shirley Chisholm announce for president that month. Lee, who had made a commitment to politics after his first round with Thurmond, was now absolutely mesmerized. "It was like throwing gasoline on a fire for Lee," recalled Yon.

Though his duties as an intern had been menial, politics now coursed through Lee's veins. It was more than a job. It was self-validation, a way for Lee to define himself. Although experience is a great teacher in politics, at the outset Lee relied totally on instinct, and his instincts were at home here. Moreover, the work gave him entrée to a world he could only dream of as a youngster when he looked forward to knocking on the senator's door on Halloween. Above all, in this business there was a constant flow of stimuli — people, messages, calls, pleadings, job requests, favors to

grant (or to deny) — all of which Atwater needed to keep from being bored by the tedium of life on this planet. And he had energy,
incredible energy. All of this, and the prospect of making a nice
salary, too? Well, OK, but for Atwater, it was different. For him it
wasn't business. It was religion.

Atwater later explained that he had been driven to enter politics because "it is applicable everywhere. The other interesting
thing, and one of the reasons I got into it, is that I *like to learn*. If you
like to learn, politics is the place to be. You've got to learn statistics,
you've got to learn history, you've got to learn math, you've got to
learn demographics, you've got to learn culture — well, you've just
got to learn something about everything."

Strom Thurmond remembered young Atwater as a prime
student. "Lee was always a good watcher," he said. "He didn't miss
a thing."

Politics appealed to the prankish youngster Lee always
remained in his heart of hearts. As he approached his fortieth birthday, Lee would later reflect, "The fact of the matter is, I never really became an adult. I don't want to be a fucking adult. I want to
be Lee Atwater." And Lee Atwater paid no attention to the rules:
"I made my own up."

On June 13, 1972, Lee filled out a bio sheet for the *Greenville News-Piedmont* and submitted it with a picture of himself for
a "story" about being a delegate at the Republican National Convention. He explained that he was state chairman of the South
Carolina College Republicans, a committeeman, Oakwood precinct, Richland county. "I am the youngest member (full-fleged)
[sic] of our delegation," he wrote. Lee listed his church affiliation
as Bethel Methodist, and under "Education" he said he was a "rising senior and history major" at Newberry College. Chosen as an
alternate for the convention, Lee had been promoted to full delegate when former U.S. Representative and 1970 gubernatorial
candidate Albert Watson decided not to attend the convention.

When the story came out, Lee was quoted as saying, "I think
the President is going to carry the under-30 vote in South Carolina.
McGovern is strong in the colleges, but that's not everything." Lee
liked the way it made him sound, the positioning it gave him. The
press could be had.

As a rising senior, he quickly noticed that the press was usually willing to run with whatever you gave them. He was better

educated politically than many of the young reporters. Besides, he had more energy and was always willing to take extra time with them to make meaningful connections for his candidate. He knew that voters often formed their opinions on the basis of reading stories written by people too busy to read and do the work necessary to connect the dots in political reporting. That's where he came in.

Lee learned early that if you make it easy for the press to do its job, the press will make it easy for you to do your own job. The easiest and best known means of gaining free press exposure was the press release — a prepared statement containing an explanation of a point or an attack on the opposition. He kept a thick file of his own crafted "stories" that had appeared in the South Carolina press, usually run without a byline and always without any indication that the "source" for the story was actually a self-serving press release. As you climbed higher up the food chain, of course, the press was less willing to regurgitate what you handed them. But at the local level, there was a lazy, willing element in the press with which a fellow could build a clip file quite readily. And what's to lose? "Even if release information is not published," said Lee, "the worst is a waste of a twenty-cent stamp."

As a delegate to the Republican National Convention in Miami that summer, Lee inadvertently drove the senator into a demonstration of peaceniks. He later told David Remnick, "Somebody yelled, 'Hey, it's Strom Thurmond, the power pig of the South!' We couldn't move." Lee thought they were in trouble. "But, man, Thurmond didn't sweat. He said, 'I'm gonna talk with these people.' Jesus! Well, he gets out, and there's TV cameras all over the place, and this eighteen- or nineteen-year-old girl confronts him. She starts callin' him a fascist pig and cocksucker and all sorts of stuff. And the whole time Thurmond is just smilin' and sayin', 'Little girl, do your parents know you're out here? Honey, you sure are a pretty little thing.' The girl's still cursing at him, and Thurmond gets back in the car and we drive away. I say, 'What were you doing?' And he says, 'Young man, that'll be twenty-five thousand votes when we get home.' Boy, did I learn from that man."

By May 1973, when he received his bachelor's degree in history along with 151 members of his class, Lee was heavily involved

with the College Republicans on a national scale. In June he became campaign manager for Karl Rove, a highly controversial candidate running for chairman of the College Republican National
Committee. The chairmanship was a full-time paid job, with influence in D.C. The CRNC comprised more than 1,000 col-
legiate Republican clubs, with a membership exceeding 100,000.
It was housed and partially funded by the Republican National
Committee.

As executive director of the CRNC in 1971, Rove, a twenty-
two-year-old Texan, had organized regional conferences for College Republicans on "the nuts and bolts of politics," talking about
pranks and campaign espionage, such as purloining the opposition party's garbage to obtain inside memos and lists of contributors. On one occasion, operatives in Illinois discovered evidence
in stolen garbage that one of their own supporters had contributed
$5,000 to the opposition. "So one of our finance guys called the
guy up the next day and told him there was a vicious rumor going
around . . . that not only was he giving money to both sides, . . .
but that they had heard he had given [the Democrat] more," said
Rove's accomplice at a 1972 seminar that was taped. "The guy got
all embarrassed, and flew to Chicago that day with a check for
$2,000" for the Republican candidate.

On another occasion, Rove had assumed a false name and
posed as a supporter to enter the campaign headquarters of a
Democratic candidate for state treasurer in Illinois in 1970. Rove
took some of the candidate's campaign stationery and used it
to fake a thousand invitations to the opening of the Democrat's
headquarters, adding "free beer, free food, girls, and a good time
for nothing" to the invitations, which were distributed at a hippie
commune, a rock concert, and soup kitchens in Chicago.

Despite Lee's best backstage effort to steer Rove to victory,
the CRNC convention ended in confusion, dissension — and the
election of two rival chairmen, Robert Edgeworth and Karl Rove.
The standoff was forwarded for settlement to the Republican National Committee, not the most propitious setting in the summer
of Watergate, with allegations of dirty tricks and political espionage
in the air in Washington. Chairman George Bush established a
grievance committee to look into the CRNC, but his people did
not consider the tapes and transcript submitted as evidence against
Rove, for fear of dirty tricks — "one of the things with tapes is that

they can be doctored by editing," said one investigator. On September 6, 1973, Atwater's candidate was notified of his victory in a letter from Bush. Karl Rove promptly appointed Atwater to his old post, executive director of the CRNC.

At the elevator on the fourth floor of the RNC building, Lee stuck out his hand to a chipper, good-looking middle-aged man. "I'm Lee Atwater," he said, "the new head of the College Republicans."

"Well, it's good to meet you, Lee. My name is George Bush."

Lee knew who he was, of course. He proceeded to do what he would later refer to as "a brazen thing."

"Mr. Bush," he said, "I know you're the chairman here, and I've got a few things I want to tell you about what I can do for you with the College Republicans."

Without batting an eye, Bush said, "Well, come in and tell me." Bush took him into his office.

"I was in hog heaven," Atwater would later say, deeply impressed by Bush's willingness not only to talk to a young Republican, but to listen. "I couldn't believe a guy in his position would spend that kind of time with me."

After twenty minutes of listening, Bush inquired, "What do you want to do in politics?"

"Someday," said Lee Atwater, "I'd like to be sitting in your chair right there."

Bush adopted him at once. "Lee Atwater became one of the five thousand friends of George Bush at that point," recalled a member of the Bush clan.

Atwater began receiving the famous Bush personal letters. "Unreal," said Lee, who was soon using the same tactic with his own acquaintances. "You couldn't make a move without getting a note from the guy." Lee tried to keep all of Bush's notes in an orderly file, but volume made it impossible. "He uses funny but different analogies on each and every one. The interesting thing about these notes is (a) they're personal; (b) they have a meaningful message; (c) they're short but sweet; (d) he knows how to get them out quickly; (e) they're part of his personality; (f) they work."

Although Lee had visited Washington, D.C., and been a temporary resident in the past, moving to the city was a culture shock to him. Lee's folksiness and good ol' boy demeanor — assets back home in South Carolina — left people in D.C. with the impression that his future was seriously limited. He was also a member of his city's minority race for the first time. There were many different kinds of police, guards, and security people around, everywhere. Everybody wore uptight business suits and took themselves so seriously. The established, professional men were lifeless and slender, and their female counterparts were so tough they seemed sexless, even masculine. Conversations about policies and political punditry went on incessantly, in the most minute detail. They talked fast, they walked fast.

Lee was rooming with Stuart Barnwell, another good ol' boy from the College Republicans back home, in an apartment with ambiance somewhere between ratty and cruddy. Mike Ussery, a fraternity brother, recalled visiting the duo and going out for dinner, where Lee was very impressed with the Steak & Ale concept of "all you can eat for five dollars!" That night, Ussery slept on a straw mat at Lee's place.

Gradually, Lee began to blend in, even becoming just a bit affected as he walked around the halls of the various Senate office buildings, the Capitol, the Library of Congress, the White House. The Hill. He began to feel a sense of privilege and access that others would never understand, a feeling underscored when a hotshot senator passed you in the hall and gave you a nod. He knew of behind-the-scenes details when Something Big was going to happen. The goal now was to be able to take it all in without that bumpkin look on your face that the tourists have.

Lee and Bush began meeting regularly. "I was trying desperately to pick up a girl who was interning for Strom Thurmond, and I was getting nowhere in record time," Atwater told *Rolling Stone*. "So I asked George Bush if I could bring this girl by to get a picture made with him and for him to mention that I was doing a vital job at the Republican National Committee. So he did that, and when she walked out of the office, he said, 'I don't think she really got the full meaning of that. Maybe something else will work.' " That weekend Bush loaned Atwater his boat, docked on the Potomac.

Lee tried to impress the girl, Sally Dunbar, with his boatsmanship, but she quickly realized that he didn't know the first thing about steering the boat. Yet he had a boyish quality that appealed to her mothering instinct. When they were stopped for speeding on the river, she thought: This guy needs somebody to take care of him. The rapport was instantaneous. Lee looked Sally in the eyes, listened intently, and had a hundred questions. He wanted to know everything about her.

Sally had been happy as a child, born and raised in Union, South Carolina, which proclaimed itself "the city of hospitality" — a town of ten thousand in a rural county where the largest employer made tassels for curtains and braided ropes for places as far away as Buckingham Palace. She had been a majorette in the band at high school and the first in her family to attend college. Sally's father Curtis was in the federal soil conservation program; her mother, called Theo (for Theodosia), was a secretary to the superintendent of schools.

Life had been very secure for Sally during the growing-up years. Curtis was forty when he married Theo, forty-four when Sally was born. Curtis Jr. was born two years later. At thirty-six Theo knew that she didn't want to stay home and rear kids full-time, so she returned to her job, and Sally's father played a formative role in the rearing of his children. Theo, a Baptist, yielded to Curtis, a devout Methodist, on Sundays, so he started taking Sally to services when she was two. When Sally turned five, he took her to Sunday school afterward. She cried when he started to leave. At the end of that year, the teacher told the class how much she was going to miss the seven students, "and our eighth student, Mr. Dunbar." Curtis, sitting in a small chair at the back of the room, had attended every class with his daughter.

While dating, Lee and Sally talked about what they wanted to do in life. Lee wanted to pursue politics, but not as a politician. He wanted to manage campaigns. He talked about his value system, how you needed an alert mind in politics, and how you had to be careful about money. He had seen too many people corrupted when money was a consideration.

How you handled money was important to Sally, too. Like Lee, she had been raised in a family where there were memories of the Depression. When Sally's grandmother was twenty-six, her husband died, leaving her to raise three children alone, including six-month-old Theo. There was some insurance money, which she put in the bank. But when the banks closed during the Depression, she had to work extremely hard just to make family ends meet, and the children had to rear themselves. Sally's mother often spoke of these hard times with her daughter, and she kept such meticulous records of *every* family expenditure *every* day that the

idea that money was a form of security made a strong impression
on Sally.

Politically, Sally was indifferent. She liked studying current
events at school and watching political conventions on TV, staying
up late for vote counts. But she had no sense of party loyalty; in fact,
her parents were Democrats. After Sally posed for the picture with
Bush, Lee mailed it "To Sally Dunbar's Mother," in Union, trying
to impress her parents by making their daughter seem important.
Have the young man come by, they said.

Sally had a lot of the qualities Lee wanted in a wife. She
wasn't clingy, didn't get jealous. Sally liked the fact that Lee didn't
hover, didn't use a full-court press on her. No, he would talk with
other people, liked to tell stories, was comfortable being the center of attention, while Sally stayed on the sidelines, pleased just
to enjoy the total atmosphere of the evening. Like most southern
girls, she had been taught to defer to men, and as an attractive
small auburn-haired collegian, she had learned to beguile them.
Although she was attending Winthrop, a women's school, Sally
had been pinned to Bill Lucas, a senior at The Citadel, whom she
had met at one of that school's legendary weekend beach parties.

An opposing candidate did not hinder Lee, who began a
campaign for Sally's love. Lee could relate to everything about
her — the beach parties, of course, but also his mother had
attended Winthrop for one year before returning to enroll at
Wofford and study Spanish. Sally was a special-ed major and
wanted to teach. Toddy was a teacher, of course.

Lee wanted Sally to meet his mom. They went to his home
for a weekend, and Sally delighted in Toddy's hospitality, except for
one thing: Lee got his old room, and Toddy arranged for Sally to
sleep on the couch. Lee was a mama's boy, totally, thought Sally.

The Dunbars were not without some misgivings about this
young man. When Lee arrived in Union to meet them, he surprised everyone by bringing along Beechie Brooker, a high school
pal who served as driver and Lee's traveling audience. The
Dunbars told Sally's old beau, Bill, not to give up. Lee was just a
summertime fling, they thought. Bill was the real thing.

But Lee was different and immediately captivating. Sally
parted ways with Bill and let herself fall hopelessly in love. She and
Lee went to the movies, to parties where he played his guitar. He
made Sally feel like she was going to be part of an exciting team.

At political picnics, he and Sally arrived together, went their separate ways, worked the crowd, rejoined at the end. "I'm gonna put that man in the White House!" Sally told her parents one day.

Lee liked Sally because she was more secure than he was. He always sought her approval — "Did the speech go well? Was I all right?" — but rarely her advice. Once, at a political workshop he conducted with Karl Rove at American University, Lee bragged about some of his old favorite strategies, including the "diamond" trick for rigging audiences.

"Lee, you shouldn't be teaching dirty tricks," cautioned Sally afterward, reminding him of Watergate.

"Don't worry about me," Lee replied. "I know what I'm doing."

3

THE EDUCATION OF
A CONSULTANT

Handlers and consultants and managers always tend to
view the candidate as a necessary pain in the ass.
— David Keene, Bush campaign manager, 1980

When Lee returned to Columbia, South Carolina, in late '73
to enter the political consulting wars, he moved back in with his
parents, assuring them that the arrangement would be strictly temporary. Not only that, he brought along Stuart Barnwell, his roommate and political cohort in Washington. By day they jammed the
phone; by night Stuart crashed on the couch. The family room
was off-limits to the normal. "This," Harvey said, "has got to end."

At the age of twenty-three, Lee left home for an apartment — and an office with a firm that he called Baker & Associates. There was no Baker. Lee had distanced himself from this
endeavor, as he had done with *Big At's Comedy Ratings*. The
agency was named after a man whose portrait Lee had purchased
at a garage sale. Except for Stuart, there were no associates. Lee
usually flew solo. The office was two blocks off Two Notch Road,
on Beltline Road — above a chicken-wing restaurant. Lee resisted
the temptation to sneak downstairs.

Six days a week, he ate right, jogged, and didn't smoke. Discipline. He called Friday his junk day: He ate bacon and hot dogs,
sat around unshaven, and smoked a pack of Winstons. Friday night
he drank, lots.

Lee worked with ferocity, from early morn till late night. How else could you become a political consultant? There was no coursework, no school of training, no degree in the world of political operatives. No, you learned by trial and terror. After all, if George Washington's military training consisted of reading two books on the art of war and taking fencing lessons, how difficult could it be to teach yourself to be a consultant?

One thing that Lee thought he had going for him was a dream candidate: Carroll Campbell. They had met several years earlier at a state convention for College Republicans. On that occasion Campbell and his wife stood amazed as Atwater bounced around onstage, shouting at the top of his lungs, windmilling his arms, exhorting the students to fight the good Republican fight. They had never seen a convention speech quite like that. Lee's arms didn't hang at his side; they stuck out, palms outward, and moved up and down and up again. "But there was a message," Campbell later said, "and he mesmerized the young people." After Lee's speech Campbell introduced himself, sensing in Lee a kind of youth and commitment that reminded him of his younger brother, Richard, who had been killed at the age of nineteen in Vietnam two years earlier. The men bonded quickly.

Campbell was impressed by Lee's drive. Here was someone who could motivate people, and who had good instincts. "He could see around corners, anticipate what was going to happen. He was good at it, and this led to some strategizing."

As for the immaculate Campbell, he reminded Lee of Robert Redford in *The Candidate,* the political movie of '72. Lee admired Campbell because he was "the epitome of a self-made man." When he was in his teens, his parents had divorced. Much of the responsibility of raising a younger brother and four sisters fell to him. That burden was not lightened when his brother was killed.

Carroll Campbell had actually backed into a political career. From Greenville he had run congressional campaigns for Democrats in the late 1960s; there was no South Carolina Republican Party to speak of at that time. In the process he got a bird's-eye view of rigged elections and beatings for those who got out of line. In one Democratic primary he found himself in a meeting with his candidate and a ward heeler, who told them how much five boxes of votes would cost: "Pay for the boxes and I'll deliver them to you."

Campbell said no deal. When those boxes came in, Campbell's candidate got three votes and lost. In 1968 Campbell volunteered to be a poll watcher — for Nixon. He served as campaign manager for Cooper White, the first Republican mayor of the city of Greenville. The following year Campbell ran for a seat in the state house of representatives in a special election and lost. In 1970 he ran again and won.

Carroll needed help with some bills he was trying to get through the state legislature, including a constitutional amendment that would give eighteen-year-olds in South Carolina the right to vote. Carroll was ahead of the wave and spoke with special conviction when he used the slogan "If you're old enough to go to war, you're old enough to vote." Lee organized the state campuses, and the amendment passed in South Carolina before a federal constitutional amendment gave the vote to eighteen-year-olds nationally in 1971.

Lee and Carroll became political brothers. Campbell, about the same height and heft as Atwater, was ten years older, with just enough seasoning to control Lee without squelching his delightful, youthful exuberance. Campbell was also hardworking, with a sharp business mind. At thirty, he owned Handy-Park, a parking-lot franchise that had become the largest of its kind in South Carolina. Then he purchased several Burger King restaurants in Florida and Tennessee. Along the way, he became what Atwater would call "a natural politician. He has handled with equal ease the president of a major textile firm, a cabinet-ranking diplomat, and a filling station attendant." Campbell firmly grasped state and national issues, and he was adept at taking reporters in hand.

Campbell was a patient, trusting mentor to the youthful manager. Lee would later say that he learned much from Strom Thurmond, whose name carried more clout as a reference on one's political résumé; but he had learned to be a political handler in the grassroots campaigns of Carroll Campbell.

The Republican Party had only been on the ticket in South Carolina since 1952, so Campbell tried to make himself a spokesman for reform. He was reelected to the state house of representatives in 1972 with 42,000 votes, more than anyone had ever received in Greenville County. Now, in 1974, he was planning to run for lieutenant governor — with an eye on the U.S. Senate, and perhaps someday on the White House. Atwater wanted to hitch his wagon to that star.

But then along came William Westmoreland, and Lee Atwater thought he'd found a faster-moving star.

William Childs Westmoreland was a native son. Born in 1914 in the mill town of Pacolet (population 500), twelve miles outside Spartanburg, Westmoreland quickly sprouted wings and made his first trip to Europe at fifteen. By the age of eighteen, he had left South Carolina for West Point and an army career that would include seventeen battle campaigns in three wars, the U.S. command in Vietnam, and a Man of the Year cover on *Time* magazine in 1965. After retiring to Charleston in 1972, Westmoreland signed on with Democratic governor John West to head a task force for economic growth, which entailed extensive travel around the state.

"You know, you should run for governor," said the governor.

"If I do, it'll be as a Republican," replied Westmoreland. Shortly after, the general was coaxed by state Republicans to enter the state's first Republican primary.

While stationed in Washington with the College Republican National Committee, Lee had heard of Westmoreland's next campaign. Lee sought out Harry Dent, the Republican operative who ran the White House political shop during Nixon's first term, and who was now coaching the general. Dent introduced Lee to Westmoreland, who rather liked the energy that Lee exuded. Lee later told Campbell that Westmoreland had asked him to run his campaign. Campbell was enraged. Lee tried to assuage him, saying that, after the primaries, he envisioned a Westmoreland/Campbell ticket.

Westmoreland's campaign for governor peaked the day it was announced. "I didn't know beans about politics, and Lee didn't know beans about the military," recalled the general. "I was internationally oriented, and this was the first time I was ever in the trenches. But Lee liked to quote from Sun-tzu's *The Art of War*, and I knew Sun-tzu well, and somehow we put a campaign together, though I can't say my heart was ever in it." When James Edwards, a dentist and Republican Party regular, entered the primary, the old-boy constituency kicked in. Edwards won the nomination handily.

The loss didn't bother Westmoreland. *C'est la guerre*, he

thought, considering it a sacrifice for the cause of the party in South Carolina, where Republicans were still a rarity in office. Lee, ever an ungracious loser, had the dry heaves for two days.

In the meantime, Campbell had won his primary with 70 percent of the vote. When Lee wanted to return to Campbell's campaign for lieutenant governor, all was forgiven. It was a shoe-string operation, and Lee was tying all the shoes. "He struck me as being very tense," Campbell said. "He took the job of politics and campaigning very seriously. He developed a sixth sense, an ability to anticipate what a candidate might do and the impact it might have." Still, Campbell — who had managed campaigns himself in the 1960s — regularly overruled his inexperienced manager.

In 1974, as community battles over utility rates proliferated, one of the least popular institutions in the state was South Carolina Electric & Gas. To position Campbell as a populist, Atwater developed what he called "a long polarizing TV spot that I could not guarantee would win the election, but it would have broken the election wide open because it was the issue of the hour." The utility president phoned Campbell, saying the ad would damage his campaign. "Which was bullshit," said Lee, "because Carroll was not getting a cent from those people." Regardless, Campbell had Atwater pull the spot the next day.

"It was one of the two or three most effective spots I have ever seen," Atwater later said. "I will never forget that event. I have often thought of it as a time where I absolutely knew the right thing to do. I absolutely did, but at twenty-two I did not have the self-confidence to slug it out."

Although Brantley Harvey outspent Campbell three to one, the polls showed that the race was close all the way through. "We got on a plane in Greenville the last day and were ahead," Campbell said. "Flew into Columbia, and we were behind." Some boxes came in late. "A few rural counties, some money exchanges hands, and there's one hundred percent control by the Democrats," Campbell theorized. "That was politics in our state at that time." Carroll lost by 6 percent, with 239,317 votes to Brantley Harvey's 272,493.

"Lee ran a terrific campaign," said Campbell. "It almost killed me." It almost killed Lee's ambitions as well. "I got over it," Lee later told Columbia journalist Jan Stucker, "but I never want to get to where I can stomach losing."

For those aged twenty-three, failure can be a great instructor. "I tried to do too much, too fast," Atwater explained. "So I started all over again. First I had to win local. Then state. Then regional. Then . . . more."

He worked a series of twenty-eight winning campaigns over the next four years, starting with the lowly city council. In 1975 he managed Joyce Hearn's campaign for the state house. "He really made politics fun," she said. "He dragged in all sorts of volunteers from the campuses around Columbia — the College Republicans were like a standing army for him — and they worked ungodly hours. When things got down to the wire, I remember going into the office and seeing Lee in midnight meetings with his staff. For them it was the excitement, the win factor. He had a real insight into motivating others."

It all required confidence. "Self-confidence versus cockiness mean two different things," Atwater said later. "I have been both. I had to go out and manufacture self-confidence." Hamlet could never have won a political campaign. "The single most important component in politics is decision making," Atwater observed. "When you need to make a decision, (a) make the damn decision, and (b) implement it — quickly."

He was a man of action who wanted to convert others to lives of action. Lee took graduate courses in journalism at the University of South Carolina. (Sun-tzu: "When you have assessed the opponent and seen the opponent's formation, then you can tell who will win.") "I was in college one day, and I sat up looking at this professor talking about campaigns and politics," he recalled. "I guess the best way to put it is this guy was an egghead. This guy wouldn't know a vote if he saw one. I said to myself I am going to teach college one day, but I'm not going to do it until I go out and get enough practical experience and really learn the business and accumulate enough knowledge and wisdom to where when I go in a college classroom there won't be a kid sitting there saying, 'This guy doesn't know what he's doing.' There's plenty of room on college campuses for eggheads and people who are professional scholars. But I think, as a novelty, you ought to have a few people who have actually gone out and spent a lot of time and effort on the practical side."

Having reinvented himself as a consultant to his satisfaction, Atwater started looking for a race that would return him to the limelight. It came in 1976, when Campbell announced that he was running for a state senate seat representing Greenville and Laurens Counties. The seat was left vacant when Richard Riley resigned to chair Jimmy Carter's state campaign. The heir apparent was Daniel Yarborough, Riley's cousin and a fellow member of his law firm. Yarborough was thirty-one and attractive; he had a pretty wife and child. His campaign chairman and father-in-law, former Furman University president Gordon Blackwell, promised to use his extensive contacts to organize and finance the campaign.

Once again, Atwater became Campbell's manager. Both were taking a small step backward, with hopes that it would someday lead to a giant leap forward. Instead of a statewide race embracing all forty-seven counties, this campaign would cover just two. It would give Atwater a small lab in which to try out techniques that he would later apply to presidential campaigns. He took careful notes throughout, chronicling the campaign in a thesislike "work project" he submitted as part of the requirements for the masters of mass communication degree he was eventually awarded by the University of South Carolina in May 1977.

At this point Atwater and Campbell had worked with each other for five years. Atwater had managed Campbell's only statewide campaign, and he had raised funds to help pay off its $50,000 debt. They knew each other's weaknesses. Campbell, for instance, had trouble keeping his hands off the campaign wheel. "It is hard for a man whose political career is on the line to surrender details of his campaign," said Atwater. To Lee, the campaign manager had to be in control. He had once trained a manager of Joyce Hearn's campaign with this advice: "When she panics over something, tell her *anything*, get her off your back, lie to her, if necessary. Then run the campaign exactly as you planned it."

For his part, Lee shot from the lip. No longer the gawking boy of '74, he now manufactured self-confidence by the truckload. "He was a BS artist of the first order," Campbell remembered. "We put out more than one fire that was his. But that was just Lee. If he didn't know the answer, he'd make up one — and generally get by with it. Because he was a spin doctor." For politicos like Lee, spin wasn't lyin' — not at all. Spin was making public logic out of a situation, providing an analysis that made perfect sense and even made it look as though you'd thought everything out beforehand, when in fact the explanation was always ex post facto.

At first both Atwater and Campbell thought that victory in the state senate race would come too easily to require Lee's full time. They soon reconsidered. Lee feared that Carolina Democrats would ride the coattails of Jimmy Carter, then rising like a meteor out of Plains, Georgia. Meanwhile, Baptists from Bob Jones University had taken control of the local Republican Party at precinct meetings. Lee thought them decent but politically naive. They "were considered extremist by most of the community," he said.

To make matters worse, Yarborough became chairman of the Greenville County Democratic Party, a forum for free media coverage. His father-in-law was generating Old Greenville support from the pillars of the community. "This was especially alarming because this group was conservative and usually voted Republican," observed Atwater.

With a flow chart, Atwater and Campbell mapped out a fivefold strategy. First, Campbell would act as the front-runner throughout the campaign. His landslide victory in 1972 and his 72 percent margin in Greenville County in the lieutenant governor's race in '74 had made him well known. Yarborough was the new kid on the block. Campbell would remain aloof, as if he had no opposition. His campaign would never mention Yarborough or even answer charges the Other Guy would level at Campbell. Atwater also decided to avoid debates.

Second, they would target the independents. "The political realities of 1976 indicated the folly of riding an elephant down Main Street in Greenville," said Atwater. Only 18 percent of the voters considered themselves Republicans, so the media campaign would seek out the 40 percent who considered themselves independents or "soft" Democrats. All campaign literature, commercials, and speeches would avoid the R-word — *Republican*.

Third, the campaign would focus on Campbell's natural base, Greenville County. The hard-core rural Democrats of Laurens County would be at the bottom of the dance card.

Fourth, this time they would raise money first. They had to. The campaign was so starved for funds that Atwater managed it from the back room of a potato-chip factory. "We had no assets except potato chips," Campbell said. They began with 3,000 direct mailings — signed by Governor Edwards's personal autowriter machine, typed on watermarked stationery, individually stamped (to avoid the "Dear Occupant" look), and thoughtfully accompanied by a self-addressed, stamped envelope. The response was almost $10,000, twice what they had anticipated.

Encouraged, Carroll and Lee drew up a list of business leaders and political action committees from whom they expected contributions of $100 each. But this appeal produced only $3,000. Atwater thought they lacked the right "horse" — someone to solicit funds directly. Campbell's campaign chairman Dick Greer was good, but at thirty-one he was probably too young to wow Old Greenville. In the closing days of the campaign, Atwater directed a phone solicitation of physicians and businessmen, "emphasizing that Campbell could win with or without their help, but that Campbell personally reviewed all contributions and would be disappointed if their names were absent." Cha-ching: $4,000 more. This time the campaign debt was only $1,800 — Carolina peanuts.

Finally — and perhaps most critically — Campbell and Atwater would campaign through all media. They agreed that television alone was too costly and too risky. This campaign needed diversity: television and radio, billboards, newspapers, brochures, telephone, *and* direct mail. They had concluded that spending $20,000 more on TV would have pulled off the 1974 race. "When television spots are well produced, winning is considered inevitable," said Lee. "Obviously, there are other factors to be considered, but if television can sell soap suds, it can sell politician appeal." The big problem with Campbell's television area was cost. Campbell needed to reach only two counties, but he had to pay for the privilege of reaching the entire three-state audience. Still, his group made three new campaign spots — which usually cost $1,000 each — for a total of $250 by using footage from the lieutenant governor's race.

Atwater concentrated the advertising budget on spots airing during news programs at WFBC in Greenville, appealing to the news junkies whose votes would matter the most to the election. He made an exception for a Spartanburg station, at which he placed several spots on country music shows for the "good ol' boy" vote. He rolled out the spots about a week before the election, relying on his shortest, cheapest spot of ten seconds. The spots showed Campbell chatting with the good folks, riding a horse, tossing a football to his son, working on the legislators. "Issues were still important," Atwater said, "but they remained general." He yanked off the air a spot about education after two showings when polls showed it wasn't a hot issue.

Lee believed in radio. It was cheap: the Federal Communications Commission forced stations to offer candidates time at their lowest rates, from 90 cents to $15 for thirty seconds. But there was a catch. The candidate's voice had to be in the commercial. Atwater tagged Campbell's voice to the end of spots, intoning, "This ad paid for by the Campbell for Senate Seat Number 3 Committee."

As with television, Lee picked his radio stations carefully. He knew that Nixon had carried the state with 68 percent of the total vote but had received only 3 percent of the black vote. So he bought no time on black stations. Instead he bought up "drive time" — between seven and nine A.M. and four-thirty to six P.M. — in the cities, where commuters stuck in traffic were held captive by radio; and out in the country, where farmers lent an ear to weather and agricultural news as well as to talkfests. Campbell wrote his own scripts. Lee also struck a deal with the Bob Jones University radio station to produce high-quality spots gratis, with a $2 charge for each copy of the tape ordered. The total radio budget was $25.

Atwater thought that billboards fired up the faithful. Campbell's campaign bought fourteen at $100 apiece. In fact, Campbell turned out to be the only candidate in Greenville County to use billboards. "Anytime one can totally dominate one form of advertising, impact upon the voter is enhanced tremendously," Lee reflected.

In the neighborhoods, Atwater used stick signs — two three-by-five-foot boards placed on either side of a pole and stuck into the ground. The top board said CAMPBELL; the bottom, S.C. STATE SENATE. Atwater thought that the stick signs had the same impact as billboards but were far cheaper. In addition, he said, "should Campbell ever run for another office, the bottom board can be replaced with another one indicating the new office."

Atwater considered newspapers the least effective mass medium. Less than 20 percent of the public read newspapers; far fewer read the political ads. The key with newspapers was to maximize impact and minimize cost. There were two dailies in the district, the *Greenville Piedmont* and the *Greenville News*, both owned by the same company. Thus, Lee could take advantage of "combo" rates by placing an ad for both publications for the same day. But he felt that people in this rural state scrutinized the rural weeklies more carefully than they did the dailies. "In a town like Clinton, everybody reads the *Chronicle*, and all of its stories and items are pored over and discussed exhaustively in local gossip sessions," said Lee. Vital news, like farm reports, traffic accidents, 'driving while under the influence' offenses, divorces and weddings, are culled from its 24 pages until the next Wednesday's edition comes out." Accordingly, he placed half-page Campbell ads in the *Clinton Chronicle*, the *Laurens Advisor*, the *Greer Citizen*, and three other weeklies in the district for the two editions before the election. The ads cost from $38 to $80 per insertion. "Pound for pound, this money was as well spent as any other financial outlay in the campaign."

Paid media was the greatest part of a campaign budget. Timing mattered. "Billboards come first, because they are the best at instilling name recognition in voters," Atwater said. According to him, they should go up forty-five to thirty days before the election. Radio spots should start twenty-one to fourteen days before the election. Television should begin twenty-one to seven days before the election, converting the candidate from a name into a human being. Newspapers, serving as a reminder, should begin during the last week.

Direct mail was more focused than mass media advertising. "As an old pro said, 'If you are splashed all over billboards, radio, television and the newspapers, you are never sure whether Bill Boogles gets the message,'" wrote Lee, "'but if you sent him a letter, you know that he at least opened it and saw your name.'" During Campbell's state senate campaign, Lee's goal was a cost-effective mailer that wasn't packaged so unattractively that it would be discarded with the rest of the junk mail. Lee's total budget for the direct-mail campaign was $3,000. The campaign couldn't afford to send a letter to every potential voter, so Lee had to choose with care.

He decided to focus in part on absentee-ballot voters. From September to the week before the election, the Greenville and Laurens County election commissions received daily ballot requests from students, military personnel, and the hospitalized. Atwater figured that the average absentee voter would make an extra effort to vote in a presidential election, but "all the other races would be postscripts to him." A letter from a candidate in a lesser race might provide the needed nudge.

Lee's assistant Jeannie Bettis went to the election commission every Wednesday and took down the names and addresses of everyone who requested absentee ballots for that week, and then she sent them campaign letters that reached them two days before they got their absentee ballots. Some University of South Carolina students who received the letter asked Lee, "How in the hell did Carroll know I intended to vote absentee?" The campaign manager pleaded ignorance, "helping to perpetuate the myth of campaign magic," he later observed.

Atwater also sent direct mail to more than three thousand potential voters who had been identified as undecided in phone polls. Letters went to independent Republicans and to people who seemed disposed to vote for other Republicans on the ticket. Lee said, "The theory was that a letter to those who appeared to be Democrats would only serve as a reminder to vote, and vote they would — for the opposition."

Lee considered the mail campaign satisfactory. He had less faith in giveaways. A candidate for the state legislature once handed out "Frisbees, measuring cups, sponges, pens, combs, mirrors, key chains, and pot holders, all of which had his name engraved on them," he recalled. "This is absurd." He yielded to staff requests for calendar cards and bumper stickers but nixed buttons. "Buttons are great at conventions and political party gatherings," he said, "but very few people in the real world wear them in public."

One giveaway that Atwater insisted upon was a brochure. When someone dropped by headquarters and asked for something to do, Atwater would hand him or her a fistful of brochures to distribute. The key to an effective brochure, according to Lee, was to remember that "because most people do not like politics or politicians, the brochure should be as 'nonpolitical' as possible."

At least a fourth of campaign publicity should be free, said Atwater. He had an assortment of devices to resort to: press releases, radio appearances, press conferences, appearances on television, and staged human-interest events.

For local or county campaigns, one press release a week was enough. In 1976 Atwater maintained this pace for the Campbell campaign — except for a flurry of releases around a visit by vice-presidential candidate Bob Dole — and found the results gratifying. Only one release failed to get published during the campaign.

By now Lee had become an expert at feeding the press. His press releases were hand-delivered, never mailed, to increase reporters' "feelings of importance and help them feel appreciated and taken into confidence," he said. They had to be delivered an hour before deadline so that reporters could work the "news" into their day's work. A release rarely ran longer than one page; the lead was no more than twenty-five words. Reporters had to be able to read it at a glance. Atwater never played favorites among reporters, but he did mimic their styles in his releases. "The average reporter is lazy, as the rest of us are," he said, "and sufficiently harassed by deadlines that he will want to use material as 'filler' without need for an extensive rewrite." The ideal day for a release was Saturday, when newsroom staffs were small and inexperienced.

Lee viewed press conferences as risky "pseudo-events." Rare was the candidate who could sidestep their pitfalls. Usually the candidate reads a prepared text — but then must answer reporters' questions on anything. Lee liked to schedule press conferences for Monday — "because after a fun-filled weekend, reporters are usually content to hazard a good 'pseudo-event.' " He plied them with coffee and doughnuts as well as with press releases, for those among them who were intellectually impaired.

Before press conferences Campbell recorded a tape of thirty to forty-five minutes with the meat of his text; this was delivered by telephone to all area radio stations. After all, radio announcers "have to stay at the stations and prefer to have the story come to them," Atwater noted. Campaign workers often offered radio stations a recording that summed up a recent Campbell speech. Atwater knew that most radio stations used the "rip and read" method of newscasting — ripping sheets off the United Press International teletype and reading them directly on the air. They would be delighted to give listeners — via canned speeches — the illusion that they were doing live news reports.

FCC rules required that equal time be given to both sides of an issue by two opposing candidates, and Campbell appeared with his opponent twice on the NBC television affiliate in Greenville. Lee knew that it would be more difficult for the opposition to monitor the dozen or so radio stations in the district and to demand equal time from each, so he decided to concentrate on radio as a forum for airing Campbell's views. The week that Campbell returned from the Republican National Convention, Atwater contacted every station in the district and asked if it would like to have Campbell drop in and discuss convention activities — including the textile plank of the platform, which Campbell had helped draft; it was an issue of intense local interest. "This helped to circumvent FCC regulations," Atwater reflected, "because Campbell could drop by and talk with them as a convention delegate and citizen, not as a candidate."

Campbell's stately bearing would prove useful later in the campaign when Dr. Bob Jones III, one of his backers, referred to Betty Ford as a "cheap slut who should be done away with, not by divorce but by drowning." Jones, a Republican and fundamentalist Baptist, controlled four thousand votes, a bloc that Campbell could not alienate. With friends like Jones, however, Campbell didn't need enemies like Yarborough, who, in his capacity as chairman of the County Democratic Party, criticized Jones for his commentary. Lee and Campbell agreed that, under the circumstances, silence was golden. Campbell said nothing about the matter, and it passed over.

Lee also worked the press from the human-interest angle. A sixteen-year-old student volunteer had been coming into campaign headquarters to stuff envelopes after school each day. Lee arranged for him to bring in a $50 cash donation for Campbell, and $100 for President Ford — supposedly representing nearly two years of tips from his job as a Winn Dixie bagboy. Then Lee casually mentioned the donations to a couple of reporters, who came out the next day to do interviews. The results were superb — a piece in the local human-interest column, and a four-column front-page story and picture of the student handing out bumper stickers in the afternoon paper.

To develop media strategies, Atwater and Campbell prepared surveys to find out what voters thought of issues and candidates. "The key to a well-implemented survey is interviewing the 'right' people in the 'right' places," said Atwater. Because 81 percent of the vote was expected to come from the more populous Greenville County, of the 300 interviews conducted, 243 (81 percent) were from Greenville and 57 (19 percent) were from Laurens. A formula was developed based on the statistics of voter turnout in

three earlier elections. "If 20 percent of the vote came from the upper urban area, take 20 percent of 243 — or 48 interviews — from
that particular category," said Atwater. "If there are eight wards in
the upper urban area, then break them down numerically by precinct." Demographic and census survey maps were also used to
balance such factors as age, race, sex, and occupation.

The real issues for voters in the district related to money.
Jobs, taxes, government spending — these were "mom and apple
pie" issues that cut across party lines. "Obviously, no American
was opposed to pocketbook conservatism as polls across the country clearly indicated," Atwater said. Because Campbell had been
addressing these three issues during the previous year, they were
"his." He added two more issues — the need for quality education,
and a get-tough-on-crime policy. That was enough. Campbell
recalled a guy who ran a country store who had told him to try not
to talk about more than three issues. "Every time you add to it, you
risk losing more."

Campbell's five-issue agenda put him in the driver's seat and
left little for the competition to claim as its own. Said Lee: "Confederate General Nathan Bedford Forrest answered the question
of how he developed his battle strategy with the reply: 'You git thar
the fustest with the mostest.' The same strategy holds true with
campaign issues. One must be quick to seize the initiative and
capture the fertile ground, making any response of the opposition
look like the typical 'me too' guy answer."

It worked. One evening at a "Meet the Candidates" program
Yarborough listened to his rival's speech and commented, "Well,
I certainly can't disagree with anything that Mr. Campbell has
said."

Campbell had high (and positive) voter recognition. Still,
for a newcomer, Yarborough's name recognition was surprisingly
high. Atwater attributed this to Yarborough's connection with incumbent Riley and his recent primary victory. Even though
Campbell had a 23-point lead in the polls, Atwater was not comfortable. Too many voters were undecided (29 percent), and most
of the undecided were from traditionally Democratic groups:
blacks and unskilled and textile workers.

Atwater also worried that Campbell was still below 50 percent in surveys. "A candidate who exceeds the 50 percent mark in
a poll has excellent chances in the election, because the only way

to defeat him is to provoke a voter defection," he said. "Breaking a prior commitment is something the average South Carolinian is loathe to do." In late September Atwater did a stripped-down poll to find out how Republican candidates stacked up against their opponents. Even if Yarborough's popularity were to boom and Campbell's to bust, a month still remained for plotting a media blitz to boost Campbell right before the election. Atwater and Campbell had tried this in the lieutenant governor's race, but "there the gamble did not pay off," conceded Atwater. This time Campbell received 52 percent of the survey. Although the undecided voters still heavily favored Democratic candidates, Campbell had over the 50 percent edge that could be expected to put him over the top.

Lee learned early that every vote counted. Only 60 percent of the eligible population in the United States was registered to vote. Of those registered, only half participated in the general election. In the primaries, voter apathy had an even more profound effect, with only about 15 percent total participation. In close elections, therefore, 15 to 16 percent of the eligible population was electing candidates for president and senator. If the campaign manager knew the candidate's base and could identify it, he could win a primary with 10 to 15 percent of the voter population. Because of these basic circumstances, Lee said, "The precinct is the key to the whole election."

There were 115 precincts in Greenville and Laurens Counties. "Ideally, a chairman was necessary in each of these to canvass the precinct and make sure every voter identified as a Campbell supporter showed up at the polls on election day," Lee later said. Because there were up to 3,000 voters in each precinct, comprehensive canvassing would be a massive undertaking. Rather than organize every precinct, he ranked them in the order of importance to Campbell's winning. If the top 45 precincts were effectively organized, and if the second group of 30 were somewhat organized, then Campbell would win Greenville County by at least 55 percent. Atwater knew from experience that you couldn't depend on any one precinct chairman to do the job; on election eve some will plan to be out of town until after the vote, he said. So he placed four volunteers in each of the 45 key wards, confident that at least one would finish the job.

Almost as much as votes, what every candidate needed was

time. Atwater kept a large posterboard behind his desk with information on Campbell's schedule. Each Wednesday morning, he and Campbell reviewed the events of the previous week and planned the week to come. Atwater never scheduled more than two weeks in advance. "Accepting invitations months in advance, the schedule may demand attendance at 20-member meetings of the Young Republican Club, sparsely attended and all supporters anyway, while an invitation to the textile show, with 3,000 attending, must be turned down," he explained. Once he gave his word, however, Lee never broke a scheduling commitment. Reliability was key to preserving Campbell's image as "the man who was as good as his word."

Greenville media would not print or broadcast a press release unless the candidate addressed a recognized group. "One does not write, 'Campbell, speaking today on the legislature,'" Lee said. "One writes that he spoke before the Greater Greenville Jaycees concerning his remarks to the legislature." Therefore, Lee tried to secure at least one speaking engagement a week with one of the hundred or so civic groups in Greenville, many of which influenced voters. If Atwater needed a quick public pronouncement, he would schedule an "emergency meeting" of the five-member Young Republican executive board at campaign headquarters.

There was also unstructured time, during which the candidate would visit barbershops, stores, and factory gates. Atwater had determined that Campbell would spend about 30 percent of his time in Laurens and other rural, traditionally Democratic areas. "People in urban areas are usually too busy to bother with politicians," said Atwater. One could reach the urban voter most quickly and effectively through television, but the rural voter wants a personal appearance. "Someone in a country store or in a mill will appreciate the candidate's visit because it provides a break from his routine."

Lee liked to say, "A good political organization is worth 3 to 5 points in an election, and if that won't make the difference, you aren't going to win anyway." In the Campbell campaign, the candidate could veto any campaign decision but would have no role in the campaign structure, which was lean. For instance, Atwater felt that the candidate should know where the money was going but should not co-sign bills. Strom Thurmond once said that he had never touched a penny of campaign money in more than thirty years of politics. "This," Atwater said, "is the best policy for all candidates."

As always, volunteers played a key role in the Atwater-managed campaign. Atwater knew of campaigns where candidates and their spouses had been forced to stuff envelopes because of lack of manpower. Not here. Lee could inspire anyone, especially young students, to work long and hard for nothing more than the political thrill of it all. Volunteers stuffed envelopes, put together information packets, answered the phone, took surveys of voters to determine Campbell's popularity, and more.

Atwater had observed that in a campaign, "almost anyone who talks to the candidate will ask him to 'let me know if there is anything I can do.'" It would be impossible to follow up on this kind of request effectively. "Generally, when the candidate gets around to contacting these people, they are preoccupied with their own affairs and do not have time to undertake any heavy campaign responsibilities." So Lee created a brochure, which the candidate carried with him at all times. The brochure had space for ten names. "Anyone who wanted to help was given such a packet and told to locate ten prospective supporters and return the packet in a prestamped envelope. This identified more than 1,000 supporters."

A general campaign committee was named. Usually such committees are a formality, merely a means of enlisting fifty or so community leaders. Some members were rich prospective contributors. Others were regular party leaders or headed particular factions that might be at odds if not stroked in public. Still others were hardworking volunteers who deserved recognition if not riches. Putting a battery of names on campaign stationery gets the bandwagon rolling and impresses letter recipients.

Usually dinners with famous speakers were "far more trouble than they were worth," Atwater said. In the 1972 presidential campaign, he had seen several "surrogates," celebrity stand-ins for Richard Nixon — including Mrs. Herb Klein, wife of the president's press aide — at programs that were usually threadbare. One name event, however, paid off for Campbell in '76.

Campbell had served on a platform committee at the National Republican Convention, chaired by Bob Dole, the vice-presidential nominee. Later Dole wanted to make a stop in the South. Campbell could only come up with a little barbecue they were planning out at his farm in Fountain Inn; maybe two hundred would attend. Too small.

Then Lee got on the phone, determined to make this event a turning point in the campaign. "There will be four thousand votes there," he assured the Dole staff. Dole said OK, he would show. Now the barbecue had become a national media event; Lee had a host of details to tackle.

He had to find a flatbed truck for the band, erect a platform for the national media, figure out parking for several hundred cars, place signs along the road to direct people to the farm, and erect a tent rented from a small-time local evangelist, just in case it rained. He also recruited food servers, car parkers, and ushers. Campbell spent three days grooming the grounds, mowing pastures, and cleaning up beer cans along the highway leading to the farm. "Very seldom does a man in his position perform this type of menial task himself," Atwater said, "but he wanted things to be done just so."

Then there were the mysteries of protocol. Who would meet Dole at the airport? Who would ride with him to the farm? Who would sit with him on the speaker's podium? "Hundreds of egos were in balance," remembered Atwater, "and the campaign manager was charged with their tender care and maintenance." By the time Dole arrived, there were more than four thousand voters on hand, due to Atwater's hustle. "This is great!" he said, taking the head count and running into the kitchen to grab some pots and pans. "Pass 'em around and we can finance our own campaign!"

Some egos mattered more than others. The Dole visit enabled Lee to pull off a little trick that endeared him to the local press. The night before the Thursday barbecue, a Secret Service agent was checking out the Campbell house as part of the process of "protecting Dole from would-be assassins," recalled Lee. When the agent went to the bathroom, he left a bag of Priority Clearance badges on a table. "In his absence, the badges mysteriously disappeared," said Lee. The next day, local reporters showed up with Priority Clearance badges and took their places in the press bullpen — in front of members of national media, who had mere routine press passes. Turning to a bitter-looking blonde correspondent from NBC, Atwater explained, "Honey, we don't need any votes up in New York. We need 'em in Green Pond, South Carolina."

Meticulous planning was Atwater's hallmark. But some

things couldn't be planned. During the campaign, Campbell had
said that Yarborough supported collective bargaining for educa-
tors and had indicated his support in writing. Yarborough denied this, issuing a press statement the Thursday before election
day that insinuated that Campbell was a liar. This proved too
much for Campbell. He denounced Yarborough, who denounced
Campbell's denouncement. In the final four days of the campaign, picture stories covered the candidates' charges and counter-
charges. Atwater felt that this coverage was bad for Campbell.
"He was the clear favorite, but he appeared to give Yarborough
credibility by answering his attacks." Campbell admitted he had
overreacted and told Atwater he would not do so again in future
elections.

On November 2, 1976, Carroll Campbell was elected to the
South Carolina state senate by a margin of more than ten thousand votes. In a year when Carter was sweeping South Carolina,
Campbell was the only Republican to win a new seat in the state
senate.

After the campaign, Lee was exhausted. He vowed never to
manage more than one campaign at a time. Managing *any* campaign, whether for the school board or for the U.S. presidency,
was "an all-encompassing job and a manager should have minimal
outside distractions," he later said. Then — as he had done after
the '74 defeat — he took stock of the victory, drawing up a list of
mistakes to avoid in future campaigns. He felt that Campbell had
been scheduled into too many meetings — Republican functions,
voter fairs, "Meet the Candidate" events sparsely attended by the
media. In the future, the candidate would go to "events attended by
media and groups with many nonpartisan and independent voters.
Campaign workers, not the candidate, should attend the voter fairs
and hand out brochures and buttons." Lee also thought that the
finance committee had been poorly developed. Ninety percent of
the funds were solicited by four or five people; at least twenty committee members should have made "heavy personal solicitations."
He should have started identifying precinct workers at least eight
months before election day — the previous February or March.
His organizational efforts had begun in July, too late to use volunteers effectively. In the future, a campaign chairman would exert
early and total control over volunteers. Direct-mail lists would be
double-checked to make sure that they included important names.

As far as Lee was concerned, only the deserving would be rewarded. After Campbell won, an aide to Lee who had left Campbell's earlier losing campaign called and asked for a job. "No, I can't help you," said Lee. Toddy was puzzled when she heard about this. The guy had a wife and family. "If he'd stuck with me," Lee said, "he could have any job he wanted."

From others Lee demanded loyalty. From himself he demanded all. One Saturday Lee and fellow political consultant Roger Stone went for a six-mile run at the Isle of Palms in South Carolina. It was 90 degrees, every one of them humid. After running three miles, Stone was exhausted, dying. He could see that Lee was miserable, too. "Why don't we knock this off?" said Stone.

"We have to finish."

"Nowhere is it written we have to finish. We ran yesterday, we'll run tomorrow, we're both in perfect physical shape. Why do we have to finish if we don't feel like doing it?"

"Because we have to finish."

Three miles later, Lee lay spent in the grass for fifteen minutes while Stone vomited. "Lee had enormous self-discipline," Stone recalled. "Mind over body. Make yourself do what you don't want to do."

Lee was ready for bigger races.

• • •

Lee and Sally Dunbar were married on June 24, 1978, at the Methodist church in Union, South Carolina. After the ceremony, Lee ushered his mom from her seat to the church door. Everyone laughed, but for Lee it was a tender acknowledgment of respect. Afterward Toddy drove the couple to find their car. To startled onlookers, it seemed as if Lee's mother was going off with the couple on their honeymoon.

Toddy had never thought Lee would marry. Neither had his friends. In truth, he had been a balky bridegroom. Over the years, he and Sally had come to converse easily but superficially. He still could not talk to her about his brother Joe, who traveled with him like a palpable presence. Once, during their engagement, Sally was talking with Lee's sister, Anne, about Joe's death when Lee entered the room. "You weren't there, and you didn't even know him!" he exploded. "That's something I don't discuss, and I don't want you to *ever* talk about again!"

When Sally's brother Curtis was two and a half, he was trailing after his mother in the kitchen one day as she concentrated on making strawberry Jell-O. Theo Dunbar poured the boiling water into a measuring cup and watched it turn red as the crystals dissolved. She turned to carry the Jell-O to a table when the cup burst before her eyes, the steaming red liquid spilling onto Curtis's neck and chest and scalding him. The little boy screamed in pain. Mr. Dunbar came running from the living room, and they bundled the boy off to the hospital, where he spent a week recovering from the scalding. The symmetry of this event and little Joe's death always haunted Sally. But she never mentioned it to Lee.

Despite the usual mugging for the cameras by the wedding party, Lee had a noticeable pallor that day. Later he would tell a friend that he had felt ill. Not that he didn't love Sally! But he was twenty-seven, he was 150 percent into his career, and the whole thing seemed pretty damn stupid.

Lee's domestic skills were slight. In the early years he could be found painting an apartment bedroom with Sally or helping at the grill when friends came over for a barbecue. Afterward, nothing. Washington friends sometimes speculated that the marriage was mostly an arrangement. Lee had charm, but he could also be cold, even cruel. Sally had a dazed, small-town quality and was given to malapropisms: "Lee reads vivaciously!" she would exclaim. Many thought her the salt of the earth; others found her somewhat detached from Lee, except during state occasions. She seemed to love Lee's life of friends, travel, and visibility.

Despite others' speculation, Lee and Sally shared a real fondness for each other. "I think they reached an accommodation," said a friend of theirs. "There was no way to leash Lee's energy and drive. She was always very good about Lee's career. Never made demands on him, never gave him a hard time. She managed all of their finances. Lee gave her his paycheck. She managed the money. They had some apartments in Columbia. She was sort of running the marriage, and Lee was doing his career and his politics. Sally was the ideal political wife because she didn't make demands on him. His time was his time, and his political life was his political life."

Sally had just completed coursework for her master's degree

on the Friday before the Saturday wedding. Lee told Sally they could have a one-day honeymoon. She said fine, and they decided to go to Charleston to stay at Hill's Hyatt House, which Sally had heard was romantic and stylish. They made the three-hour drive from Union. Lee went in and came out to Sally, waiting in the car. "They had to give up the honeymoon suite," he said.

"Whaaattt?" said Sally. "To whom?"

"The Rolling Stones!"

One night in a Charleston motel, and then Lee was back working on Strom Thurmond's campaign for reelection. "Call me Strom," said the senator to his youthful aide.

"Yes, Senator," Lee replied.

• • •

Lee not only abandoned Sally for the senator; he jilted Carroll Campbell, too. Campbell had assumed that Lee would run his campaign for a seat in the U.S. House of Representatives against Max Heller, a popular mayor from Campbell's home base, Greenville. But in conversations with his mother's old schoolmate Warren Abernathy, Lee had discovered a chance to join Thurmond's campaign. Fare thee well, Carroll. Campbell's campaign was managed instead by Sam Dawson, who had worked with Lee briefly at Baker & Associates. Lee asked Mike Ussery, an old ATO fraternity brother, to be Campbell's deputy manager. After working as a liberal Democratic operative in Atlanta, Ussery was now making the rounds at the state house in Columbia as a medical lobbyist. Ussery missed politics and needed the work. Lee liked it when someone he had left in the dust came back to him for a job — it was like homage to the king. Ussery was Lee's man to keep an eye on Dawson and to keep Lee abreast of developments, so that he could help out if Campbell needed another man in his corner. Meanwhile Lee was off to a real prizefight.

Strom Thurmond's race in 1978 looked to be the toughest since he had beaten Edgar Brown in 1954 as a write-in candidate. Lee had called that campaign "one of the most amazing precedent-setting elections in the history of the entire country" in a term paper he wrote for a history class at Flora. The senator's opponent in '78 was Charles "Pug" Ravenel, a young, attractive Democrat whose nickname originated on the playing fields of his youth after he flattened his nose during a third-base encounter in a sandlot game. For the first time, age was an issue for the senator.

Pug had quarterbacked the football team for the Harvard class of '61, graduated from business school in '64, made a fortune on Wall Street, then returned to South Carolina in 1972 as an investment banker. In 1974 he had defeated Brian Dorn in the Democratic primary for governor and was 37 points ahead of his Republican opponent in the general race when he was undone by enemies in his own party. They dug up an 1895 residence rule that disqualified carpetbaggers from seeking office, requiring five years of in-state residence for candidates, even though Pug's was the tenth-straight generation of his family to be born in South Carolina. As Atwater well knew, Carolina politics was a mud bath. The same residency requirement could have been leveled against his own candidate Westmoreland in 1974, but it hadn't been. Now Ravenel was back, residency in place, hat in the ring.

The senator, at seventy-six, had long relied on a coterie of old cronies, most of whom were conservative Democrats who thought it unfortunate that their leader had become a Republican. Youth and the GOP were still somewhat suspect — although the cronies were perfectly willing to let this dynamo Atwater, brought in by Abernathy, do all the fieldwork. Lee was gaining experience and momentum, but in the eyes of the Thurmond camp, at age twenty-seven he was still too raw, too young to be campaign manager. Abernathy hired Allison Dalton as campaign coordinator to oversee Lee and to make all of the egos mesh. The group would later be called "The Class of '78," because members of that team would later rise to some measure of political glory.

Besides Lee other staff member included John Carbeau, later to become adviser to Jesse Helms; Robin Roberts, who would head the National Media political advertising group; Warren Tompkins, who would become chief of staff to Governor Carroll Campbell and a leading consultant in Columbia (he had been part of the famous Flora backfield that had included Steve Sisk). The press secretary was Mari Maseng, who was just out of college and had put in a brief stint at the *Charleston News and Courier*; she would later become a speechwriter in the White House and the wife of political columnist George Will.

The chief consultant to the campaign, at the senator's insistence, was Arthur J. Finkelstein of Brooklyn, New York. He was hired ostensibly as a pollster, but since polling was key to the Thurmond campaign, Finkelstein would also plot strategy from on high. Already he was known as a masterful Republican strategist and senior adviser to focused, hard-nosed campaigns. A reclusive conservative ideologue, he shunned publicity; there was no known picture of him until 1996, and he avoided speaking to the press.

Lee's job was to execute Finkelstein's strategy. Or so Finkelstein thought. Finkelstein and Atwater were strong-willed players who contrasted dramatically in age, experience, and vision. Arthur had already run Jesse Helms's campaign in North Carolina. Thurmond's campaign was Lee's first big race, his shot at the big time.

Finkelstein was a wise, absentminded professor with a medium, nondescript build — and a regal bearing. Walking back and forth in stocking feet on the bed of his hotel room, he would discourse poetically for hours about his vision of the campaign's destination. Allison, Mari, and Lee sat and watched in awe. Atwater, still trying to hide his insecurities, was learning what northeasterners would call chutzpah; he was learning how to do things that would stick in people's minds.

The two men differed even in grooming and cuisine. The rumpled Finkelstein discharged his obligations to the world of fashion by hanging a loose, unknotted tie around his neck. Lee, still the self-doubting pupil, always wore a tie neatly knotted by somebody else. Lee wanted to dine on green beans, turnip greens, and corn bread at Ray Lever's or Maury Bessinger's barbecue places. Finkelstein's idea of a real meal was right out of New York: a two-inch steak at Peter Luger's or the Palm with fried potatoes and onions.

"Finkelstein and Atwater had a very healthy distrust of each other," recalled Roger Stone, who worked as an aide to Finkelstein during the campaign. "Two very smart guys on a collision course. Both concerned about who would get credit for Thurmond's reelection." They ended up working together well because both wanted the senator reelected. "I don't think they ever particularly liked or trusted each other. In Lee's case, it didn't matter. Lee would work with anybody as long as it meant getting the job done." The question was how.

Finkelstein liked the statistical approach. He was a pioneer in the use of prodding questions in polls to estimate the candidate's core support: Would you vote for Strom Thurmond regardless of who ran against him? If 40 percent said yes, that was Thurmond's base, to be protected at all costs. Finkelstein's polls drove his strategy. How, Lee thought, can a carpetbagger come down here with his numbers and tell us how to run a race for Strom Thurmond? What does Brooklyn know about the good ol' boy system?

Lee came to the campaign with a negative, nearly evangelical pitch. He wanted to paint Ravenel as a young, liberal Johnny-come-lately who had never held elective office, had never done anything for the good folks of South Carolina. To Finkelstein, Lee was too raw and took too many risks.

When he was not spouting Sun-tzu, Lee was dipping into the tomes of the War Between the States (never the Civil War), looking for political lessons. In his southern heart of hearts, Atwater was fascinated by Robert E. Lee, Stonewall Jackson, and A. P. Hill, but he also studied the generals of the north, especially Sherman, because he was the only one who understood the value of *total* war.

"Lee would be guilty of overkill," said Allison Dalton. "All I wanted to win was 51 percent. He wanted to win every vote. The big risk was to overplay the aggressive nature of the campaign, to put down Pug Ravenel with a negative approach. In some campaigns that's the way to go. But we had this guy, Senator Thurmond, with these huge positives. And what we needed to do was to protect the positives and not worry too much about building the negatives on the other side. . . . We used to sit around and argue about it at night. 'Well, yeah, sure, we can drive this guy up against a wall — but do we need to do that? And, in doing that, do we take an unnecessary risk?' " Lee would argue for total war, but he was also a good soldier. "Great idea," Dalton would tell him, "but I don't think we need to do it at this point," and that was that. After going round and round in their discussions, the campaign chiefs finally decided to give the Thurmond campaign a positive theme: *He's earned your respect. He deserves your support.*

To reinforce Strom as an icon, a statesman larger than life, they used line drawings instead of photos in ads and press handouts. Finkelstein liked media presentations that he could control. No ad agency was allowed to intrude. The group wrote their own scripts for TV spots, hiring a camera crew and makeup staff to carry them through. Still it was a close race — that is, until Roger Stone bought a box of frozen tacos at D'Agostino's, just a few miles from Brooklyn.

Stone had an apartment in New York. Standing in a checkout line at the grocery on Third Avenue, near Thirty-second Street, he idly picked up a shopper newspaper. Lo and behold, there among the ads was editorial filler about a local fund-raiser hosted by a New York couple for their Harvard classmate, Pug Ravenel. Addressing a crowd of twenty-five in their apartment, Ravenel said that if elected to the U.S. Senate, he would like to be the third senator from New York. Stone dropped his tacos and went to a pay phone. "You're not going to believe this!" he told Atwater in South Carolina. He read the story over the phone.

"You've got to get that down to me," said Lee.

Stone shipped the article via Express Mail and flew to Carolina two days later. A group of Democratic state legislators berated the would-be third senator from New York. An anti-Ravenel commercial featuring Pug's old primary opponent Brian Dorn kept up the heat. Ravenel denied making the comment, but the damage was done. Television, which thrives on the caustic encounter, had caused Ravenel's negative rating to jump from 12 to 43 percent.

Looking back on the campaign, Lee later explained, "We had to use guerrilla tactics." For instance, the singer Jimmy Buffett had let the Ravenel staff raise funds by buying choice concert tickets and reselling them at $50 apiece. Atwater sent a teenager into Ravenel's Columbia office to buy a ticket. Thirty minutes later the kid returned — with two cops, who arrested a Ravenel staffer for scalping.

"We knew as much about them as we knew about our own campaign," recalled Allison Dalton. "Any news conference for us, he took no chances — he built a crowd with our own friendly people. For Ravenel press conferences, Lee had our people there to raise tough questions."

"Republicans in the South could not win elections by talking about issues," Atwater said. "You had to make the case that the other candidate was a bad guy." Hereafter, Lee would market himself as a Machiavellian political warrior, skillful at using ad hominem strategies and tactics, characterized by personal attacks, dirty tricks, and accentuating the negative.

Thurmond won the election with 56 percent of the vote.

Throughout the campaign, Ravenel had called for a debate, which the senator had steadfastly refused. Now, on victory night, Atwater and cohort Gene McCaskill unfurled a banner behind Strom Thurmond: THE DEBATE IS OVER.

But another debate began: Who would get credit for Thurmond's win? Finkelstein told others that Atwater's role in the campaign had been relatively minor, and he tried to keep it that way. Finkelstein might have wanted credit, but he was not about to ask for it. Lee won a debate with himself: If there's some credit to hand out, why can't I claim it? I was here before them all.

Speaking of Lee, Dalton said, "We are talking about an ambitious guy who worked nineteen, twenty hours a day, trying to do things that would bring him credit."

"He was very gifted," recalled Richard Quinn, a colleague from Baker & Associates. "Perhaps not as gifted as he said he was. But a lot more gifted than his enemies think."

Strom Thurmond became Lee's passport to a future. History shows that out of the dust of '78 Lee got credit; Finkelstein got lost. As the years rolled by, Lee's role in the Thurmond campaign gradually expanded along with his reputation, until, on January 29, 1982, he oversaw an effusive White House announcement that incidentally noted that he had been "the manager of Senator Strom Thurmond's 1978 reelection."

As Lee Atwater moved up the political ladder, he often wondered aloud if Finkelstein would ever go public and the '78 bubble would burst. But he was safe. Finkelstein was one of the most private players in Republican politics. He didn't believe in telling tales about past campaigns in order to drum up business.

• • •

Meanwhile, in Carroll Campbell's close race against Max Heller for a seat in the U.S. House of Representatives, a smear attack was underway. The wild card was the third-party campaign of Don Sprouse, known as "The $12 Man" because he would tow anyone for $12. Sprouse, a high-school dropout, had moved to Greenville in 1976 and had been conducting a legal war with the mayor's office in his attempt to get his wrecker service on the city's rotation list to do business with the police department. Two months before the election, Sprouse got onto the U.S. congressional ballot by petition. He began a guerrilla campaign against Heller, driving around the state in a motor home, playing a jingle on radio stations — even doing an interview with Roger Mudd of CBS. Two days before the election, Sprouse called a news conference and attacked Heller for refusing to "believe Jesus Christ has come yet." He declared that a Jew should not represent South Carolina's fourth congressional district.

"What about Campbell?" the press asked.

"Why, he's an Episcopalian!" said Sprouse.

Campbell had been campaigning in Liming, a small town in Spartanburg County, when Ussery reached him by phone with the news. "That's it, my goose is cooked," he said. Carroll thought that Sprouse's statement would create a sympathetic backlash for Heller. He condemned the statement immediately. To his surprise, Campbell won the race.

Where had Sprouse's religious charge come from? Accounts vary. Indeed, Campbell had hired the elusive Arthur Finkelstein in July to conduct a poll consisting of forty-eight questions, including two that touched on religion and ethnicity:

• Which "personal qualities" would make voters more or less likely to vote for the candidates? (Among the qualities listed were "a Jewish immigrant" and "a native South Carolinian.")

• Choose from the following characteristics that best describe Campbell and Heller: (a) honest, (b) a Christian man, (c) concerned for the people, (d) a hard worker, (e) experienced in government, (f) Jewish.

Alan Baron, a Democratic analyst who published a newsletter for political insiders, discussed the poll over dinner with Finkelstein in 1983. "Finkelstein's survey sought to determine the impact on voters of information that Heller was (1) a Jew; (2) a foreign-born Jew who [3] did not believe Jesus Christ was the savior," Baron told his readers. "He learned that Heller could win with the first two pieces of information out — but not the third." Enter Don Sprouse, who met with Campbell's campaign manager Sam Dawson in a Greenville parking lot, spreading the word that Heller did not accept Jesus — and Campbell wins. "Finkelstein told friends that the onus of the attack was on Campbell," added Baron, "and that he just provided the candidate with the 'numbers.'"

Marvin Chernoff, however, remembered that the topic had come up in a conversation with Lee Atwater after breakfast at the

Elite Epicurean Restaurant in Columbia in 1985. In the midst of political war stories, Lee recalled the Finkelstein poll, adding that he had passed on the information to Sprouse with a wink and a warning: "Now don't use it, because we're going to do it right before the election." Lee told Chernoff, "I knew goddam well, Marvin, the guy was going to go right out and do something with it. Sure enough, the next day he called a press conference and said Max Heller doesn't accept Jesus Christ as savior." Was Atwater telling the truth? Sprouse said he never spoke with Atwater. As Marvin walked away, he heard one of Lee's cohorts say, "Where'd you get that fuckin' story from?"

"Lee liked to brag about his dirty tricks," said Campbell, dismissing the episode as another Atwater embellishment. "He did it all the time."

Atwater didn't help matters in August 1986 when Sam Tenenbaum, a prominent Jewish businessman and Democratic fund-raiser in Columbia, accused Campbell of having exploited religion as an issue against Max Heller. Lee called Tenenbaum a "Gestapo-type politician," comparing his accusations to the big lies of Adolf Hitler. When Tenenbaum raised hell in the press, Atwater met with him at the Madison Hotel in Washington to apologize in person for his poor choice of words. Roger Stone thought that Atwater's insensitivity was due to his upbringing in South Carolina, that Lee had had no intention of wounding Tenenbaum. Stone said that he had once tried to explain to Lee how his Nazi reference offended: "He didn't understand why it was offensive. There was never any understanding of ethnic politics, which is solely a northeastern and midwestern phenomena."

On balance, the Carroll Campbell campaign had been even harsher than Thurmond's. But some people saw one man behind both. "How is it that things like this always happen in races with which Atwater is associated?" asked Sam Tenenbaum.

CHAPTER

4

LEE ATWATER'S OFFICE,
CAN YOU HOLD?

I don't want loyalty. I want *loyalty*. I want him to
kiss my ass in Macy's window at high noon and
tell me it smells like roses. I want his pecker
in my pocket.
— Lyndon B. Johnson

In 1979 no one could tell how the Gipper would play south of
the Mason-Dixon line. Even Haley Barbour, head of the Mississippi Republican Party and a Reagan supporter at the 1976 GOP
National Convention, turned down Mike Deaver's offer to run
the South for Reagan. He signed up with John Connally and
tried to coax Atwater into running the campaign in South Carolina. Governor Edwards was in their camp, and Strom was leaning. No, said Atwater, he didn't think Connally was a winner. The
Westmoreland campaign had taught Lee to look before leaping
into a race. Even when Senator Thurmond endorsed Connally
and asked Lee to run South Carolina, he said no.

From the outset, Lee thought that Connally was a loser. Perhaps Strom was relating to Connally because, like the senator, he
had switched parties. But that was only seven years ago — and now
Connally wants to be a Republican president? To businessmen
Connally may have looked like a president, as someone remarked
on viewing his chiseled features, but to Atwater there was no way
that Connally was presidential.

The only primary campaign that Lee Atwater wanted to manage in 1979 was Ronald Reagan's. Lee was working as a pollster in state campaigns, and he was beginning to develop a theory that had its origins in the Thurmond race. Atwater's axiom: No candidate can succeed with negatives of 35 percent unless his positives are at least 5 points better. The negative factor, he explained, meant that voters don't like much of *anything* about a candidate for any of various reasons. As Lee saw it, Connally's negatives were at 37, with positives of 26. The campaign was terminal at the starting gate.

Ronald Reagan was the horse Lee wanted. The candidate also had a quality that Atwater would spend a lifetime trying to achieve: self-confidence. Though the press made fun of Reagan because he seemed forgetful, he was a symbol of strength to anyone who met him. "The guy just did not let anything or anybody intimidate him," said Lee. "He did not want anything from anybody, and I felt he was the single most self-confident guy I have ever run into." Lee liked the way Reagan defined himself from within, knew what he believed, and refused to live his life by the daily public opinion polls that guide so many politicians. Reagan let others worry about that. Lee wanted to be one of Reagan's others.

Reagan had enlisted John Sears and Charlie Black to run his national campaign. Sears didn't think Atwater was worth having around, but Black was a pal from the College Republican days, when he had led the North Carolina delegation. Lee learned that Sears and Black wanted Carroll Campbell, then a freshman congressman facing his first reelection campaign in the fall of 1980, to chair Reagan's South Carolina campaign. He told Campbell, who seemed surprised. "If you will agree to be chairman of the Reagan campaign," said Lee, "I can be campaign manager." They agreed.

Meantime, after Richard Quinn mentioned to Lee that he knew the cochairs of the Reagan campaign (who would have to sign off on the campaign manager), Quinn quickly found himself urging them to hire Lee Atwater. By the time Ronald Reagan got around to calling Carroll Campbell to ask him to chair the campaign, Lee's appointment was a formality. Campbell said yes, if he could have Lee handle the day-to-day details. No problem, said Ron, whose staff seemed to be quite knowledgeable about this young operative.

During a trip to South Carolina in the early days of his campaign, someone asked John Connally, "Have you run into Atwater
yet?"

"What's an Atwater?" he asked.

"You'll see."

For Reagan, this was a critical campaign. His primary
opponent George Bush, borrowing a page from Jimmy Carter's
playbook, got out early in 1978 and organized intensively. Iowans
showed up in unprecedented numbers to give him 31.6 percent of
their delegates and an upset victory; Reagan came in second with
29.5 percent. Many cited Reagan's aloof posture as the cause of his
poor showing. By refusing to debate his opponents and limiting
his public appearances, he was campaigning like an incumbent.
Reagan needed a victory to get back on track.

In New Hampshire, not only did Reagan underwrite a debate
against Bush, but he also demolished his main rival with his onstage presence when the moderator insisted that his microphone
be turned off during a rules dispute. "I paid for this microphone,
Mr. Green," proclaimed Reagan (a line borrowed from an old
Spencer Tracy film). Reagan won in New Hampshire, but his
campaign was still bleeding internally. Before the results were in,
he fired John Sears, Jim Lake, and Charlie Black, and named
William Casey as his new campaign director.

Bush was changing players as well. Rich Bond had coordinated the attack in Iowa. David Keene came up short in New
Hampshire. Now Harry Dent, a savvy veteran of the Nixon political office (and one of Lee Atwater's early mentors), was
running things for Bush in Columbia. And Connally, who had
Governor Edwards and Senator Thurmond on his side, needed
a win more than anyone. Thus, the South Carolina primary
loomed as an encounter of even greater importance than had been
originally thought.

General Lee was ready in South Carolina, calling himself a
"political nymphomaniac." At the age of twenty-eight, with the experience of seventeen campaigns behind him, he had a desire for
political success that was insatiable. Indeed, he seemed oblivious
to all else. Lee had his first run-in with Nancy Reagan on January
8, 1980, at a rally in Charleston after she learned that Sally was
back in Columbia giving birth. Nancy gave him hell. He flew to
Columbia, where his assistant Linda Reed met him at the airport.

Lee was nearly four and his brother Joe was thirteen months old in this portrait taken for Christmas 1954, the year before Joe's death. Lee told confidantes that he heard his little brother's screams every day for the rest of his life.

Lee at 13: Though in this eighth-grade photo he didn't show it, in junior high school Lee was unanimous choice for class clown. Next stop, military school.

In tenth grade, Lee starred as Conrad Birdie in the Flora High production of *Bye Bye Birdie*. The audience loved him, but when the director failed to single out his performance, Lee thought he had failed.

Courtesy Joe Sligh

In high school Lee assembled his first rhythm-and-blues band, the Upsetter's Revue. Lee is squatting front and center. Clockwise from Lee are Larry Lovell (wearing a wristwatch), Buzz Peele, Chuck Powers, Benny Goodwin, Dale Gunter, Joe Sligh, and Doug Ballentine, with Tom Burton in the center. For cufflinks Lee was wearing two aluminum tabs off pop-top cans.

June 24, 1978: Lee Atwater and Sally Dunbar on their wedding day in Union, South Carolina. Sally was a beautiful Southern bride. Lee had a noticeable pallor. Friends and family were shocked that he was getting married.

At his wedding reception, Lee talked politics with Carroll Campbell, then a candidate for Congress. Lee and Sally's honeymoon lasted one day.

Lee with his parents, Harvey and Toddy, and his political father figures, Strom Thurmond and Ronald Reagan, at an '88 fundraiser.

The White House Office of Political Affairs, class of 1981: Ed Rollins, Paul Russo, Lee Atwater, and Lyn Nofziger.

Lee with Michael Deaver and James A. Baker III, two of the Reagan White House's Big Three, in 1983. Jim Baker's ultra-loyal assistant, Margaret Tutwiler, could recognize politicos in packs: "When Ah see them together, Ah just call them the baaaaad boys," she said.

Credit: White House

One of the best perks of working in the White House was showing celebrities around the place. Lee hosted a musical idol, James Brown, in the White House mess in 1981.

Lee often called up Washington columnists Robert Novak and Rowland Evans when he wanted to spin news stories his way.

Lee provided his own caption for this photo taken on Air Force 2 during the 1988 campaign.

OH Shit o⁰

At the New Orleans Republican convention, America first met a "kinder, gentler" George Bush and started to read his lips. Network correspondents Connie Chung (NBC), Jim Wooten (ABC), Diane Sawyer (CBS), and Charles Bierbauer (CNN) muzzle Lee. He had this photo blown up and hung it in his office at the RNC.

His first child was a girl, though Linda wouldn't tell him that because he had fixated on the name Sara Lee after seeing a frozen-food commercial. Linda knew Sally wanted to talk him out of that name. At her bedside, though, Lee explained how he wanted their little girl to have a name that combined Sally (Sara) and Lee. Sally gave in.

Five days later, Sally's parents brought mother and child home from the hospital. Sara Lee had been delivered by C-section, and Sally had a long recovery ahead. Lee, back on the road with the campaign, pulled in a few days afterward. When he asked Sally to iron his pants, Sally's mother hit the roof. "She has just had major surgery," Theo Dunbar informed her son-in-law. "Sally will *not* iron your pants." Sally had never seen her mother so angry.

Lee was seeing the Reagan primary campaign as a two-step version of the race he had run for Campbell in '76. First there was voter identification. Lee set up phone banks to call people most likely to vote in the GOP primary; by the first week in March, more than a quarter million voters had been called. Then came the Gipper in TV ads and personal appearances aimed at influencing the undecided voter. In late January, the television campaign consisted of eight different spots running on eleven stations.

Atwater knew things they didn't teach at Harvard's Kennedy School of Government from his training as a good ol' boy who loved wrestling and soul music. He told a journalist that his motivation for winning was "to show the Harvard crowd that a redneck from South Carolina could come out on top." Lee had hired Richard Quinn as media consultant for the campaign. Quinn contacted J. Evatts Haley, a respected western historian and author of the best-selling political hatchet book A *Texan Looks at Lyndon*. They brought him to South Carolina for scathing presentations called "A Texan Looks at Connally," portraying Connally as just another LBJ.

As Connally's prospects stalled, Lee worried that Bush might catch fire. Quinn then created several ads that attacked Bush as a liberal. The ads featured Reid Buckley, a friend of Quinn's — they were founding partners in a speakers' school Buckley ran in Camden. Buckley was a South Carolinian and a conservative with good ideas on how the ads should be written. Unbeknownst to him, he was also enlisted because his voice sounded like that of his brother, William F. Buckley. The ads were recorded in Reid's living room, with Quinn referring to his friend as "Mr. Buckley." People listening to the ads cold would swear they were hearing beloved conservative William F., holding forth on the liberal tendencies of George Bush. Lee roared. As did Harry Dent, when he heard the ads on his favorite radio station, WIS in Columbia. Furious, Dent called a news conference to defend Bush — and suddenly South Carolina knew a lot more about Bush's vote for federal handgun control in 1968.

Atwater and Campbell had placed their old fund-raising pal Dick Greer under Harry Dent's wing for the purpose of subterfuge. Two weeks before the primary, an internal memo from the Bush campaign was leaked to a UPI reporter, stating that Connally had endorsed gay rights years before in San Francisco. Greer said that he and Dent had written the memo to give Bush supporters ammunition in case Connally should attack Bush or misrepresent his stands on the issues. "The only reason I mentioned it was because the Connally people were out calling Bush a liberal," he added.

Connally called the attack memo "a self-serving, scurrilous piece of propaganda" from the Bush camp. Connally, once considered the leading challenger to Reagan, had fallen to third in the polls. Meanwhile, the Bush campaign got the blame for slinging mud.

During the last gasp of their campaign, Connally and his staff failed to recognize that while they had the support of Senator Thurmond — they did not have that of the senator's wife. Lee later told colleagues that he asked Nancy Thurmond to make a call to a reporter saying that she had heard rumors that Connally was buying black deacons' votes so they could stand before congregations and influence parishioners. In addition, Lee gave Harry Dent a tape of black ministers supposedly talking to a Connally operative about selling out. Dent called the *State*'s top political reporter, Lee Bandy, and played the tape for him in a room at the Heart of Columbia Motel. "A black individual in Washington was saying, 'How much is it going to take?,' " recalled Bandy, who broke the story — and Connally's chances — the next day in the *State*, South Carolina's most influential paper.

"This is typical of his underhanded politics," said Connally, accusing Harry Dent of planting the story. "He's an expert at this. . . . I'd say that's where he gained his fame." Lee Atwater had turned the Bush and Connally camps against each other, and his own candidate took the high road to a lead in the polls.

Lee loved to spin the press. He was especially fond of Lee Bandy. "He would plant stories, or give you the dirt on somebody. 'You might want to check this out,' he'd say, 'but you didn't get it from me. Call me up, I'll give you a quote,' " recalled the *State* reporter. "Lee was accused of a lot of things, and he may have been involved in a lot of them, but Lee was good at making sure his fingerprints weren't on them."

Because Reagan didn't do many appearances, when he did show up in South Carolina, Lee aimed for maximum impact. For an event in Columbia, Lee sent out a personal note from Reagan on monarch-sized stationery, signed by autowriter, in hand-stamped envelopes to thousands of donors, past and potential. A very effective pitch. Hey, the first word in *president* is PR! Then, to maximize appearances, Lee had the room cut up with drapery so that maybe eight hundred people looked like a packed house. A couple of hundred were personal friends of Atwater and company. Finally, Lee got the fire marshal to tell the police, and the police to tell reporters, that there were more than five thousand people in there, and they couldn't allow any more in or the fire marshal would have to close the place down.

The Reagan campaign ran out of money the last week before the primary, so Lee arranged for Reagan to come through the state for a whistle-stop tour by bus from Charlotte down to Florence. Because there were no funds to build audiences in advance, Lee took advantage of captive audiences. He scheduled Reagan for stops at schools, where students filled the auditorium, or luncheon meetings at civic clubs, where the members turned out full force. Lee's early genius was creating audiences on short notice, just in time for the cameras and the cherished coverage on the evening news.

For his candidate's final visit to Columbia, Lee put together one of the biggest political rallies ever assembled in the state. The advance team brought the Reagans to the back side of the state capitol. Because the building looks the same on both sides, there was a momentary gasp — no one was there. Then Lee directed them to move around to the front, where he had assembled over twenty thousand true believers (as well as several hundred personal friends), along with signs, balloons, cowboys on horses — it was a great day in America for the Gipper.

The Gipper won South Carolina in a landslide. Lee and Carroll Campbell were credited with helping Reagan erase the political momentum Bush had gained with his win in Iowa. As for John Connally, before it was over, he would spend some $12 million and get but a single delegate (from Arkansas) at the Republican convention. In South Carolina he earned and learned nothing in 1980, except perhaps a painful lesson in what an Atwater was.

• • •

Despite the high marks he achieved for the victory in South Carolina, Lee had a hard time breaking into the general election. The first impression of a lot of California-cool Reaganites was, Hey, who is this bumpkin, anyway? Some thought he had a chip of class resentment on his shoulder.

One of Reagan's national advance men had even dropped in on Lee during the primary and announced that he was going to run the South Carolina campaign that week. Lee welcomed the Reagan intruder graciously and asked his assistant Linda Reed to show him the town.

When the outsider finally crawled back to his hotel room in the wee hours, he was blasted. In the morning, when he flushed his toilet, the bowl runneth over. Some culprit had flushed a face towel down the toilet — accidentally, to be sure. By the time the advance man got over his hangover, called the hotel housekeeper, and arrived at campaign headquarters, Lee had issued marching orders and everyone was gone. The manager of the week soon retreated. "Oh, it was excellent," Reed recalled.

Reed was a Thurmond volunteer whom Lee had befriended and whose toughness he admired. He once played in a band with her brother. "She's as mean as a rattlesnake!" moaned a state GOP director after one encounter.

"Oh, no," said Lee. "You can defang a rattlesnake."

The need to win South Carolina had forced some of the upper-crust Reaganites to come to Lee, but even with a victory they didn't like the aftertaste. Nothing personal, really. They just didn't care about Lee, or South Carolina, or the South insofar as the presidential campaign was concerned. For this was not going to be a regional campaign. The Gipper was a national commodity. After South Carolina, Lee flew up to New York to assist Roger Stone with the primary in fifteen upstate congressional districts and to ask Stone to push for him in the Reagan camp. He also asked Carroll Campbell, Strom Thurmond, and the usual suspects to push his résumé. Lee was named a regional political director (RPD), overseeing South Carolina, Georgia, Alabama, and West Virginia. So he decided to take advantage of the anarchy of a campaign that was run off the plane like a massive advance operation. He viewed his job as his license to roam, to go to other states and announce, "I'm with the campaign." After all, Lee had no real boss up the line who wanted to hear from him — "no adult supervision," he would later say. To some, Lee Atwater was crashing a party with no formal invitation. To Lee, though, it was just an exercise in political crowd control: If you can't join them, lead them!

Lee loved to visit the Georgia campaign, stop in at town after town. In Carter's home state the GOP did not plan to expend meaningful resources. To some onlookers, it appeared that the bosses had written off the state and assigned a kid to do the job. To Lee his was a responsibility of the highest order. The Reagan campaign against Jimmy Carter wasn't negative. It was almost condescending. Carter had traveled the long road from the governor's office in Atlanta to the Oval Office in Washington, but his handling of the hostage crisis in Iran indicated to most Americans that he didn't have the stuff to remain in office. Lee called him "an incompetent dud."

State cochairman Margaret Holliman, twenty years Lee's senior, had been in many losing Republican campaigns and was feeling just a bit downtrodden. Lee arrived, optimistic, full of energy; he was an invigorating presence for a campaign that was an older, all-volunteer army. "That's youth!" she thought. "He thinks you can't lose." Lee had such bounce! "He energized others," she remembered. "He'd come into town and you knew he had been in and out of airports, working himself to death. We were all tired, but he would make you feel, 'Gee, you don't have any right to be tired. Let's go!' He was like a preacher. To him, it was the gospel. He felt that strongly about the campaign, and it came across. He left a real impact — especially important when working with volunteers."

Lee earned the respect of the campaign workers in Georgia

and taught the older ones to compromise a bit in order to reach their ultimate goal. The Reaganites had serious doubts about putting George Bush on the ticket, for instance. Atwater assuaged their conservative fears. "Hey guys, Bush will do what Reagan tells him," he assured them.

"The RPDs were all big talkers," recalled John Ellis, a nephew of Bush who was then a producer with NBC television news. "Lee was funny, had this odd persona, a hipster among the Reaganites, and he was so much smarter than the rest. A real student of politics, he took pains to talk about how things had gone historically. When you talked to him, you felt you were learning something, not just getting twaddle that the Reagan people were putting out. Atwater was in a class by himself."

In most political wars, the survivors in the winning camp are only as big as they can convince others they are. Within two years, Lee would be issuing "for immediate release" a White House announcement declaring that he had been "a delegate to the 1980 Republican National Convention, where he served as Reagan's assistant floor leader. Shortly after the convention he presented, and subsequently saw adopted, his campaign strategy for the southern states."

If ever there was a truly national election, it was 1980, and the Gipper won states everywhere. The notion that *any* RPD had "won" states for Reagan was a false argument — but one that Lee promoted as a matter of self-interest to journalists working with tight deadlines on books about the campaign, and to poli-sci profs at the University of South Carolina who saw him as a political folk hero.

"I don't remember what Lee did for the Reagan campaign," said Reagan's chief political adviser, Stu Spencer, who would later become one of Lee's mentors in the White House. "Something in the South" is all he could recall. (Carter did carry Georgia, after all.)

Lee took a step toward cementing his national image when, while serving as RPD for the Reagan campaign, he also signed on to work as a pollster for Congressman Floyd Spence's campaign in South Carolina's second district. Spence's Democratic opponent was Tom Turnipseed, a forty-four-year-old maverick who had been a tactician for the George Wallace presidential campaign of '68, which he had left at Wallace's insistence after several episodes of heavy drinking. Twelve steps later, Turnipseed turned up as a Kennedy-style liberal, heading a consumer organization, the People's Voice, in the early '70s. In 1971, when Lee was governor of the state student legislature, Turnipseed had tried to enlist him in a citizen's movement for lowering taxes. Lee said no thanks. Turnipseed went on to lose a 1974 race for attorney general, then won a state senate seat in 1976. In 1977 he entered the Democratic gubernatorial primary. He eventually withdrew for health reasons, but not before revealing that as a teenager he had undergone shock treatments to treat depression. He knew that the truth would eventually come out during the campaign anyway.

Spence campaign manager Joe Wilson knew Lee from the Miami convention in '72, where they had both worked as Strom Thurmond's bodyguards. Wilson hired Baker & Associates to conduct a preliminary poll for the five-term congressman, as well as a status poll midway through the campaign. The results of the latter were so pleasing — Spence had 52 percent of decided voters; Turnipseed had 27 percent — that they decided to go public. "This is the most open and shut race of the thirty-two I've polled this year," said Lee, embellishing his commentary with the claim that polling techniques were the subject of the Ph.D. dissertation he was working on at the University of South Carolina. "The point is that Turnipseed is not a viable candidate. His negative rating is eating away at him like a cancer."

Turnipseed erupted, claiming that the poll was fraudulent. In October he released the results of a poll he had commissioned, which showed Spence leading him by only 3 percentage points, 44 percent to 41 percent. Who's fraudulent now?

"Anybody who gets more than a 35 percent negative factor can't win an election," according to Atwater's axiom. Turnipseed, by Lee's calculations, had a positive rating of 32. "If his negatives are 35 percent and his positives aren't at least 5 percent higher, it's politically fatal. And these figures are not likely to change. This race ended back in the summer sometime." Lee showed the public's negative opinion of Turnipseed by quoting from actual questionnaire responses: "big-mouthed, obnoxious, crazy, lacks foresight, overboard, shoots bull." "I never heard of anyone who disliked Turnipseed," he added. "But he's not going to convert any new people. It's too late to change his image."

Turnipseed's campaign style *was* erratic. To counteract Spence's paid television commercials, he held press conferences several times a week — in soybean fields to dramatize farm problems, at gas stations to decry the tactics of oil companies, and in front of the Public Service Commission to call attention to inflation. "We can't match them dollar for dollar, so we have to depend on free media," he said, referring to his lack of campaign financing. He scoffed at Atwater's notion that he had an image problem. "The biggest feedback I've gotten is that people want me to rant and rave more," he said. "That's my style, to create public awareness of the problems."

The battle between the pol and the pollster continued to the final days of the campaign, with Turnipseed complaining that he had been "done in" by Atwater. "What do you expect from someone who's a walking joke?" Turnipseed asked. "Nobody believes anything that he says." At one of his press conferences, he accused Atwater of using the telephone "push poll" technique to falsely inform voters that Turnipseed belonged to the NAACP.

Atwater erupted. "I'm not going to respond to that guy," he said. "What do you expect from someone who was hooked up to jumper cables?"

The whole thing was like a slap fight, the type of exchange that could make two people friends, or enemies, for life. Atwater struck first with the poll and his cutting remarks; Turnipseed hit back with impact; then Atwater, the counterpuncher, hit below the belt. At the time the exchanges weren't picked up by the press. "Lee came up with so many cheap shots, you couldn't print them all," said Henry Eichel, a reporter on the beat. "That one *was* particularly scurrilous, though."

Toddy Atwater saw Tom Turnipseed on the evening news, ranting and raving, as was his style, about her son. "Lee, this man said the most terrible things about you on TV, that you were a dirty-tricks artist," Toddy said tearfully on the phone.

"Mother, I'm gonna be in politics all my life, and people are gonna say things like that," said Lee.

"I know, Son," said Toddy, "but don't let these people get close enough to you to know you."

The Turnipseed-Atwater fracas didn't effect the election outcome. That was foreordained: Spence won 92,306 votes (56 percent) to Turnipseed's 73,353 (44 percent). But the "jumper cable" remark would be branded on the political soul of Lee Atwater, leaving him with some negatives of his own.

• • •

In the confetti of the Reagan victory over Carter, Strom Thurmond put in a call to James Baker, the incoming chief of staff. The senator wondered whether Baker could find a place for Lee Atwater in the White House. Thurmond liked the idea of having his own man on the inside. During the Nixon years, he had had Harry Dent positioned there as political director. Mighty convenient when you need the president's attention, or even something as menial as a White House tour or a state dinner.

As chairman of the Senate Judiciary Committee, with a stranglehold on federal judgeships, the senator had enormous clout in Baker's office. Baker, who had also received calls from Harry Dent and Carroll Campbell endorsing Atwater, could hardly wait to meet this guy himself. He called Lyn Nofziger, head of the Office of Political Affairs. "Will you talk to a guy named Lee Atwater who wants a job?" he inquired.

Nofziger said yes and found himself in the company of a fidgety young man who resembled a lot of young Turks that Nofziger had seen over the years, guys who "never lost a campaign," who forged a future by making a forgery of the past. "I pick up résumé after résumé of people who have worked for me, and I am constantly surprised at the work they have done," said Nofziger in bemusement. "Why, I was hardly needed at all!"

Something about Lee triggered suspicion in Nofziger. This South Carolinian struck him as someone who might be a bit tricky, a little too clever for his own good.

"Atwater, do you think you can keep liar politics out of the White House if you come in here?" Nofziger asked.

Lee was stunned. "Yes, sir," he heard himself say. "Absolutely."

Nofziger still didn't feel confident or comfortable enough to offer Lee a job. "I'll think about it," he said. Lee *did* have a lot of campaign experience for a young man, thought Nofziger. He seemed easy to get along with, a good person to have working in your shop. He exuded energy and might need to be controlled from time to time.

Over the next several days Nofziger found himself running

into the antsy Atwater. "Well, have you made up your mind yet?" Lee kept asking.

Finally, Nofziger gave in. "Well, OK, you're hired," he said. For Lee the anticipation was over. Now he could tell the press back home that he had accepted a job and would be leaving South Carolina, somewhat reluctantly. But he would ever wonder why Nofziger asked that question. Liar politics. Had Lyn heard about the Turnipseed campaign?

So it was that Harvey LeRoy Atwater at the age of twenty-nine became a walk-on in President Ronald Reagan's Office for Political Affairs. The little one-man band that had begun as Baker & Associates above a chicken-wing restaurant six years earlier was now doing business from the White House.

One afternoon in that cold January of 1981, as Sally's parents looked at their invitations to the inauguration of Ronald Reagan, Curtis Dunbar conceded that their daughter just may have picked a winner after all. "I guess," he said to Theo, "Lee is smarter than we thought he was."

In Washington Lee set up residence in a Harbor Square condo on the Potomac, sharing it with Jim McCabe, his old frat brother. Sally stayed in Columbia, finishing up her teaching duties and tending to their firstborn. Though it was a commuter marriage, the couple didn't exactly burn the long-distance lines keeping in touch with each other. "Lee didn't do too much parenting because he was so involved with his career," said Sally. "It wasn't his fault. It's the nature of what politics is. Luckily, I understood that. I knew what the deal was." Later she began to view it as a family-based decision. "When you hired Lee Atwater, you got Lee Atwater — and when he decided to do politics, we as a family all decided to do politics."

This time D.C. was more comfortable for Lee. Washington was a men's club, basically, where the key to success was building relationships. Washington was also about men making deals, using a smiling face and gracious manners as a front for carrying on with some of the most ruthless behavior in the land. Lee's favorite book in these years was the first volume of Robert A. Caro's biography of LBJ, *The Path to Power*. He ordered three copies — one for the office, one for home, and one for traveling. When Lyndon Baines Johnson got on the phone to someone, perspiration was known to break out on the top of the head of the recipient. "One thing you'll learn someday is that you have to be a demagogue on a lot of little things if you want to be around to have your way on the big things," said LBJ. Lee carried the book everywhere, discussing it with anyone who would listen. It was required reading on his own path to power.

Washington was a southern city in some ways: it was mannerly — you called the hostess the next day to thank her for a lovely party. But Washingtonians were much more self-absorbed than southerners ever were. They might tell you if your hair was on fire, but only if you asked. It was also a city in which politics and sex and domination got mixed up. People showed up at a party because they were networking: lobbyists, strategists, consultants, people trying to become hard-wired into the White House, overpaid people who made their oversized livings with retainer fees based on influence rather than ability, people who could not explain what they did for a living in less than a paragraph.

In D.C. one either had sophistication imposed on oneself at an early age, or one arrived at it after considerable effort. For Lee Atwater, a combative man, proud of his heritage, the social expectations were a challenge. He must have seemed an odd figure to the Washington regulars with his drawl, his awkward clothes, his thick mop of hair atop piercing altar-boy eyes. His small lips pursed above a pixieish chin were always poised to reply as he listened. His voice was a smoky baritone that seemed to embody the South of an earlier era, when politicians were like preachers on the street corner. It was the voice of an older man.

Reagan speechwriter Peggy Noonan ran into Lee at a dinner party at the home of Donald Graham, son of Katharine and publisher of the *Washington Post*. "Hi, this is nice," she said. "I don't know why I'm here, do you?"

"Ah don't know," he replied, "but Ah think this is meeting the Yuppih Republicans." They chatted over a dinner of stuffed sole, salad, raspberries and cream, followed by coffee, cognac, and laughter that Lee probably had to force a little. He was always uneasy around gourmet delicacies.

In these months Lee's struggle for sophistication reached an impasse, raising serious questions as to where his true heart resided — in the sharp-edged, networked world of Washington power politics or in the small-town laid-back byways of Spartanburg, Aiken, and other burgs of South Carolina. There he could eat collard greens, black-eyed peas, fried chicken — food a man could understand. The answer, ultimately, was both places, and neither. Lee Atwater was a world unto himself.

Because he wore khaki slacks and a blue blazer to work every day, some colleagues thought that Lee didn't have a suit. One afternoon Roger Stone took Lee to Britches in Georgetown, then the premier men's haberdashery in D.C. Stone was very high fashion, sartorial even — wearing ascots, patent leather shoes, incredibly expensive clothes. Sometimes it was hard to tell whether Roger was wearing the clothes or the clothes were wearing him. "Atwater, you've arrived," he told his friend that day. "You've got to dress like you've arrived. You're not going to be taken seriously dressing like a teenager."

Lee bought a dark blue suit. One Saturday afternoon later that year Stone was walking past Britches when he noticed Lee inside trying on a double-breasted suit in front of a three-sided mirror. Stone walked in. "What the hell are you doing?" he asked.

Lee seemed embarrassed, like a little boy caught playing dress-up. "Oh, I just wanted to see how this looked on me," he said. Then he looked at the clerk. "It looks ridiculous. Get this off me." He left quickly. He certainly didn't want to turn into a dandy like Stone.

Gradually, Lee arrived at a definition of his own sense of style: a navy blazer with slacks, which he wore even when everyone else was in a suit; or a double-breasted navy or gray suit for deluxe occasions. For a speech, a trip, a photo shoot, he began to dress as if his tailor liked him. After hours, of course, it was still khakis and loafers.

And movies. Lee loved B- or even C-flicks. He told a reporter his favorite movies were in the "art cult, bizarre cult, sci-fi cult, horror cult" genres. Favorites included *The Undertaker and His Pals, Hillbillies in a Haunted House, 2,000 Maniacs, The Corpse Grinders, Pink Flamingos, Shanty Tramp, Night of the Living Dead*, as well as the Ma and Pa Kettle series, the Francis the Talking Mule series, and anything with the Three Stooges. The more outlandish the plot or title, the more he got a kick out of it. Anything loosely existential — Lee's definition: "man exists as an individual with free will in a hostile environment" — he was likely to memorize. *The Ultimate Warrior*, starring Yul Brynner, was a favorite, as was *The Last Man on Earth*, starring Vincent Price, later remade as *The Omega Man*, starring Charlton Heston.

Of course, there would always be little occasions when the irrepressible bad boy still arose from within the man in the blue flannel suit. Lee found it impossible to control his desire to debunk the values he was endeavoring to take on. At an early gathering of the Reagan kitchen cabinet, Lee found himself in conversation with one of Nancy's closest friends, Charles Z. Wick — an impresario at the inaugural and a member of the Reagan power team on his way to becoming director of the United States Information Agency. "You're Charles Z. Wick!" said Lee.

"Yes, I am," said Wick as onlookers — mostly California millionaires and expensive-looking wives — gathered around.

"You're one of my heroes!" said Lee.

"Really?"

"Yeah, you produced *Snow White and the Three Stooges*," said Lee. "Didn't you?"

Wick, horrified, got away as quickly as possible.

• • •

The Office of Political Affairs was located, appropriately enough, in Nixon's hideaway office in the Old Executive Office Building (OEOB), a short walk from the Oval Office. This was where Nixon made some of the greatest decisions of his presidency, including the decision to mine and bomb Haiphong Harbor. Later, under conditions of political war, this was the place where Nixon, his presidency crumbling, asked Henry Kissinger to get on his knees and pray for him. Since then it had become a series of four interconnected high-ceilinged offices, with Nofziger stationed in the big room. His deputy, Ed Rollins, and two special assistants — Paul Russo, an operative from the Midwest; and Morgan Mason, the twenty-six-year-old son of actor James Mason — were in connecting offices. Down the hall a couple of doors was Lee, who was just a staff guy with no mess or parking privileges, nothing much at all except for a balcony that he liked to brag about, where he could smoke his Friday cigarettes.

In the confusion of the day, no one knew that Lee was just a staff guy. Lee certainly wasn't going to let on. Meantime, Mason served as emissary to the Reagan court. He arrived at eleven most days, was Mike Deaver's tennis partner, dated starlets, and lunched with Nancy. Nofziger, an egalitarian, thought that Lee and Russo were equals, and he treated them accordingly. Lee went on missions with the president and soon acquired a reputation as a doer. Lee was there to fill the vacuum, as always.

The Office of Political Affairs was dedicated to divvying up the spoils of war — that is, jobs for the faithful. Nofziger, a Reagan loyalist, wanted to make sure that deserving Reaganites got jobs. He turned the mechanics of that task over to Lee, a guy for whom it was easier done than said.

Two weeks into the chaos, Kelly Sinclair dropped by. He and Lee had done some time together back in the College Republican days. Once, in Louisville, Lee had slept on a floor mat in Sinclair's garage apartment for three days while they organized a campaign on campus. Lee's waiting room was jammed that day, but when he spotted Kelly, he asked, "Can you volunteer today, maybe tomorrow?"

Sinclair said yes and was immediately introduced to Judge Guy Hunt, who had just lost the governor's race in Alabama. "This is my assistant," Lee told the judge. "Kelly will get your people placed in the administration." Then Lee left for a meeting. Sinclair bluffed his way through that and similar encounters all week.

By Friday Lee was suitably impressed and offered him a job. "There's something you need to know," said Sinclair. Lee closed the door. "I worked for George Bush."

Oh, Lord. Lee's first staff hire, right under the nose of Nofziger the Mad Reaganite, was a Bushee. "Were you on payroll?" asked Lee.

"Nope."

"Does anybody around *here* know about it?"

"No, they don't."

"Then let's play dumb," said Lee, opening the door, "and just keep movin'." The next week Sinclair was on the payroll for Ronald Reagan.

The federal government — a faceless and all-powerful blur to most onlookers — is composed largely of small-time clerks holding the best jobs they will ever have. Above them the "Schedule Cs" come and go: political appointees who come in with salaries that are higher than those of the career bureaucrats. They are roundly hated, and with good reason. Most Schedule Cs are not qualified for the jobs they assume, though they quickly adapt to a lifestyle based on salaries around $85,000 — only to be devastated when they are booted out by a new administration.

The so-called Plum Book, published every four years, lists all appointed political positions in the federal government. It enumerated some 4,200 in 1984. Not a big number, when you consider the hundreds of thousands of volunteers who are part of any major political campaign. Therefore, those chosen to fill political jobs have done the right favors for the right people on the right campaign. By the end of Reagan's first four years, a majority of these appointees had come through Lee Atwater's office.

At the outset of the Reagan revolution, career bureaucrats were playing games, so none of the Reagan political appointees were getting onboard. Think of a transaction with a postal clerk, or someone at the registry of motor vehicles — and then multiply the slow-moving ordeal by thousands. For example, for the infamous "Schedule C" form, required for all appointees, information had to be copied from the appointee's résumé to a government personnel form, along with gross compensation numbers, which included health insurance and benefits. The information had to be letter perfect, of course. If someone didn't put the numbers down just right, the compensation could be screwed up, the form would be kicked back, and the whole process would go round and round.

Lee found this fascinating — not because he wanted to wander down the labyrinthine ways of the federal bureaucracy; rather, he knew that if he could break through the logjam and get the Reaganites hired, then he would start getting some "stroke"; that is, would be perceived as *the man who can deliver.* And that was the path to power.

"We're losing the revolution!" Lee told Nofziger. "Presidential personnel is processing the high-level appointments, waiting for congressional approval. Meantime, the campaign workers are starving." Although each department and agency ostensibly had one person in charge of personnel to get the Cs hired, none of *them* had ever worked in the government, either, so the problem was getting worse. Lee was ecstatic when he got the go-ahead to start processing the Cs. To ground-level appointees, Lee was a godsend.

Lee moved up politically because he helped thousands of people — and you are never more vulnerable than when you are unemployed. When someone gets you a job, you never forget. The people he had helped were all over government, happy to answer questions, get him information, respond to his needs. Atwater's Army. "Give them a schedule C job at the Dept of Interior," Lee later wrote, "and then they are there for me. They will do anything I want them to do."

In order to get blacks in the Republican ranks, Atwater would "work with the résumé" of Cs who had not come up a straight Republican path. One black who had worked for a Democratic congressman, done favors for other Democrats, and was altogether lacking in the pedigree required in the Reagan administration became a pure Republican on paper after being processed by Lee. His single reference, should anyone ask: Lee Atwater.

Kelly Sinclair, already masquerading as a Reaganite in Lee's office, caused some consternation at Christmastime after one of his guests was shot while arriving at his apartment to attend a party. The police were called, and word got back to a higher-up in the administration, who told Lee. "I understand the party at your place the other night was a gay party," Lee said to Sinclair.

"I don't know if you ever knew that about me," said Sinclair. "I'm not going to embarrass you or the president or anybody else, Lee. I'll resign."

"Nothin' doin', Kelly," said Lee. "I don't *give* a shit. Let's play dumb and just keep movin'.'" Of course, nothing was a free ride in the world of political plums. Kelly now owed Lee a couple of times over.

In political parlance, *owed* means that if you do a favor for someone — especially someone who doesn't know you — that person owes you a chit in return. Not immediately. And maybe not ever. But it's there, waiting, to be collected in a time of need. "The game of politics is like a bank account," said Lee. "You put chits in, and you take chits out." Even if you move on and take another job. In a world where there was lots of job flipping, where people moved from position to position after a year or two, you never knew where your chits were going to end up. Not that you really wanted to *buy* someone's favor and full attention, but you may want to rent him or her for a while.

When Lee first started, the people in his office answered the phone with, "White House political affairs." Then Lee asked them to answer it, "Lee Atwater's office."

Whaatt? Who the hell knew who Lee Atwater was? thought Sinclair.

Soon the phones were ringing steadily as the Schedule Cs checked in for clearance. The phones rang all the time — one day Kelly tallied over nine hundred calls — and the lights on each of the four hold buttons blinked all day. The standard response to incoming calls became, "Lee Atwater's office, can you hold?" By now thousands of rising young Republicans knew who the hell Lee Atwater was.

Lee kept his army happy, going from department to department to address the Schedule Cs, to remind them that they were not lost in the bureaucracy and that they worked for the White House. He sent each appointee a picture of Ronald Reagan with a pseudopersonalized message and the president's autowriter signature. More important, enclosed with each picture was a note from Lee: "I hope the enclosed photograph will serve as a reminder that we are all part of the same team." As photos of Ronald Reagan began to appear on office walls all over bureaucratic Washington, the buzz that followed was Lee did that. Lee got the picture, in more ways than one.

Lee worked at loyalty. He had always been a tense, overworked man in whom conscience battled with ambition — and usually lost. Now he was trying to change his habits, trying to lay a political foundation for a new persona. Loyalty became the building material. One day Lee asked a volunteer, "Do you know what the three most important things in politics are?" She didn't know. "Loyalty, loyalty, loyalty!" he said. It was a return to the old-fashioned notion — which Lee found in the writings of Jeremy Bentham — that people should not make decisions based on what is best for themselves, but instead based on what is best for the group, the team. This meant you don't desert someone as soon as you think you might do better elsewhere.

Lee was known for generosity, for the extravagant gesture — giving jobs to friends, paying special attention to birthdays, family considerations, and the details of protective power. Of course, it was easy to be generous with other people's money, which is the coin of politics. Yet, even by these standards, the Atwater style of largesse and loyalty went beyond business as usual in Washington, a town where the definition of a friend is someone who will stab you in the chest.

Lee's staff became like family. His highest compliment was to say that someone was "one of us." "You need a certain honor code, and you've got to be very devout about it," he said. "Loyalty is very, very important. . . . This is not a business in which liars are going to be around a long time."

Of course, loyalty *sometimes* occasioned a lie, but only when the cause was right. Lee also used the code of loyalty to keep the details of his personal life away from outsiders. His attitude was what goes on in this office or in my life after hours is nobody else's business.

Amidst the hundreds of letters that Lee received daily from well-wishers and job seekers, one day a note arrived that jolted Lee backward. "You're the biggest scumbag I know," the letter read, "and if Ronald Reagan is going to run this country with bastards like you, then I know America is going to hell." It was from the woman he had tried to dupe back at Newberry the night he became Brother of the Month.

Lee showed the letter to a friend who knew about the episode. "What are you gonna do about that?" the friend asked.

Lee shrugged. "Just keep movin'," he said.

After settling into his office, Lee was frequently the contact for elected and party officials who needed favors. The Senate, of course, was a club with rules designed to protect the weak. This meant keeping small disputes out of public view, treating rivals with deference, and avoiding any conflicts that might show up a colleague. In short, to get along, go along. Because Lee was young, some senatorial aides thought they could intimidate and ruffle him. They didn't. Two freshmen Republican senators from the New South wanted their respective candidates to be named to a big regional appointment. Each senator was important to Reagan to maintain a slim Republican majority in the Senate; each was putting pressure on Lee for his candidate. One day Lee called each of the dueling senators, saying, "I've done some checking on that appointment, and I know it's really important to you, but I need to tell you that Senator Thurmond from South Carolina has somebody he wants in that job. If you want to talk to his office about your candidate, . . . " No thanks, said the frosh at the prospect of a conflict with one of the Senate's top guns.

Then Lee called Strom Thurmond. "Senator, this is Lee down at the White House," he said. "We've got an opening here for a regional job. You got anybody from South Carolina you want to put in it?" He did. Perfect. Nobody was mad at Lee. Nobody went over his head to Nofziger or the president. And Thurmond owed Lee another favor. Classic Atwater.

In order to wield political power in Washington, you have to be able to do three things, according to conventional wisdom. First, deliver the message and be able to move people with it. Second, mobilize followers for the cause. Third, raise money to pay for items one and two. By far the most important and powerful feat to accomplish is number three. After all, Washington is filled with talented message makers and staffers who can rustle up a crowd on short notice. Real clout comes to those who can raise money.

A relatively new fund-raising phenomenon when Lee arrived in Washington was the political action committee, or PAC, dedicated to raising money for a particular cause, usually from individuals and corporations with vested interests. In the wake of Watergate and the Campaign Finance Act of 1974, with all its limits on political donations, business groups had started forming PACs in 1978 in order to influence legislation. The Carter administration didn't let them into the White House. In Nixon parlance, that would be wrong.

Well, the Office of Political Affairs was new, too, so Atwater decided to invite the PACs in to brief them on what the office was doing. He wouldn't solicit money from them, of course — that *would* be wrong. But we might as well say hello, tell each other what we do, so his thinking went. It was good politics for the political shop, an opportunity to learn what issues were of importance Out There. The invitation was also perceived as a gracious touch of southern hospitality, a gesture that seemed more genuine than the trinkets many politicians liked to hand out. Lee was beginning to understand that infamous maxim from LBJ's infamous aide Bobby Baker: "No man's price is too small." Sometimes you can buy someone off for life with a carefully timed set of cufflinks.

In the first year, Lee invited corporate PAC representatives to meet him in monthly gatherings of ten to twelve. By the end of the year, he had met with 150 of the top PAC players in town from oil, manufacturing, paper, agricultural, and other groups. Each attendee received a personalized picture of Ronald Reagan. The second round of PAC meetings involved breakfast at the White House mess, followed by the presentation of a set of presidential cufflinks. Finally, at the end of 1981, there was a reception in the Indian Treaty Room for all of the PACsters.

There were no solicitations for funds during the first series of meetings, but 1982 was an *election* year, so the second series took a different turn. They were located outside the White House and led by staffers from the Republican National Committee who briefed attendees. "Lee will be here shortly," the staffers explained, while they discussed key Republican races and priorities with the PAC representatives.

Finally, Lee entered, shaking hands all around, recognizing some big givers, linking them by name to specific pols on the Hill, connecting the necessary political dots, and then giving his view on the national political scene. At the end of his talk, he would say, "I know that you all want to discuss who you're going to support in these campaigns." Then he would leave. The RNC staffers would close the meeting with a roll call of Who's Giving to Whom.

"Lee understood where the line was legally, and he understood power intuitively," recalled Don Fierce, a consultant Lee befriended in his first year at the White House.

What he did *not* understand were issues. In fact, he took pride in saying, "I don't know 'em. I don't *want* to know 'em." He never got involved in any of the lobbying problems PAC players were prone to, though he was not averse to making a friendly phone call to the appropriate political liaison. (Lee always made sure that the White House liaisons were hard-wired to him.) "There's someone here who needs to talk with you," he would say. "He's got a problem. Would you see him? Set something up?"

Lee Atwater raised millions. No one had ever raised money this way before. His fund-raising, which he kept under wraps, was important to the party and to the White House, where he became part of an "assets and priorities group" that directed campaign money to chosen candidates. Thus, some thirty senators and congressmen whose campaigns would have gone broke without this found money began to realize, too, that Lee Atwater was a guy who could get things done in a big way. Easier done than said; that was Lee.

● ● ●

To work with Lee Atwater was to be consumed by him. Your time was his time, and that was twenty-four hours a day. The day started with a staff meeting at seven. He insisted that calls be answered the same day, that people be tracked down and forced to respond to requests. "I put a call in to him, and he hasn't gotten back to me," a staffer once explained.

"Well, is that how things get done?" asked Lee. "Follow up! Get home numbers so that you can return calls in the evening!"

Mail had to be handled within three days. The rule was if you do not have the answers, tell them you are working on the answers. Lee abused staffers, using fear and intimidation. In order to learn from Lee, you had to put up with a lot of yelling and screaming but not take it personally. By this point Lee had developed an intimidating stare as well. He could be scary.

Lee took an interest in staffers, asking them why they were vegetarian, what they saw in a particular boyfriend they were dating. It didn't come off as someone being nosy, just curious: "How do you *know* God's in your heart?"

He usually carried a legal-size yellow pad to take notes during a meeting. It also gave him something to hold onto, for he was still fidgety. He liked to maximize the moment, never doing one thing at a time. He usually ate at his desk so that he could make phone calls, which were more important than the meal. A cold hamburger didn't bother him — he doused everything with Tabasco sauce anyway. He went through three bottles a week. "I'd put it in my iced tea if my wife would let me!" he liked to joke. Jogging was still Lee's main tonic, though: a jog meant he could release the stress, keep his weight down, and engage in useful conversation or expand his mind by listening to a book on tape. One rainy afternoon in New York City, he ran up and down the ramps of a parking garage — taking a ticket and paying the attendant afterward for one hour (or six miles).

Craig Helsing, a young law student working in Presidential Personnel, met Lee walking around the Old Executive Office Building in a bright green jogging suit. Lee had discovered the bathroom in Nofziger's office and explained with delight how he showered in Nixon's old stall after a six-mile run. They fell into discussions of Machiavelli, and within a month Helsing was working for Lee. In exchange for a tutorial on politics, Craig agreed to become Lee's driver, working every day of the year except Christmas and Thanksgiving. Helsing picked Lee up at six-fifteen sharp every morning.

Once, due to snow, Helsing arrived ten minutes late. He waited in the driveway another ten, fifteen minutes. Finally, he knocked on the door and found out that Lee had already left. Helsing drove to the office for the seven o'clock staff meeting and was ten minutes late for that. When he knocked on the door, Lee's secretary told him he should wait outside. Lee wouldn't let him in the meeting. No matter what the weather, what the conditions, Lee expected Craig to *anticipate* these things and still be on time. Normal impediments were never to be an issue. Helsing was never late again. "Life is not horseshoes," Lee said. "You don't get credit for leaners — only ringers count."

Lee wanted to keep up, to have the best information. And if information was power, *timely* information could be awesome. At eleven-thirty each night he had a staffer deliver the next morning's *Washington Post* to him at home so that he could read it and start making phone calls at five A.M., telling others what they should be ready for. If he was on the road, he had a staffer call him at night and read key stories from the *Post* to him over the phone. Next morning, same routine — early-warning calls at five. He read the news magazines on Sunday, before they came out on Monday. Thus, he became perceived as a *source* of information to others, even though his own sources were standard publications.

Lee was fascinated by writers. He told students and anyone who would believe him that he read two books a week, although in fact he was unable to sit and read for long periods of time. Instead, he became a highly skilled browser, going to the index for key ideas, underlining passages, focusing on maybe fifty pages in a four-hundred-page book, memorizing small sections. He could skim a book in half an hour and had tremendous powers of recall. Certain epigrammatic books he knew word for word, the result of multiple browsings of the Cliffs Notes version. He bragged to Don Fierce that he had read *The Prince* fifteen times. "Anybody who understood Machiavelli would never admit that," replied Fierce.

Lee *did* understand the need for surrounding himself with very bright staffers. (Machiavelli: "The first impression that one gets of a ruler and of his brains is from seeing the men he has about him.") There was money to hire assistants. As the political shop grew to twenty-four, Lee's support staff included a brain trust led by James Pinkerton, whom Atwater, ever given to nicknames, dubbed Pink. Pinkerton was seven years younger than

Lee. While attending Stanford, he had won $5,000 on *Knockout*, a short-lived TV game show hosted by Arte Johnson, because not only was Pinkerton smart — he was quick. After a brief stint as a failed screenwriter, Pink had volunteered to answer phones at the Reagan campaign in Los Angeles, where his specialty was handling "nut calls." "I'm worried about UFO infiltration of the U.S. space command, and I want to talk to Governor Reagan about it," a caller might begin.

"Let me put you through to the governor's special assistant, Jim Pinkerton." Then Pinkerton would talk the caller down from the psychological ledge with assurances of governmental action soon.

Pinkerton also began to write letters and memos for the campaign, so when the Reagan team moved East in 1980, Pinkerton ended up at campaign headquarters in Arlington, Virginia, working as a researcher and "clipper," responsible for reading a dozen newspapers a day and culling relevant clips for the Reagan cause. Pinkerton, a newshound and speed reader, was in heaven. After the victory in November, he was assigned to the White House as an analyst in the policy office, where he felt seriously underutilized. To Pinkerton — surrounded by Reaganite technocrats with cufflinks and slicked-back hair — Lee Atwater stood out.

To Atwater, Pinkerton stood out. For one thing, he was six nine with long blond hair and a tendency to speed-talk. And talk they did. As they talked about political strategies, Lee saw Pinkerton as someone with a brilliant, disciplined mind who could research and explore difficult questions about crime, the media, the welfare state, the gender gap, patterns of political discontent — and be meticulous and thorough in reporting his conclusions. He could also be fearless, even if what he said flew in the face of conventional wisdom. Atwater had enough faith in him that he would advocate Pink's conclusions once they were shaped and supported by facts.

With the '82 elections on the horizon, Lee hired Pink at a salary of $24,000 to read the papers, looking for items of political interest. Pinkerton arrived at six-thirty each morning and discovered that Lee was already there. He was amazed at how hardworking and supportive Lee was.

Lee knew how to motivate nerds with his affable arrogance. Though Pinkerton was serious, even scholarly, he had a humorous underside that Lee loved to provoke. Lee would deflect visitors to his office, telling them that they would be meeting a short Jewish fellow named Pink, "short for Pinkenheimer."

Lee was in favor of anything that could make his way easier. As his life became more chaotic and his schedule more turbulent, he developed great skills as a delegator. Eventually Pinkerton brought in another research sleuth, Gary Maloney. Their jobs were, in part, to keep Lee au courant on the latest intellectual happenings, providing synopses and critiques of books, plays, and events so that Lee did not need to read or attend them himself. Lee liked the way Reagan used three-by-five index cards for speeches and even offhand remarks. Accordingly, Lee's staff gave him their summaries on index cards, which he often memorized.

Although Lee operated largely by instinct, he used Pinkerton to establish credentials for himself with Reaganites who preferred to operate by memos. To Pinkerton it was like being in graduate school, with Lee acting as professor. Lee had the ideas; Pinkerton had the time. Lee would call him, tell him what he wanted to say, and then Pinkerton would go off for a few days, or a few weeks, and produce a memo, much as a student would hand in a term paper. In addition to the pay, there was plenty of psychic income for a young student of the political wars.

Unlike other departments where Pinkerton had worked, with Atwater he never felt like he was covering for the boss; rather, *everyone* was working hard. In addition to putting in long days, Lee was in the office weekends and on his way to an event most evenings. At the end of the day, he would always holler to his hardworking staff as he headed out the door, "Thank you! Thanks for everything!" Atwater wouldn't ask for anything that he wouldn't do or hadn't done himself. To Pinkerton, it was like the motto of the Israeli officer corps: Follow me.

With his staff in place, Lee could now concentrate on becoming what he *really* wanted to be. A legend.

CHAPTER

5

THE PERMANENT CAMPAIGN

When men in politics are together, testosterone poisoning
makes them insane.
— Peggy Noonan

"**O**nly two things are important," said Lee Atwater. "Important
things, and things that are important to important people."
Footloose in the Reagan White House in the early '80s, Lee
quickly surmised who was important, and who merely had the
trappings of importance. Among the Reaganites, two forces had
emerged — the hardliners, led by Ed Meese, who wanted an ideo-
logical presidency; and the pragmatists, led by James Baker. Anything that went into Meese's office was subject to so much delay,
you might never see it again; Lee called Meese's briefcase "the
black hole." So when Mike Deaver, the president's image maker
and confidant to Nancy, sided with Baker, there was no stop-
ping the two of them. Then Lee knew where the *real* power was:
Margaret Tutwiler.

Margaret Tutwiler, a few months older than Lee, was also
a high-energy southerner. From a prominent wealthy Alabama
family, she had been Baker's assistant since the Ford campaign of
'76, with a stint as Bush's scheduler in '80. She was not married,
and, aside from a passing interest in oriental rugs, her life was
whatever Jim Baker touched. As the right arm of the chief of staff,
she was very organized, methodical, with a pleasant yet demanding demeanor. She expected results, and if you didn't deliver you
were taken off her list. "Let me give you a bit of advice," she once
told Atwater after Rollins had failed to come through on some

routine request. "If Baker asks you what's the weather like today, you'd better send over a weather map."

"When Tutwiler calls, get me on the phone immediately," Lee instructed an aide. "She's Baker's right-hand man."

Initially, Tutwiler was skeptical about Lee. She thought he was a bit cagey, but aren't most white southern men that way? Gradually, he worked his way into her organized heart. Lee was such a doer! Whether it meant getting tickets to a ballgame or coordinators to work a precinct, Lee delivered. Baker's aides watched him deliver even more. "Lee played Tutwiler like a violin," recalled one assistant. "Day after day he was in her office as if she were the font of political wisdom: 'Oh, what do you think of this?' or 'Let me bounce this off of you,' or 'I need Jim to do this. How's the best way to approach him?' he'd say. It was a beautiful thing to watch." Lee understood that Margaret was the conduit, Baker's wholly owned subsidiary, and when you got your message to Margaret, and she believed it, it was like whispering in Baker's ear.

At first, Jim Baker — who had made a career of finding and using talented people he didn't approve of socially — thought Lee was crude but useful. With a B.A. from Princeton and a law degree from the University of Texas, Baker was a lot of things that Atwater would never be. If Baker was debonair, liked order and follow-through, and was a model of consistency, Atwater was still a work in progress. Initially, Baker could seem mirthless, but after a few encounters his sense of humor usually emerged. He even liked to chew tobacco, tell ribald jokes, and be a good ol' boy when necessary. Baker and Atwater got along. Lee saw to that.

Baker soon recognized in Lee someone who, like himself, wanted to get ahead; someone who was not sentimental, except given good political cause; someone who was rarely interested in ideology; someone who loved to play the inside power game of politics. Moreover, Lee wasn't pestering him about sitting in on cabinet meetings. Atwater was actually of value in helping to line up votes for initiatives among southern Democrats, to help develop switchers. Lee knew how to execute. Margaret was right. Lee Atwater was a *doer*.

If there was a core Atwater ideology, it had to be pragmatism. "I feel that I have an intuitive grasp of the political scene," he once said. "I can't always cite statistics, but I can feel what's in the air."

Indeed, Lee had no interest in the policy loop. In the Reagan revolution, he called himself "like Jefferson, a conservative libertarian," something hinted at as much by his shaggy hair and taste for blues music as by his aversion to various functions of official government. He believed in Reagan, but not everything on the menu. Lee would laugh at jokes that poked fun at Reagan for not being alert, but he never violated the respect he had for the president. Lee was personally in favor of legalized abortion, referring to far-right ideologues as the "extra-chromosome" crowd. He felt that the more heat Reagan took from the right, the better he looked to the moderate and liberal press covering him.

Once Lee got a call from the Oval Office. The president had a few minutes between appointments and wanted to see him, immediately. Oh, boy, some face time at last. What would he want to talk about — the southern strategy? "They tell me you know a lot about the movies," said the Gipper.

While Ronald Reagan held forth as the nice grandfather figure, the Office of Political Affairs often had to deal in tough love, an Atwater specialty. After barely six months on the job, a cocky Atwater explained to journalist Hedrick Smith how the Office of Political Affairs was using scare tactics — direct mail, radio and TV ads, speakers — to put heat on congressmen who wandered from the program. "A congressman's behavior on legislation can be affected more by pressure from within his own district than by lobbying here in Washington," Lee explained. "The way we operate, within forty-eight hours any congressman will know he has had a major strike in his district. All of a sudden, Vice President Bush is in your district; Congressman Jack Kemp is in your district. Ten of your top contributors are calling you, the head of the local AMA, the head of the local realtors' group, local officials. Twenty letters come in. Within forty-eight yours, you're hit by paid media, free media, mail, phone calls, all asking you to support the president."

Lee made it part of his day's work to befriend reporters, especially the southern press. "Come by the White House when you're in town," is a hard invitation to ignore. Lee would establish rapport, feed a reporter some information — the coin of the realm — maybe even throw in lunch at the White House mess. Before long there was a self-manufactured story about this young gun from the South. Hey, no ink, no glory.

One sun-flecked afternoon, as a reporter from the *Atlanta*

Constitution sat in his office, Lee lounged shoeless on his couch, deep in dispute over the phone with someone he assured the reporter was a southern Republican senator. "I ain't gonna get into that crap," Lee growled. "Do me a gargantuan favor. Get me a good guy who was with Reagan *before* the general election. You follow where I'm coming from?" Lee hung up, confiding, "Everybody wants to be the big man. It's a mess."

Later there was a photo opportunity on Lee's balcony, with Lee supplying all the revisionist history of his life the Atlanta reporter could handle. With Lee's coaching, the focus of the piece became "what shrewd political operatives believe is becoming the Lee Atwater factor in Southern politics." He explained how John Connally was an odds-on favorite to win in South Carolina until Lee managed the campaign that saved Ronald Reagan. "After the victory, Atwater was quickly whisked into the inner sanctum, where his help in designing and implementing Reagan's assault on President Carter's home region, some contend, contributed to the Georgian's humiliating loss of every Southern state but his own," wrote the reporter.

"If I've done an innovative thing," Lee said cockily from the couch, "it's consciously having this working formula, which has proved invincible in every campaign." He explained how he went through polls looking for negative attitudes toward an opponent, and then cross-referenced those negatives by age, sex, race, and economic group in order to develop negative themes to hammer again and again to raise the opponent's negative rating. For example, "Connally had so many negatives, it was absolutely lethal. Republicans hated him because he was for LBJ. Democrats because he was for Nixon. Little people because of big oil. Intellectuals because of his tough talk. You name it."

Lee then went on to explain another favorite strategy, drawing an opponent's fire to himself, thus leaving his own candidate above the fray. He pointed to the job he had done when running the Spence race the previous year, for instance. "I knew Tom Turnipseed didn't have enough self-discipline to keep from attacking me, so I released this poll showing he couldn't possibly win," said Atwater. "He took out after me the next day. Then, a reporter asked me about his mental history. He had once had a problem. I said that that issue had no place in the campaign. Then, I added that I heard he once had to be hooked up to some jumper cables." Atwater grinned impishly as he told the story. "The guy lost control of himself. I just made myself a tar baby and sat in the road, where he couldn't get past me. That became the issue."

While we find it admirable when someone powerful channels his force into service of the good, it's downright mesmerizing when someone equally powerful channels those same powers into destruction. That September the *Atlanta Constitution* reported that if indeed there *was* a big man in the White House, insofar as the South was concerned, it was Lee Atwater. A guy who, after all, had read *The Prince* twenty-one times!

In subsequent interviews, Atwater would revive the Turnipseed tale for *Esquire*, the *New York Times*, NBC-TV, and PBS. "Why did he keep fucking with me?" Turnipseed wondered years later. "Lee seemed to get sadistic delight out of making fun of a sixteen-year-old who was treated for depression with electroshock treatments. Perhaps it enhanced his take-no-prisoners media persona." It also turned Turnipseed into Atwater's own tar baby as he pushed forward on the slippery slope of American politics.

• • •

Lyn Nofziger had made it clear that he was getting out after a year. Immediately, there was jockeying for position — who would succeed Lyn? Although Ed Rollins was Nofziger's deputy and had known him since the late '70s, he was not considered the operative apparent.

In his younger days, Edwin J. Rollins had been one tough son of a bitch. As an amateur boxer, he won 164 fights, losing but twice, with one draw. He lifted weights, once pressing 385 pounds — remarkable for a middleweight. Now, as deputy to Nofziger, Rollins was not physically intimidated by anyone, but mentally he'd taken a few hits. Though only nine years Lee's senior, Ed Rollins at thirty-nine looked — and acted — older, *much* older. His laid-back California demeanor was in sharp contrast to the Eddie Haskell gyrations of Lee. The only thing the two shared in the early innings was a sense of awe at how far they had come. "Sort of the imposter syndrome," recalled Rollins. "We felt any day they'd come through the door and say, 'What the fuck are you two guys doing here?'" Rollins and Atwater bonded in a classic alliance of two unlikelies who needed each other for political survival. There was no choice.

Reagan's political adviser Stu Spencer had heard so many errant things come out of Rollins's press encounters that he was convinced that there was no biological connection between his brain and his mouth. Some of it was innocent stuff, and it was rarely mean-spirited; in the final analysis, though, Ed Rollins just didn't get the concept of spin. After six months on the job, Rollins had given an interview to his hometown Vallejo, California, paper, *The Daily Republic*. It was the sort of interview that every White House staffer looks forward to, then lives in fear of, lest the braggadocio bounce back. Ed presented himself as the guy who "works right next to the president as one of the top 20 assistants," adding, "I'm with him almost daily."

Atwater highlighted the self-serving quotes and made up a memo to Ed from Baker aide Richard Darman, adding the pointed observation, "Perhaps we should discuss this," with c.c.'s to Baker, Meese, Deaver, Rich Williamson, and Nofziger. Rollins squirmed for a day before Lee confessed to the prank.

Rollins's mouth nearly cost him his job after a lecture he gave to a Georgetown University class meeting on the eve of the Senate vote on the sale of AWACS planes to Saudi Arabia. There had been an all-out White House effort to lobby senators to support the sale, and one student asked Ed how the political office had pressured Republican Senator Roger Jepsen, from Iowa, to switch his vote. "We just beat his brains out," said Rollins. "We stood him up in front of an open grave and said he could jump in if he wanted to." Unbeknownst to Ed, he was speaking to a correspondent for the *Des Moines Register*, and his lighthearted response ended up in print. Senator Jepsen called Jim Baker and asked that Rollins be fired. Thus, one of Lee's early campaigns in the Office of Political Affairs involved saving Ed Rollins's ass.

Rollins was traveling with Reagan when the story broke in the *Post*. Lee immediately called the Georgetown teacher and students, conducted interviews, and pulled the facts on the incident together. He told the reporter his story was wrong. Instead of spinning it as a reporter's misinterpretation, though, Lee called syndicated columnists Rowland Evans and Robert Novak and pointed out that the humorless senator from Iowa had overreacted. The next day Rollins's assistant Michele Davis read the columnists' take to Ed by phone. Lee's spin had created a story that absolved the wayward press and focused on the senator's heavy-handed tactics, pointing out that taxpayer-funded staffers had been sent on a witch hunt. "Reagan insiders are convinced that Jepsen will not get Rollins' scalp, certainly not for using a pugilistic idiom as common on Capitol Hill as in the ring," concluded Evans and Novak.

"Lee turned it around, didn't he?" said Rollins from Air Force One, his voice relieved.

"You bet he did," said Davis.

"Lee's role was protecting me and making sure that I didn't get blown up," said Rollins, "knowing full well that if I didn't get blown up he could ride along on my coattails and wait for his opportunity to go by me."

If Rich Williamson didn't go by Rollins first. And indeed, there was much in favor of Rich Williamson's advancement. In '80 he'd been deputy to Paul Laxalt, the president's soul brother, when Laxalt was chairman of the Reagan election committee. Before that, he was top gun for Illinois congressman Phil Crane, one of the first to support Reagan in the famous primary challenge of '76 that fell short at the convention. Moreover, Williamson now had additional clout as assistant to the president for intergovernmental affairs — working with a former California governor who favored state responsibilities. With a deputy assistant, three special assistants, and a staff of eighteen in the White House, Rich Williamson was certifiably a big foot, EEE width for extra clout. He even had the right pedigree — he had been president of his class at Princeton, Baker's school. Hell, he'd even been a wrestler in college, and at six feet and 190 pounds, he got up at five-thirty each morning to do six miles on a bike. Talk about discipline!

To position himself for Nofziger's job and the role of campaign manager in the '84 reelection, Williamson set up Laxalt and Frank Fahrenkopf from the Republican National Committee as allies. Lee countered by lining up support for Rollins from the South and the West — elected officials the White House responded to, as well as important Reagan backers in the states. Lee also watered a few lawns in the press, alerting friendly reporters that a little war was underway.

Then a third contender appeared. Lee learned that Haley Barbour, the Mississippi operative, also wanted the job and had arranged to meet with Jim Baker. Lee knew that Haley was a family man, a deacon at the First Presbyterian Church in Yazoo City, where he had taught Sunday school. He called Haley, suggesting that he and his wife Marsha stop by after seeing Baker. What could be friendlier?

Baker told Barbour that he was his choice to run the political shop, but others wanted Rollins, and Williamson was also in the wings. Baker didn't want to put Barbour into the running unless he was ready to fight for the job. Barbour sparked to the idea. Yeah, he said. Let's do it. He told Marsha his decision, and they left to visit Atwater.

"I know you're Baker's choice," said Lee, "but I've been working with Rollins, and I have to be for him." Then he looked Barbour in the eye, seemingly oblivious to Marsha's presence. "It's hard. I don't know whether you'd like the job or not," he said in his best good ol' boy tone. "I'll tell you one thing about it, though — you can get all the pussy you want up here. You can sleep with a different woman every night!"

Haley Barbour decided instead to run for the Senate back home in Mississippi.

Back to Williamson. The National Conservative Political Action Committee had asked the Office of Political Affairs to endorse a conservative Democrat over Kathy Whitmire, a liberal Democrat, in the Houston mayoral election. Nofziger refused; it made no sense — there was also a Republican in the race. NCPAC then went to Williamson, who promptly denounced Whitmire as "quite liberal" and "not sympathetic to President Reagan's goals." Whoa. Why was Williamson sticking his oar into Democratic waters? Lee fed that one to Tutwiler instanter.

Baker, stunned by the news, turned on his aide. "Rich Williamson's chances to replace the retiring Lyn Nofziger as White House political chief slumped when he intervened in the Nov. 3 Houston mayoral election without authorization from his superiors, who promptly repudiated his action," quoth the wire services. "Favored until now by Baker as first choice to replace Nofziger, Williamson has a host of enemies in the White House and among Reaganite grassroots politicians."

On Friday, November 13, Baker announced that Ed Rollins would succeed Lyn Nofziger as director of the Office of Political Affairs. Shortly afterward, Rich Williamson dropped by to see Lee. Their conversation quickly turned caustic. "You want to be master of the universe!" Williamson said. Atwater had heard that one from Rich before. He just smiled. "Someday I'm gonna take over this office," said Williamson, heading for the door. "And the first motherfucker I'm gonna fire is you!"

• • •

On Friday, January 15, 1982, Lee was honored by the Jaycees as one of the nation's "Ten Outstanding Young Men," along with a young congressman from Indiana named Dan Quayle. Lee flew to Tulsa for the event, after a stop in Orlando. A reporter from the *Tulsa World* interviewed Atwater about the Mickey Edwards race in Oklahoma. "We will do anything to help re-elect him," said Lee. Edwards was the state's only Republican congressman, and "one of the first ten congressmen to endorse Ronald Reagan."

Since Lee had just flown out of D.C. on Air Florida, the interview turned naturally to discussion of the plane that had crashed in the nation's capital on Wednesday. Air Florida Flight 90, delayed nearly two hours owing to snowfall, had taken off for Fort Lauderdale and hit the northbound span of the Fourteenth Street Bridge over the Potomac. The disaster gripped the nation's headlines after passersby made dramatic life-saving attempts, plunging into the icy river near the Jefferson Memorial.

Lee confided to the Tulsa reporter that he had actually had a seat on that ill-fated plane. "I told my secretary to cancel the flight at the last minute because I just had too much to do. About twenty minutes later she came in and told me. At first I thought it was some kind of morbid joke." Obviously, it appeared this young Atwater was enjoying some sort of charmed life. "I live on the waterfront about fifty yards from the site. When I got home, I could see it right out my picture window," Lee added. "It really made me think how easy life can come and go."

Eerie. Or perhaps a little too pat. In fact, on Wednesday Lee had an interview scheduled with Dan Balz of the *Post*, followed by a four o'clock meeting with Tutwiler, Russo, and Rollins. Everyone in the political office was looking forward to the black-tie farewell for Nofziger at the Sheraton that night, hoping it wouldn't be canceled because of the snow. With all that going on, would Lee really have booked a flight to Fort Lauderdale? Or was he adding just enough zest to his flight aboard Air Florida the next day to make a memorable lead for this nice reporter? Or was Lee simply spinning the anxiety he no doubt did feel? Clips from the *Tulsa World* Sunday edition began to circulate in the political office. The story featured a front-page photo of the crash site with searchers looking through the debris near the Potomac. An office wag drew an arrow to the Jefferson Memorial, about fifty yards from the site, marking it "Lee's House."

• • •

On January 29, 1982, Lee Atwater was named deputy assistant to the president for political affairs. In addition to watching Rollins's backside, Lee's duties now included being point man for the 1982 congressional elections. Lee saw to it that the official White House announcement of his promotion enhanced the role he had played in a few earlier campaigns. This was the release that called him "the manager of Senator Strom Thurmond's 1978 reelection" and the mastermind behind the 1980 "campaign strategy for the southern states."

Reagan's second year was a crisis point in his presidency. A recession had pushed his popularity below 50 percent. Lee began to work the Hill, taking care of congressmen who needed a favor. Immediately he clashed with Ken Duberstein, a veteran who was running the office of Congressional Affairs. "I don't want you on the Hill," he told Atwater. But by now numerous congressmen from the conservative South were quite concerned about Lee's political well-being. When the dust settled, it was agreed that whenever Lee went to the Hill he would touch base with Duberstein.

Lee loved access. By picking up the phone, he could issue an invitation to lunch at the White House mess, the dining room in the basement run by the Navy. Lee used the mess as though it were a four-star restaurant. The food was great. There was a main room with a huge round table for the staff, as well as an executive mess, which was no bigger than some people's dining rooms — but it was right next to the situation room, conversation was usually conducted in a whisper, and there was likely to be a cabinet secretary at the table. Very intimate, quiet, with place cards — and no press allowed. Lee became a regular, lunching with James Brown, his childhood idol, *Pink Flamingos* director John Waters, or wrestlers like Big John Studd.

After lunch, Lee liked to take guests on a backstage tour of the White House, where the intimacy could be disarming. In addition to the Oval Office, the main floor included the chief of staff's office, the vice president's office, with the national security adviser and the press secretary nearby. And how unplush it was, with all the big guys sharing one little bathroom just off the hall that led to the West Wing lobby. Apart from Secret Service agents, no one was here without an invitation. Lee loved access.

One day Lee was lunching with Don Fierce, and the talk turned to Nixon. "Go see him," said Fierce. "He's got one of the greatest political minds in the country. Go pick his brain."

"He won't see me," said Lee.

"He'll see you in a minute."

When the two met, Richard Nixon may have seen a bit of himself in the young operative. Nixon admired Atwater's combativeness, his scrappiness; and, of course, the fact that he came from "humble stock." Atwater saw Nixon as someone who knew how to bounce back. That went beyond book learning; that was *street* smarts. It was the beginning of a beautiful political friendship. Lee asked Roger Stone, a Nixon confidant, if he could get the former president to attend a state Republican dinner honoring Strom Thurmond back in Columbia. Nixon agreed. Afterward, Atwater, Stone, and Nixon retired to the former president's hotel suite and talked politics till three in the morning.

In February 1982 Lee and Nixon met again, and Nixon coached Lee in the expectations game as the congressional elections drew near. Don't raise hopes needlessly, he said, pointing out that historically there had been a thirty-eight-seat loss for the incumbent party. Nixon also suggested that Lee try to neutralize Reagan's California friends, who were causing him damage, and that the president should "get away from the millionaire image." (Nixon allowed his own well-heeled friends to come in only once every four years for a state dinner.) In order to keep some discipline on the Hill, Nixon said that "when some members go off the reservation, strategic press leaks saying the White House and the president are upset and don't understand" could be disciplining, along with one-on-one chats reminding them that the second year of an administration "is always the bad year, and things will be getting better in the third and fourth years, and that nothing should be done in 1982 that will rupture a friendship in 1983 and 1984." Nixon also said, "It is time to go after the media again," calling for "a nut-cutting spokesman to go on the attack in the same manner that Agnew did in 1970."

Finally, Nixon stressed that "those in executive positions

should concern themselves with the big picture and not get preoccupied in details." In Nixon's opinion, "the good executive can sign a bad letter without trying to make a bunch of changes in it." A telling observation, and one that made its mark on Lee. For more than a year now, Lee had been consumed with details in the White House, "the things that were important to important people." If Lee was going to become important himself, he had to impress others that he was capable of big-picture thinking. The day after his meeting with Nixon, Lee distributed a sixteen-point memo to colleagues summarizing the ex-president's recommendations. Other memos would follow as Lee undertook a paper campaign to show others what a big thinker he could be.

• • •

Meanwhile Rich Bond was riding high. After delivering Iowa for Bush in '80 — a win that still had Reaganites brooding — he had come to the White House as the upstart young strategist, with far more credibility than Lee had. Bond, who played racquetball with Rollins, was a shrewd high-stakes poker player and now Bush's political director. Like Lee, he was intense, loyal to his friends, a highly competitive street fighter, and someone who didn't forgive or forget anyone who crossed him. The wrath of Bond. Lee hated him immediately. "They were absolute total rivals — the same age, the same party, the same circle, the same hot-bloodedness," recalled a D.C. journalist who listened to their outpourings about one another. "They had this rivalry going over who was going to replace Stu Spencer and the older guys who had run Nixon and Ford and, to a lesser extent, Reagan's campaigns. Running a winning presidential campaign makes you an icon in the political world. Everybody wants you then."

At the end of the first year, Bond, at odds with Bush's executive assistant Jennifer Fitzgerald, wanted out. Besides, he didn't want to wait around for seven years while Bush considered running for president. Meanwhile, Lee had been conducting an underground campaign against Dick Richards, the amiable head of the Republican National Committee who had started withholding poll data — the stuff careers are made of — from the Office of Political Affairs. Using unsigned, undated memos addressed to the Big Three (Meese, Baker, and Deaver) chronicling all of

Richards's misdoings, Lee began inflicting death by a thousand paper cuts. He suggested that Rollins put Bond over at RNC to keep an eye on Richards. Once Bond had left the White House, Lee offered his own services to Bush as political counselor. To Lee, Bush looked like a strong contender for '88, and waiting around for seven years was not an issue. The campaign could begin *now*.

The White House Office of Political Affairs viewed the RNC as a checkbook, and Lee viewed South Carolina as his special province. Therefore, when Carroll Campbell needed money for his '82 reelection campaign, Lee said no problem. He called Bond, now the RNC political director, who said no way. Lee called Ron Kaufman, an offbeat operative at the RNC who was seeing quite a bit of the town's nightlife with Lee. "Listen, I know you have money in your budget," said Lee. "Just give Carroll the money. Don't tell Rich."

Kaufman told Bond, but he also told him that supporting Campbell was the right thing to do. "Fuck him!" said Bond. "We don't give him a dime!" The war became a jihad. Lee had a messenger ceremoniously deliver to Bond an index card on which was typed: "*Traitor*, n. One who betrays one's country, a cause, or a trust . . . from Latin, past participle of *tradere*, to betray." Lee made sure that the veep heard the worst about Bond, determined to ace him out of the Reagan/Bush reelection.

Rollins tried to mediate, but he had bigger problems. Monday, October 25, 1982, started as an easy morning for Ed, followed by lunch at the mess with Tug McGraw, the colorful Mets reliever, and his family. Ed returned to his office aglow. By the end of the day, though, he was feeling dizzy, his blood pressure moved up precipitously, and the last thing he remembered seeing as he stumbled to the couch was a soft white flash going off inside his head. Stroke. By the time Lee returned to the office at six-thirty from a run, an ambulance had taken Rollins to George Washington University Hospital. During the operation that followed on November 16, Rollins had a second seizure. Partial paralysis on the left side. When Lee learned of the second stroke, a light flashed before his eyes: even if Ed survived, this could kill the reelection job for them both.

Lee's calls began at four the next morning. Calmly and deliberately, he made the rounds, shoring up support for Rollins, briefing Tutwiler, explaining that they wanted to keep the second stroke *real* quiet, spinning the press with tales of Ed telling jokes ten minutes after entering the hospital. "He was the man with the focus and the plan, the one clear-thinking adult among those who loved and wanted to protect Ed," recalled Michele Davis. "I never looked at Lee as Eddie Haskell again."

There were other setbacks. On November 2, the Republicans lost twenty-six House seats in the midterm elections. If 75,000 votes had gone the other way, it would have been truly disastrous. Considering the fact that Reagan had been shot, there was a recession, and unemployment was its highest since the depression — the Reaganites hung on pretty well at midterm.

Lee was distraught. Despite Nixon's advice, Lee had bragged up Republican hopes in the '82 elections. He had told *Post* columnist David Broder that they might lose six or eight seats, hoping he "wouldn't write lousy stories before the races began." Of course, Lee's "spin" memo had media messages for all outcomes, no matter what happened. In Arkansas, for instance, where Bill Clinton was running against Frank White, a win by the Republican candidate, according to Lee, meant "Voters had a clear choice between a Democrat retread and Governor White." A loss meant "1980 was an aberration. Arkansas is a Democratic state. Only three Republicans ever elected including Reconstruction."

"I was just dead wrong," said Lee about '82. "I should have said we were going to lose thirty seats. We could have gotten away with that because some expectations were that we would lose forty. But I didn't understand the expectations game very clearly back then. I should have kept my damn mouth shut." The stress landed him in GW hospital one afternoon with chest pains. Exhaustion. A doctor put him on an IV, took some blood for tests, and left, saying he would return. Lee insisted that a phone be installed in his room. He completed his calls, and the doctor still hadn't returned. Lee waited for no one, except perhaps the president and his cabinet officers. He took the IV out, left the hospital without being discharged, and returned to work.

Lee had to hold down the fort against another onslaught by Rich Williamson. As assistant to the president for intergovernmental affairs, Williamson was one of the dozen or so equals reporting to Baker. He had crafted Reagan's New Federalism program and was back in Baker's good graces. So when he began marshaling support for a takeover of the political shop while Rollins was in rehab, it was a duel to the death with Lee.

One day in late November, Pinkerton was reading his customary eight newspapers when he ran across an article in the *Philadelphia Inquirer* about Rich Williamson visiting the homeless, complete with quotes from the president's aide that suggested regret for not doing enough to help. Atwater sent a memo around with the clip, saying Williamson was breaking ranks with Reagan. "It's not a question of anybody enjoying people suffering," he said. "The question is: Do we want White House aides agreeing with our enemies?"

In a two-week period, Lee managed to steer ten of the dozen or so presidential deputies to Baker with complaints about *something* Williamson had done. The coup de grâce occurred when Lee got a copy of a memo Williamson had written to a constituent group, bragging in effect that, you don't need to worry about Baker. I have him in my back pocket. Well, now. When Margaret Tutwiler saw that, she said it was a breach of loyalty. In the spring, after Rollins had completed his physical therapy and returned to the office, Williamson was given his walking papers — and sent all the way to Europe.

As Williamson became ambassador in Vienna, a farewell gift from Lee appeared in the *Post*, a story chronicling his enemy's fall from power. "You sons of bitches," Williamson told Rollins when he saw the story. "The day I'm leaving, and you're still shooting arrows in my back."

"Rich, I had nothing to do with it," said Rollins. "You just picked a fight with the wrong guy."

•   •   •

In January 1983 a Gallup poll of registered voters placed Walter Mondale, the likely Democratic candidate for president, at 51 percent and Ronald Reagan at 33 percent. Atwater was worried about the gender gap, Hispanics, the education "blitz," and other issues related to the '84 election. He also wanted Baker and Bush to think of him as a big-picture guy, as a thinker as well as a doer. Jim Pinkerton was the perfect instrument for Lee's campaigns. "Jim, I want to talk about the southern fortress," Lee said one day, looking Pinkerton in the eye, as if to say: If this thing blows up, you're fired.

"I didn't need a baby-sitter," recalled Pinkerton, who by now had an office on the fourth floor of the OEOB. "I needed fear, a sense of dread over what would happen to me if it didn't work."

Lee called in people. Pink did the same. Then they huddled. At first Pinkerton wrote term paper–like tracts, complete with footnotes. Lee read the drafts quickly but closely, tossing footnotes, muttering: "That's a dumb word. . . . That's stupid. . . . That'll get us in trouble. . . . When that leaks, we'll all look like idiots." Although he had a master's degree and was completing coursework for a doctorate, Lee was largely an autodidact. He retained an unintellectual demeanor, which enabled him to fool others when he wished. But these memos were his most important tool.

Once the memos were up to snuff, they began to float around the West Wing. Written for the Big Three, plus Paul Laxalt, but with no names on them. No dates. Hand-delivered. Prepared as blind items, untraceable if leaked. Or at least deniable. Intended to impress his elders — or to influence history as written by reporters with book contracts and tight deadlines. Rich Williamson once accused Lee of misdating his memos and leaking them to the press. "Hey, don't worry about it, Rich," said Lee. "It works!"

With a Ph.D. from the University of South Carolina and his White House experience, Lee could fulfill his dream and teach anywhere. He started to work on a dissertation, telling inquiring reporters it was about — what else? — negative politics. Actually, it was about the "permanent campaign" a president conducts in office, with a staff at the ready for the reelection effort. With the assistance of Pinkerton and Gary Maloney, Lee completed five of the eight chapters he outlined for *The Campaign to Re-Elect the President, 1981–1984*. The study gave special attention to Harry Truman's 1948 campaign, which showed "the first evidence of a 'permanent campaign' type of operation within the White House," Atwater observed.

"The key figure in this groundbreaking concept was Clark Clifford," the legendary Democratic counsel who drafted a forty-three-page double-spaced memo, titled "The Politics of 1948," on legal-size paper in November 1947. Lee called this memo "not only thorough but amazingly prescient." It had a major impact on his strategic thinking. He could identify with Clifford, an outsider raised in Missouri who came to Washington and after less than a year became special counsel to President Harry Truman in 1946.

At age thirty-nine, Clifford had helped mastermind Truman's come-from-behind election victory in 1948. In "The Politics of 1948" Clifford predicted Thomas Dewey would be the GOP candidate, predicted Henry Wallace's third-party candidacy, boldly proposed a strategy of confrontation with the Republican 80th Congress, and foresaw Truman's victory, even with the assumption that he would lose many of the major states in the East. "So deep and original is the Clifford memorandum," Atwater wrote, "that one can scarcely believe it was not produced by a full-time political consultant with years of experience and study." Now, *that's* a compliment.

Lee was especially smitten with Clifford's comprehensive geopolitical strategy, based squarely on the politics of the electoral college: "If the Democrats carry the Solid South and also those Western states carried in 1944," wrote Clifford, "they will have 216 of the required 266 electoral votes. And if the Democratic Party is powerful enough to capture the West, it will almost certainly pick up enough of the doubtful Middlewestern and Eastern states to get 50 more votes. We could lose New York, Pennsylvania, Illinois, Ohio, Massachusetts — all the 'big' states — and still win."

Thus was born Lee Atwater's "southern strategy": basic Truman electoral politics with a Republican spin built on Lee's gut understanding of racial politics and southern traditions. Accordingly, based on his research, in March 1983 Lee Atwater drafted a seventy-two-page single-spaced memo on standard-size paper with forty-two tables, twenty graphs, charts, and maps. He called it "The South in 1984." In it Lee analyzed the state of the party and racial politics in the South as the '84 reelection beckoned.

Because Reagan had still not announced his candidacy for reelection, Lee had to play a cautious hand. "In 1980, Ronald Reagan persuaded Southerners to vote against one of their own," he wrote. "Southerners are fiercely proud of their region, and yet they cooperated in the ouster of the only President from the Deep South this country has had in 130 years." If Reagan ran again, he "would run better in Dixie than any other Republican," added Lee. Reagan was the candidate most likely to inspire southerners to once again violate their Democratic heritage. "The South's gut instincts are still Democratic," he added. "*Southerners only vote*

Republican when they feel they must." To win in '84, "we must re-member the fundamentals of Southern politics," an electorate di-vided into three groups: country clubbers (Republican), populists ("usually Democratic; will swing to the GOP under the right cir-cumstances"), and blacks (Democratic). "In 1984 we must assem-ble coalitions in every Southern state largely based on the country clubbers and the populists," said Atwater near the end of his trea-tise. "We must stave off Democratic attempts to forge a strong coalition of populists and blacks, by targeting both."

The memo was a giant step toward establishing Lee Atwater as a cut above the usual operative, with a keen understanding of race as a political force, ostensibly in the South — but with impli-cations that crossed all state lines. The memo created delicious buzz in the White House, where Lee was now positioned as one of Jim Baker's acolytes. Certainly it served Lee well in his campaign to help run the Reagan reelection.

For months, Baker, Deaver, Laxalt, and Spencer discussed various candidates to run the '84 campaign. Baker wanted to take care of the California coalition by giving Rollins the somewhat re-strictive title of campaign director. If Rollins messed up, they could bring in former transportation secretary Drew Lewis as campaign *manager*, a position that had real clout. Spencer said fine, but he insisted that they put Atwater on Ed's tail. Lee had more politi-cal smarts, and everyone considered Rollins a media slut. Baker couldn't say no to Spencer. He owed Stu big time for his basic training and his access to the Reagan court. Besides, Baker liked sending Rollins "over there" to the campaign, because he wanted to run the show from the White House. One thing he had learned in '76, when he ran the Ford campaign while Dick Cheney ran the White House, was that a campaign divided left the candidate adrift. You needed full control. So Baker wanted a lightweight in charge of the campaign, someone who wouldn't make — or dispute — decisions. Rollins was perfect.

• • •

Rollins was a perfect cover for Lee, too. During the campaign Lee would be able to operate at will. In part, Rollins still wasn't up to the job physically. The stroke had left the old boxer on the ropes. But Lee doubted that Rollins *ever* read the briefing memos he signed before the president attended a political event. To win an office bet, Lee began to insert offbeat items into his text. To show the president in a Hispanic setting, Reagan was scheduled to appear in San Antonio on May 5, 1983. Lee's briefing memo for Rollins included a cautionary thought: "On September 30, 1976, while campaigning for the Hispanic vote in San Antonio, President Ford attempted to eat a tamale without removing the husk. This caused serious embarrassment for the President, and cut into his Hispanic support — possibly costing him Texas and the election. If the President chooses to eat a tamale," wrote Lee, "the husk should be removed first. It is then appropriate to eat the tamale with the fingers or a fork. (If the tamale is sauced, it would not appear Presidential to eat it with the hands.)"

For days, Lee studied the campaign office floor plan, moving people around as a battlefield general might arrange his troops. Rollins scoffed, dismissing the blueprint as a "seating chart." All he wanted was a corner office. When the Reagan/Bush campaign moved into headquarters at 440 First Street, N.W., on October 17, 1983, Rollins got his wish. Then he learned that his office was a sleepy corner. It was near Spencer, but Stu was based in California and rarely on the premises. It was right next to the office waiting for Drew Lewis, who was supposed to leave his post at Warner-Amex and take over the campaign, but Lewis never showed up. At the other end of the hall was Lee's corner office, surrounded by Pinkerton, Kenny Klinge, Rick Shelby, Roger Stone — the real players. That was where everyone went to find out what was happening. Including Ed, whose staff was perplexed by the strange sight of their leader trundling down to his deputy's office all day long.

In addition to being Ed's deputy, Lee was the campaign's political director. Whenever anybody wanted anything done, they went to Lee, whose responsibilities included directing all fifty state campaigns (divided into six regions, each with its own director), as well as voter registration drives and campaign scheduling. An immense undertaking. "Lee always did his best to acquire political power for his boss, and to make him look good," said Roger Stone. "But at four-thirty on Friday, Ed Rollins was going to the mountains. Atwater was the guy in the office all day Saturday and Sunday."

Rollins never caught on. As he got more enmeshed in high-level liaison with the White House, the burden of developing campaign strategy fell to Lee. The deputy's seminal document was an eight-page memo completed on November 5, 1983, and titled "Building an Electoral Fortress in 1984." In it Lee laid out the Reagan/Bush electoral game plan, emphasizing that "securing the South would mean the difference between a close election and a landslide in 1984." He advocated a plan that would "secure Ford's snowbelt states as early as possible," then "take the fight to Democratic states in the Northeast." Key to victory here was a plan to "drive a wedge between the liberal (national) Democrats and traditional Southern Democrats." California, Texas, and Florida would be the "anchors" of an electoral strategy in the Sunbelt. The South was the key, however. "If our campaign can get the South firmly in tow before the general election . . . few states will remain beyond our grasp," he wrote.

From the campaign's inception, the fortress strategy would guide basic budgeting decisions, scheduling recommendations for the president and his surrogates, and the White House posture toward all Democratic endeavors. Of even greater significance, however, was the emphasis that the fortress memo placed on geo-political considerations — the politics of the electoral college and the fifty states, as opposed to demographic considerations. While the Mondale campaign went off in pursuit of constituencies and special-interest groups, the Reagan/Bush strategy from the beginning was rooted in the reality of the electoral college, with special thanks to Clark Clifford.

By early 1984 Lee was turning out strategy and research memoranda at a furious pace. His writings addressed the Iowa and New Hampshire primaries, the surprise Gary Hart candidacy, plans for key states, and issues such as crime, unemployment, and the deficit. With the southern strategy in place largely along the lines suggested in his fortress memo, Lee initiated a study of the industrial Midwest and the Northeast. The result, in May, was a sixty-two-page memorandum titled "Winning the Snowbelt in 1984," in which Lee outlined the electoral dynamics of three voter blocs crucial to a Reagan victory in Democratic strongholds: suburbanites, Yankees, and blue-collar ethnic Catholics. Because the campaign's most precious resource was the president's time, this memorandum led to the scheduling of campaign appearances at a Pennsylvania Polish Catholic shrine, Michigan assembly lines, and other sites.

Atwater could not recall a single meeting that lasted for more than an hour when someone didn't say, "How will this play in the media?" He drafted a memo, "A Media Strategy for 1984," which outlined Mondale's weak points: having been Carter's vice president, being a tool of special interests, and pushing Big Government policies. He called for an "inoculate and attack" strategy using presidential surrogates to speak out, thus keeping Ronald Reagan out of the fray while stirring up constituencies in order to "prevent the Democrats from unifying their party." Lee was learning how to play the expectations game, too. When Mondale decided to mimic Jimmy Carter's 1976 vice presidential selection by interviewing potential running mates at his Minnesota home, Lee suggested that Strom Thurmond say that the Democrats were giving the cold shoulder to the South. Thus, no matter what Mondale's final choice might be, the heightened expectations of various Democratic factions would be shattered.

Lee held Sunday morning seminars at campaign headquarters for Young Republican volunteers who did the grunt work all week: a mini McLaughlin Group. Lee realized that effective leadership meant keeping one's followers, not barking orders. He developed an audience — and a following — with preacherlike talks that inspired both loyalty and fear. He was so insightful about what was *really* going on that his people felt constantly that they were sharing an epiphany: *Here's the light. Here's what's happening.* That would bind them to him. Simultaneously there was also some fear about being around Lee. People knew how smart he was and how aggressive he would be in getting what he wanted. If you think you've got an education in politics, went one maxim, go South and get a graduate degree. Politics there was a blood sport.

Honesty was always the best policy, of course — unless it was being done to you. And then you might have to take an evasive action. Lee sent a messenger to MTV to fetch a John Cougar Mellencamp video to show to the president. At least, that's what he told MTV. For one solid week, their announcers reported Lee's request, interspersing their music programming with a picture of Reagan, asking, "Does this man like MTV?" Reagan was already asleep as his image flashed on the screen. If Lee committed little political crimes, it was purely from passion.

Lee was also making valuable allies. To him, John Buckley

was a renaissance man. In addition to being a member of the conservative Buckley clan, John had been a rock critic for the *Soho News* and *Rolling Stone*. Now he was writing novels and working on the reelection. And he was a runner! One day, after George Will wrote a column comparing Gary Hart to Jay Gatsby, Lee and Buckley jogged together, talking about this literary archetype. Lee, at Pinkerton's urging, had recently read *The Great Gatsby* and was fascinated by the idea of the self-invented American. Buckley suppressed a smile as they ran along. Like many of Lee's friends, he saw a similar transformation underway in Little Harvey — the kid who had arrived in Washington with a jacket and a pair of khaki pants with no crease and who had evolved into someone extremely precise about his dress. Lee had learned how to fit into an environment while leaving just a touch of mystery as to where he had been and where he was going.

Andy Card observed the transformation in Lee from a unique perspective. Card graduated from the University of South Carolina in January 1971, a few months before Lee's political epiphany in Thurmond's office. Card had even seen a band play around the Five Points neighborhood of Columbia with a fat, obnoxious party animal at lead guitar. Card had befriended Jim Baker during the '76 campaign, then worked for Bush in '80, and eventually he had moved from Massachusetts to the Reagan White House. Not until years later, when Lee spoke with him about his college days, did Card even connect *that* Atwater with the one he met in Washington through his brother-in-law, Ron Kaufman. Lee was still a bit cocky for Card's political taste. "He liked to sit around trashing Northeast establishment Republicans," said Card. Lee's targets included many figures Card had grown up emulating in Massachusetts: Bill Saltonstall, Frank Hatch, Elliot Richardson, Henry Cabot Lodge — politicians who emerged after years of public service as statesmen. Card added, "I don't think Lee ever worried about trying to become a statesman."

● ● ●

On a trip back to Columbia after his first year in Washington, Lee was pulled aside by a friend in the Thurmond office. "You'd better get Sally up there," he was advised. There was some concern about what Lee was doing to his reputation in a city that didn't talk so much as it liked to whisper. Didn't he understand the political consequences of living separately? Sally joined Lee in the winter of '82, but, for all the discipline he could bring to his life — running six miles a day, being meticulously on time, compulsively attending to details — Lee Atwater continued to push all discipline aside when sexual temptation reared its beautiful head. "He had two obsessions — politics and women," recalled a colleague. "Sex was as much a driving part of his life as anything else."

Perhaps it was a southern thing, friends theorized. Men were different down there, more rambling, reckless even. Southern men even had a flippant name for it: sportfucking. In the minds of many stereotypical southern men, southern women were expected to be adept at cooking and makeup application. In the South, there was also a basic dichotomy in the concept of womanhood. Older conservative Bible-thumpers abhorred the sins of the flesh, yet recent generations have been raised in a society that glorified baton twirlers, beauty pageants, and bathing-suit contests.

Although he admired female colleagues, Lee once stated that no woman would be elected president: they stayed out of the economic mainstream, didn't take enough risks, used too much of the emotional right brain. One-on-one Lee was the quintessential southern cad. He called many women "baby doll" in a manner that would have gotten him a look, even a slap, in other parts of the country. He reveled in telling stories of conquests, sharing details with office colleagues. Braggin' rights were more fun than the actual sex act. The women he chased were interchangeable. Disposable sex without commitment was a huge piece of his ego, a badge of honor. "Screwing was Lee's hobby," observed a colleague. "That, and he ran."

• • •

"Lee was always loyal to Ed," recalled John Buckley. "Whenever there was a trouble spot that threatened Rollins, Lee was there to smooth it over." Rollins called a meeting one day to discuss how the reelection campaign would mesh with other state campaigns. But Ed was late. Meantime, Baker, Tutwiler, Card, Richard Darman, Haley Barbour, Atwater, and others made small talk. "It was almost uncomfortable," recalled Card. "I think most people were hoping Jim Baker would start the meeting." In previous meetings chaired by Rollins, Atwater had been a note taker. This

time Lee moved into Ed's chair and outlined the objectives for the
meeting. "That was the first time I remember seeing Lee step up to
the plate and drive the discussion with some pretty heavy hitters,"
said Card. By the time Ed arrived, embarrassed and annoyed
at his deputy, Lee was in charge.

Mr. Outside and Mr. Inside: Ed and Lee became a great
team in spite of themselves. Ed did the ceremonial stuff; Lee
was the man with the plan. Ed wore his best suit for meetings
at the White House while Lee worked the phones in his war
room, wearing no socks, scratching himself, talking to the people
making it happen in the field. Rollins's battlefield duty consisted
largely of running interference with Nancy Reagan, who thought
he was incompetent. Lee gratefully tried to stay out of Nancy's
crosshairs. He had grown accustomed to dealing with candidates'
wives — Nancy Thurmond and Iris Campbell both could be for-
midable on occasion — but there was no one quite like Nancy
Reagan.

Ed returned to his office after a wardrobe harangue one day.
"I walk in and cross my legs and see that I have a *hole* in my shoe,"
he said. "I knew I was doomed."

Stu Spencer came in behind him, chortling. "Fear!" he said.
"Ed, she could *smell* fear in you. You didn't have a chance!"

Once Mrs. Reagan asked Ed why there wasn't a Reagan campaign office in Beverly Hills. The campaign director promptly set
up a new office, a satellite to the headquarters near Los Angeles
International Airport, so that Nancy and Ron's friends had a place
to go to do their volunteer work.

One of Lee's most challenging tasks was to keep Ed from
being the honest no-spin guy that he was. Honest — to a fault,
thought Lee. One week after taking over from Nofziger, Rollins
had told a correspondent for the California-based McClatchy
Newspapers that Maureen Reagan, a Senate hopeful, "has the
highest negatives of any candidate I've seen. . . . She's been strident on some issues, and, while the President has been scrupu-
lously neutral, there's an impression that Maureen is not the over-
whelming choice of the Reagan boys." Whoa. That little assessment earned Ed a summons from the president, who instructed
him to watch his tongue. Which Atwater did from that day forward.

In his office planning, Lee had assigned John Buckley to the
same office as Sherry Sandy, whom Ed was dating (and would later

marry). When Ed set up a luncheon interview with the *New York Times* squad, Buckley showed up at the car. Ed asked, "What are you doing here?"

"Lee asked me to come along." It would be Buckley's task to kick Ed under the table in order to keep him from saying something impolitic to the reporters.

By this point, protecting Ed had become a thankless task for Lee. Besides having loose lips, Rollins's biggest problem was his inability to share credit or to allow any praise of his staffers to go unintercepted. In April 1982 Lou Cannon of the *Post* gave Ed a big wet kiss: "President's Chief Political Aide Emerges as a Tough 'Enforcer,' " a story that positioned Ed as the new tough guy running the political shop. "He has chosen the role for himself, sort of like Charles Bronson in *Death Wish*," said one of Cannon's sources. Which wasn't Lee. He was feeling a bit downtrodden when Michele Davis asked him what he thought of the piece.

"To be honest with you," he said, "I'm just too jealous to say the words out loud."

Eventually Ed noticed that Deaver and Baker weren't even calling him when they had a problem; they would call Lee. Though Atwater and Rollins were successful as a team on the surface, the distrust between them began to bubble up. "Friends of mine were always saying, 'Look out for Lee. The guy is undercutting you,' " recalled Rollins. "Unless it was obvious, I took it as part of the mix — the good, the bad — and I have to say I enjoyed him. Lee was a character." A character who required some vigilance. But not only did Ed want to keep an eye on his deputy; he wanted to out*do* him. The competition became more overt. When Lee hired Pinkerton as his thinker, Ed hired a brain trust — John Roberts, then Jim McNeill — but it never quite kicked in with the same impact. When Lee gave a girlfriend a mink teddy bear for Christmas, Ed gave Sherry a fur coat.

"The wizened elder and the young upstart," recalled Michele Davis, "both teeming with testosterone."

• • •

Back in April of '82 an ABC News poll had shown that only 42 percent of female respondents approved of Reagan's job performance (a drop of 25 points since February 1981). Lee had drafted a report called "Ronald Reagan and the Gender Gap" that had led to more women appointees, increased sensitivity to women's issues, and the placement of at least one woman at the state cochair level in each of the fifty state Reagan/Bush organizations for the reelection campaign. The strategy peaked at the Republican National Convention in Dallas in '84, where Lee boasted that an unprecedented 46 percent of the delegates and alternates were women.

There was no gender gap for Lee at the '84 convention, either. Lee had arranged to have a "workroom" adjoining his two-room suite with Sally. Colleagues tried to caution him: If he wasn't going to be discreet, couldn't he at least be a little bit smarter? During the convention, Lee escorted women in and out of his workroom like clockwork. One of his visitors left her earrings. Later, when Sally returned, she saw Lee on the couch and seemed to notice the earrings. "It was all I could do not to panic," Lee told a friend afterward. Sally said nothing.

Finally a White House staffer sat down with Lee and told him he was afraid Nancy Reagan would find out about the bimbos on parade. Then Lee would be in trouble with the president. Not only that — if the Religious Right found out how he was behaving, he'd be damaged there, too. Lee never understood the Far Right, which always seemed to love feeling virtuous. To him it was hypocritical, especially in a city where politicians stood up and declared themselves in favor of "family values" while shedding the wives they had brought from the home district for younger, glossier versions. For Lee, extracurricular sex was part of the political landscape. Sure, it posed some tricky ethical — and logistical — problems, but stepping out was like a private campaign.

Lee assured his worried colleague that he was being very careful, and Nancy Reagan would be none the wiser. Then the staffer's curiosity took hold. He said, "I can understand how you get them to come to your room in the first place, but how do you get rid of them?" Lee explained that he told his visitors that the Secret Service had to sweep his room for security every three hours, so they would have to be quick.

The Mondale campaign began to unravel when Geraldine Ferraro first promised to release her husband's tax returns, then reneged. That was an open invitation for the Republican Party to strike. Rollins brought everyone into Lee's suite at the Anatole Hotel during the second day of the Republican platform hearings in Dallas to review the situation. In attendance: Nofziger, Atwater,

Rollins, communications director Jim Lake, Charlie Black, Roger Stone, Pinkerton, Spencer, and Buckley. Initially, Lee was highly excitable; he saw this as a major break — a flaw in the other candidate, a chance to take full advantage of some secret debility. Then he went into a Zen-like state of total concentration on what Republicans should do. Command focus, he called it. Lee could dilate his attention either big or small. When the refraction was at a pinpoint level of precision, he was like no other operative in politics. Everything had to stop. The question was: What resources are there *in the entire world* that we can line up *right now* in order to turn this thing?

When they met again at eleven-thirty that evening to agree on a Ferraro strategy, Rollins was the chair of the meeting, but the focus was on Lee. He came out of his command focus with a single belief: They should do *nothing*. "We don't have to do a thing, and this will destroy Geraldine Ferraro," said Atwater. "The one thing that will save her is if we get into it." Oh, sure, maybe they could do some small things — have Bob Dole talk about how he always files his returns; have Lynn Martin speak as a woman in public life, noting that she always includes her spouse's returns as part of her filing with the House of Representatives. But they should not push the topic with reporters. Lee quoted Napoleon: "Never interfere with the enemy when he is in the process of destroying himself."

When Mondale refused to insist that Ferraro disclose all, the damage continued for two weeks. Charges of suspect real estate deals and unethical campaign funding floated through the slow-news month of August. Finally, some financial improprieties were disclosed, and Ferraro's husband was shown to be mostly to blame. Late that month Ferraro held a marathon press conference to clear the air, but the campaign was wounded. The whole affair played out exactly as Lee had hoped. All he did, with discipline, was nothing.

The only anxious moment in the rest of the 1984 campaign occurred after the first presidential debate, when Reagan's performance raised questions about his abilities. Most baffling was his contention that Social Security was somehow not part of the federal deficit. *Newsweek* said that, at seventy-three, Reagan appeared "shaky." "People in the White House tend to get old mighty quickly," said Speaker Tip O'Neill in his morning-after press conference. A few days later a front-page story in the *Wall*

Street Journal asked, "Is the Oldest U.S. President Now Showing His Age?"

Atwater mapped a contingency plan, to be executed if Reagan did poorly in the second debate. "The single most important mission of the fog machine will be to shift the emphasis to Mondale, and to drive up his negative rating," he wrote in a strategy memo. Lee called for loyalists to dismiss the debates as a "bizarre ritual" that had no place in the civilized process of choosing a president, and to attack Mondale's support of big social programs and his opposition to new weapons systems. As a campaign tactic, it was an example of Lee's brinksmanship that he had intended to impress his elders by having a strategy in place if the second debate went poorly. It didn't.

Lee watched media guru Roger Ailes engineer Ronald Reagan's comeback. Reagan, overcoached and uncertain, had looked like a doddering incompetent in the first debate. In the second the Mondale threat passed when Reagan declared, "I will not make age an issue in this campaign. I am not going to exploit for political purposes my opponent's youth and inexperience."

In September, victory was apparent. With Reagan leading in the polls in every state, Lee called a news conference declaring that the Democrats had pulled out of the South. On November 5, Lee predicted that the Reagan "electoral fortress" would hold more than 400 electoral votes. Clearly, Lee had worked on his expectations game. The Reagan/Bush ticket swept forty-nine states, bringing in 525 electoral votes and 59 percent of the popular vote, including 54 percent of the women's vote. The boys in the reelection had themselves a landslide.

Near the end of the election, another campaign had begun — between Lee and Rollins to claim credit for the victory and, by doing so, move on to the next round with Bush. Lee fumed as Ed stepped in front of the cameras and took the glory. "The biggest disappointment of the campaign," Rollins told the press, "was not taking Minnesota." To ensure his own place on the victory platform, all along Lee had been leaking his memos and "on background" insights to the reporters doing campaign books. Readers (and that included the Bush family) would know that Atwater had run the show, while Rollins had run around making sound bites.

During a lull in the final weeks, Lee asked Ed to give an interview to Leslie Sewell, one of his TV producer pals. She had been covering the Ferraro campaign and was in some difficulty with the network, Lee said. This piece would be a real coup for her. Rollins agreed, thinking he was being a nice guy, but when he sat down to do the interview, he found himself being cast as the bad guy. Reporter Jamie Gangel charged him with running an undercover operation that included setting Lyn Nofziger loose to play dirty tricks on the Democrats. She suggested that Ed and company had orchestrated hecklers against Ferraro. This was the friendly interview set up by his buddy Lee?

Rollins's jaw dropping ran as a lead story on the evening news. Ferraro responded, "If all this stuff is true, if they're organizing from the White House, my reaction is why don't they come out and fight like men?" (Earlier in the campaign, Rollins had stumbled into an embarrassing double entendre when he declared that Ferraro could be "the biggest political bust of recent years.") Jim Baker got on the phone to Rollins, furious. Six weeks before an easy election day, and Rollins was muddying up the track.

NBC stood by their story. Rollins was about to take the fall when television reporters covering the presidential candidates came to his rescue, saying there was no evidence to prove such allegations — and wondering how someone on Ferraro's plane could find mischief in the Reagan campaign. Baker cooled. Rollins confronted Lee, who denied any knowledge of the setup. "I was a perfect foil for Lee because I have a tendency to be too honest, and I'm absolutely too trusting," reflected Rollins. "Lee had a pathological side. If you lied to me — and if you lied passionately enough, as Lee always would — I believed it." But who else could have done it?

For Ed Rollins, this was the last betrayal. He could never trust Lee Atwater again.

CHAPTER

6

THE ODD COUPLING

The true test of a first-class mind is the ability to hold
two contradictory thoughts in your head at once.
— F. Scott Fitzgerald

Rollins may be a wonderful guy, but Lee is the guy you want
to run the campaign," Ron Kaufman told George Bush. "He is
the one with the most talent, and it's growing every day." Few of
the brain trust gathered at the vice president's residence in June
of 1984 agreed with either of Kaufman's assessments. For many,
Rollins was like having the press in your living room, and Atwater
represented an ethical divide between the Reaganites and the
Bushees. They couldn't understand why Bush was even *thinking* of letting Lee into the select circle of advisers. The kid was
wenching around. Was George crazy?

Like a political fox, perhaps. Bush had been surrounded
by establishment Republican thinking all his political life: Nick
Brady, the Dillon Read investment banker who had backed into
politics as First Friend to the veep; Bob Mosbacher, finance chairman of the campaign and a thirty-year friend from the Texas oil
days; Jim Baker, Reagan's chief of staff who was grooming himself for bigger things in a Bush administration; Dean Burch, the
former Republican National Committee chair who was staying
out of the mainstream now but wasn't afraid to tell George when
he was acting stupid; Malcolm Baldrige, the commerce secretary,
very establishment in his thinking; Craig Fuller, former cabinet
secretary for Reagan who had become chief of staff for the vice

president; Bob Teeter, the pollster who thought he was a strategist; and author Vic Gold, the resident cynic.

But Bush was beginning to realize that he needed Reaganites. That's why, despite Burch's bias toward selecting Rich Bond as campaign manager, Atwater had such appeal. Sure, there was the ethical thing, but Bush had to like a guy who exuded such energy, who like himself was an early riser, always on the phone, constantly in motion, a runner, moving moving moving. Both men believed that the race went not necessarily to the swiftest, but to the earliest. Hell, Lee didn't even pause to tie his ties in the morning. Lee's ties were *pre*-tied, so he just flopped them over his head, pulled the knot, and he was off for the day. And, while others called it an "odd coupling," Bush and Atwater had another thing in common, which was only everything: intense ambition to make it to the top of the political mountain.

George Bush represented everything for which Lee Atwater had an unaffected scorn. The son of a white Anglo-Saxon senator from Connecticut, Bush had attended prep school, then Yale. He was your basic WASP who wanted to be president. He had moved from Connecticut to Texas, where he made money in oil after a big loan from Daddy, and he had been elected a carpetbagger congressman for two terms in an affluent Republican district — no heavy lifting. By the late '60s he was aligned with the more traditionally conservative pragmatists, among them Richard Nixon. As payment for losing a senatorial race twice (in 1964, against Ralph Yarborough; and in 1970, against Lloyd Bentsen), he led an appointed life for some time — ambassador to the UN, chairman of the RNC, envoy to the People's Republic of China, and head of the CIA. His 1980 primary campaign was financed with Texas oil money, with input from conservative advisers who seemed moderate compared to Reagan. In a defining moment of the campaign, Bush labeled Reagan's supply-side nostrums "voodoo economics." Bush won the 1980 caucus in Iowa and four primaries — Massachusetts, Connecticut, Pennsylvania, and Michigan — and then ran out of money.

As a candidate, George Bush's major problem was that he had shown such a willingness to change his positions over the years that he seemed to lack any real philosophical foundation. He was like Benedict Arnold in Republican tights, distrusted by moderates for flip-flopping on abortion when he remade himself in 1980, and by Reaganites who were suspicious of Bush's conservative pedigree ever after. Reagan picked him as a running mate to make it easier for eastern country-club Republicans to vote for a California B-movie actor. As vice president, he was still a Connecticut Yankee with a condo in Houston that he declared home for political purposes, although he spent every spare minute he could at the family ocean estate in Maine.

And now here was Bush (like Fitzgerald's Tom Buchanan, a varsity athlete from Yale) considering Lee Atwater (like Jay Gatsby, a product of his own invention who wanted what Tom Buchanan had). For such a coupling to work, each would have to overlook the character flaw he perceived in the other: Bush's Republican promiscuity, Atwater's womanizing.

In mid-1984 Bush and his brain trust made no decision about who would serve as campaign manager. To cover all of their options, Ron Kaufman was told to get close to Lee, to keep an eye on him through the rest of Reagan's campaign. Kaufman found this an easy task; in fact, he and Lee struck up a great friendship. Like Lee, Kaufman was a workaholic. In the late '70s he had been managing supermarkets in Massachusetts. He took an interest in politics when his brother-in-law, Andy Card, urged him to get involved. By 1980 he found himself running state primary campaigns for George Bush, which led to the job of political director at the Republican National Committee when Lee was in the Office of Political Affairs. The two clicked. Lee was the first guy to arrive at the White House every morning, and Kaufman the first to arrive at the RNC. "The phone on my desk would ring at six-thirty and it was Lee," recalled Kaufman. They ran together by day, and also at night, since Kaufman was separated from his wife and was living alone in Washington.

One evening they came out of the Kennedy Center, where Lee and Sally had entertained a group of power couples in the president's box. Although Lee hated classical music and couldn't sit still for a play, he knew the allure of those tickets. Kaufman pulled Lee aside. He had heard a lot of criticism aimed at this young punk, and Kaufman, who considered himself a shrink at heart, didn't hold back. "You know, Lee, I'm new at this game, but I've watched everybody for a while, and you understand it better than anyone I've met. You understand the power and the history and how it all connects," he said. "If you play this thing right, there's no doubt in my mind but that you'll be the star. Someday we'll all be working for you."

Atwater laughed. He barely knew Kaufman, but here was this northerner, this Jew, this guy on a fast track from Bush's camp acting subservient. What was the deal?

"My whole thing is to make George Bush president some day," said Kaufman. Lee backpedaled. He told Kaufman that he certainly wanted to run a presidential campaign one day, but he didn't leap at the mention of Bush.

Shortly afterward, Kaufman had a blowup with Frank Fahrenkopf, the new RNC chair, and left his job. As soon as he heard the news, Lee called Ron. "Tomorrow morning, we are having lunch at the White House mess," he said. By putting his arms around Ron in that little showroom, Lee was letting everybody know that Ron Kaufman was still a player. Indeed, Kaufman returned to the Bush camp, ostensibly to run the VP leg of the '84 reelection campaign. His real assignment, though, was to size up the field so that if Bush decided to run for the presidency four years hence, Kaufman would know what players they wanted for the '88 campaign. As Kaufman told the brain trust, that meant Atwater.

• • •

When George Bush started out back in the '60s, there were no political consultants. Instead there were "campaign specialists" or "communications consultants," operatives who wielded considerable power yet were content to divert fame and glory to the politicians who paid their fees. After all, candidates were generally chosen by party bosses who made deals and decisions in smoke-filled rooms, often oblivious to — or turning a blind eye to — the downside of their candidates' private and political peccadillos. This world came to a screeching halt in the '70s with Watergate, Woodward and Bernstein, the Freedom of Information Act, and a journalistic game of "gotcha" that turned reporting into flank attacks. Candidates needed more protection.

Thus was born a new breed of political hired gun, consultants who brought a specialized knowledge of today's enormous communications network and sensitivity to the perversities of human nature. They ran polls, conducted focus groups, and created a candidate's image. They manipulated the press and invented news; they also designed highly suggestive advertising. Their work was actually an offshoot of what used to be called PR, because so much of what they do resulted in the molding of public opinion — the textbook definition of public relations work.

Growing up politically in the '70s, Lee Atwater was the right person at the right time to recognize that political consulting was a newly powerful — and lucrative — science. There were some six thousand political consultants in the country. About one hundred were well known. Lee, at thirty-three, was moving up in that pack like a rock star with a hot album. During his hitch in the Reagan White House, working alongside Mike Deaver & Co., PR took over politics. There was far more emphasis on processing the candidate, sanitizing the message, and orchestrating the response than had ever been seen before. And if the first word in *president* is *PR*, the first word in *consultant* is *con*.

Lee, as one of the new aggressive breed of consultants, liked to get credit for his work, liked to see his name in the Style section of the *Post*. "That was one thing he did *not* learn from Thurmond," said Bush's ghostwriter Vic Gold. "Thurmond would cut your head off, and you wouldn't know it until you tried to turn around." Atwater brought to his task a specialized knowledge of how the media fed on the political process. Unlike other consultants, he boasted about his methods because he knew the press loved the backstage angle. They began to perceive him as a strategic guru. "Strategizing in public is something I didn't approve of," added Vic Gold. "But it is necessary if you are going to try to impress people with how smart you are."

You only had to be a student of history (which Lee was) to see Bush's inside edge. Of the ten men serving as vice president since World War II, half had become president (three by direct succession upon the president's death or resignation), and two more had been their party's presidential nominee. Of course, Bush had no political infrastructure. He wasn't a governor, or a senator with an electoral base. All he had were two enormous Rolodexes of friends, many of whom thought they were better friends than they actually were. He had a one-on-one relationship with thousands of people. He was always writing personal notes to people. He was a master of retail politics, but he wasn't a retail politician. He wasn't a populist. He wasn't a glad-hander. He did it because he was so damned disciplined. Now that is about as pragmatic as you can get, thought Atwater, no slouch himself in the discipline department. For Lee, George Bush was a winner — only he didn't know it yet. "The secret to being a good consultant," said Nofziger, "is to find a winner and stick with him."

Shortly after the Reagan/Bush landslide victory in 1984, the vice president called Lee. Thence began a political courtship that culminated in a forty-page "Memorandum to the Vice President" that Lee sent to Bush on December 19.

The real power of a campaign manager is in the role of strategist. The campaign manager creates and crafts the strategy for a campaign, establishing the guidelines, the events, the momentum — all of the elements that lead the leader. Lee laid the foundation for that strategy in this memo, largely crafted by Pinkerton. "The 1988 presidential nomination is the VP's to lose," was the opening statement.

"It is helpful to think of the next four years as a layer cake," wrote Lee. "The bottom layer is 1985, the next layer up is 1986, etc. Each year will bring with it new tasks, which must be completed before we can begin adding the next layer." Lee then proceeded to analyze all of the media, categorizing various members of the press "in and around the echo chambers" of Washington.

"A cosmology that no politician to my knowledge has yet appropriated comes from Alvin Toffler," he said. As outlined in Toffler's *The Third Wave*, the first wave of human social evolution was agriculture. The second wave was industry. "The third wave is more than just computers and high tech," however, argued Lee, taking the theory into the political arena. "The third wave is decentralization, de-massification, and the entropy of giant institutions. It is entrepreneurialism. It offers new freedom and independence to the individual. . . . It is the third wave, Toffler would say, that had been disrupting American politics in the '60s and '70s." Thus, the third wave was threatening "to those whose livelihoods and outlooks are firmly wedded to the much different values of the second wave, e.g., unionized workers, government bureaucrats, family traditionalists, and TV network executives."

Lee called for a thematic campaign, one that would have crossover appeal to both the second and third waves and mainstream appeal to populists. "Populism, as opposed to conservatism, isn't so much an ideology as a set of attitudes," Lee said. "Populists — generally middle and lower middle class — across the country are 'anti' in outlook. They are anti–Big Government, anti–Big Business, and anti–Big Labor. They are also hostile to the media, to the rich, and to the poor. They are often called 'Middle American Radicals.' Because populists are opposed to a lot more things than they are for, it is difficult to mobilize them. When they do get mobilized, it is just about as likely that they will support a liberal, or Democratic, cause as a conservative or Republican cause," added Lee.

In his judgment, the question that Bush had to answer from the get-go was, "What would be the purpose of a Bush presidency?" He warned, "This question, which I guarantee is coming, is a close cognate of Roger Mudd's 'Why do you want to be president?' query that undid Teddy Kennedy in '79. The VP is forewarned that even an answer very much more glib and articulate than Kennedy's stumbling ramble will be judged insufficient by many '88 echo chamberites."

Lee had no specific themes in mind for the campaign at present. "I'm a political operative, not a philosopher," he said. The key to a successful campaign would be coming up with themes that had a duality to them, so that Bush could appeal to Reaganites yet "carve out a sharper and clearer identity as someone who is his own man, with his own ideas" for populist consumption, observed Lee. "The VP's message needs to encompass the simultaneous desire of the American people for the status quo *and* for change, for continuity *and* innovation." Then Lee waxed just a bit philosophical to underscore his point. "The VP will have to search out themes with which he feels comfortable, but it seems to me that an essential aspect of any effective theme is the quality of dualism. After all, life itself is based on dualities. Life and death. Black and white. Yin and yang. Heaven and hell."

George Bush was impressed. "Christmas might seem like a peculiar time to read a brilliant somewhat provocative paper on a possible future for the V.P.," replied Bush, pecking away at his typewriter on Christmas Day, "but I did read it today and I am staggered by its thoughtfulness, its clarity of thought, and its brilliance. . . . Thanks for a superb bit of analysis. I agree with your conclusions." No real decision, however. Bush was off to do some quail hunting in Texas.

• • •

"I can say in all honesty that the two of us together were a far better team than either one of us were separately," Rollins later reflected on his relationship with Atwater. Each was indebted to the other, and when you're indebted to someone, inevitably you come to hate him. After the reelection, the pair went their separate ways — Lee to make some money at the consulting firm Black Manifort Stone while Bush made up his mind, and Rollins to shop around. He looked into the chair at RNC, but Fahrenkopf was solid. Then he looked into the possibility of becoming postmaster general. That went nowhere. Secretary of labor? Absurd. When Ed ended up back at the White House working as assistant to the president for political and intergovernmental affairs, Lee told friends it was a dumb move. Rollins thought that Lee was young and impetuous, lacking in political maturity.

Black Manifort Stone had a reputation for throwing a lot of money at campaigns. They were a bright bunch of guys who seemed to be saying, "If you've got the cash, we'll spend it for you!" Now that Lee had some experience in the world of presidential power plays, he was very much at home in this group — all Young Republicans from the '70s with lots of Carolina linkage. Charlie Black was the smoothest, the leader of the pack; when he was going through a divorce in 1984, Charlie had lived with Lee in a townhouse at a time when Sally had gone back to South Carolina. Paul Manifort was known as a convention man, but not much else. Roger Stone had a reputation for being very smart, and very sleazy. With Lee onboard, there were whispers about a rivalry between Stone and Atwater to see who was the smartest, and the sleaziest.

In March of 1985, Lee called on Michele Davis, Rollins's former assistant and now director of the Republican Governors' Committee. Lee was happy to be out of the White House. "Now I'm going to have to act more like an adult," he said, referring to his new job pitching for clients at Black Manifort Stone & Atwater. "It's a tough transition I'm going to have to make," Lee confessed. His immediate goal was to sign up Bush as his biggest personal client.

With Reagan, all you had to do to make him focus on your agenda was get your message to Stu Spencer and cut off other sources of information. Bush was more complicated. He had so many friends and acquaintances who fed him information that even the most straightforward issue could get muddied. Everything was a balancing act for him. Atwater would tell him something, and Bush would get on the phone to some county chairman, who would tell him the opposite. Round and round they would go, for Bush seemed to have an endless tolerance for trivia from the trenches. Besides, there was the Family.

What started out as a Camp David briefing for the veep on Saturday, April 27, 1985, at eleven A.M. turned into a gong show for the whole Bush clan, which George had assembled. Bar, of course; the five children; George's sister and his three brothers; plus spouses. Fuller was there. Teeter brought charts. "Now, I am not going to do this if we don't have 100 percent behind me," said Bush to his family. "I cannot do this without your support and feeling that you are all with me, because it is going to be a hard thing to do."

Lee tried to cover his impatience with the committee, but they picked up on his mood. Some of them felt, correctly, that Lee was a self-promoter. As John Sears once observed, Lee did not have "a passion for anonymity."

"I think he felt this was an unnecessary weekend, really," Nancy Bush Ellis told a journalist afterward. "I don't think he realized in the beginning how important it was to my brother. It was enormously important to him."

Others were deeply impressed by Lee's presentation. "The guy knew his stuff, worked without notes, and he could really talk," recalled another member of the clan. "He knew how to do the campaign, and he left his audience feeling confident that he could deliver the result they wanted."

George Jr. had his doubts about Lee's ability to remain loyal while working as part of the Black Manifort Stone machine, which was courting other candidates. "I had real trouble understanding how loyalties would work," said Junior. "Who would he be loyal to? Charles Black, hence Jack Kemp, or George Bush?"

"If there's a hand grenade rolling around George Bush, we want you diving on it first," Jeb Bush told Atwater.

"Are you guys really worried about my loyalty?" asked Lee.

"Absolutely."

"Well, if you're so worried about loyalties," said Atwater, "then why don't one of you come here in the office and watch me, and the first time I'm disloyal, see to it that I get run off?"

And so it was that George W. Bush — aka Junior or "W" —

became an early member of Atwater's staff. Skeptical in nature, blunt to a fault, Junior was contemptuous of haughty D.C. insiders. As such, he and Lee were kindred spirits — they just didn't know each other yet. Junior, four years older than Lee, had lost a run for a Texas congressional seat ten years earlier, so he had a bit of seasoning and some experience that counted. And, of course, he had the right last name. Lee had seen Nancy Reagan, who also had the right last name, take aim at Ed Rollins and disarm him from a distance. That wasn't going to happen here! Pragmatically speaking, Lee observed, "I'd rather have him inside the tent pissing out than outside the tent pissing in."

• • •

On Friday, May 24, 1985, Lee took the aisle seat, bulkhead, of Eastern's 11:25 flight to Columbia, with every intention of reading *The Kennedys*, when he found himself sitting next to Donald Regan's assistant, Brooke Vosburgh. Lee struck up a conversation. He remembered her from the '84 campaign and wanted to know how she had ended up working for Regan, who had just switched jobs with Jim Baker and was now chief of staff; Baker became secretary of treasury. Brooke felt certain that Lee wanted to read his book, not listen to her boring life story, but he prodded her on.

Some of the parallels between their lives were remarkable. Brooke had attended Catawba College, a small North Carolina liberal arts companion school to Newberry College. She had spent summers at a camp across the lake from where Lee and Steve Sisk were lifeguards. Their birthdays were a few days apart in February. They both ran! Brooke had married her college sweetheart, had two children, separated, and gone to live with her sister Tracy.

Tracy's roommate, Carol Lancaster, had been Lee's first secretary in 1981. Lee dropped things off at the apartment for Carol occasionally, and Brooke remembered him as being very pleased with himself, carrying Caro's biography of LBJ, and going on and on about power politics. She knew nothing about politics then, and he made her nervous.

To make ends meet in D.C., Brooke at first worked at an ice cream shop, then at Talbots clothing store. She had no office training until Carol Lancaster arranged for an interview with Atwater's old crony Linda Reed, director of administration for the '84 reelection. Brooke was put in charge of supplies and got to know everyone on the campaign who needed a pencil or a typewriter. She watched Lee growing bigger, even a bit too big for reality, and she didn't like the groupies he began to attract — young things whom Lee would flirt with nonstop. She didn't want to be someone he flirted with, or someone he humiliated — since she recalled stories about Lee in the early days. Once he had declared it galosh day in the office, and Craig Helsing had shown up wearing galoshes. On another occasion, Lee had urged Craig to wear a Halloween mask to a meeting with Ed Meese. "Meese will get a kick out of it," he said, and Helsing nearly fell for it.

Brooke went to work for Craig Fuller in the White House after the reelection, and when he left to become chief of staff for Vice President Bush, she interviewed for the job of staff assistant to Donald Regan. Now Brooke was torn between family and career. A congressman had offered her a job in North Carolina, where her sons were living with their dad. She could take it and be closer to the boys, but that would take her away from all that she wanted to do professionally. Brooke was heading to Hilton Head for a short holiday to think things through, and to spend some time with her kids.

Lee was commuting to Columbia himself, he explained, where Sally was living with Sara Lee. They were expecting their second baby in the fall. He had balanced career and family considerations all his adult life, and for him career always came first. "Know what your goal is," he told her. "Don't pay attention to what anyone else is thinking. Stick to your goals."

Even after this conversation — Lee never lifted the book off his lap — there was an untamed quality to Lee Atwater that Brooke found both intriguing and frightening. Then she remembered a vow she had made to herself after hearing the stories her sister's roommate used to tell about her crazed boss — a vow that she would never work for this man, never find herself alone with him, never be one of those people whose lives he took over.

For the last week of September 1985, Lee followed a typical schedule: staff meetings; dinners; cocktail parties; over one thousand phone calls; a birthday party for Linda Reed; a trip to Michigan to huddle with Teeter and Ailes over polls; an interview with *Time*'s Margaret Carlson; an appearance at the Madison Hotel as speaker for Americans for Responsible Government; PAC meetings with Bond, Pinkerton, Ede Holliday, Ron Kaufman; a meeting with Mrs. Bush on Friday, October 1; leaving for Columbia that night to be on hand for the arrival of Ashley Page Atwater, 8 pounds, 14 ounces, on Saturday, at three o'clock in the afternoon.

• • •

In December of 1985, George Bush announced that Lee Atwater would chair the $5 million Fund for America's Future, the political action committee that would launch his presidential campaign. "Ed never knew what hit him," recalled a member of the Bush brain trust who met with Rollins shortly after the announcement. Rollins wanted to know, "What happened?" What happened was Craig Fuller, Bush's chief of staff who was also from California, didn't want Rollins on his turf. What happened was Rollins was becoming one of the *few* people George Bush really disliked; Ed was always prowling for candidates, blabbing to the press for glory. What happened, too, was Bush recognized the real killing field of presidential politics: the South.

Tip O'Neill's pronouncement that "all politics is local" had no bearing on the care and planning of a presidential campaign, where all politics was *regional*. As early as 1982 Atwater had been developing a strategy for the Republican Party after Reagan. He concluded that the candidate who could lock in the South before 1988 would have a running start toward the party's next presidential nomination. He had worked with George Bush and saw in him a potential that other professionals did not perceive. While scheduling White House political events. Atwater made certain that Bush met the key political players in the South. "Let me tell you something," said Bush to Vic Gold, his confidant and ghostwriter. "It's all going to be over on Super Tuesday." Lee had built a firewall for him on that day when primary votes clustered in the South.

After Bush made Lee chair of the PAC, Lee resigned from Black Manifort Stone & Atwater, accepted a salary of $120,000 a year, set up shop in the Ring Building on Eighteenth and M, hired some of the usual suspects and additional visionary grunts, and went about the business of inventing George Bush's political future.

Lee had met with Allan J. Lichtman, the coauthor of "Thirteen Keys to the Presidency," which Lee dubbed a fascinating "parlor game." According to Lichtman, thirteen situations had remained virtually unchanged during more than a hundred years of American history. The situations were expressed in the form of yes/no questions such as: Is the incumbent-party candidate the sitting president? Was there major third-party or independent campaign activity during the election year? Is the election year a time of recession or depression? Etc. Using responses as "keys" to these situations, Lichtman and his associates had correctly identified the results of each presidential election from 1860 to 1980. After analyzing thirty-one elections, Lichtman arrived at one basic rule: "Anticipate an incumbent-party victory in years with fewer than five discrepant keys; anticipate a challenging-party victory in years with more than five discrepant keys; suspend judgment in years with exactly five discrepant keys."

"By my calculations, we had ten or eleven of the thirteen keys turned in our favor in '84, which was one or two more than we needed," Lee told Bush. "I am convinced that Lichtman is onto something."

Within the Republican Party, Lee anticipated a challenge from the Right. In his December 1984 memo to Bush, Lee had written that he felt this was a challenge they could overcome, even learn from. "Assuming that the wounds heal," Lee said this would make Bush "a stronger candidate in the fall." A bigger problem would be if a hopeful emerged on the Left. Then "the world will discover that the early caucus and primary states aren't that conservative. We know that is true of Iowa, but the common perception that New Hampshire is a bastion of right-wing nuts and nothing else is simply wrong. New Hampshire's trend rightward is the result of the influx of high-tech Yuppie tax refugees pouring across the border from Massachusetts. They are economic conservatives, not social conservatives. A candidate with a more libertarian outlook could do very well there." Bob Dole, for instance.

Lee's biggest concern, however, was an election after eight years of Ronald Reagan. On the surface, Bush's candidacy resembled Nixon's first run for the presidency in 1960. "Eisenhower was very popular, but after eight years of his leadership, the people were ready for a change. It was the GOP's misfortune that

John Kennedy represented such an enormous contrast. Kennedy represented change. Nixon represented the status quo."

Lee had seen the possibilities of another JFK-style campaigner in Gary Hart during the '84 election. "Nobody in 1983 thought that he'd ever break out of single digits. He probably never would have, either, had not he and [consultant Pat] Caddell gotten together late in the year." Hart lost the nomination to Mondale, owing largely to Mondale's early start and party allegiance from the Democratic old guard. But Mondale's embarrassing defeat in '84 "sets the stage for mainstream Democrats to get control of the party machinery and run a strong, centrist candidate," said Lee. This was likely to be Hart or someone with similar appeal. Moreover, the Democrats had a counterpart to Lee Atwater in their camp. "It is also likely that Caddell will either find the Democratic nominee, or that the nominee will find Caddell. Either way, Caddell will bring his enormous intuitive and analytical powers to bear on the central goal of convincing the voters that it is finally time for a change."

In early February 1986, Lee sent Bush a six-page memo titled "Gary Hart's Long March." His purpose was to scare Bush, to point out that Hart was a superior candidate with a sense of historical destiny (thus the reference to the "long march"), who had made some peace with Reaganism and was now talking about using that as a foundation for doing better things. Lee pointed out that Hart, who was smarter than Mondale to begin with, was also young, urgent, and dynamic.

Then there was the wimp thing. After the *Challenger* catastrophe in January 1986, Lee suggested to Bush that he take charge of the commission to investigate the tragedy. That would put Bush in the news every day for six months. Why give the seat to William Rogers, former secretary of state? He's not running for anything. Likewise, after the Chernobyl disaster that year, Lee suggested that Bush head a commission that would investigate nuclear power in the United States, making sure that every last nuclear reactor in the United States was safe. Lots of photos of Bush in a hard hat looking at pipes, maybe even an opportunity to rake some corporate nuclear bureaucrat over the coals for sloppiness, a trip to Chernobyl to look at two-headed fishes and show fearlessness — that would pack some political drama.

Nada. Lee was determined to create a new, improved Bush,

but he couldn't make a dent. "We're dealing with a stubborn, not-too-smart guy," Atwater told Pinkerton. Nothing was ever easy or evident to Bush. If it involved writing a thousand thank-you notes to every key voter in Iowa or Michigan, he'd actually take the time to write them by hand. But if it involved "thinking outside the nine dots," no deal.

The nine-dot metaphor was a favorite Atwaterism. Using four straight lines, and without lifting your pen from the paper, how do you connect these nine dots?

•   •   •

•   •   •

•   •   •

Most people sit looking at the nine dots, trying to solve the problem *within* their perimeter. There is no rule that says you can't go *outside* the nine-dot perimeter, which was the way Lee liked to attack things. When George Bush was in trouble, he had a tendency to keep trying to do the same thing as before, only harder. But once you're in a hole, the solution is not to continue digging.

In April 1985 Lee spoke at a Cato Institute conference entitled "Reassessing the Political Spectrum." Playing the role of political theorist as well as hardball tactician, Lee discussed "The Politics of the Baby Boom," saying that the generation of 75 million voters born between 1946 and 1964 was coming on in such force that it was "probably going to be the single most important political phenomenon for the next fifteen or twenty years." By 1988, they would represent about 60 percent of the electorate. Speaking as a baby boomer, he analyzed the political inclinations of his generation. "I do think that we're off the flat liberal-conservative or Republican-Democratic continuum, and into a four-pronged continuum composed of populists, libertarians, conservatives, and liberals. Each year the populists will probably diminish in number, and the libertarians will grow larger and larger as a result of the influx of the baby boomers into the decision system."

Why were the baby boomers different? First, they grew up during the television revolution of the '50s, going "from nothing of this kind to five and a half hours of uncontrolled information coming into their homes a day." Second, boomers were highly educated. "Education looms very large in understanding the difference between the baby-boom and other generations." Another demographic change that had occurred since the '50s was the integration of women into the workforce. Leisure time was something the group had in abundance. The materialism of the fifties, offset by the new consciousness of the sixties, led to what Lee called the "new values" of today. He shifted into the briefing he had given Bush in December. "I think that in order to examine these new values," he said, "you've got to think of them in conjunction with what else is going on, and that is a technology revolution. When you move from an industrial age into Alvin Toffler's *Third Wave*, or into the communication or information age, you've got two forces working simultaneously that are very important — a cultural value revolution and a technology revolution. They add up to what I call a 'new synthesis,' for lack of a better term."

One of the components of this new synthesis was the concept of "self-actualization" or "inner direction," said Lee, acknowledging the work of Daniel Yankelovich in *New Rules*, and Arnold Mitchell in *Nine American Lifestyles*. "Once you get certain materialistic needs taken care of," he said, "you start looking for self-actualization and inner-directedness. This inner-directed movement is characteristic of the baby-boom generation." This phenomenon manifested itself in several ways. "One is the concept of quality. Bigger is not better anymore — better is better." Although others might parody the Yuppies as measuring excellence in terms of Rolex watches and BMWs, Lee felt that "if you read books such as *In Search of Excellence*, you will understand that there is a new drive for true excellence in this country that's very important. The concept of opportunity is also a part of this new value synthesis. It involves equal opportunity and upward opportunity, and I think the role of minorities and women is an integral part of it. Baby boomers feel that all groups should have opportunity. It's popular to say that baby boomers are economic conservatives but liberals on social issues," Lee added, "but I don't quite look at it that way. Rather than viewing them as 'liberal' on social issues, the concept and the word should be 'tolerance.' In other words, there is almost a new traditionalism. . . . The family's very important to them, but they understand that the very structure of the family unit has changed. The concept of hard work is still intact, but it's not hard work for the sake of money or for materialism; it's hard work with a notion of success in mind, instead of just money. On the other hand, on issues such as sexual mores, smoking marijuana maybe, cohabitation, and so on, you find them liberal or at least open-minded."

Lee said that the boomers have a social conscience, one that had "developed in this group in the 1960s" and stayed intact. Thus South Africa was emerging as an issue. Likewise, boomers saw women as "coequal with men. The integration of women into the workforce has helped create this, but baby boomers generally feel that equality is the name of the game."

Boomers are "anti-big," a notion that Gary Hart had used effectively in his New Hampshire campaign. "Baby boomers are by and large anti–big government, anti–big labor unions, and anti–big institutions in general," Lee said. "What we as Republicans have always got to be aware of is that they're also anti–big business, and if we once again become viewed as the party that caters solely to big business, we would be in trouble with this group."

Boomers "will be by and large more receptive to change throughout their lives than any other group." Finally, Lee said that there was "a broad concept that I don't know how to articulate concisely." He had looked over surveys with baby boomers, "and even those who are supposedly happy — both economically and with their families — feel there's something missing in their lives. . . . Their lifestyle is somewhat different from their expressed values, and this gulf of cognitive dissonance, if you want to use the scholarly term for it, must be closed."

Lee felt that candidates who understood this gulf and tried to "make values and lifestyles work together for this group" would do well. Key issues of the future for boomers would be pocketbook issues. "Tax reform, particularly the flat tax, is going to be right at the top of the agenda as these people get squeezed economically. Education will be a critical issue, and health care is very important." Concern for the environment was a consensus issue among boomers, no longer a liberal-conservative debate.

Lee's nemesis Pat Caddell was on the same panel. "Lee Atwater got to the heart of the problem," Caddell said. "This is a generation with a collective social conscience, a collective sense that they can do great things, yet they are leading a life right now that's fairly mundane (even if they like their lifestyles) in terms of changing the world. This is a generation that grew up believing it was going to reshape the world, and that's where its power is." How can you communicate with this power base? "Those of you who saw *The Big Chill* know that the movie depicts a generation in which pictures, remembrances, ideas and experiences are shared universally," said Caddell, "and music is the greatest conductor of these." Lee, former head of the Upsetter's Revue, couldn't have said it better.

When a slim book based on the conference was published the following year, called *Left, Right & Babyboom*, Lee gave a copy to George Bush. He told the vice president that he could not expect to win as just another Reagan. He had to develop some *ideas*. As the boomers came on strong, Lee said that future Republican coalitions would have to be built on "a combination of business-minded conservatives and baby-boom libertarians — people who oppose government intervention in both the economy and personal life — rather than the 1980 Reagan coalition of country-club, Main Street conservatives and populists — people who support a government role both in the economy and in restoring traditional social values." In fact, Reagan could create a backlash for Bush. Though correct in assessing Reagan's plan as voodoo economics, Bush had swallowed his words and became vice president in an administration that had amassed a trillion-dollar debt. Some Wall Street execs, with considerable influence in Republican party fund-raising circles, considered the ol' supply-sider Reagan a traitor. Would this deficit come back to bite the Bush campaign in the butt?

Lee viewed the campaign from another direction as well. One of futurist John Naisbitt's major themes was making big institutions customer-friendly. "That's what politics is," said Atwater. "It has to be more consumer-driven, in touch with the customer/voter." Lee spent time with Naisbitt, who, with his wife Patricia Aburdene, had written several best-sellers that tracked trends by measuring the amount of space local newspapers gave to topics. For years Atwater had been sifting and analyzing the news each day; he saw his business as being much the same as Naisbitt's. After reading *Megatrends*, Lee began to think of himself as someone who could identify *political* megatrends, someone who had learned how to arbitrage the future. Ultimately, he concluded, it's

not what happens to us that matters — it's how we *interpret* what
happens to us. The interpretation establishes an attitude, which
can then be catered to emotionally. Therefore, the political goal
was to get in *front* of the interpretation — mental crowd control:
When we want your opinion, we'll give it to you!

Accordingly, Atwater made an important distinction between "attitudes" and "opinions." He cared little about opinions, but voter attitudes fascinated him. "Attitudes are deeply
ingrained," he explained. "You can't even necessarily verbalize
them." These attitudes could leave voters open to negative stimuli, especially boomers who were open to the allure of change
and were anti–big status quo. In December 1984, shortly before
signing on with Bush, Lee had told Thomas Edsall of the *Post* how
he had cut his political teeth in the early '70s playing on attitudes
to break the partisan loyalties of white Democrats in South Carolina. Before going negative on an opponent, he explained, he
made certain that his own candidate cultivated strong positive *attitudes* among the electorate. He used impressionistic images and
symbols to depict his candidate in such a way that the perception
"can't be busted up even with opinion changes on specific issues
that my opponent might accomplish."

The average voter could absorb only a limited amount of information about his candidate, Lee thought, and should never be
bewildered with specifics. The average voter was kind of slow, actually — would perceive facts as ideas, as an index to superiority in
thinking. So you could throw fact after fact at a voter . . . who might
never be able to connect the dots. In 1984 Reagan education secretary Terrell Bell spoke of the "dumbing down of America." Well,
here we were moving toward '88, and how far had we progressed?
Lee realized that in order to get swing votes, Bush had to tap voters'
emotions instead of their brains. It was Lee's job to find the specific
example, the outrageous abuse, the easy-to-digest tale that made
listeners *feel* — usually, repulsion — rather than *think*. Like the old
carnival barker, he needed a hook to get them into the tent. And so
began the search for wedge issues for George Bush — simple, impressionistic issues that appealed to attitudes, created a reaction,
not a thought.

In '86, when the rest of the political world was watching the
Senate races, Lee made sure that George Bush paid attention to
the thirty-six gubernatorial races. Lee had Bush go into the states

and raise money for GOP candidates, thus creating a political infrastructure of governors for Bush. "Make the governors your best friends," Bush heard from Andy Card, now in Rich Williamson's old slot as Reagan's liaison with the governors. "A congressman or a senator can walk away from a failed campaign," Card continued. "Not a governor. Governors have a stake in your success in their state. If they are with you, they can't afford to lose because it tarnishes their image." Governors can also command local press attention on short notice.

Andy Card became a mole in the Reagan network, handling the governors for the president but also setting up an infrastructure for Bush. Card had a direct line to the VP in the White House. He also maintained a good working relationship with Craig Fuller, a fellow E-mail nut. There was no paper trail between Card's office and Lee Atwater. An ideal situation. Governors were courted and lined up for Bush: Carroll Campbell, Tommy Thompson in Wisconsin, John Engler in Michigan, George Deukmajian in California, Bob Martinez in Florida. The key player was John Sununu in bellwether New Hampshire, the state the whole world would be watching on primary day.

In 1971, as a member of the planning board for Holbrook, Massachusetts, Card had attended a regional meeting in Pittsfield. There he met John Sununu, also an engineer, and his wife, Nancy. Instant rapport. In 1980 Card served as Bush's campaign manager in Massachusetts, and Sununu was running against Warren Rudman for the Senate in the New Hampshire Republican primary. Card and Sununu kept bumping into each other at rallies. In '82 Sununu ran for governor of New Hampshire, and Card ran for governor of Massachusetts. Sununu won; Card lost but went to D.C. to work with Reagan. One of his first calls was to Sununu, who began to use Card as his pipeline to Reagan.

In 1984, the day after his second nomination for VP at the Republican National Convention in Dallas, George Bush — at Ron Kaufman's insistence — was on Air Force Two to New Hampshire to attend a fund-raiser for Sununu. In the fall of 1986 Atwater called on the governor in New Hampshire to ask for his support for Bush. Lee drew the governor in with a discussion of his governor-focused strategy, which Sununu delighted in refining. Shortly afterward, Sununu called Lee in Washington. OK, he would endorse Bush one year before the primary. Now

Card's orders from Atwater were to get to know Sununu *really* well.

The only bright spot for the GOP on election day 1986, when it lost control of the Senate, was that it picked up eight gubernatorial seats. Bush picked up "a ton of chits." Atwater picked up something else from Campbell — a wedge issue. In the closing weeks of Campbell's campaign against Mike Daniel, Lee went to South Carolina and worked with Warren Tompkins. During a televised debate, the candidates were asked, "Where do you stand on taking the Confederate flag off the top of the statehouse?"

"I really don't have a position on that," said Daniel.

Campbell had a position: "I'm opposed to taking it down." Simple as that. This was the only time the issue came up. It put the other guy in an indecisive mode; whereas Campbell appeared decisive — and *that* became the cutting-edge issue. The flag was a perfect wedge issue: it wasn't a fact, it was a feeling.

Lee had seen that approach work in county and state elections. He was sure you could go national with wedge issues — working outside the nine dots — and come up a winner.

●   ●   ●

There were over ten thousand journalists permanently stationed in Washington — a lot of anxious mouths to feed. Back in 1984 Lee had asked John Buckley to put together a select list of emerging reporters, young guns who would be important in the next three years. Then he arranged for get-togethers — interviews, ostensibly, but always taking place in the context of catching some music, eating ribs, doing the things that boomers do together. Charm and disarm. Hey, good ink was better than good luck.

Now that newspapers had lost the footrace to the networks and *Nightline*, reporters were shifting from news to analysis in order to survive. Lee had the goods reporters wanted: the backstage version, the strategy behind the events, the political process itself! You give a little, and pretty soon the press learns to give a little. Lee gave plenty of access to the chroniclers of campaigns, fully expecting history's admiring glance in return. Their books were often filled with inside info on phone calls, privileged conversations, reconstructed private meetings, and memos — things that Lee leaked.

As for the national press — well, there was none. Lee only

cared about five papers: the *Washington Post*, the *Washington Times*, the *New York Times*, the *Wall Street Journal* and *USA Today*, which he called "the television of American newspapers." Except for the networks and a few major newspapers — the *New York Times*, the *Los Angeles Times*, and a handful of others that maintained bureaus in a few major cities — all media fed off the Washington press corps. That corps was led by the *Post*, whose big-foot reporters and columnists swarmed around the same stories on the political beat. Thus, to hold sway with a handful of reporters in the Washington press was to control the perceptions of millions.

Unlike Bush, who distrusted journalists, Lee liked to let reporters hang around him. Interviewing Lee was like interviewing a celebrity in reverse. With a celeb, the outer life is a matter of record; the goal is to find out some surprising insights into the inner life. Atwater turned the tables by trying to create the impression that his inner life was on display in intimate detail. He provided a list of ten close, personal friends who would tell you all you wanted about Lee's background. (Afterward, he went through the articles, calling sources who had given what he considered bad quotes, and putting them "on notice.") South Carolina reporters swapped stories of Lee's flagrant womanizing, even in front of female journalists. "He has no morals and will freely admit that," a reporter jotted in interview notes. "Messed around on wife . . . took girls back into bedroom." Reporters never wrote about Lee's personal flaws, however. It was *too* personal a story, and there would be many innocent family bystanders hurt. Once, when Lee learned that a reporter following a campaign couldn't get a hotel room for the night, he offered his own, which he wouldn't be using — with the proviso that if Sally called, the reporter was to say that Lee was at a meeting. (No deal.)

Although Lee brought considerable talents to his work, his true genius was devoted to marketing himself. In Washington Lee conveyed the attitude that he had nothing to hide — and a hell of a lot to be proud of. That meant that reporters were left to find out some surprising truths about his public life, his professional persona, what made him so effective as a political manager. In effect, he turned unwary members of the press into his own personal press agents. "He was amazingly insecure," recalled Ann Devroy, White House political reporter for the *Post*. "He would give a speech that I wouldn't normally pay any attention to; it didn't have any news value. And he would call me up, saying, 'What do you think? What do you think?' — as if I was supposed to be sitting there watching his speeches."

By now Lee's molding of his own persona was well underway. The press had respect for him because he kept winning campaigns — and because he was a helpful leaker. The media often assumed, with no real evidence, that Atwater stage-managed certain events. He got credit for triumphs he didn't even have to claim. Exaggeration, repetition, inadequate reporting based on handouts, follow-up reporting based on erroneous clips — such is the stuff on which political reputations are built.

Before an important interview Lee would rehearse phrases he wanted to insert in answers, especially if the piece was a profile of himself. But his defensiveness, his fears, his powers of denial — these emotions were on the surface for anyone to see, covered over lightly with a touch of the outrageous, even the bombastic. He was transparent, not subtle; even heavy-handed at times, and always insecure afterward. "How was I? Was that OK?" he would ask *Post* columnist David Broder at the end of an interview. "How did I do?"

Lee nearly did himself in with the Bushes when he let journalist David Remnick into his unvarnished life during the summer of 1986. They did the usual lunch at the Palm, played guitar at the house with Sally and the kids, did a road trip to Texas. Then Remnick made the rounds with Lee's top ten sources — and others that Lee didn't know about until the profile appeared in the December issue of *Esquire*. Lee had asked Remnick to drop by his hotel room for a midnight interview. When the writer arrived, Lee answered the door wearing nothing but boxer shorts and socks. They started talking, then Lee went to the bathroom, and, with the door open, kept talking while he peed. "I read that Johnson biography by Robert Caro," he said. "You know that book? I'm a student of power, and man, that Johnson knew everything about power." Lee flushed, put on a T-shirt, settled into a chair, and continued the interview.

Remnick recognized the casual attempt to disarm him as a Machiavellian touch. It was "a trick he may have learned from reading about Lyndon Johnson, who used to quiz his aides while he sat on the toilet," said the journalist. Remnick also reported on how Lee liked to check out the unwashed masses, the "swing vote" as he called them, while on road trips. During one after-hours tour in Austin, Atwater, giggling like a college boy, peeked into a massage parlor.

"You wanna massage, dahlin'?" asked the receptionist.

"Uh, no," he said. "We were just lookin', really." Outside, he laughed hysterically. "It's a little different outside Washington, isn't it?" he said. "You think that girl gives a damn about the contra vote?"

With Bush fighting off critics for his role in the Iran-contra scandal, this comment infuriated Bar. Not only that, Lee came off sounding like a punk, not a Republican: "I'm tellin' you," Lee told David Remnick for the record, kicking up some dust, "this here's a young man's game. This is stress, high motherfuckin' stress. When you're working with the front-runner, you're gonna get shot no matter what you do." Especially if you talk like that in front of Mrs. Bush. After the article hit the newsstands Lee needed damage control.

"If the wife of the candidate doesn't like you," observed Ann Devroy, "you're a dead man." Bar was miffed. Thus, George Jr. earned some of his early campaign experience trying to stage-manage a mea culpa from Lee. On the suggestion of Bush's nephew John Ellis, Lee wrote a letter to Mrs. Bush saying it wouldn't happen again. He began to walk the straight and narrow around the Bushes, placing pictures of Sally and the kids in every corner of his office. Lee was good at acting good. It took time, sending lots of little notes and exchanging books and courtesies, but gradually Lee got their confidence in good working order again.

Lee still had to work to keep his sexual adventures from the Bushes. He had fallen in love not with women, but with a lifestyle that included dalliances in a city where single women vastly outnumber single men (which is not to be confused with *available* men). In the office Lee could charm and flirt his way through an evening, get work done, and enjoy the assortment of friendships that he needed to feel complete. Lee could seduce a vulnerable woman with his troubles, real or imagined; with his attention to details, his desire to make things easier for her. An unattached woman usually liked the attention. For Lee, infidelity wasn't really about sex. It was about control and power. As in politics, for Lee the lure was the hunt itself, not the prize. For months he told one of his ladies that she was the one, that he and Sally were no longer having sex. She was startled when she learned that Sally was pregnant.

Lee's marriage was more of a working partnership than a perfect union. Everything he did was based on getting the maximum amount of work done every moment of the day. He measured the cost of every act — watching his kids, giving time to Sally — against what else he could be doing. On average he got two or three hours of sleep a night. Sally arose at five each morning to fix him a big breakfast (he loved fried shrimp and pork chops), to press his shirt (a portable iron rested on Sally's nightstand), and to review a three-by-five-inch card listing the things Lee wanted her to do that day. Sally became the full-time designated driver so that Lee didn't have to worry about traffic and directions. He sat beside her, sometimes reading aloud for discussion.

Sally had taught special education in grade school until she moved to D.C. in 1982; then she had worked in special ed programs at the Department of Education. But she soon became overwhelmed with the responsibilities of motherhood and maintaining family appearances. "I stopped working outside the home in '84 because it got to the point where one of us had to go to the grocery store," she explained. She put Sara Lee in a parochial school because she felt her daughter needed more structure. During campaigns, Sally even had to take Sara Lee to headquarters to see her father, because that was where he slept. In October 1986, when the Atwaters were moving into a new home, Sally gave Lee instructions on a slip of paper as he left for work at five-forty-five A.M. "This is where you will live this afternoon," she said. "Please show up."

Marriage is hard enough for ordinary couples; for political couples it is nearly impossible. Lee wanted a family, yet he was more than work-oriented; he was work-obsessed. Theo Dunbar recalled visiting Lee and Sally at their first residence in Washington, a fifth-floor apartment with a back room where Lee would often retreat. It was his space to read, to be alone, on the job. In every home thereafter he had a similar place where he could close out the distractions of family in order to give command focus to his work.

"I saw all sorts of women throw themselves at Lee, but I never saw Sally swoon over Lee," recalled one of Lee's lifelong pals. "Every now and then Lee would put his arm around Sally and say something sweet, but they were not a publicly affectionate couple. It seemed like a practical arrangement. Lee's view seemed to be, 'This is my wife, the mother of my children.' I never saw him hanging his head about his marriage, or being unhappy with Sally. But there was not a lot of passion there." Lee's emotional need for Sally was tinged with the fear that she would throw him out, and this would kill him with the Bushes.

One woman wanted to break up Lee's marriage. She called his home regularly and would hang up when Sally answered. She would intentionally scratch Lee's back with her fingernails during their sessions, drawing blood so that Sally might ask about the marks. The spin at home ended when Lee used one of his closest buddies as an alibi one night, and Sally called the next day to ask what he and Lee had been doing. "I don't know what you're talking about," the friend told her. Like many of Lee's pals, he felt sorry for Sally. And helpless.

Sally's beautiful fixed smile grew more forced. Perhaps it was too many parties, too many fund-raisers at one-night chic hotels, with Lee holding forth about the same old stuff. After that phone call, the spirit seemed to go out of Sally, a friend observed. "She just seemed to be tired of hearing Lee's shit sometimes, his pontifications and everything. Normally she was a chirpy, cheerful person. Eventually, she bounced back. I think she began to understand Lee for what he really was."

Lee had always thought that, in accepting him, Sally *understood* him, and that she understood that success wasn't a threat to their relationship. But it wasn't the success that bothered Sally; it was Lee's other women. His attitude was comparable to what some call a European style of marriage — that is, the wife is honored as the woman of the household, the sacred shrine with the child; the husband goes out with the women who aren't important to him, but who relieve him . . . and he always comes back. In Europe this is considered sophisticated and is rarely a problem in politics. In the States it is considered reckless and potentially destructive.

In May 1987 Gary Hart's campaign ran aground on just this reef. John McEvoy, a friend and political ally, told *Newsweek* that Hart would win the nomination if he could keep his pants on. Despite warnings that his alleged womanizing would be an issue, Hart invited scrutiny, telling E. J. Dionne of the *New York Times*, "Follow me around. I don't care. I'm serious, if anybody wants to put a tail on me, go ahead. They'd be very bored." The press soon disclosed that Donna Rice, a Miami model and pharmaceutical sales rep, spent the night of May 1 in Hart's Washington home. Then a photograph surfaced showing Rice sitting on Hart's lap a month earlier as they sailed off to Bimini on a yacht called *Monkey Business*.

The day before the story broke, Lee and Charlie Black were driving to Ed Rollins's wedding in Roanoke. "You know, this guy is a terrific front-runner on paper," said Lee, "but he's not going to make it — just no way — because we have ten months left in this contest, and he can't have a story written about him that doesn't talk about him changing his name, talk about him changing his age, and talk about him being a womanizer."

Lee watched his candidate's most feared enemy self-destruct on television: Hart offered an apology and an admission of adultery on *Nightline*. Although the words were real, Hart seemed more defiant than penitent — the apology failed to bridge the gap between his candidacy and his monkey business. When Hart decided to reenter the race for the nomination months later, his future was already behind him. Again watching on TV, with Rich Bond and others in his office, Lee jumped up, grabbed his hair, started pacing. "This is good! This is good!" he said. "This is helpful! This is helpful!"

To many journalists covering the election, Gary Hart's "seven days in May" looked like a setup. Wayne King of the *New York Times* theorized that Rice might have been recruited to sink Hart. "Hart meets her in Colorado [at a New Year's Eve party], then he runs into her on a yacht in Miami because she happens to be at an adjoining disco. Those things can happen, but it still looked a little funny." One suspect, of course, was Lee Atwater. After all, Donna Rice was from Columbia, too.

"Nothing ever happens that I'm not blamed for," replied Atwater with a laugh. "I wasn't behind it, but if I had been, I would have waited until the son of a bitch got the nomination and I'd have broken it then!"

Later that year a rumor about Bush's alleged affair with a longtime assistant nearly derailed his campaign before it started. Bush's enemies were not averse to spreading stories about him having a mistress. Aides in both the Dole and Kemp camps pushed rumors to the press, playing one media outlet off against the other. "There were some Kemp people who were masquerading as Dole people — a double whammy, that's a great technique," explained

Atwater. "I'm Kemp, right? I want to get it out. I get a 'twofer' if I get the rumor out to fuck Bush and I also get the Dole people fucked in the process because they're being blamed for the rumor."

During preparation for the debate at the Iowa caucuses, Bush staffers arranged for the rehearsal moderator to ask, "Yes or no — have you ever committed adultery?"

Bush snapped, "None of your damn business!" That only heightened the press hysteria.

The next day the rumors hit Capitol Hill; Atwater received fifty calls. "The third day, it started melting down, and we were getting calls from the states," said Lee. "At that point what I figured would happen, after observing the Gary Hart episode, is that a favorite game would be played. It's the old game we saw a hundred times: *Time* calling up and saying, 'Well, *Newsweek* is going with it.' "

Atwater decided to take action. "What crossed my mind was that we needed to get it out on our own terms and in midair to shift the nature of the story from the rumor to who was the dirty trickster putting out the rumor." Lee decided to handle this the same way he redirected the "open grave" incident when he was Rollins's deputy. He would shift the story from its substance to how it was being spread. He met with George Jr., who said he had asked his father about the rumors "point-blank." "The answer to the Big A question is N.O." Lee met with Howard Fineman of *Newsweek* for an off-the-record lunch and gave him Junior's quote. The item ran in *Newsweek*'s Periscope column on June 27, and the issue was defused.

"Within twenty-four hours it was flat dead," reflected Lee. "Why? Because the whole story shifted to whoever was putting this out was a dirty trickster and this was vile, etc., and no one would put it out." In defining events like this, George Bush could not have been in the hands of a more capable operative than Lee Atwater.

• • •

On October 18, 1987, Lee's "children's crusade" began in earnest. So called because of the young aides who surrounded Lee, the campaign moved into headquarters in the Woodward Building at Fifteenth and H Streets. The building featured erratic heat in the winter, uncertain air-conditioning in the summer, a tiny elevator that rarely worked — and cheap rent. The staff called it the Temple of Doom. There was even a rumor that the building had been condemned.

On the wall behind the chairman's desk was a framed photograph of wrestler Big John Studd clasping Lee in a headlock. An appropriate image, since Lee viewed wrestling not as a sport, but, rather, as a morality play in which good usually triumphs, but bad boys seem to have all the fun. Desperados, of course, do whatever it takes to win — right down to, yes, dirty tricks. But compared to football, say, this sport had integrity. Hell, you couldn't even bet on its outcome, even though it was fixed. "I tell candidates to look at a wrestling interview," said Lee. "It's a caricature of a politician's press conference. And I tell 'em I learned a lot about politics from going to wrestling. Audiences at professional wrestling matches are the swing voters in elections."

Having formulated strategy, Lee was now in charge of inspiring his troops to carry it out. He had been a showman all his young life. He enjoyed playing the bad boy. Indeed, much of his power came from knowing it *was* a role. He was a fake, sure, but an *honest* fake, right at home in a city filled with people leading lives of quiet obfuscation. In Washington you could move up quickly by being good at "personal" skills — which usually meant outrageous flattery followed by backstage savaging. Lee liked to say that the thrill of Washington politics was that it could be over in a day. The trick was to play dumb and just keep movin'. "I always wanted to be a creative artist," Lee had explained to David Remnick. "I wanted to create something. I take a campaign with great pride, the way an artist would view his work. A client feels that. In other words, I'm not doing it for the money. Sure I get paid, but if you take my attitude about quality, you're just gonna end up getting bigger bucks in the end anyhow. I try to tell that to the young kids I see."

"He had a way of making everybody feel special — a great trait, which most leaders have," said Ron Kaufman. Anyone who worked with Lee and visited him at home was likely to end up lying alongside him on the bed in front of the big-screen TV. Sunday mornings Lee liked to huddle with aides and political buddies and "watch the shows" — *Meet the Press, Face the Nation, Brinkley*. They'd discuss the news, eat "something fried," maybe head to Olsson's bookstore in Georgetown to buy a handful of titles people were talking about, snack at Hamburger Hamlet, thumb the books and discuss them. Then back home to plug in a movie in the bedroom, flopping down on Lee's king-size bed as if it were a giant beach blanket, while Sally and the kids disappeared. "Yet everyone was self-contained and in a box," Kaufman added. "None of us ever really knew Lee. He would give you that little piece of him that he found necessary to make that box work, but no more — and usually less."

One of Lee's Sunday buddies was Ed Rogers, a lanky young tireless, disciplined worrier who usually carried a legal pad with a list of to do's. Lee had carried a pad like that back in his White House days, but he had taken to using custom-printed note cards, usually tucked into a leather Jotter by T. Anthony's of New York. To get Lee's attention with an idea, a request, a strategy, you had to give it to him on an index card. "Lee believed that if your campaign plan didn't fit on a three-by-five card," recalled Rogers, "you're gonna lose." Rogers, from Alabama, had been an advance man during the Reagan campaign; then he'd handled Lee's old territory as deputy regional campaign director during the '84 reelection. He worked in the White House political office until February 1987, when he became Lee's deputy at the Bush campaign.

Like Lee, Ed Rogers was a doer. He was also a grinner. Try as he might, Rogers could not stop from grinning, even at the most inappropriate times. Once Lee learned that he could provoke a grin from Ed with theatrical hand gestures or animated conversation, it was like Curly and Moe in the boardroom. They would be in a serious meeting with someone going on about problems. "You're kidding me!" Lee would say. "You're telling me you don't think we can get the Hispanic vote in California?!" Then he would look at Ed, who would have a grin on his face. "Ed, this is not funny!" Lee would say, feigning seriousness and making a spectacle of his fellow stooge.

"There was never a minute, no matter how serious, that was off-limits to some sort of frivolity, gesture, or inside joke, often at the expense of someone who didn't get it," recalled Rogers. "Every day was a day at the improv." Rogers was the straight man for many of Lee's machinations. Nonsensical one-word phone calls: "Grapefruit." Returned by Rogers later in the day, as though it were a secret code word: "Grapefruit!"

Shortly before the Bush campaign began, Haley Barbour had

met with Lee at his favorite spot on the Tow Path that meandered beside the C & O Canal on the outskirts of Georgetown. That was where Lee liked to run, where he gave command focus to problems that seemed insoluble in the office clatter. As they walked, Barbour urged Lee to bring Rich Bond into the campaign. Bond was ready to work for Lee, and the old battles were forgotten; moreover, Bush wanted to get his old political director in the loop.

Lee had serious doubts about this shotgun marriage, but shortly afterward Bond came aboard. He and Lee became almost inseparable — because of their jealousy and distrust. Rich, in turn, had another person he wanted to bring aboard: Mary Matalin. In 1982, when he had gone to the Republican National Committee to keep an eye on Dick Richards, Bond had discovered Mary working as a secretary in the bowels of computer services. She was a former homecoming queen who once worked in Chicago's steel mills before becoming a law-school dropout. When Frank Fahrenkopf became head of RNC, Bond left to form a consulting firm, taking Matalin with him as his deputy. Now he wanted Lee to approve her as a field organizer in Iowa. She had aspirations of becoming the midwest regional political director, and this was an opportunity for her to get her hands dirty, expand her portfolio, become one of the boys. Lee was not enthusiastic, but Bond reassured him. OK, said Lee, and the honeymoon continued.

If Atwater was the dark prince among political handlers, he met his counterpart in Roger Ailes, the legendary dark prince of political advertising who had repackaged Richard Nixon as a TV personality in 1968 — as chronicled by Joe McGinniss in his surprise best-seller *The Selling of the President, 1968.* Ailes had been most generous toward McGinniss, leaking internal strategy memos to the young reporter and turning himself into the star of the book — a tactic that Lee could certainly relate to. Like Atwater, Ailes was from common stock: his father was a foreman at the Packard Electric plant in Warren, Ohio. Ailes liked to nurture his image as a tough, pugnacious player. "Don't go looking for a fight," his father had told him after he was bullied at the age of nine, "but if you're hit, *deck* the bastard. The worst thing that can happen to you is you can die. If you're not afraid of that, you don't have to be afraid of anything." Ailes trained himself to think that way for life. Not unlike how young Lee Atwater manufactured his self-confidence.

"He has two speeds," Atwater said of Ailes to *Time* reporter David Beckwith. "Attack and destroy." At five ten, Ailes wore a white goatee and 250 pounds on a frame more corpulent than combative, far removed from the lean and mean physique of Lee. Intellectually, though, they were like bruise brothers.

Ailes could produce and capture the vision, but he was not a visionary. That's where Atwater came in. Lee's initial problem was to turn around Bush's negatives. According to Lee's *revised* theory, no candidate was electable with negative poll ratings over 40 percent. In 1988 Bush's negatives had reached 44 percent; he was being derided as a wimp. Of course, Reagan had had similar problems at the outset of his 1980 campaign; that February his negatives had been 46 percent, with polls showing that he was perceived as being too old, not very bright, and trigger-happy. Reagan had wiped the slate clean in one debate with Jimmy Carter. Couldn't something similar be done for George Bush?

Atwater and Ailes remade Bush's image in a series of planned encounters, including a testy confrontation with Dan Rather on the Monday evening of January 25, 1988. An interview had been set up the preceding Thursday through a series of phone calls between Pete Teeley, press secretary of the Bush campaign, and Tom Bettag, executive producer of *CBS Evening News*. Bettag stressed that the interview would follow a long, pointed story about the Iran-contra affair, that it would be tough and focused on the content of that story. "I just smelled setup," said Atwater. "Rather was a middle-aged guy with a sagging career who remembered what the Ted Kennedy interview did for Roger Mudd." On Friday Atwater warned his candidate to stay away.

"Lee, I know you're looking out for my best interests," said Bush, "but Dan has been a friend of mine for twenty-five years."

The night before the interview, Ailes called a source inside CBS News. The source called him back from a pay phone to say that the network had hired a Democratic consultant to work with Rather. When Lee heard this news, he called Bush. "I know how you feel about this interview," he said, "but just in case I'm right and you're wrong, I've asked Roger to meet you to go over a few things."

"God, Lee, you just don't give up," said Bush.

The interview was conducted with Rather in New York at his anchor desk and Bush at his Capitol Hill office. Ailes stood a few paces from Bush, off camera, writing key words on a yellow pad to remind Bush what to say. Classic Ailes scripting and Atwater strategy: when attacked, hit back so hard that your opponent regrets getting tough in the first place. After a five-minute report on Iran-contra, Rather asked his first question on that issue, and Bush came out firing away. "I find this to be a rehash and a little bit, if you'll excuse me, of a misrepresentation on the part of CBS, who said you're doing political profiles of all the candidates. It's not fair to judge my whole career by a rehash on Iran," Bush told Rather. "How would you like it if I judged your whole career by those seven minutes when you walked off the set in New York?"

The previous September, Rather had walked off his program because the evening news broadcast was delayed by CBS's coverage of the U.S. Open tennis tournament. The network went black for six minutes while producers coaxed the anchor back to his desk. When Bush landed that blow, thanks to Ailes's coaching, Rather seemed to lose his composure. The interview was a verbal slugfest for ten minutes, and most viewers agreed that Bush had decked the bastard.

Ted Koppel of *Nightline* observed that Rather had allowed himself to be maneuvered into serving as "a high priest in the ceremonial de-wimping of George Bush."

"I think it was the most important event of the entire primary campaign," said Atwater. "It was stronger than grits in the South. Rather is a guy people love to hate down there."

• • •

Nevertheless, Lee's campaign got off to a poor start when Bush finished third in the Iowa caucuses, trailing Kansas senator Bob Dole and TV evangelist Pat Robertson. There was also a problem behind the scenes in the White House, where the infighting between the Reagan and Bush wings had become intense. To some Reaganites, a candidate like Robertson was more consistent with conservative principles than the wily George Bush would ever be. As a result there was no unified effort behind Bush, despite the perception that he was heir to the Reagan legacy. Bush may have been the incumbent candidate, but he was not a popular one. His support was a mile long and an inch deep.

In Iowa, Lee did manage to achieve one goal: to throw Dole off balance. Lee had a theory that people were divided into two camps — Adults and Kids. He was a Kid, of course, with a curious mind, and he could be a pain in the ass if he didn't get things his way. Bob Dole was an Adult with zero tolerance for pranks, so it was Kid's play to rattle him. (Sun-tzu: "If your opponent is of choleric temper, seek to irritate him.") Atwater distributed Kansas newspaper clippings that questioned a Dole associate's handling of the blind trust set up for Elizabeth Dole after she had resigned as secretary of transportation to work on her husband's campaign. Dole's famed temper, which his advisers had been trying to keep under wraps, came out in the open. Atwater responded by calling Dole "a typical schoolyard bully," adding, "He can dish it out but if someone hits him back, he starts whining." Atwater sent a ten-page letter to Dole detailing the negative campaign tactics he said the senator had employed in the campaign. George Bush may have lost the Iowa caucus, but Atwater had scored by getting under the skin of his key opponent.

Iowa was one of those wrestling matches Lee just couldn't fix. For weeks he had received daily poll reports from John Ellis, the veep's nephew who was working for Tom Brokaw at NBC. It was no surprise when Bush lost. Perhaps, in light of Bush's lethargy, it was even a necessary loss. In the media, however, Bush was declared dead politically, with the implication that Lee might be fired or — what Lee was more afraid of — layered, with a new boss installed above him. In that case, he'd have to quit. Meantime, there was the matter of damage control, and someone had to take the fall.

Lee flew into Des Moines the night of the caucuses with Bush on Air Force Two. He sent an aide to get Mary Matalin, whom he had heard plenty about from Rich Bond, of course, but never met. She seemed to be doing a fine job, reporting in advance that Bush was probably going to lose because of the proximity of Dole's state, Kansas, and "this huge Robertson thing" just below the radar screen.

Matalin was terrified. Though only two years younger than Lee, she felt like a neophyte, and he sensed this instantly. He also sensed that the best way to enter her mind was through emotion, not logic. Lee stared at Mary in disbelief for three minutes. "I can't believe this!" he said. "I can't believe it!" This little caucus was a mechanical exercise that *anybody* could do. He was absolutely *amazed* that they had lost. What had gone *wrong*? Matalin squirmed. Lee's face was gray, washed of color. He kept shaking his head. After staring for another five minutes he said he would talk to the veep about the situation, and Matalin left.

The next day a more composed Lee Atwater made a conference call to the Iowa field reps for the sole purpose of firing Mary Matalin while everyone was on the line. She had failed them all, he said. While the boys on Air Force Two roared off to do battle in New Hampshire, Matalin, in tears, called her supervisor, Janet Mullins. "Look, you're not really fired," said Mullins. "Just don't let him see you for a while."

Ironically, New Hampshire was a grassroots campaign — something that Atwater had cut his teeth on back in the '70s. Perhaps he had outgrown this sort of politics. Lost touch with it. Certainly it wasn't the kind of politics that would work in South Carolina or in any part of the South at this time. You had to count on the media to win down there, and that meant you had to create momentum. If Lee failed in New Hampshire, Bush would lose both his momentum and his fund-raising base. If Dole won, he would have more momentum, more money — and Lee's southern firewall would most assuredly be at risk.

The Bush campaign in New Hampshire had a lot of assets — and a few liabilities, often in the same suits. John Sununu was brilliant, with a great political mind; he was also smug and difficult to work with. Starting in '86 Ron Kaufman had set up a Bush political base in New Hampshire, lining up legislators who did not like Sununu but would hold their noses. A group called the Freedom Fighters had been meeting in Concord with Kaufman every Monday at six A.M., driving from all over the state where they were sheriffs, state reps, town officials. Gradually, Kaufman — very intense, very driven — wore out his political welcome, not only offending Sununu and his wife, but also about twenty state officials who began to moan to Atwater.

In late 1986 Atwater had asked Andy Card to take over the New Hampshire account. Card wavered. After all, his family was just settling into Washington, and Kaufman was his brother-in-law. Lee knew how to cut through the wavering: "Well, if the vice president asks you to do it, would you do it?" Card had to say yes. Kaufman was kicked upstairs as regional coordinator for New England, and on March 15, 1987, Andy Card arrived in Concord as New Hampshire campaign director. For a year he slept in a sleeping bag on a cot in the office on School Street as he soothed the pols whom Kaufman had wounded. Each day began at six-thirty with a conference call from Lee. The campaign plan was laid out day by day and posted on a closet door in the little house that Kaufman had rented as campaign headquarters.

Although the Bush strategy came from Lee, he didn't micromanage. Andy Card had carte blanche. As in the '76 Campbell campaign, his key task was identifying the vote and getting it out. Tactics included everything from passing out bumper stickers and hosting coffee parties to volunteers going door-to-door and calling potential voters. There are 113 precincts in New Hampshire. In each one there was a Bush campaign chairman. Card called on each chairman and devised 113 different campaign plans, each written up by the precinct chairman and based on the number of votes needed to win that precinct. "In New Hampshire, you don't elect the president," Card later said. "The public wants to believe they do, but I told them to think of their job as electing George Bush the chairman of the precinct." If they needed 85 people in a precinct to vote for Bush, he insisted that he get each one's name.

The precinct strategies were in place, the vote identified and counted, long before the Iowa caucus began. Card knew how many votes Bush needed, and he felt they had 60,000 votes accounted for. But by the time Bush arrived in New Hampshire, the "overnights" were bad. Daily polls showed him losing 2, 3, 4 points a night. Sununu said they had to run the campaign his way or they would be in deep trouble.

In the beginning there was little trust between Lee and Sununu. Lee didn't especially like the governor, though they shared a common dislike of the old Yankee domination of the Republican Party. Sununu, of course, looked down on Atwater; there could be no political equality between a governor and a campaign hack. "I don't think they ever became fast friends, because Sununu always felt he was better than Lee Atwater," said Andy Card. "Certainly not social friends. But Lee had such arrogance and such confidence in his abilities that he never *presumed* John Sununu was any better, so they got along pretty well. Remember, Sununu had a vowel at the end of his name, and Atwater *fought* like he had a vowel at the end of his name."

Gradually, the two grew to respect each other, even found

themselves linked by their status as outsiders inside the Bush camp; they weren't blue suits. To make the most of his association with the New Hampshire governor, Lee was characteristically Machiavellian. "What do you think about this?" he would say to Sununu. "Tell me what your thoughts are," stroking away, with no intention of following Sununu's advice. The hard-charging governor just loved what Lee would tell Bush: "Do whatever Sununu wants out there. Listen to Sununu." That Lee was *smart*, thought Sununu.

In New Hampshire Bush abandoned all the trappings of the vice presidency and campaigned as if he were running for the state legislature. He dropped in at truck stops, fast-food joints, and drove a tractor around a parking lot for one photo op. "I am one of you," he said, shamelessly borrowing Dole's approach.

Sununu knew how to work the New Hampshire media, recognizing the value of live TV rather than videotaped news, especially at WMUR-TV, Channel 9, in Manchester. After going live, a TV station couldn't edit Bush's comments. "No matter what they ask you, here is the message we want to get out," Sununu would tell Bush. He was also adept at getting an ad on the air at short notice. He took crap from no one and doled it out to station managers everywhere. Not only in New Hampshire, but also in Boston, where he called owners of TV stations: "We want to change an ad. We've already purchased the time. We've got a new ad that we've got to get *on the air*, and it's got to be on TONIGHT, and your people are saying it's going to take another day to get it!" Sununu's hold on the media gave Bush virtually instant response to any Dole attack.

"I think we're six to eight points up," Atwater told John Ellis three days before the vote.

Ellis's information from NBC indicated that Bush and Dole were even. "You just have to own the weekend on television," Ellis told George Jr. By now the stations had closed because of snow. Sununu would have to stir some station managers out of their homes to get the ads on.

Ailes had a commercial called "Straddler" ready to take a piece out of Bob Dole. The ad wasn't pretty. Even Bush winced when he first saw it. It featured a two-faced picture of Dole, with dual images pointed toward each other and the word "Straddled" across the screen. The senator was portrayed as waffling on oil-import fees, arms control, and tax hikes. "Taxes — He can't say no," said the screen, with a voice-over intoning, "Bob Dole straddles, and he just won't promise not to raise taxes. And you know what that means."

"We have to go negative. We have to go negative," said Lee. On further consideration, Bush was willing. Lee loved to tell the story of laboring all night over the ad, then running around in the closing hours of the campaign with Sununu in the snow in New Hampshire to deliver the tape to television stations. The ad ran. The next day "Straddler" moved New Hampshire's undecided voters to the Bush column.

At least that was how the media and Roger Ailes played it. Sununu, Card, and Atwater had estimated 60,000 votes for a 10-point victory. Bush won by 9 points over Dole with 58,656. Did the ad make a difference? Probably not. Did it make a good story? Yes indeed, and that's what the media needed.

Lee Atwater knew that the press liked to play winners and losers and was fascinated with the tactical process. So he told reporters that three nights before the polls opened, he had spoken with their colleagues. "I talked to 36 reporters — I counted them . . . 36 out of 36 said George Bush did not have a chance," he later spun columnist Marilyn Rauber. "I've been in politics for eighteen years, and the eighteen years combined weren't any more intense than the last seven days," he said. The victory had the usual Atwater earmarks, he advised her: solid grassroots organization, the door-to-door get-out-the-vote drive, and some killer ads attacking Dole at the finish line.

The Dole campaign never recovered from the shock of losing in New Hampshire. Every campaign has a series of what Lee Atwater called "defining events" — dramatic vignettes, usually occurring at critical junctures, that become ingrained in the nation's consciousness principally through being constantly replayed in the media. One such event occurred at the end of the New Hampshire primary, when Tom Brokaw, on a live remote with NBC, asked Bush if he had any message for Dole. "Naw, just wish him well," said the veep. "And meet him in the South." Then the camera picked up Bob Dole sitting in a hotel room.

"Senator?" said Brokaw. "Any message for the vice president?"

"Yeah," said Dole. "Stop lying about my record."

In the days that followed, the "stop lying about my record" comment was played over and over on television and repeated in newspapers and magazines — not as an indictment against the Bush campaign, but rather as a way of explaining that Dole had blundered. "I'm sure Dole wished even as he said those words that he had been more gracious in defeat," observed Dayton Duncan, press secretary for Michael Dukakis. "One of the values we are all taught while growing up is to be a good loser, and his remarks clearly put him out of that category. . . . But even in the hyperbolic language of politics, 'lying' is a highly charged word, and, at least where I grew up, being a liar was considered even worse than being a poor sport." Did the "Straddler" ads lie about Dole's record? Didn't matter. Meanness was more fun for the media to focus on.

Toddy Atwater told Lee, "I thought Dole looked like a sore loser."

On the Roger Mudd show Lee shared Toddy's comment. "I called my mother and she said, 'I think Dole looked like a sore loser.' Now if my *mother* thinks that, what do you think everybody in the United States thinks?"

At the end of the show, Mudd observed with tongue in cheek, "Well, if we have any political problems, we'll be sure to check with Lee Atwater's mother."

A writer for the *Washington Post* reported that Lee was using his mother as a ploy in order to sock it to Dole. Toddy wanted to write her and say it wasn't a ploy; he *had* asked her about Dole. "Leave the press alone," Lee told her. "Ignore it. Play dumb and just keep movin'." After all, hadn't complaining gotten Dole in trouble?

Whether or not the TV blitz made a difference, in New Hampshire George Bush looked into the abyss and agreed on the necessity of going negative. Once Bush had got a taste of it, going negative against the Democrats would be easy.

With its GOP primary scheduled three days ahead of Super Tuesday, South Carolina was positioned as the New Hampshire of the South. On Saturday, March 5, 1988, Bush won nearly half the vote there, with Dole and Robertson far behind. On Tuesday, March 8, Lee's firewall strategy led Bush to a blazing victory in fifteen primaries in all the southern and border-state contests.

Dole still had a pulse, so it wasn't quite over until March 12, when the Bush campaign headed for Illinois. Lee got word on a bus that Dole had canceled his Illinois media. George Bush had the Republican nomination.

Next stop: Michael Dukakis.

CHAPTER

7

THE HAZARDS OF DUKE

He who is skilled in attack flashes forth from the topmost
heights of heaven, making it impossible for the enemy
to guard against him. This being so, the places that he
shall attack are precisely those that
the enemy cannot defend.
— Sun-tzu, *The Art of War*

In 1987 political guru George Will wrote a book called *The New Season: A Spectator's Guide to the 1988 Election* in which Lee Atwater's name was not mentioned once. "A negative tone has served Republicans (and Democrats) well when out of office," quoth Will. "But by autumn, 1988, a Republican will have been at the head of the government for almost eight years. So the old-style negativism will not be a useful arrow in the Republican quiver." It didn't exactly turn out that way.

From the outset, the 1988 election saw heightened coverage of what the press called "character issues" — revelations about Gary Hart and Donna Rice, Joe Biden's exaggeration of his college career and plagiarism of other politicians' speeches, and Bruce Babbitt's and Al Gore's confessions that they had smoked marijuana. Even the *Wall Street Journal* jumped in, revealing that Pat Robertson and his wife had conceived their first child months before their marriage.

Some candidates made a point of speaking out against the negativity. Massachusetts governor Michael Dukakis dumped his field general, John Sasso, for distributing the "attack video" that disabled the Biden campaign. The Dukakis people thought the integrity their candidate showed would be his competitive advantage. "I believe that 'character' in the broad sense is the most important criterion in assessing who should lead the nation," said Dukakis's press secretary Dayton Duncan. Character certainly included whether a candidate "spends weekends on yachts with young models, inflates his academic record, once used an illegal drug, [and] led a wild life before a religious conversion. . . . They are bits of information the public deserves to know before choosing its president," he added, noting that such bits of information are not to be found in a candidate's speeches and pronouncements during a campaign; rather, "they most likely can be found in exhaustive searches of a candidate's personal history and political record."

James Pinkerton agreed wholeheartedly. As head of research for the campaign, Pinkerton had a staff that Lee liked to refer to as "the thirty-five excellent nerds." Actually, including volunteers, there were more like one hundred researchers working around the clock, in three shifts, with a budget of $1.2 million to spend on the sleuthing of Michael Dukakis. Foremost nerd was Don Todd, Republican National Committee director of opposition research, a rumpled fifty-year-old chain smoker from Idaho, who liked to compare his job to his father's old profession: panning for gold. "Back when gold was thirty-six dollars an ounce, a prospector had to get four ounces of gold out of a ton of ore to be successful," he recalled. Likewise in "oppo," where to get a few killer quotes you have to wade through thousands.

The search for an opponent's skeletons is a long tradition. When research is done right, it isn't defense; it's solid offense. After all, who can remember everyone they slept with and everything they did, said, smoked, or profited from during their career? Revelations are characterized by an element of surprise, too, which Atwater loved. Nothing like a few sticky details and the public glare of full disclosure years after the fact to throw an opponent off course. "The only group that I was very interested in having report to me directly was opposition research," said Lee.

Todd sent six young ops up to Massachusetts in a motor home. They went through twenty-five years of the daily *Boston Herald* and the weekly *Phoenix* by hand, then on to twenty-five years of the *Boston Globe* (indexed, thank God), thereby culling some 135,000 quotes in a two-week blitz. Their search led to the Brookline city council minutes for 1949, where they found a letter written by Dukakis and several Swarthmore classmates protesting the Korean War. They discovered that Kitty Dukakis had served as president of her high school girls' club; in her yearbook she had written a statement on the club's efforts to stop male oppression. Though this information was never used, it gave Lee a portrait of the opponent as a liberal from way back.

Back in South Carolina, Republicans won elections when an opponent was identified as a liberal. By the late '70s liberalism had driven the country toward a form of socialism that had resulted in what some were labeling a new welfare nation, and conservatives were arguing convincingly that the government was now in the welfare business. Ronald Reagan's candidacy was just conservative enough to draw ambivalent Democrats into the ranks of the "swing vote," and to change the political landscape of the '80s, where Atwater was on patrol. Lee liked the basic insecurity that was the underpinning of most liberal thinking. What was it that Justice William O. Douglas had once remarked? That liberalism is the spirit that is not too sure it's right. And if ever there was a candidate who exuded uncertainty, it was the Duke of Massachusetts. In the Dukakis campaign, the point was to know yourself. In the Atwater camp, the key was to know your enemy.

Lee asked Pinkerton to look for examples of Dukakis liberalism. He wanted to pin Dukakis to his liberal roots and deny him upward political mobility. Of course, Lee wanted only the "best" issues — that is, the most damaging ones — on one three-by-five-inch card. So many issues. So little time.

Pinkerton and Todd wanted to relate Dukakis's state actions to federal issues. With the governor in office, his current files were off-limits. But Dukakis had had a break in service, after he lost to Ed King in 1978, and all of the records for his first term had been sent to the state archives — correspondence, interoffice mail, you name it. So the oppo squad dug deeply into the past, assembling a 312-page textbook called *The Hazards of Duke*. This outline of the key issues in the campaign ahead was distributed to reporters, county chairmen, and other onlookers. Ads and speeches all were based on this core material. In *Hazards*, there were chapters on the five key issues of the campaign, from the Pledge of Allegiance on down. The prison-furlough issue came late and wasn't given much weight as a victims' rights concern at first, but it was all there in the textbook. Atwater's game plan was, literally, an open book.

The only thing Lee was missing was an anecdote that would put storytelling power behind his portrait of Dukakis as liberalism run amok. He needed something like the obscure but damaging "third senator from New York" moniker that Lee had stuck to Pug Ravenel back in South Carolina. As Dayton Duncan put it, "examinations of character often rely on the 'telling anecdote' — the vignette or story that illuminates a larger point and, in a vivid shorthand, explains more than the vignette itself."

• • •

On the Sunday evening of December 6, 1987, writer Robert James Bidinotto was attending a retirement dinner in Irvington, New York, for Paul Poirot, editor of *The Freeman*. Among the fifty guests was Howard Dickman, an editor at *Reader's Digest*, where Bidinotto had recently published an article about a one-man radio station in Massachusetts. Bidinotto and Dickman fell into conversation about another Massachusetts piece Bidinotto was working on, this one about how the state's prison-furlough system was stirring up a citizens' revolt.

It had all begun the night of October 26, 1974, in Lawrence, Massachusetts, when William R. Horton Jr. stabbed Joseph Fournier to death during a gas-station robbery that netted $276.37. Horton stabbed the seventeen-year-old attendant nineteen times with a knife at least six inches long, then stuffed the crumpled body in a garbage can. It was a grisly crime scene, with blood all over the floor. After serving ten years for first-degree murder, Horton skipped out while on a weekend pass from state prison in Concord. On April 3, 1987, he broke into the Maryland home of Clifford Barnes and his fiancée Angela Miller. He pistol-whipped Barnes, cut him twenty-two times across his midsection, then raped Miller twice as Barnes, bound and gagged, listened in helpless horror to her screams. Horton terrorized the couple for twelve hours before Barnes broke free and called the police. After a chase and shoot-out, Horton was captured and charged with eighteen crimes, including rape and kidnapping.

As Lawrence legislators launched a probe into why Horton had been released on an unsupervised furlough, four women from

the area, including Joseph Fournier's sister Donna, began to collect signatures to ban furloughs for first-degree murderers. This
furlough program had been enacted under Republican governor
Francis W. Sargent as part of the Penal Reform Act of 1972. Nevertheless, Governor Michael Dukakis was its steadfast and loyal supporter. In 1976, during his first term as governor, Dukakis had
vetoed a bill that would have modified the program by banning
furloughs for first-degree murderers — like William R. Horton Jr.
That veto had set the stage for the evening that would shatter the
lives of Angela Miller and Clifford Barnes.

The controversy heightened when the Dukakis administration, citing confidentiality laws, refused to release Horton's records or explain why the inmate had been furloughed. On October
20, 1987, Maryland Judge Vincent Femia sentenced Horton to
two consecutive life terms plus eighty years, adding that Horton
would never be returned to Massachusetts. "I'm not prepared to
take the chance that Mr. Horton might again be furloughed or
otherwise released," he said. Meanwhile, Miller and Barnes were
threatening to sue Massachusetts for having released Horton, and
the success of the signature drive was calling into question the
judgment of Governor Michael Dukakis.

Dickman listened to Bidinotto with guarded interest that
night at the retirement dinner. "We do a lot of victims' rights
stories," he told the writer. "Maybe we can do a reprint when
your story runs." A week later, Dickman was reading a draft of
Bidinotto's story. The magazine that had commissioned the piece
had folded. Dickman asked Bidinotto for a revised outline, something with more edge to it. By now the signature drive had become a crusade, and the Lawrence *Eagle-Tribune* was coming
down hard on Dukakis. On January 10, 1988, Bidinotto pitched a
hard-hitting version of the story to the *Digest*. Editor in chief Ken
Gilmore liked the idea of a small newspaper taking on the state
bureaucracy, so three days later Bidinotto was on assignment. He
spent two days at the *Eagle-Tribune* office photocopying nearly
two hundred stories and interviewing the staff. For newspaper editor Dan Warner, the stories weren't part of a series; they weren't
a vendetta; the paper was just providing steady coverage of an
ongoing local news event that Dukakis was trying to ignore. "He
just thought it was a bunch of housewives who would go away,"
recalled Warner.

"Who are the good guys and the bad guys in this story?" Bidinotto asked Warner one day.

"The real bad guy in this is Dukakis," replied the editor.

In February 1988, responding to public pressure, Dukakis began to distance himself from the program, acknowledging that it "worked effectively until a fella named Horton came along." On March 17, meeting in secret session, the Governor's Anti-Crime Council told Dukakis the legislature would overrule him on the furlough issue. Five days later, on March 22, Dukakis announced that he would no longer oppose a ban on furloughs for killers.

By backing off, Dukakis avoided certain defeat on the issue in Massachusetts. The question now was whether the controversy would come back to haunt him in the fall. "There's no doubt that this will be part of the debate in the general election campaign if Michael Dukakis is the nominee," Andy Card told an *Eagle-Tribune* reporter after the Dukakis flip-flop. "I don't know why the Democrats haven't used it. People care about crime."

"If someone really wanted to do it," said Merrimack College political science professor Eugene DeClercq the day after Dukakis's turnabout, "they could make a devastating ad using Horton."

On March 30, Robert James Bidinotto sent the first draft of "Getting Away with Murder" to the *Digest*. On March 31, the *Eagle-Tribune* received a Pulitzer Prize for its articles on the furlough program.

The next month, Bidinotto and the magazine's editors huddled with fact checkers and went through the article line by line. By now the villain in the piece was the Democratic Party's leading candidate for president of the United States. Dukakis had refused an interview before, but Gilmore sent another request by registered letter. The answer was still no. Horton's picture, which had appeared sporadically in the *Eagle-Tribune* coverage, did not appear in the *Digest* — but Dukakis's did. In his article Bidinotto described an encounter between the governor and several furlough opponents at a police station in Andover. Mary Gravel told Dukakis about her own daughter's unsolved murder. "What if Claire's killer is caught and convicted, then furloughed?" she asked. "What do you think it would do to my family if they were walking down the street and saw this person?"

"I'd probably feel the same way you do," said Dukakis. "But, unfortunately, it's not going to change my mind."

The hazards of Duke were mostly self-inflicted.

• • •

As Dukakis began to pull away from the pack in the New York primary, Al Gore started to worry. Gore had not won a state outside the South, and if he failed to win 20 percent of the vote in New York, he would lose his federal matching funds. And crime was a major state issue. What to do? Attack.

On Wednesday, April 12, during a Democratic candidates' debate sponsored by the *New York Daily News*, Gore called Dukakis "the principal advocate and defender" of weekend passes for first-degree murderers. "Eleven of them decided their . . . passes were not long enough and left," said Gore, drawing a laugh from the crowd. "Two of them committed other murders while they were on their passes. If you were elected president, would you advocate a similar program for federal penitentiaries?"

"The difference between you and me is that I have to run a criminal justice system, and you never have," Dukakis fired back. "I'm very proud of my record in fighting crime."

James Pinkerton wondered what Gore was so angry about. He pored over the Lexis-Nexis transcript of the debate, then phoned Andy Card in Boston. Card faxed him nearly one hundred stories from the *Eagle-Tribune*. Pinkerton read the stories, then drafted his index card for Atwater, jamming it, front and back, with state tax increases, state spending stats, Duke's support of a nuclear freeze, the veto of a bill that would require schoolteachers to lead students in the Pledge of Allegiance — and the prison-furlough controversy. "The great thing about the issue was that any way you spin it, Dukakis loses," said Pinkerton. "It was a tar baby."

• • •

Early that spring Pug Ravenel met with Dukakis in Boston, along with a handful of other Democratic operatives brought in as a national brain trust. Dukakis recalled Ravenel from their Harvard years together, before Pug went on to be beaten by Atwater-managed opponents in two South Carolina campaigns. Pug told the candidate that during his own campaign his big mistake had been not responding fast enough to Atwater. He also cautioned Dukakis to get ready for the negatives. Pug suggested a fast-response mechanism of some sort in research, "because they're gonna try to tear you a new one."

"I've been in negative campaigns before," said Dukakis, recalling his primary battles with the feisty conservative Democrat Ed King.

"Whoever ran that campaign was no Atwater," Ravenel replied. "Atwater is the Babe Ruth of negative politics."

To emphasize his concern, Ravenel sent a letter to the Dukakis staff in May. "My very strong belief is that Lee Atwater is the premier negative strategist in American politics," he wrote. "I have the deep suspicion that Atwater will begin hitting at Dukakis very early, perhaps even before the convention. . . . If Mike does not respond right away, he could risk having the negatives well set in the minds of Americans before he could begin to change them. The Bush campaign has all the money in the world and can afford to do this on a massive scale and do it early. If you are weeks or even a month behind in terms of preparing countering ads and buying time, it may be too late. It would be fighting an uphill battle for the rest of the campaign. I strongly urge that a full-scale defensive effort be made ready right away."

Atwater's suspicion that the Dukakis campaign lacked the intensity for responding to a negative campaign was on target. Dukakis recalled, "I think we were just feeling good about the primary, about the very positive tone of it, and we thought that the country had been badly polarized under Reagan for eight years. I felt that keeping it positive was (a) the way we wanted to do it, and (b) the way that we *should* do it — not in just an ethical sense, but because that was what people were looking for."

In early May, the July issue of *Reader's Digest* went to press. "In Massachusetts, convicted killers roamed the streets on weekend passes," blared the world's leading magazine for the masses. "Then a crusading newspaper and outraged citizens took action." Bidinotto's story "Getting Away with Murder" would become the most influential piece of journalism in the campaign.

● ● ●

Nicholas Brady, Craig Fuller, Robert Teeter, Roger Ailes, and Lee Atwater — the entire Bush command — had shown up to watch focus groups through a one-way mirror in a black-windowed office building near a shopping strip in Paramus, New Jersey. Two groups of fifteen "target" voters — all Democrats who had voted for Reagan in 1984 and were now inclined to vote for Dukakis — responded to leading questions from the moderator: What if Dukakis opposed capital punishment for murderers? What if he had vetoed legislation requiring teachers to lead school-children in reciting the Pledge of Allegiance? What if he had per-mitted murderers to have weekend passes from prison? Quickly, the groups turned on Dukakis. Majorities favoring him became majorities opposing him. Positive attributes were forgotten. He was a liberal, he was red meat, he was a goner.

Atwater was ecstatic. If they could turn around voters in New Jersey, think what they could accomplish in more conservative parts of the country! He realized that he had the issues he needed to drive Dukakis's negatives upward. But could he drive George Bush toward a negative campaign?

By Memorial Day, a Gallup poll showed Dukakis leading Bush by 16 points, 54 to 38 percent. More ominously, Bush's nega-tive rating was beyond Atwater's definition of terminal status. More than 40 percent of the voters held an unfavorable opinion of Bush — the highest negative rating ever recorded for a presi-dential candidate before a fall campaign. (To put this in context, other candidates whose early negatives presaged a November de-feat included Barry Goldwater with 36 percent in 1964, George McGovern with 27 percent in 1972, Jimmy Carter with 28 percent in 1980, and Walter Mondale with 29 percent in 1984.) Bush's favorable rating was 53 percent; Dukakis was viewed positively by 70 percent of likely voters. Worse, Bush was still plunging in the polls, while Dukakis was on the rise.

The next day at George Bush's family home in Kenne-bunkport, Maine, Atwater and Teeter gave Bush videotapes of the Paramus focus group so he could see the transformation in voters for himself. At Yale few things were admired more than that old-fashioned virtue, sportsmanship. Ferocity did not come easily to George Bush. Atwater argued that Dukakis's lead in the polls would be roughly 15 points going into the Democratic National Convention in mid-July, and that the lovefest and Republican-bashing in Atlanta would bounce him 10 points higher. In order to offset this, Bush could attack at once, hoping to knock Dukakis's lead below 10 points by the end of June. In that case Dukakis's lead shouldn't surpass 20 points after the Democratic convention, a dangerous but not impossibly high margin. Dukakis might still be ahead, but he wouldn't have the initiative. With the Republican convention still to come, the momentum would then go to Bush. What did the veep want to do?

Attack.

• • •

We are all replaceable. In politics the switch happens often, and somehow the republic survives. From the moment George Bush seriously dreamed of running for president, long before he talked to Lee Atwater, it was ordained that Jim Baker would run the general election campaign. Baker would return from the Treasury Department to the playing field sometime during that summer of political sport.

The problem was that Bush had never really explained things. He just had this notion that everyone would understand that Jimmy was going to come in and run the show. To make matters worse, Baker toyed with the press, feeding them stories that he would never go back, it was demeaning, he loved his role at Treasury. All pure ego, pure stroke. But those stories meant that when Bush pulled Baker back onto the campaign field, the press would have to come up with a rationale — a reason for this action, something that was counter to their previous reporting. The spin was going to be that Atwater couldn't handle the job.

On Sunday afternoon, June 5, Lee arrived in Los Angeles at 1:20 and checked in at the Four Seasons Hotel. He told reporters that he wanted to do some fieldwork, get back in touch with the swing vote, walk along the beaches and byways of Orange County. Mostly, he wanted to get out of the pressure cooker and talk with Stu Spencer about Bush's plan to make Baker campaign chairman. The move surprised none of the Bush brain trust, but Lee — master of surprise — was shook. He refused to be layered. He worried that Baker would oversee a very punctual, orderly, on- or under-budget state funeral. Insiders knew that Baker was a timid politician, someone who didn't want to make people mad. Super careful. When the '76 Ford campaign came up just a point short at the finish line, Baker had almost $2 million left over — he didn't

spend it! — to be sure all the bills would be paid. One thing that
Atwater and Spencer agreed on was that first you go all out to win
elections, and *then* you worry about paying your bills. Once you
have elected the leader of the free world, you can pay your bills
pretty easily.

Lee wanted to vent his anger and establish his indispensabil-
ity with Spencer. Stu knew Baker better than most; he'd brought
Jimmy into the Ford campaign and taught him politics. He also
knew how badly Baker needed Lee. Hell, Atwater had been in
forty campaigns, emerging victorious in all but a handful. Baker
had been in just a handful, winning but one — the '84 reelection,
and anyone could have put up Ronald Reagan, said it's morning
again in America, and gotten 59 percent of the vote.

Lee and Spencer walked from the hotel to a small park a
few blocks away, where they sat on a bench. "I'm gonna resign,"
said Lee. He felt he didn't deserve this kind of treatment. He had
delivered the nomination for Bush — and now this?

Spencer tried to turn him around. They talked for more than
an hour. "You're looking at it the wrong way," Stu said. "Hey, you're
not going to get hurt by this. . . . It's gonna be a plus. Baker knows
what your strengths are, he knows what your assets are, and he'll
leave you alone if you do your job right as political director. It's a
great opportunity for you, if you do it right."

Spencer was one of Lee's gods, and the soothing words meant
a lot. Lee had been unhappy before, when he was forced to hire
Bond. But, ever the pragmatist, he'd done what he had to do. Hell,
he'd been on this job for over three years; he didn't want to quit
now. A few more months and it would be over. Two days later, as
Lee took the red-eye back to D.C., Spencer gave Baker a heads-up
on Lee's delicate condition.

Shortly afterward Lee went over to Treasury and spoke with
Tutwiler. "All I ask is just make sure that I have my dignity," he
said.

In a short meeting, Baker said, "Don't worry about it." Now
Lee was *really* worried.

•   •   •

On June 10 *Reader's Digest* shipped copies of the July issue to
West Coast subscribers. Radio talk shows picked up on the prison-
furlough issue immediately, and word doubled back eastward on

the airwaves, just in time for the June 25 arrival of newsstand copies across the rest of the nation. Pinkerton received a bagful of mail forwarded from the White House — letters from *Reader's Digest* Republicans with the Bidinotto story attached, saying "Use this against Dukakis."

Bush already was. The furlough program featured prominently in Bush's first pointed attack on Dukakis on June 9 in Houston before the Texas Republican Convention. The following week, in a speech to the Illinois Republican Convention in Springfield, Bush said voters should ask Dukakis why he let "murderers out on vacations." On June 22, in Louisville, Bush mentioned Horton by name for the first time in a speech to the National Sheriffs Association, explaining how the convict had escaped while on furlough and attacked a couple in Maryland. Clint Eastwood's answer to crime was "Go ahead, make my day," Bush said. "My opponent's answer is slightly different: 'Go ahead: Have a nice weekend.' "

For the July Fourth weekend, Sally, Lee, and the girls drove to the Luray Caverns in Virginia, about a hundred miles from D.C. The caverns are enormous, and a church organ hooked to the stalagmites provided a musical light show that Lee loved. The family checked into the Ramada Inn on Route 211, three miles west of the caverns, then went for dinner at Brown's Chinese & American Food in Luray. There Lee heard some middle-aged motorcyclists in the next booth talking about the *Reader's Digest* article they had just read. "My god, they're talking about Willie Horton!" he told Sally. He joined the conversation, sensing the bikers' political fury. This was what it must have been like for the petition signers in Massachusetts. This wasn't an issue, thought Lee. It was a crusade.

Everyone knew that Willie Horton was black, and everyone had to be disciplined: the issue was crime, not color. May the two never intersect in Bush ads or admonitions. The problem was Lee's delight in using the Horton episode to drive up Dukakis's negatives: his preacherlike enthusiasm smacked of lynch-mob tactics to some onlookers. But to others on the inside, it was just pure Lee. Hey, the shortest way around something is right through the middle.

On July 9, two weeks before the Democratic convention, Lee met with southern Republicans in Atlanta to pump them up for the campaign. With Dukakis moving up in the polls, Lee wanted to drag him down in front of a home crowd. "I can't wait until this Dukakis fellow gets down here," he said with glee. "There are quite a few questions he ought to have to answer every day he's down here, and every time he gives the answer, there's going to be votes coming up just like in a cash register. Can you imagine him trying to answer how in the world as governor, a responsible position like governor, he was in favor of this furlough program that allowed first-degree murderers and drug pushers to go on weekend vacations where they could murder, sell drugs, and do all the rest of this stuff?"

Lee took a shot at Dukakis's labyrinthine procedure for selecting a running mate. "There is a story about a fellow named Willie Horton who for all I know may end up to be Dukakis's running mate. Dukakis is making Hamlet look like the rock of Gibraltar in the way he's acted on this. The guy was on TV about a month ago, and he said you'll never see me standing in the driveway of my house talking to these candidates [referring to how Walter Mondale had interviewed vice-presidential candidates at his Minnesota home in 1984], and guess what? On Monday I saw in the driveway of his house: Jesse Jackson. So anyway, maybe he'll put this Willie Horton guy on the ticket after all is said and done. And Willie Horton is the fellow who was a convicted murderer and rapist who got let out on eight of these weekend furloughs, and on the ninth one he brutally and wantonly raped this woman. . . . And do you know what the response was from the Dukakis crowd? 'Well, he didn't do anything on the other eight.' "

At the Democratic convention, Michael Dukakis won over his audience by choking up about his late immigrant father, through evidence of his thrift (his actress-cousin Olympia Dukakis reminded the crowd of the candidate's trusty twenty-five-year-old snowplow), and the onstage embrace of his family. "The entire evening focused attention on the idea that this otherwise quintessential technocrat didn't borrow symbols, he embodied them," observed U.S. News and World Report.

It's hard to be mean if we think about it beforehand and reflect on it afterward. Lee didn't do enough of either. The morning after Dukakis's Atlanta acceptance speech, Lee decided to establish a tone for the campaign ahead. "I'm going to scrape the bark off that little bastard," he declared at a meeting of top Bush staffers.

Atwater used the prison-furlough issue to create the perception that Dukakis was one of those fuzzy-headed liberals who is sympathetic toward criminals. When coupled with his opposition to capital punishment, Dukakis's furlough for Willie Horton would prove to be most damaging indeed. The governor said it was a bad rap. Actually, violent crime had dropped 13 percent in Massachusetts during his administration, drug convictions were up fivefold, and the homicide rate was the lowest among the major industrial states. When he saw that the furlough-program issue was slicing him apart, Dukakis said, "You're looking at the guy who repealed it." But it was a half-truth, and he knew it. The issue continued to erode his campaign.

• • •

It was time for the Republicans to start advertising. Lee had recruited Sig Rogich, a Paul Laxalt campaign manager who ran the largest marketing firm in Nevada, as director of advertising for '88. Sig, seven years older than Lee, knew every episode of the *Andy Griffith Show* — an Atwater favorite, and the subject of numerous Trivial Pursuit challenges between Lee and Ed Rogers. Sig and Lee had bonded in 1984 when Sig went to Lee with an idea: "Why don't we get Ray Charles to sing 'America the Beautiful' at the convention?"

"I love it!" said Lee. It cost the GOP $25,000 to get Ray Charles and the Raylettes singing in harmony that summer, but it sent the proper message: No racists here, thank you.

Ailes was the Bush campaign's senior media advisor, overseeing ad buying and the whole media operation, but Rogich was responsible for coming up with ideas, hiring the creative teams, and producing the ads. Sig came into Lee's office with a guitar one day and started strumming "I Remember You" with customized Republican lyrics. "I love it!" said Lee. Another defining event.

Rogich's commercial premiered on July 22. With the song "I Remember You" striking a friendly, nostalgic tone at the outset, it suddenly turned grim: "You're the one who made me feel so blue. . . . It's true. . . . It's you." Then came the images: Jimmy Carter on TV, long lines at gas stations, smiling Arabs meeting to raise oil prices, collages of newsclips showing unemployment up, high interest rates, and long lines of worried-looking citizens. Then the voice-over intoned: "You're seeing what America was like just seven years ago. The Republicans have worked very hard to make sure you'll never have to see it again." Another burst of song so that viewers knew where to direct their anger: "Tell them you remember. . . . Tell them you remember, tooooo." Closeout onscreen: The Republicans.

The ad ran unanswered as a generic RNC message for the four weeks between the conventions. The party spent some $5 million, a huge expenditure to establish a buffer zone that neutralized some of the shrillness from the Democratic convention, with all its Bush-baiting. Meantime, Lee was settling in for a long summer's attack. This was the emergence of a new type of campaign, dominated by fast-moving events and overnight poll results. It was a campaign that called for a master tactician — someone who could assess the opportunities of the day and act on them. "Lee was born to take Dukakis on," said Bill Carrick, a Democratic operative who had battled Atwater in South Carolina. "Dukakis was too good to be true."

Atwater told Ron Kaufman his job was to get under Dukakis's skin, doing damage with random acts of senseless politics. (Suntzu: "All we need to do is throw something odd and unaccountable at the enemy.") Kaufman probably overachieved. He put a volunteer in front of Dukakis's Brookline home each morning with a BUSH/QUAYLE sign. He arranged to have Boston Police endorse Bush and pose for a photo in Dukakis's political backyard. He put Bush in a boat for a ride in the polluted waters of Boston Harbor, with the press clicking away. He rented the only billboard in the whole campaign behind the state capitol in Boston, knowing that every day as Dukakis went to work he had to see BUSH/QUAYLE in forty-foot letters. He arranged for pickets at the statehouse and at Dukakis's home whenever a special-interest group was disgruntled with the governor. He hired college kids to line up with BUSH/QUAYLE signs in front of the Callahan Tunnel to Logan Airport whenever Dukakis had to fly out.

Once, when Dukakis was scheduled to give a speech on education at Bates College, the governor flew into Lewiston, Maine. The press was to travel by plane to Portland, then by bus to Lewiston. As the press corps got on the bus in Portland, a member of the Young Republicans gave each member an L.L. Bean canvas bag with reading material for the trip — an educator's report card for Dukakis (Honesty: F; Conduct: F, etc.) as well as a book by Dave Cowans, former Boston Celtic and current environmentalist, trashing Dukakis for lying — extracts kindly highlighted. After the press conference in Lewiston, the bus took reporters back to L.L. Bean for shopping, then on to Boston. The Dukakis press plane returned nearly empty. A wayward press, indeed.

Atwater's old unit, the College Republican National Committee, distributed small yellow cards that depicted a man flying from an open cage like the drawing on a Monopoly game card, with bold text: "GET OUT OF JAIL, FREE. Compliments of Michael Dukakis." On the back, the card said: "Michael Dukakis's furlough plan allowed convicted murderers to take a weekend leave from prison. One, Willie Horton, left and never came back. He viciously raped and beat a woman while her fiancé was forced to helplessly listen to her screams. This is only one example of many. In the last several years, Mike Dukakis has furloughed more than one murderer per day. Mike Dukakis is the killer's best friend, and the decent, honest citizens' worst enemy."

At three o'clock one morning in late July, the phone rang in the Michigan hotel room of Duncan Dayton. At his editor's insistence, a reporter from a large West Coast paper wanted to know if it was true that another large paper was about to publish a story about a rumor that Dukakis had once secretly undergone psychiatric treatment for clinical depression after the death of his younger brother in a car accident. Duncan was disgusted. It had come to this — a reporter calling about a rumor about a story based on a rumor.

Who started that rumor? Atwater insisted that he told aides that anyone who trafficked in rumors would be fired. But John Sununu had publicly warned reporters to check into Dukakis's mental health. After all, the Massachusetts governor had not released his full medical records. When a representative of third-party candidate Lyndon H. LaRouche asked Ronald Reagan during a televised news conference if he thought Dukakis was "fit to govern," the president replied: "Look, I'm not going to pick on an invalid." Though Reagan later said he intended the remark as a "joke," his comment lent credence to the rumors. The whole affair had a disassembling effect on the Dukakis camp. A precious week of campaign time was consumed as newspapers published stories about the rumors being unsubstantiated, and Dukakis was forced to deny something that no one had even charged. In a matter of

days, he dropped 8 points in the polls. "I sincerely believe, knowing Atwater, that he did this to Dukakis," said Tom Turnipseed.
The episode bore a striking resemblance to the "jumper cable"
incident. "He's a master at doing things to purposely shake the
confidence of the other side."

"This episode angered Dukakis, and a number of us on his
staff, more than anything else during the campaign," said Dayton Duncan. Did Dukakis hit back hard? Critics said that Mike
Dukakis would rather make policy than make war. "His only re-
venge was to invite the press corps to accompany him on an early-
morning 'power walk' in Denver," added Duncan. "If they were
interested in health, he figured, at least let them work up a *legitimate* sweat about it." A handful of reporters rented a limousine to
follow the power striders.

● ● ●

On August 6 James A. Baker III resigned from Treasury to join
the Republican campaign. With one of his peers in charge of the
troops — Baker was twenty years older than Lee — Bush felt comfortable. Baker's first concern was to keep Lee out there working hard, to make certain that his presence was perceived as
creating a move over, not downward, for the campaign manager.
Wisely, Baker left Lee's corner office untouched and moved into
Rich Bond's office across from Lee, thus nudging the deputy director into another office down the hall. Lee liked that. What counts
is not only who you are, but *where* you are. A campaign is, after
all, just another bureaucracy on wheels.

Baker calmed Lee down and made it clear that he had no
intention of humiliating him in public. This was just the way
George wanted to do things, and, of course, Lee understood that
he would never sitteth at the right hand of Bush as long as Baker
was around. And if Lee ever forgot this, Baker had the press around
to remind him. Baker had constructed his career as a plenipoten-
tiary source who gave quotes to political reporters; they paid him
back the favor by making Baker seem more important than he
was. This time, no matter what happened, Baker couldn't lose.
If Bush's polls went up, Baker did it. If not, well, Baker got there
too late.

Baker and Atwater turned out to be perfect for each other.
They were like Bradley and Patton in World War II. General

George S. Patton, commander of the Third Army, was charming and inspiring, but his emotionalism was so extreme that he was also considered dangerous. Patton was the likely choice to lead U.S. ground forces into Normandy — until he slapped a soldier around. Then Omar Bradley replaced him. Without Bradley over him, Patton would not have been the success he was perceived as being. Likewise, given the rawness of the campaign, it was more appropriate that Atwater devote his complete enthusiasm to working in the trenches rather than in the command bunker.

For Lee, Baker's great skill was organizing decisions. He was a master political facilitator. Lee didn't have enough clout to override the Bush inner circle, and he understood that he couldn't push for that kind of clout, either. He didn't have what he called "the right cologne." (Appropriately enough, Lee's favorite cologne was Obsession.) But Baker was a southerner he could talk to, and Lee knew Baker could get those six guys heading together in the same direction. "It's going to be good for me," he told his old pal Mike Ussery. "I *need* this. There's been too much pressure on my shoulders, and I don't have the clout with George Bush to always sit around and beat back the Nick Bradys. If Brady and others take a different point of view than I do, heck, it comes down to a vote on what to do." When Baker came, the appeal process ended. Bush didn't have to get involved in making decisions anymore. Now Lee could cut through the committeelike deliberations and get on with the campaign, hardball style.

Of course, his old boss Ed Rollins didn't help. Lee was in a rage when Rollins told the press, as the Republican convention drew near, that the campaign needed "adult supervision." Then, when Baker arrived on the scene in August, Rollins was there with another stinging sound bite: "Lee Atwater will never be on television again."

• • •

Although George Bush had been in national office for eight years, Atwater put Dukakis on the defensive, casting him in the role of the incumbent candidate with a record to defend. Throughout the summer, the GOP leveled charges at Dukakis, ranging from being in favor of nuclear disarmament to preventing schoolchildren from reciting the Pledge of Allegiance, from wanting to confiscate hunting rifles while furloughing murderers and rapists to supporting grain embargoes against farmers while opposing military strikes against terrorists. Atwater was dismayed when Dukakis resisted making forceful responses. How would Dukakis get any press that way? And the response, when made, rarely caught up to the original charge.

Lee was running such a relentlessly negative campaign that Dukakis thought it would backfire. Having already campaigned in a score of states during the primaries and having addressed the nation in his convention speech, Dukakis thought that people knew him well enough that they would discount the charges. He didn't believe the negativity would sink in. He called Mario Cuomo, whom he considered politically smarter. Cuomo said, "Hey, don't pay any attention to that stuff. Just let it go."

"After the campaign was over," Dukakis reflected, "I realized that was the worst advice he had ever given me."

For the majority of Americans, Dukakis was still an unknown quantity — and Atwater was defining him as a candidate who refused to defend himself. In the end many voters considered that trait worse for a would-be president than being willing to wage a nasty campaign. Atwater's campaign also had a devastating effect on Dukakis and his staff. They were immobilized by it. Atwater just kept coming at Dukakis (whose name Lee intentionally mispronounced as Du-*kay*-kis) with one charge after another, setting the agenda, the tone of the campaign. Dukakis was busy promising "good jobs at good wages," and by September reporters had been there, done that. Sure, columnists wanted to inform as well as to report, but there was very little time to do in-depth reporting, and in the harried world of deadlines and crunch competition, no one wanted to be scooped. Atwater knew that the press wanted "news" — something new, something that hadn't been said before, something that represented a change in the campaign. When there wasn't a story about the candidate, there was one about the campaign strategy. Press manipulation means creating pseudo-events that become pseudo-news.

Lee used isolated facts out of context to create a negative view of Massachusetts and its governor, painting Dukakis as the elitist in the race: the creature of Harvard and the ACLU, too "sophisticated" to say the Pledge of Allegiance or to kneel in prayer. Dukakis had vetoed a bill passed by the Massachusetts state legislature requiring teachers to lead students in the

Pledge of Allegiance in 1977, but the Bush campaign treated the event as though it were recent. Bush stuck to Atwater's script, making the Pledge of Allegiance the centerpiece of his campaign. He recited the Pledge constantly, attended the "First Annual Flag Festival" in Findlay, Ohio, toured a flag factory in New Jersey.

Bush also worked on another Atwater theme — that Dukakis had proudly claimed to be a "card-carrying member of the ACLU," and that meant he was an ultraliberal and out of the mainstream of American values. A master at what he called "strategic misrepresentation," Atwater used an obscure publication as the source of an inflammatory quote. Bush and Quayle both gave speeches claiming that Dukakis had once said, "I don't believe in people owning guns, only the police and the military." Dukakis said that the quote was a fabrication. It turned out that the quote came from a gun-lobby leader who had met with Dukakis once in Boston, and who was being quoted in *Gun Week* magazine. Late August polls showed Dukakis and Bush running even. Finally, the real guns came out.

On Labor Day in California Bush cried, "No more furloughs for people to rape, pillage, and plunder in the United States!" The next week, the National Security Political Action Committee, founded by Elizabeth Fediay and doing political business as Americans for Bush, announced that it would launch commercials focusing on the furlough issue. NSPAC's two ads were created by Larry McCarthy, an alumnus of the Ailes office now working on his own. One of the spots, "Weekend Passes," featured visuals of Bush and Dukakis side by side. "Bush supports the death penalty for first-degree murderers," said the narrator. "Dukakis not only opposes the death penalty; he allowed first-degree murderers to have weekend passes from prison." Then the visuals shifted to photographs of Willie Horton, with the explanation: "One was Willie Horton, who murdered a boy in a robbery, stabbing him fourteen times. Despite a life sentence, Horton received ten weekend passes from prison. Horton fled, kidnapping a young couple, stabbing the man and repeatedly raping his girlfriend." Then to a closing close-up of Dukakis. "Weekend prison passes," concluded the narrator. "Dukakis on crime."

NSPAC's "Weekend Passes" ads ran only on cable TV and only for fourteen days. But the national media picked it up as a news item and showed snippets of the ad over and over as an example of how negative the campaign had become.

The Bush campaign's own ad blitz had begun on September 9. As a candidate for governor, Dukakis had called Boston Harbor an open sewer. That observation led Rogich and his film crew to shoot the harbor one drizzly morning. The spot entitled "The Harbor" rubbed Dukakis's nose in images of environmental damage and despair in his own home port. Theoretically the environment issue was Democratic territory, but Lee viewed it as a boomer issue — open territory. The ad also worked in states that did not have strong environmental concerns because its message went beyond Boston Harbor; it said that Dukakis was a fraud. "As governor, he had the opportunity to do something about it," the narrator said. "He chose not to. The Environmental Protection Agency called his lack of action the most expensive public policy mistake in the history of New England. Now Boston Harbor, the dirtiest harbor in America, will cost residents $6 billion to clean. And Michael Dukakis promises to do for America what he's done for Massachusetts." The ad ended with the sound of gurgling water, which may have been the sound of the Dukakis campaign drowning.

Three days later another Bush campaign ad hit, called "A Crime Quiz." The crime quiz consisted of three questions — Which candidate gave weekend passes to first-degree murderers not eligible for parole? Vetoed mandatory jail sentences for drug dealers? Even vetoed the death penalty for cop killers? The answer was a close-up of Dukakis, looking like he was taking the fifth. Fourth and final question: Which candidate for president can you really count on to be tough on crime? Close-up of Bush, looking quite presidential.

The first time Sig Rogich heard the name Willie Horton, he thought Atwater was talking about the '60s outfielder for the Detroit Tigers. They had agreed immediately to leave Horton out of their ads — instead, hit the idiocy of the furlough program. At the Old Ebbett Grill, Rogich brainstormed with Dennis Frankenberry. A "revolving-door policy," someone said, and they had their image.

The next day they read through a script and got approval from Lee and Baker. Rogich flew to Provo, Utah, where he rented prisoner uniforms and recruited students at Brigham Young

University to be models. Rogich shot the ad in both color and black-and-white, with ominous images of a prison tower, a guard carrying a rifle, then a stream of convicts moving through a rapidly revolving door, with a brooding narration that paralleled that of "The Harbor": "As governor, Michael Dukakis vetoed mandatory sentences for drug dealers. He vetoed the death penalty. His revolving-door prison policy gave weekend furloughs to first-degree murderers not eligible for parole. While out, many committed other crimes like kidnapping and rape. And many are still at large. Now Michael Dukakis says he wants to do for America what he's done for Massachusetts. America can't afford that risk." From idea to ad in seventy-two hours. Of the nineteen "convicts" visible on camera in Rogich's final edited version, two were black, one Hispanic, sixteen white. Everyone felt politically quite correct when "Revolving Door" was released in living black-and-white on September 26.

John Sasso had returned to oversee the Dukakis campaign in September, but it was too late. On September 13, Dukakis decided to reply to Bush, who had been banging away at him on defense. He visited a General Dynamics facility in Michigan and went for a spin in an M-1 tank. The helmet was too large. The grin on his face was sickly. "Dukakis looked like he wanted to call for his mother," said Sam Donaldson as the cameras whirred.

By October Bush was leading in the polls, gaining momentum against a candidate who didn't know how to fight, never mind how to fight *back*. On October 6 in Fort Worth, Bush began a new offensive with Willie Horton as the centerpiece. "Previously Bush had implied that the case demonstrated bad judgment on Dukakis's part," said David Hoffman, political reporter for the *Washington Post*. "Now he said it was a sign of bad personality." He charged that Dukakis presided over a criminal justice system that was "completely out of whack." According to Bush, Dukakis had expressed "unrelenting opposition" to changes in the furlough program; thus he was crowned the "Furlough King."

In a speech to police officers in Xenia, Ohio, the next day Bush was relentless. "On no other issue is the dividing line so clear, on no other issue is my opponent's philosophy so completely at odds with mine, and I would say with the common-sense attitudes of the American people, than on the issue of crime," he said. "There are some — and I would list my opponent among them — who have wandered off the clear-cut path of common sense and have become lost in the thickets of liberal sociology." He described criminal justice under Dukakis as "a *Twilight Zone* world where prisoners' 'right to privacy' has more weight than the citizen's right to safety."

Later that month, in a phone interview with a reporter, Horton was asked whom he supported for president. "Obviously, I am for Dukakis," he replied.

In Michigan Lee spun traveling reporters, "Did you hear about Willie's endorsement? I assume the reason he endorsed him is that he thinks he'll have a better chance of getting out of jail if Dukakis is elected. I don't know if Dukakis would let him out, but I think there'd be a better chance."

The candidates met for a debate on October 13 at UCLA's Pauley Pavilion. The first question from moderator Bernard Shaw made reporters gasp. He asked Dukakis whether he would favor the death penalty if Kitty Dukakis were "raped and murdered." "Our surprise at the question was quickly overtaken by our surprise at the answer," said David Hoffman of the *Washington Post*. "Without flinching, Dukakis delivered his standard answer against the death penalty, shedding not even one hypothetical tear."

In reply, Bush scored big, saying he supported the death penalty for "brutal" crimes. "And so we just have an honest difference of opinion: I support it and he doesn't."

"Dukakis became a defense attorney for the murderer, as opposed to the outraged husband of the victim," said Roger Ailes. "That said it all." Later that evening, there was a message from the Bush camp for *Post* reporters at their hotel saying, "NSR." No spin required.

The day after the debate, emotions were running high in the Bush camp. At a rally in Cerritos, the advance men hoisted a balloon labeled SAY GOODNIGHT, MIKE as a rock band blared a song with the same lyrics. Atwater kept a straight face as he told reporters it would be "sheer folly" to get "smug or overconfident." When asked about the message on the balloon, he replied, "Well, it wouldn't make much sense having a balloon saying, 'We're not overconfident.' "

On the news one night, Sig Rogich saw the footage of Dukakis riding atop a tank. He quickly got rights to it and was negotiating for rights to the song "Hang On, Sloopy" when Atwater told him to get that film on TV *now*. Thus was born "Tank Ride," a hilarious ad that featured long-range images of a tank doing light maneuvers on a nonthreatening practice field, with assorted sounds of an engine belching, gears shifting. Dukakis's attempt to look like a strong leader was subverted by images suggesting a kid caught up in forces he couldn't control. The narrative took dead aim at the candidate: "Michael Dukakis has opposed virtually every defense system we developed. He opposed new aircraft carriers. He opposed antisatellite weapons. He opposed four missile systems, including the Pershing 2 missile deployment. He opposed the Stealth bomber, the ground emergency warning system against nuclear attack. He even criticized our rescue mission to Grenada and our strike on Libya." The camera then moved in tight for a close-up freeze-frame of Dukakis smiling uncomfortably in a tank helmet. "And now he wants to be our commander in chief. America can't afford that risk."

Rogich thought they should ease up, put out some positive ads. But few can resist the appeal of laughter, and Lee loved it. Rogich called Baker, complaining that the campaign had no endgame. "We just took a vote around the table here," answered Baker. "You lost." The tank ad rolled over Dukakis on October 17. The Bush campaign kept hammering away with a $32 million TV ad campaign.

On October 27, Dukakis attended a town meeting in Independence, Missouri, Harry Truman's hometown. In these closing days of the campaign, going wild about Harry and his come-from-behind victory in '48 was the Democrats' only source of hope. Already Dukakis's staff was devoting precious resources to ads complaining that Bush's handlers didn't fight fair! When Lee and Ailes saw those, they knew the race was over.

In Colorado two days before election day, Bush responded: "I am getting sick and tired of my opponent's complaining about the rough-and-tumble of this campaign. He seems to forget those personal attacks, night after night on me, on my character at that idiotic Democratic convention. . . . The American people are fair — they see through this last-minute smokescreen, and so now all that's left is this daily whining about a negative campaign. Let me give the governor a little advice." Then, his voice rising in a pretty fair imitation of Harry Truman himself, Bush said, "If he can't stand the heat, he ought to get out of the kitchen!" For a guy who seemed reluctant to go negative in the early rounds, Bush was pounding with delight. Victory was at hand.

On Tuesday, November 8, at 9:18 P.M. eastern standard time, George Bush was declared leader of the free world by a margin of 54 to 46 percent. He won 426 electoral votes to Dukakis's 112. In victory, Bush called for national unity. In conceding the race, Dukakis criticized the GOP campaign.

Lee met with reporters briefly. On his face was a look of enormous satisfaction. "My job is over, my friends," he said.

Lee was considered a kingmaker in most political quarters for turning a bland candidate given to gaffes and wimp tendencies into a near landslide winner. Some wanted to keep Lee just a bit humble. "Four years ago the gun was loaded and aimed at Dukakis," Rollins told the *Wall Street Journal*. "Baker walked in, pulled the trigger, dumped the gun on Lee Atwater and Bush won." Good ol' Ed.

A few weeks before the election, Lee had felt confident enough to kick back and attend the MTV music awards in Los Angeles. He had been practicing his guitar in private at least an hour a day, trying to get back in shape while developing his theory that music would provide strong political linkage for the future. It was something he saw around the corner, not just down the road, and he wanted to tap into the MTV generation. From time to time, Lee even played his guitar to entertain the political troops.

Late in October Lee packed up his guitar and called up his old ATO buddy Mike Ussery. They snuck off to Newberry College for homecoming weekend. Despite the hero's welcome he received at his old campus, Lee seemed worn by all the attention and adulation. Politics was wearing him down. He was maneuvering for the job at RNC, but Bush was being indecisive as usual. Lee thought he might finish his Ph.D. and teach — be someone who sat on his porch while others came to him for advice. "There is no way I could ever do another one like this," he said to Ussery. "I'm too old to run these things. This is my last campaign."

CHAPTER

8

THE TAR BABY

Lee Atwater is probably the most evil man in America.
— U.S. Representative Pat Schroeder
(Democrat, Colorado)

On a clear, sunny election day in November of 1988, Lee Atwater found himself jogging around Houston's Memorial Park with George Bush. "Lee, what would you like out of all this?" asked the presumptive president-elect, who knew exactly what Atwater wanted: to be head of the party. For weeks, Junior had been lobbying his father for Lee. Yes, we owed the guy; and paying your debts is everything in politics. Yes, like his Quayle decision, this would show we're not just the party of old white guys anymore. We've got this rock star–crazed pol here, an inspiration to a lot of young operatives around the country. They'd adore him. They'd hang on him: "Mr. Atwater, Mr. Atwater . . ."

Bush considered Lee tough, aggressive, loyal, and dependable, and the boy needed no coaching. Still, he wavered. Rich Bond would die for the job, and there were others. Maybe it was the immaturity thing, the reaction to Jimmy taking over the campaign. But Junior was insistent.

"How about a job I used to have," said George Bush in a tone that sounded more like a decision than a question. "The chairmanship of the Republican National Committee."

Lee Atwater was a highly unorthodox choice. He was the first professional political consultant to head either political party, the first "hired gun" to make it to the top of the mountain. In September of that campaign year, Stephen Hess, a senior fellow at the Brookings Institution, had discussed the idea of increasing the political status of the chairman of the party in a paper prepared for the annual meeting of the American Political Science Association. It would be a good idea, wrote Hess, "to give the party chairman the additional title of assistant to the President and transfer the duties of the political office to the national committee, which would, at the same time, breathe new life into the party system and leverage the President's political outreach." Put that on an index card, and you could call it Atwater's strategy for the next year.

The RNC chairmanship was the fulfillment of Lee's dream. The man with the plan had told friends that he wanted to accomplish two things before the age of forty: manage a winning presidential campaign and become head of the Republican Party. Now he had a new plan: he was determined to make the GOP the dominant political party by the year 2000. "For Mr. Atwater, for whom politics is the love, and government simply the thing that happens after a campaign, this job is just right," reported the *New York Times* when the appointment was official. And what a campaign it would be! Hey, wasn't it about time for a real change in the Grand Old Party? You know what they say about the importance of being different: you only outlive once.

Lee came back from the jog with Bush elated but businesslike. "OK, it's done," he told Ed Rogers. "He asked me to do it, and I said yes." Then, lying on the bed in Lee's room at the Houstonian, staring at the ceiling, they started plotting the Sununu scenario. Craig Fuller and his backers were vying with John Sununu for chief of staff. Lee, who knew what the outcome would be, called Sununu to sell him on Rogers. Lee knew that the RNC could easily become a political orphan with someone as savvy as Sununu running the White House. "If you get this thing, I hope Ed will come with you and be your multipurpose guy," he told the governor. Then he went into a little sales pitch. Lee wanted linkage. Ed had worked there before; he knew the political byways; he was a planner, an organizer.

For Sununu it was a no-brainer. "We'll do it," he said matter-of-factly. With that, Atwater had his eyes and ears in the White House.

Inviting Lee Atwater to leave the campaign wars and shove his feet under the desk at the RNC could be a brilliant choice, or it could be a disaster. Traditionally, the RNC had been a po-litical bank. Its sole purpose was to collect and disburse money. Lee wanted to turn it into a *materiel* command post for the total reshaping of the Republican Party, to make the party ready for the millennium. It would be a permanent campaign — just what his still-unfinished doctoral thesis called for. He would staff the com-mittee with people like himself, ops who were hopelessly addicted to the campaign, the game, the show. Why go into government and worry about governance when you can play politics seven days a week? The wheel would always be in spin. The question was, would the wheel spin out of control?

Bush's choice caught many by surprise. Did this mean that the permanent campaign was going to be a negative one? Or would Lee shelve his bad-boy style and lead by persuasion? To lead by persuasion, you need people's confidence, and there was some doubt in the Republican community that Atwater could in-spire much of that. Of course, Republican presidential wannabes liked him just the way he was, even hoped that Lee would return to the battlefield. Drug czar William Bennett asked him to come by for a visit, saying he was going to run for president someday and wanted Lee to run his campaign. Lee returned from the meeting with a sense of political bemusement. "There is not a chance," he said. "This is not my man. A nice guy, but not the guy for the job. Not going to make it."

"You're not going to believe this!" fumed Mickey Edwards as he stormed into his office after hearing the news. "That little squirt is going to be chairman!" During the campaign, Bush had planned a stop in Oklahoma, and Edwards was told to come to the fund-raiser casual — it was a hoedown. The congressman showed up in gingham, only to discover that everyone else was in presidential jacket and tie. As they say in Carolina, Mickey Edwards looked like country come to town. The congressman was sure it was an Atwater prank. He had been brooding on it ever since. Now he realized he would probably need Atwater's help to become chair of a congressional committee.

Edwards asked his assistant, Brooke Vosburgh, to arrange a meeting with Atwater. Vosburgh called Lee's secretary, Rhonda Culpepper, and they fell into an easy conversation about the campaign. Since sitting next to Lee on the flight to South Ca-rolina, Brooke had served as Donald Regan's assistant for two

years, and one year post–Nancy Reagan while Regan wrote his
book. Vosburgh then joined the '88 campaign briefly as assistant to Pete Teeley, the communications director. Lee seemed
bigger, more confident during the campaign than the good ol'
boy she remembered from their early days in D.C., and she felt
more comfortable around him. When Teeley left the campaign
in a power struggle with Fuller, Brooke took a job with Edwards,
the smart, colorful eight-term congressman who represented a
chance for Brooke to establish some longevity on her well-traveled
résumé.

Culpepper told Brooke that she would not be going to the
RNC with Lee. Two years of working for Lee from six-thirty to
midnight had left her fried. He loved to shock her, lifting his shirt
and baring his midriff, asking, "Do you think I look fat?" She liked
to tell the story of her first day on the job, when Lee had to attend a black-tie event. He called Rhonda in at the end of the day
to review phone calls, and while she sat in front of the desk he
proceeded to change his clothes. She turned the chair to face the
wall, and by the time Lee was dressed, they had gone through the
phone sheet for the day. She turned back to see the little smile
on his face; she had passed the test to see if she could handle his
weirdness.

Recently, though, Rhonda had been in Lee's office, and
when he started asking questions, her hands shook and she burst
into tears.

"Oh, my God," said Lee. "Go home. Go get some sleep."
Culpepper was in a daze, exhausted. "You're doing everything for
me," he said, hugging her and leading her toward the door. "I love
you!" he shouted.

Brooke said, "Well, I'd work for Lee."

"Oh, you're crazy," said Rhonda. Another call came in, so
she put Brooke on hold. It was Lee, on his way to the office from
the airport. She briefed him about Brooke.

"I want her to be there when I arrive," he said.

Brooke told Edwards that she had a dentist appointment and
walked to Lee's office with her résumé for the interview.

"When can you start?" he said.

"Wouldn't you like to look at my résumé?"

"No. When can you start?"

"Do I get parking?" she asked.

"You can have whatever you want," said the little squirt.
Now Mickey Edwards was *really* going to fume.

•   •   •

As political consigliere to the president, Lee continued putting
his people into the system. He wanted the White House Office
of Political Affairs run by someone who owed him some loyalty:
Ron Kaufman. He also solidified his alliance with Chief of Staff
Sununu. Lee called Michele Davis, now head of the Republican
Governors' Committee, to inform her that he had hired someone
named Nancy as new director of special projects for her office. She
was smart, knew everyone, was an experienced fund-raiser — and
was married to John Sununu. Meanwhile, he was building his
team at the RNC.

What had started as a contentious relationship with Mary
Matalin back in Iowa had evolved into a good working friendship.
"I want to be your chief of staff," she told Lee. "I want to study
at the feet of the master." He laughed. Matalin had hidden out
during the Michigan primary, a confusing affair that Atwater had
paid scant attention to, and had later emerged from the campaign
as a somewhat blunt, focused, tireless worker who had paid her
political dues. Lee saw her as a Tutwiler in the raw. While he was
off giving speeches, traveling, being visible, and hanging out at
the White House, she would be back at the RNC keeping paper
moving, holding the division directors in line, getting fund-raising
underway. They would meet every morning, and at the end of the
day she would update him on what had happened while he would
change into black tie, eat dinner, and sign correspondence. Yeah,
he could see that.

Another key player was Mark Goodin, whom Lee had
plucked from political obscurity in 1980 after the two had met during the presidential primary in South Carolina. Goodin, who was
working for an Anderson newspaper at the time, reminded Atwater
of himself. He played the guitar, adored Strom Thurmond, was
a student of the War Between the States, and — though born in
Virginia — had South Carolina roots. His great-great-uncle on his
mother's side was Stephen Dodson Ramsuer, the youngest major
general in the Confederacy; he was killed at the battle of Cedar
Creek at the age of twenty-three. When Thurmond needed a press
secretary in 1981, Atwater recommended Goodin. That put the

young man at the altar of his god, earning twice his newspaper salary, and eventually led to his getting the post of spokesman for the
'88 campaign after Pete Teeley made a sudden exit. During that
campaign Goodin, at thirty-three became one of the most quoted
people in America, notorious for delivering hardball sound bites
that stung the Dukakis campaign. As communications director at
the RNC, Goodin would lead the media charge, like his great-
great-uncle in another great battle. Yeah, Lee could see that, too.

But first, one last duty from the 1988 campaign.

On the blustery Saturday morning of December 2, Lee was
the guy with the winning smile at Harvard's Kennedy School of
Government, right in Dukakis's backyard. Wasn't it rich? A panel
of thirty-two was conducting an election postmortem. There were
the usual suspects — Lee, Ailes, and Ed Rogers from the Bush
campaign; Rollins from the Kemp campaign; Ron Brown from the
Jackson campaign; Bill Carrick from the Gephardt campaign; as
well as John Corrigan and Susan Estrich from the Dukakis campaign. An array of high-end members of the press was also on hand:
Paul Taylor from the *Washington Post*; Linda Wertheimer from
NPR; and Judy Woodruff from *The MacNeil-Lehrer NewsHour*,
among others.

Everyone hated the campaign. "Anyone who felt good about
American politics after the 1988 presidential campaign probably
also enjoys train wrecks, or maybe a day at the beach watching
an oil slick wash ashore," *Newsweek* had reflected. It had been a
campaign during which sound bites had replaced debate, slogans
had replaced ideas, and policy had bent to the winds of television.
During the '84 Reagan campaign the average length of a TV news
sound bite had been 14.8 seconds. In '88 it had dropped to only 9
seconds. For many would-be voters, the choices and the campaign
had been depressing. The results had been more of a denuncia-
tion of Dukakis than a vote of confidence for Bush. Voter turnout
had been lower than in any election since 1924. The question for
the panel on this particular morning was not Who won it? It was
Whodunnit?

"I have always had great faith in what I call the invisible
hand," explained Lee Atwater in the opening session. "When
things get out of hand, either on our side in the political community, or in the media — it gets back fairly quickly." He was referring
to the primary season, which had turned into a kind of demolition

derby, with Gary Hart and Joe Biden both going down in trials by media, followed by a marijuana admission from Bruce Babbitt. "I think that after Biden, the invisible hand started taking effect and guiding down." Then, talking to the media, Lee admitted that after the Biden dustup, "you had two Democrats, you hadn't had a Republican in the soup. We were getting ready to man our battle stations. . . . The press view would be to go after a Republican and go after him on some main stuff. Then the marijuana thing came up, and the invisible hand took place. We got through that whole little era."

A whole big era was about to begin. Lee's counterpart, Susan Estrich, may have proven a weak strategist, unable to control the Democratic message or the candidate, but she was a master at debating issues. She had managed to defend Dukakis after his disastrous second debate with Bush, because that was her forte: post-event spin. After Quayle's weak performance in the vice-presidential debate with Jack Kennedy's friend Lloyd Bentsen, Lee had tried to spin reporters: "It was a tie."

Then Estrich had just pointed at Lee and said, "I rest my case."

In the afternoon session at the Kennedy School, chaired by Howard Fineman of *Newsweek*, Estrich shocked the gathering into silence. "I do want to talk about this furlough issue and Willie Horton in particular," she said. "I happen to have been a rape victim and taught about rape and wrote about rape. I saw that one coming right between the eyes. We tried to deal with it as an issue about crime. We tried to deal with it as an issue about furloughs. . . . But my sense is that it was very much an issue about race and racial fear. Whether it was so intended or not, the symbolism was very powerful. It was, at least to my viewing of it, very strong — look, you can't find a stronger metaphor, intended or not, for racial hatred in this country than a black man raping a white woman. And that's what the Willie Horton story was." The post-defeat spin was beginning, and soon other Democrats would be trying to rationalize their defeat and personalize the blame.

A heated, bitter exchange between Estrich and Atwater followed. Estrich elaborated: "I talked to people afterward, men and women. Women said they couldn't help it, but it scared the living daylights out of them. We're talking about the association of Dukakis with rapists. Nobody likes to talk about race, so they just talked about rapists. But I would have to add that this is America, let's be honest, with black men who come in and rape and beat and stab white women. I talked to men who said they couldn't help it either, but when they saw the leaflets later and the ads and the like, they couldn't help but thinking about their wives and feeling scared and crazy."

E. J. Dionne of the *New York Times* asked Lee why the Bush campaign hadn't focused on a case he said was similar to Horton's, "where the facts were more devastating to Governor Dukakis — where somebody was pardoned and then murdered someone. You never used that case, and it appears that the guy is white."

"I learned about that case after the election," said Atwater. "Frankly, had I known about it, we would have been smart to go with that and never mentioned Willie Horton. In other words, if the guy was white, there would have been zero question about our intent."

Atwater vehemently denied any racist intent or thinking in his campaign, pointing out that he had used Horton's name disparagingly once in public, that he had never indicated that Horton was black, and that Horton's name and face were never used in Bush ads. The Dukakis campaign, on the other hand, had produced an ad that pointed up problems in a Bush-endorsed furlough program, showing a Hispanic man with a woman in a body bag, cutting to George Bush, implying that Bush had something to do with this woman's rape and murder. Moreover, that ad ran in California, a state often defined by racial tension.

"Two sides can play this ugly game," Estrich conceded. "You want to play to fear, you've got your ugly story of a black man raping a white woman. Well, we'll tell you an even uglier story. It happened to be a Hispanic man who left a woman to die, in front of her two small children. Yeah, two people can play this ugly game. We resisted, maybe to our ultimate detriment, playing the ugly game until late October. I mean, we resisted playing it. We resisted playing it because we felt wrongly, rightly — our candidate felt — that was not the tone he wanted to set."

"I hope everybody in this room clearly focused on what she just said, because it's the most amazing thing I think I ever heard," said Atwater. "She just said three things. One, they did do something we didn't do: We never used Willie Horton, but they did use a Hispanic in their ad. Two, she clearly inferred that they realized consciously it was racism, but, three, it wasn't wrong because we had done it first and because we did it more than them. I can't believe it." That was all Atwater thought people needed to hear. "She, in effect, said they knew what they were doing but it was not wrong because we had done it first. I think that right there makes this whole thing a moot issue. You did it, we did it, let's close this off."

But they didn't close it off. Labeling someone a racist is a tar-baby tactic; it tends to stick. Usually Lee relished being a tar baby blocking his candidate's opponent, but given his new role he wanted respect as a political thinker. He wanted to lead the Republican Party in reaching out to black voters. And he was genuinely upset at being accused of playing on racial hatred.

"I'm very lucky because both of my parents abhor bigotry," Atwater reflected in a subsequent interview. "They have always been very moderate. The household I was raised in was one in which they were always open-minded. Not until I was in my mid-twenties did I realize how much I had missed, compared to a lot of people in the South. My parents instilled into me equality. My mother truly thinks that everybody on this earth is exactly equal to everybody else on this earth. She taught me that from the time I was a little boy. My father feels the same way. I'm real proud of that. My parents were conservative on most issues, but they are egalitarian. My parents believe that everybody on this earth has the same rights, is created equally and is equal."

No one who knew Lee Atwater personally — either as a pol or as a good ol' boy — ever felt he was a racist. In terms of personal rapport, Lee was more culturally attuned to black America than he was to people in the political elite, both conservatives and liberals. Indeed, James Pinkerton observed, "Atwater was drenched in black culture."

But, of course, Lee wasn't prejudiced against people with emotional problems either, and he had called Tom Turnipseed "someone who was hooked up to jumper cables." He had even bragged about that for a while. He prided himself on playing to voters' deep-rooted attitudes, he had long displayed a willingness to do almost *anything* to win elections, and he was George Bush's strategist. How much responsibility did Lee Atwater bear for how the Bush campaign pointed to a furloughed black man raping a white woman, and for NSPAC's TV ad that took the issue of the Massachusetts furlough policy and put Willie Horton's face on it?

• • •

The long, twisted story of the National Security PAC's Willie Horton ad began on April 10, 1986, when the group registered with the Federal Election Commission as an Independent Expenditures Committee. FEC regulations define an independent expenditure as "an expenditure by a person for a communication expressly advocating the election or defeat of a clearly identified candidate which is not made with the cooperation or with the prior consent, of or in consultation with, or at the request or suggestion of, a candidate or any agent or authorized committee of such candidate." When the dust settled over the primaries, Dukakis would be the Democratic nominee, and NSPAC concluded that he was the worst thing for defense policy since Julius and Ethel Rosenberg. At that point NSPAC chose to conduct its independent expenditure — and to solicit political contributions — under the name Americans for Bush.

The chairman and treasurer of NSPAC was Elizabeth I. Fediay, a fund-raiser and political entrepreneur whom colleagues called Lillie. Other than herself, the only NSPAC employees were three secretaries, one after another. Fediay was not on a political mission. The PAC was her job, and it could be financially quite rewarding. She was not unlike an independent producer doing movies in Hollywood: not all of the deals turn into movies, but along the way there are some nice producer fees. Fediay was drawing a salary of $50,000 to oversee direct-mail fund-raising efforts for the PAC that generated millions. Through the spring of 1988 the major manifestation of NSPAC's efforts was millions of Bush bumper stickers.

On May 4, 1988, Jan W. Baran, general counsel for the Bush campaign, wrote to Fediay, saying, "The Vice President has asked me to tell you that he does not endorse nor approve of your activities. The Vice President requests that you and NSPAC immediately cease using his name, the name 'Americans for Bush,' and any other name that suggests his association with you or NSPAC."

Through June of 1988, NSPAC had spent "a total of $1,211,074.96 on independent expenditures which directly advo-

Opposites attract: On a Bush '88 whistle stop through Atwater, California, Lee spotted someone in the crowd holding a sign that said, "Atwater Loves Bush." He jumped off the train and asked for the sign, holding it aloft during Bush's next speech.

On November 8, 1988, Bush showed how much he loved Atwater in return. During this jog the President-elect offered Lee "my old job: chairman of the RNC."

To Lee — On a special day in my life — a day that you did so much to make come true — Thanks a lot

Gg Bush

Houston Nov. 8 '88

Lee and President Bush mug during the January 1989 Concert for Young Americans, a defining event that introduced Lee as a rock'n'roll Republican.

Lee jams with Ron Wood of the Rolling Stones. That night, Wood gave the Stratocaster guitar he was playing to Lee.

Later that year, Lee (with Wood's Stratocaster) and B.B. King performed several nightclub and concert gigs, eventually joining forces for a Grammy-nominated instrumental, "Red Hot & Blue," featured on the all-star album of the same name.

Sally and children Sara Lee and Ashley joined Lee in January 1989 when he was sworn in as chairman of the Republican National Committee.

(top) On a trip to Israel in August of that year, Lee posed for a photo reminiscent of Michael Dukakis's ill-fated drive in a tank.

(bottom) Mary Matalin rose from being the lowly field worker Lee publicly fired after losing the Iowa caucuses to his chief of staff at the RNC, where the party rocked on.

Spin doctor at work: One week after his initial brain seizure, Lee met with President Bush and Chief of Staff Sununu in the Oval Office on March 12, 1990. Where Lee lost a patch of hair for the biopsy was still visible behind his right ear, but he was in great spirits. Bush and Sununu had been briefed by the President's physician, an oncologist, and knew the future wasn't as bright as Lee spun it.

During his battle against cancer Lee went for long limousine rides around Washington, D.C., his body swollen and his left arm useless. Looking after him were Brooke Vosburgh (*top*), Sally Atwater (*middle*), and Linda Reed O'Meara (*bottom*).

Credit: Lynn Johnson

In November 1990, Lee posed for a final portrait by photographer Lynn Johnson of *Life* magazine. When Lee's "as told to" memoir appeared shortly before his death, the photos and text created a shock heard 'round the political world.

cate Mr. Bush's election," Fediay's attorney responded. There were also some TV ads in the works.

When NSPAC disregarded the warning, Baran filed a formal complaint with the FEC on June 28, alleging violations of the Federal Election Campaign Act of 1971. Baran said NSPAC had misrepresented itself to the public, especially the elderly, as an authorized campaign committee of George Bush. "The Committee objects to the manner by which NSPAC conducts itself, actively misleading the public into believing that they are being solicited by George Bush for President, Inc." For the past year, Americans for Bush had been soliciting donations from individuals who thought they were making a contribution to the George Bush for President Committee. There had been complaints, including a letter from a New Jersey voter who had quizzed one of the phone solicitors. "The man replied that they were affiliated with Lee Atwater," Baran said. "This letter lends credence to the fact that 'Americans for Bush' is unabashedly trying to impress on those solicited that it is soliciting contributions explicitly on behalf of the Vice President and his authorized campaign committee, not on behalf of an independent expenditures committee which has the option never to contribute a single dollar to George Bush." In filing the complaint, Baran argued that "NSPAC truly spends the majority of its money to make money, not in support of the candidates for whom it claims it is raising money and making independent expenditures."

In May of 1988 Fediay had retained Floyd Brown as a consultant for $3,000 a month on issues and strategy. While working for Dole during the primaries, Brown had made the Bushees (especially Mary Matalin) pay a price in the Midwest. Every state that Dole won, he won in Brown's region: Iowa, South Dakota, Minnesota. Accordingly, Brown was consultant non grata in the Bush campaign. He signed on with Fediay, moving from campaigning against Bush to being his advocate through an independent-expenditure PAC.

In June, Brown hired fellow Dole alums Anthony Fabrizio of Multimedia Services (to plan media buys) and Larry McCarthy (to produce TV spots). McCarthy was young but had worked for the Ailes shop for nearly six years. He had met Atwater in 1985 while doing ads for the Edd Hargett congressional campaign in Texas, which got a lot of attention because it was the first real race after the '84 elections, and the Democrats looked vulnerable. It turned out that they weren't vulnerable enough; that was another loss that gave Lee the dry heaves. Larry McCarthy was on his own now. Roger Ailes called McCarthy in June, saying it was too bad that he had accepted the NSPAC position; Roger had been considering subcontracting with McCarthy to produce some spots for the Bush campaign. McCarthy cut the conversation short. FEC requirements for an independent expenditure program required that NSPAC people not have any contact, communication, or coordination with the Bush campaign.

Once onboard at NSPAC, McCarthy quickly did a sixty-second biographical spot on Bush that ran in front of the conventions, as well as a "call 800" fund-raiser for the PAC. The money raised, eventually exceeding $10 million, went to Americans for Bush from unsuspecting real Americans for Bush. With that war chest, in August Fediay retained conservative consultant Craig Shirley to create additional political strategy.

On August 24, after the Democratic convention, Fediay met with Brown, McCarthy, Shirley, and Fabrizio for a brainstorming session in Fabrizio's office in Alexandria. Fediay wanted to do low-cost cable ads. To get maximum impact, the group decided to "go out early and run in the clear" when neither Dukakis nor Bush were airing official ads.The group discussed doing a spot against Dukakis, either comparative or negative. Their strategy sprang from stories in the *Washington Post* and *Reader's Digest*. McCarthy proceeded to draft two scripts, one on the Pledge of Allegiance, another on crime, featuring Willie Horton. The group decided to go with Horton. Lillie sent an intern to the Library of Congress to get the Lawrence *Eagle-Tribune* clips, then to the AP for photos. Only two pictures existed: one arrest photo and one mug shot.

Larry McCarthy took the material to his home office on Capitol Hill. If Dan Rather did a spot on the controversy, thought McCarthy, he'd put up a picture of Willie Horton. Would that be considered racist? No way. Still, McCarthy produced two versions of the ad, one with Horton's picture and one without. He feared the ad that featured a picture of Horton might be controversial at some cable networks, and they would be under no obligation to run an unauthorized campaign committee's ads. Larry McCarthy delivered the two spots on Monday, September 5, receiving $7,000 plus expenses for his work. The spots were forwarded to various cable stations.

NSPAC held a news conference on Labor Day to unveil its ads. Media interest was slight. No film crews attended. McCarthy didn't even show. Floyd Brown blustered. "When we are through," he said, one-upping Atwater's "running mate" sound bite, "people are going to think that Willie Horton is Michael Dukakis's *nephew.*"

McCarthy considered his generic crime ad "really ugly," heavy with type. He hoped it wouldn't run for long. It didn't. After two weeks, the ad with Horton's face ran instead. Stylistically and graphically, it looked like a lot of other attack ads: very simple images, no elaborate production, standard layered background with borders around the photos of Dukakis and Bush. McCarthy had used stock images of the candidates from a photo library, with no attempt to make Bush look angelic or Dukakis unsavory. The Horton spot stopped running on October 4. It had run only on cable television, and only for two weeks. That was a very short cycle, considering the effect the ad had on media coverage of the campaign.

The ads created additional confusion for the Bush campaign. Just as Bush supporters had responded to NSPAC's direct-mail and phone solicitations, thinking they were giving directly to his campaign, viewers perceived the Americans for Bush TV ads as direct attacks on Dukakis by the Bush campaign. Because Bush was mentioning Willie Horton by name in his speeches, there was even more reason to see linkage. Fediay was delighted. Her goal was to get publicity for the PAC, to be seen as a bigger player. "Officially the campaign has to disavow themselves from me," she told the *New York Times.* "Unofficially, I hear that they're thrilled about what we're doing." She never revealed a source for that claim.

On September 8, Fediay had sent a letter to James Baker asking about his "wishes" regarding the activities of the National Security Political Action Committee, suggesting that "senior advisers" such as Baker "have remained silent." On September 12, Atwater sent her a response, and Baker replied on September 27. Both once again asked Fediay to stop using the vice president's name in fund-raising activities. Baker said there was "substantial evidence that NSPAC's tactics have in fact misled members of the public and particularly senior citizens into believing that they

are being solicited by the Vice President's official campaign committee." Both asked her to get in touch with the campaign legal
department thereafter.

The record shows that no one from the Bush campaign
asked NSPAC to stop its ads. Instead, lawyers for the Bush campaign filed a complaint with the U.S. Postal Service objecting to
NSPAC's activities. The Bush campaign sent letters to the national
television networks alerting them that the " 'Willie Horton' advertisements were not produced, authorized, or approved by the
Bush campaign," said Jan Baran in response to a complaint later
lodged by the Democratic Party of Ohio, charging that there was
collusion between NSPAC and the Bush campaign. "A request
that NSPAC cease using the Willie Horton advertisements . . . was
perceived by the campaign as legally dangerous, as it might raise
a presumption that NSPAC's activities were coordinated with the
campaign, if NSPAC complied with the request. . . . This consideration is indeed ironic in view of the fact that the effect of the
Complaint is to criticize the campaign for *failing* to influence
NSPAC's expenditures."

So there is no evidence that Lee Atwater oversaw the making
of any Willie Horton ad that showed or alluded to the man's race,
and there is a clear legal reason why either he or others in the Bush
camp did not demand that Americans for Bush stop running its
ads. But does that clear Lee Atwater of misusing Willie Horton?
After the fact his opponents presented a murkier charge that he had
set a tone in the official Bush campaign that encouraged racial ap-
peals — as long as they weren't too blatant. As Larry McCarthy put
it, the Bush campaign faced this basic question: "To what degree
could the Horton case be exploited before it started to backfire?"

Mark Goodin, as spokesman for the campaign, had Horton's
mug shot over his desk, so every reporter in the office for a sound
bite couldn't help but see it. When Lee spoke to reporters about
Dukakis's search for a vice-presidential candidate, he had said,
"On Monday I saw in the driveway of his house: Jesse Jackson. So
anyway, maybe he'll put this Willie Horton guy on the ticket after
all is said and done" — linking Horton and Jackson when they had
little in common except that they were both black men.

Atwater had swiftly denounced an "unauthorized" flyer from
Maryland state party officials that had a picture of Horton alongside a picture of Michael Dukakis. "But in the end, Willie Horton

produced tons of Bush votes from white Southerners, independents, and other swing voters such as blue-collar ethnics, whom Bush needed to win the Presidency," wrote South Carolina journalist Jan Stucker. Lee had "learned exquisitely well the South's post–George Wallace lesson about racial politics: Use it to your advantage, but handle it ever so discreetly."

"Willie Horton came as close as the Republicans needed to come" to the race issue, observed University of South Carolina political science professor Earl Black, one of Lee's graduate school teachers.

Why hadn't the Bush campaign chosen a case in which the criminal wasn't black? After all, the College Republican National Committee had claimed Horton was "only one example of many." Don Todd, the RNC's director of oppo research in 1988, said Horton's victims were key: "The reason he became the star of the program was because of the victims here in Maryland, a fifteen-minute drive for any Washington reporter. They were very vocal. They were interviewed, and 60 Minutes had done a story on the episode before Dukakis was even named as presidential candidate. It was not a racist thing. It was a policy scandal on Dukakis's part."

At the Kennedy School, Estrich said that the Bush campaign's use of the Horton story had inflamed racial fears, and she added, " 'Whether intended or not' is a phrase I think I have used each time I have said this, because I don't know if you sat down and planned it." In other words, even if Atwater hadn't set out to exploit racial fears, she felt he was still at fault for letting them bubble up, or for not recognizing that they would.

What better way was there for Democrats to cauterize the wounds sustained during the campaign than to holler racism afterward? Some of the "evidence" that Lee Atwater was racially insensitive is far-fetched. "This white southern boy, born in the same year and state as Horton, always used the diminutive in referring to Horton," wrote Boston Globe reporters Christine Black and Tom Oliphant in a book. "He called him 'Willie,' just as white men traditionally addressed black men in the South. A white criminal would be more likely to have been called 'Horton.' " But the name Willie came out of research files prepared by Pinkerton and the nerd squad, including a UPI story with a Boston dateline for February 22, 1988, in which a member of the Massachusetts

League of Women Voters says, "A Willie Horton never should have happened."

If Lee had not been a white southerner, a good ol' boy proud of his heritage, would people have so quickly assumed he was open to racism? Lee himself complained, "I knew when I got into this business that as a southern white boy, the one thing I could never do was do or say anything racist. There's a fierce prejudice in this country against southern white boys on the national political scene. It's open season on us. We can be accused of anything, and anything we say can and will be used against us."

●　●　●

Lee's tar baby came to a boil in February 1989, when the president of Howard University in Washington, D.C., one of the nation's most prestigious black colleges, appointed Lee Atwater to its board of trustees. Lee's closest advisers told him to stay away from the Howard appointment, but, ever aspiring to be the teacher, he saw it as a way to affiliate himself with an academic institution, and also a chance to wipe the Willie Horton slate clean. "When it came to his own ego, Lee was totally blind — blind to risk, blind to appearances," said Mark Goodin. "He could see it magnificently in other people, other scenarios, but when it came to his own ego, he was blind."

The problems began in the urban government and politics class of Professor Joseph McCormick one day in late February. McCormick, furious with the Howard University board of trustees for bringing Lee Atwater aboard, asked his sixteen students if they knew who Atwater was. Four did. McCormick led a discussion that soon became a lecture on why Atwater was wrong for Howard University. His main concern was Atwater's use of the "Willie Horton strategy" during the presidential race, and his association with the conservative wing of the GOP, which McCormick said prospered by "exploiting the fears of white southerners." Moreover, McCormick said, the university should not get involved in partisan politics; he would also be opposed to naming, say, Jesse Jackson to the board.

Moved by the professor's lecture, Derrick Payne — a member of the Howard student newspaper staff — wrote an editorial that held Atwater accountable for "the most racist strategy in a national presidential campaign in the 20th century." This led to a demonstration several days later.

The tactics used during the protest against Lee were those of a classic negative political campaign. If Atwater weren't the target, he might have found it admirable. On Friday, March 3, hundreds of angry students shut down a Charter Day ceremony honoring comedian Bill Cosby on the school's 122nd anniversary. The police were called, the news crews came, and suddenly Lee Atwater's bid to refurbish his image and attract more blacks to the GOP had backfired badly. Students took over the stage, pushing Cosby out of the spotlight while the cameras whirred. They said they were opposed to the naming of Lee to Howard's board of trustees — and they were also protesting delays in the school's processing of student loans. Linking Lee to financial-aid woes — guaranteed to fire things up! There was also some disinformation for the cameras. "Atwater is the man who supports the racist regime of South Africa," said one student on the evening news. "He opposed the appointment of blacks to the federal judiciary."

Like Dukakis, Lee thought he could ride it out by taking the high road. That weekend he attended a party for Ben Bradlee, flew to L.A. for an event, returned for dinner on Sunday evening with Lee Bandy of the *State* and his wife. By Tuesday, March 7, the D.C. police had been summoned to the Howard campus, where over five hundred students had blockaded themselves inside the administration building. "When Atwater leaves, the students will leave," said one student leader. The university refused to yield. That afternoon the police, with thirty patrol cars and four paddy wagons, moved in to take the building. They smashed the glass doors, only to find some students lying on the floor of the entrance-way while others chanted and cheered. The standoff lasted two hours.

Mayor Marion Barry arrived, expressing sympathy toward the students. "I think that for the sake of peace Mr. Atwater ought to find a way to gracefully resign," he said. "But my main concern up here was to make sure that the metropolitan police department didn't get involved in a confrontation situation where we need our officers on the street fighting drug dealers and dope dealers."

"It's not because he's a Republican or white," said a student opposing Atwater. "It's not a racist issue at all. It's his stance on several civil rights measures, and his traditional stance as it affects

African Americans." Support for the students began to pour in. Area restaurants and groceries sent food. The Nation of Islam sent a delegation. Jesse Jackson called the campus, leaking the story that he might pay them a visit. Rumors abounded. Lee was getting information that Jesse Jackson was chasing political ambulances again, pushing the demonstration along so that he could sweep in as the heroic black knight, a mediator.

Lee felt like an innocent pawn in somebody else's game — but that image didn't mesh with everyone else's perception of him. Lee had spent a lot of time and effort to escape his past, and everywhere he turned he seemed to be reminding people of it. Perhaps it was too much of a stretch for Lee to want what Gatsby's creator said never happened in American lives: a second act.

"He's willing to support Howard University," said a lone student on the evening news. "He said he wants to help black people. We should give him a chance!"

That day Bush gave a press conference and was asked if the students had a legitimate complaint. Talk about bad timing! "I think it's a good thing he's on the board," said the president. "I think it's a good thing he's gonna talk to these students, and I think that'll work out just fine."

Lee sent a young black aide over to Howard to get a reading on the mood there. For a while Lee must have thought he could talk his way out of the crisis. But when he opened up discussions with Jackson, the reverend made it sound like there might be a major upheaval if Lee didn't step down. Lee told staffers that Jackson said he would take care of it with everybody, would make Lee look good, that he would tell the students that Lee had their best interests at heart, that Lee just wanted to do the right thing.

On March 7 Atwater resigned from the board, saying, "I don't want anybody to get hurt, and you never know where something like this can lead." The cost was high — for both sides. Had Lee been given the chance to talk to the students, he would have asked them for a one-year term to prove himself. He would have told them that he had wanted to teach a class on practical politics, to organize a blues concert and other activities to provide student scholarships. He had wanted to begin the mother of all fund-raising drives.

In the wake of the resignation, Jackson visited the campus. He went before the cameras and dumped on Lee. "The signals that were sent in the Willie Horton ad were not so much about furloughs, but about race inciting fears in white people and creating very painful feelings among African Americans," he said. "Unfortunately, Lee Atwater symbolizes the worst of that situation."

Lee had taken Jesse at his word, and Jesse broke it for a sound bite and a photo op. Lee's staff had never seen him in such a fury. Was there no such thing as honor among pols? "I'll never trust that son of a bitch again," Lee said.

If Lee thought that resigning from the Howard board would put a lid on the Willie Horton story, he had forgotten Susan Estrich. She wrote a cover story for the April 23, 1989, issue of the *Washington Post Magazine* called "Willie Horton & Me: The Hidden Politics of Race." In that piece she revealed that it was a black man who had raped her in 1974, leaving her so fearful that for months afterward "I wanted to cross the street or run inside or lock my door every time a strange black man looked at me 'funny' — or at all. I hated myself for it, and I managed to conquer my fear, but that's not the point. The point is how easy it is to confuse race and crime."

Thus, Estrich argued, "Willie Horton didn't just 'happen' to be black, as Republicans like to claim. Half of those arrested for murder are. Blacks comprise 12 percent of the population of this country, but 46 percent of our prison population. . . . So it comes as no surprise that for too many white Americans, when we think of crime, we think of blacks. It is that association that makes the crime issue such an effective surrogate for a more explicit race-based appeal." And why didn't Estrich cry racism during the campaign? " 'We can't afford to alienate white voters,' I was told by many in my party and my campaign; whites might be put off if we 'whine' about racism," she explained.

The *Post* story included a picture of Horton with the ambiguous caption "From the ad paid for by Americans for Bush," with no clarification about the origin of this ad or the independent nature of its sponsor. The ad, as television's symbol for how the Bush campaign used Horton, clung to Lee to the end. Lee Atwater had tried to make Willie Horton into a tar baby who would stick to Michael Dukakis. Instead Willie Horton stuck to Lee.

One reason was that Lee had built himself up as a trickster, playing on the edge of the rules. "The true misfortune of Lee was that he made his own 'bad' reputation for dirty tricks," said Vic Gold. "I don't know what it is about this new generation, but they've got to go out and talk. About three fourths of the stuff that Lee said he was up to, he wasn't up to. He would talk about these focus groups, for instance. I never criticized him directly, but I would ask him, 'Why in the hell is it necessary to tell the media what you are doing?' I mean, the business about Willie Horton — did anybody have to know that they had a focus group up in New Jersey and had these people jumping out of their chairs? You don't have to tell the press that. But Lee was fascinated by the process, and he told the press, which eats up stuff like that because it allows them to say, 'Look at these conniving sons of bitches.' " Sure enough, Lee was being pointed out as a conniving son of a bitch.

Another reason Horton stuck to Lee was that he always boasted about his ability to pick up and play on deep-rooted attitudes of swing voters — especially white southern populists. If he was so sensitive to how good ol' boys and girls read things, he should have known how incendiary the figure of a black rapist would be. His memos during the Reagan years have numerous references to the black vote, to the issue of race in one campaign after another. In that context he was trying to get or overcome the black vote, not using race to get the white vote. Still, Lee knew the risks of this sort of talk. "As a white southerner," he told the *New York Times*, "I have always known I had to go the extra mile to avoid being tagged a racist by liberal northerners. If anybody from the South says or does anything, it's racially motivated." Sure enough, Lee was being tagged a racist.

And a third problem was that neither Lee nor all the vice president's men were being completely forthright in their responses to the charges about the Horton ads. The NSPAC gang and the real Bush campaign acted like unindicted co-conspirators. Lee insisted to reporter Jan Stucker, "I didn't even know Horton's name or whether he was black or white at the beginning. I just knew he was in prison for a terrible crime." Even Pinkerton said Lee must have "misunderstood" that point. Both Lee and Baker intimated that they had written to Americans for Bush asking for the Horton commercial to stop; they never did. Though NSPAC people were supposed to stay independent from the Bush campaign, Larry McCarthy and Roger Ailes communicated at least twice during the campaign, including a long conversation about campaign advertising strategies a few days after the second presidential debate. Although official Bush ads did not feature Willie Horton, a cocky Roger Ailes could not resist bragging to *Time*, "The only question is whether we depict Willie Horton with a knife in hand or without it." Thus suspicions were reinforced.

We also have to recognize one final reason that Lee and Willie Horton will be stuck together for political eternity: Lee's opponents don't want to let him go. Racism is still a problem in our society, nearly everyone agrees, but there are deep political disagreements about the effects of past racism and the best way to remedy the current problem. The Democratic Party needs its core constituencies to come to the polls, especially in the South, where it has been losing its dominance on the state as well as the national level. Just as Lee looked for issues to bring out GOP voters, so do other campaign managers, and there's little that motivates black voters more than fear of white bigotry.

Critics argued that in developing a strategy to win the White House, Atwater drew on what he knew best: hardball tactics, South Carolina style. Increasingly, what played in Columbia was also playing nationally. After managing southern campaigns for ten years, Lee Atwater knew only too well how to develop the populist "us versus them" issues — the so-called wedge issues. He handed Bush such vote getters as the Pledge of Allegiance issue (translation: Dukakis is unpatriotic) and Dukakis's membership in the ACLU (translation: Don't trust anyone who would belong to that pinko organization). He also came up with the Willie Horton furlough (intended translation: Dukakis cares more about criminals than about victims).

Yes, there's another possible translation for the Horton issue: blacks are crime-prone, and they're coming to get you. But Lee personally prohibited the use of any pictures of Horton in campaign ads and never mentioned the convict's race. "I defy you to find any other campaign I have done where race has become the issue," he added. "Race, politically, is a loser."

Hardball politics is a big tent. There's racial politics, ethnic politics, gender politics. Pols try to appeal to constituencies that will get them elected — whites, blacks, Hispanics, Catholics,

Poles, women, gays, farmers, gun owners . . . whatever it takes. Every operative in the country knew that there were numerous black pols who have been kept in office through the loyalty of black constituents. Strategies divide or multiply voters — to conquer. If the Willie Horton ad was racial politics, the post election response to it — calling the ad and the ad makers racist, and including the new chairman of the GOP with them — was also racial politics. The word *racist* is another political weapon in this dialogue.

We can't let race blind us to other issues. Crime is a problem. Willie Horton walking away from his furlough was part of that problem. Horton wasn't a Scottsboro Boy, wrongly accused of rape. He wasn't a civil rights activist whose only threat to "law and order" was trying to get a restaurant meal or a good education. He wasn't a teenager pulled over repeatedly for driving a car that cost more than the cops thought he could afford. He was a vicious, violent criminal. He posed a threat to whites, blacks, everyone. That's why the signature drive in Lawrence to change the furlough program was a success.

Did Willie Horton win the election for Bush? No. Doubtless, there was a racist segment in the electorate that saw the furlough issue as one of color, not crime, and voted accordingly. In *Chain Reaction: The Impact of Race, Rights, and Taxes on American Politics*, Tom Edsall of the *Washington Post* says, "a series of polls that tracked voter shifts through the campaign clearly suggests that the social/moral and racial issues played a critical role in moving voters from support of Dukakis to support of Bush between June and November of 1988." At the same time, economists and political scientists argue that the Bush victory margin (54 percent to 46 percent) closely approximates the outcome that could have been expected given the general economic climate surrounding the election.

Allan J. Lichtman, creator of the "thirteen keys to the presidency" concept, predicted in March 1988 that the election would be "a shoo-in" for Bush, "no matter who winds up as the Democratic nominee." Ten of the thirteen keys were tilted toward a Republican victory. Afterward, Lichtman and coauthor Ken DeCell described the campaign as being "masterful if brutal . . . devised by hardball political strategist Lee Atwater and executed by adman Roger Ailes, with unwitting assists from a furloughed murderer named Willie Horton, and the flotsam and jetsam of Boston Harbor." Nevertheless, they added, "Bush did not 'come from behind' to snatch victory from the Democrats in 1988. Michael Dukakis did not 'blow' an election that was within his party's grasp. The American public did not succumb to the manipulation of cynical, media-savvy political strategists or the influence of soundbites and television images. . . . The electorate responded to identifiable social, political and economic circumstances in a pragmatic, and clearly predictable manner — a manner consistent with the historical pattern of presidential election results since Republicans and Democrats emerged as the two major parties in our modern political system a century and a third ago."

"Candidates and their campaigns are principally responsible for their own success or failure," said Dayton Duncan, press secretary for Dukakis. "To the extent that it might ever have been ours to boot away, we did it without anyone's help. Sam Donaldson of ABC didn't force Dukakis into a tank in Michigan and place a helmet on the governor's head. Chris Wallace of NBC wasn't demanding a constitutional lecture about whether schoolchildren and teachers can be required to recite the Pledge of Allegiance. Bruce Morton of CBS neither conceived the Bush campaign's Willie Horton ads nor advised the Dukakis campaign to ignore them for a summer and most of the fall. Those were our mistakes."

Dukakis was so self-directed, the campaign became self-destructive. "These hidden races were fascinating because each side was aware of the other's strengths, weaknesses, and likely moves; and each side processed its information and made its initial judgments at roughly the same time," observed *Boston Globe* reporters Tom Oliphant and Christine Black afterward. "The difference was that one candidate acted on the information he received and the other didn't."

Lee once confided to *Time* magazine editors how he would have run a campaign against Bush by reviving the latent image of the Republican Party as "a bunch of rich, old snobs." He would have built TV ads around pictures of George Herbert Walker Bush as ambassador to the UN in the early '70s, with his half-rim glasses, long hair and sideburns, and flashy neckties. Pictures of Bush in tennis whites dancing a silly pirouette to celebrate winning a close match. Pictures of the sprawling oceanfront mansion in Kennebunkport, with a voice-over: "No wonder he wants to cut capital gains taxes on the wealthy." Of course, Atwater believed such attacks would be outrageously unfair; they would discount Bush's decency and service to his country, his hard work, and his sympathy for those who had not had his advantages. Still, he added, with a mischievous grin, "It would work."

In writing about the issue years later, *Time* magazine essayist Lance Morrow argued, "The Democrats tried to bury the issue, saying anybody talking about crime was in fact talking about race. It worked reasonably well for a while. Had a damaging effect on Lee. But eight years later, crime is such a strong issue, you can't close it down by declaring that anybody who talks about crime is a racist." Especially when the juvenile crime rate is rising, especially when voters from every part of the electorate worry about it, especially when minority neighborhoods suffer the most from crime.

Willie Horton didn't commit his crime because he was a black man; he did it because he was a flawed man and free to impose his evil on innocent bystanders because of an imperfect penal system in Massachusetts. The Lawrence *Eagle-Tribune* didn't write two hundred–odd stories about Horton because he was black. And there's no evidence that Horton was chosen by Atwater *because* he was a black man. He was chosen because he was a political bogeyman . . . someone whose activities scared voters who were about to settle for the nice-guy image that Estrich was beginning to establish for her candidate. "If I can make Willie Horton a household name, we'll win the election," Lee boasted — making no reference to Horton's race. All the same, Horton remains a household name, a national symbol of both criminal recidivism and racial politics.

Shortly before his inauguration, George Bush was asked about the campaign that had brought him to office. "That's history," he said. "That doesn't mean anything anymore." To Lee Atwater it meant a lot. It meant a piece of political history would be hung around his neck. It hurt, but when you live by spin, you die by spin.

9

TOP OF THE WORLD

A prince need trouble little about conspiracies when
the people are well disposed, but when they are hostile
and hold him in hatred, then he must fear
everything and everybody.
— Machiavelli, *The Prince*

Are you ready for star time?" asked Lee, opening the Celebration for Young Americans with a line borrowed from James Brown
shows.

It was while jogging along the Tow Path one evening shortly
after the 1988 election that Lee dreamed up the all-star musical
extravaganza. The concert on January 21, 1989, would announce
to the world that it was cool to be a Republican. "Rhythm and blues
music is part of this nation's soul," wrote Atwater in the official
press release, "and I am honored to help bring this original American art form to the youth of the United States. Never have I seen
such an outstanding array of musical talent of this caliber under
one roof." The lineup: Ruth Brown! Joe Cocker! Albert Collins!
Bo Diddley! Willie Dixon! Dr. John! Eddie Floyd! Chuck Jackson! Lafayette Leake! Delbert McClinton! Sam Moore of Sam and
Dave! Billy Preston! Percy Sledge! KoKo Taylor! Carla Thomas!
Brother guitarists Stevie Ray and Jimmy Vaughan! Joe Louis
Walker! And Ron Wood of the Rolling Stones! Even the stage band
featured Steve Cropper and Donald "Duck" Dunn, of Booker T.
and the MGs, and Anton Fig, drummer for the Letterman show.

But the biggest star was Lee Atwater.

About an hour into the program, the president arrived. Lee started to leave the stage. "Where you goin'?" said Sam Moore, starting a little routine arranged for the Bushes. "Come here!" said Sam. Lee came back onstage, dancing lightly. "The hardest man," said Moore, borrowing another line from James Brown's introductions, "the hardest-working man in show business . . ." Lee whirled about doing his best soulful strut. "Lee . . ." Now Lee dropped to the floor in a near genuine James Brown split, facing the roaring, pleading crowd straight on. ". . . ATWATER!"

Again, Lee started to leave the stage. More musical foreplay. As in politics, what seems spontaneous has usually been carefully thought out. "I'll tell ya what," said Sam to the audience. "If you put your hands together, I think we can get him to play. How 'bout that?" Wild applause. Lee still feigned modesty, walking offstage as Sam, his face beaming, entreated, "Come on, man. Come on back here, Lee. Lee . . . please?"

Oh, OK. Lee slipped beneath the guitar strap, checked the cord, and began to groove, shuffling across the front of the stage, shouting: "Is everybody having a good time tonight? Say yeah!" The crowd roared. Then a salute to the boss — "Mr. President!" Lee shouted — as Marvin Bush strapped a pair of dark shades across Lee's eyes. Delbert began to pick up the beat on harmonica, and the band moved into a soul-searing version of "High Heel Sneakers" with Lee singing his heart out.

Lee called Chuck Jackson out to sing a verse. Then Steve Cropper took some licks with Lee on dueling guitars. Carla Thomas sang, followed by Billy Preston, Joe Cocker, Percy Sledge. Lee fell to his knees on a guitar solo, leaning backward till his shoulders hit the floor, an homage to bluesmen T-Bone Walker and Guitar Slim by way of Jimi Hendrix. The crowd roared for more. Lee jumped back up to his feet. Ron Wood of the Stones moved in for a closing jam on his Fender Stratocaster soaring upward in a solo riff as Lee dropped back on his old Gibson SG to play rhythm. "How about that?!" asked Sam Moore, fifteen minutes after the number began.

The audience was on its feet, applauding wildly. George Bush came onstage. "I taught Lee everything he knows about that kind of dancing," he said. Laughter. "This has got to be the most active event of the inauguration. It is fantastic." The performers presented a special guitar to Bush, a pawnshop instrument that

Lee had picked up a week earlier and on which he had had
emblazoned THE PREZ. Bush strapped it on and feigned a little
grooving match as Lee concentrated on strumming a blues riff.
Finally Bush nudged Lee's right elbow, and Lee looked up to see
Bush mugging Atwater's blues face. Lee mugged the Prez back.

For Lee Atwater, this was a defining event, a dream realized.
Here they were, the candidate and his manager, on top of the
political world — with all of the rewards of sweet victory straight
ahead. When Bush and Bar left, Lee drifted back into a chorus
line with Delbert, Sam, Percy, Joe, Carla, and Chuck, as they all
linked arms and kicked in unison to the backbeat. Finally, as the
music ebbed, Lee broke away from the dancers and went into a
series of James Brown skips and swirls, spastic approximations of
moves that went back to his youth, when he once jumped off a balcony to impress a date. Sam Moore — the voice that Lee recalled
from all of those Sam and Dave songs of the '60s — grabbed the
mike and shouted one more time, "THE HARDEST-WORKING
MAN IN SHOW BUSINESS!"

Afterward, Lee invited the performers to Red Hot & Blue,
a restaurant that had recently opened in Arlington, Virginia; Lee
was a limited partner in the business with the title Official Music
Consultant. The restaurant's specialty was ribs and blues music.
Lee brought his cassette tapes, along with hundreds of hungry
customers and networking young Republicans, and on this particular night Ron Wood. Lee and Sally told Wood how they had
lost their honeymoon suite to the Stones back in '78, and they all
laughed into the wee hours. Then Ron presented Lee with his
Stratocaster. At first, Lee thought it was just to hold, to strum. "No,
it's yours, man," said Wood. Lee was stunned by the generosity,
the sense of musical camaraderie of the gesture. He held onto the
Strat for the rest of the evening, like a kid with callused hands
getting a $14 guitar from his mama and just counting the mo-
ments until everyone left so that he could go off by himself and
practice.

• • •

By any ordinary measure, Lee Atwater should have had minimal
effect on the Republican National Committee. Before he arrived,
the RNC was where you got a nice job if your father gave a lot of
money to the Republican cause. People there worked from nine

to five. Most previous chairmen entered the building from the basement parking garage, whisked up by elevator to their fourth-floor office, so that only their personal staff even knew whether they were in the building. Not Lee Atwater. Hey, he was the hardest-working showman in politics.

During Lee's tenure, the RNC became vital and excit-ing — regular hours were seven to seven, and many staff mem-bers put in fourteen-hour days. Lee Atwater was among the first to arrive and the last to leave the building. He made a grand en-trance — coming through the front door, shaking hands, saying hello to staffers who otherwise hardly knew him. At lunch, when he ran, it was the same procedure — shaking hands on the way out of the building, hollering to staffers on the way back in, always making it clear that he was on the job, running the shop, great for morale, especially among lower-level staff members. "If you want to be a leader, *act* like one," he said.

One of Lee's first acts as RNC chairman was to change the Muzak system from dental-office hum-alongs to hard-charging, pedal-to-the-metal blues. Sig Rogich sent a CD player as an office-warming gift, along with a massive blues collection, which Lee played over and over, sending a note to Sig: "I love love love love love love love love love love love love love love love love love love love love your gift!" — one *love* for each CD.

In 1989, according to Robert Teeter, 54 percent of Republi-cans were under forty. At thirty-eight, Atwater was the ideal leader. He led his troops with inspiration; but he was also belligerent, vindictive, a renegade loyal to some vaguely defined ideal that was part politics, part post–Civil War scorched-earth thinking. Though an inspiring leader, he was not exactly a born manager. He didn't think much of institutions in general, had a tendency to shoot off his mouth, and was too impolitic for some members of the Republican National Committee. Lee had no patience with the slow-moving aspects of his job. Once during a Republican Na-tional Committee meeting he left the stage during the reading of minutes to go back and work the phones.

Brooke Vosburgh scheduled Lee's day, but he always wanted to know how his time was being delegated. He read his sched-ule book constantly, shuffling through it. He rarely canceled appointments, even when overbooked; instead he'd reduce meet-ings from ten minutes to two. Lee fostered the image of a strong man, never canceling for illness. Once he had to stay home because of exhaustion brought on by too much exercise and pushing himself to the brink. When a receptionist said, "Lee went home sick," he ragged on her, saying, "Never tell *anybody* I'm sick."

He knew time was his most valuable commodity, and he would give others his time — but always on his terms. Things started and ended on time. If Lee said, "Call me at four o'clock," and you called a minute late, he wouldn't answer the phone. For the first general staff meeting at the RNC, Lee entered the conference room at 8:59 A.M., locking the door behind him. At precisely 9:00 A.M. he began his remarks to the group of fifty. At 9:01 the doorknob began to turn. Someone got up to open the door. "Sit down," said Lee. The doorknob continued to move. Then there was a knock.

"Lee?" asked Brooke Vosburgh, moving toward the door.

"No," he said, "don't do a thing." He continued the staff meeting. A louder knock. Then *louder*. Lee got up and opened the door. There stood a junior staffer, beet red. "You see all these people here?" Lee said to him. "All these people have is time. They aren't in politics for money. Their most valuable possession is time — and you've wasted the time of every single person in this room!" Lee gave him an intense stare, then shouted, "If you can't show up on time, don't come!"

No one at the RNC was ever late for a meeting with Lee Atwater again.

He reinforced many of his old office methods. Now he had more staffers, more money, and more power to intimidate others with. A typical day for the chairman began the night before, when one of his aides would buy an early-bird edition of the *Post*, scan it, and call Lee at eleven o'clock, reading stories that would shape the next morning's agenda. Lee was up at five A.M., on the phone to Ned Tupper, an old ATO buddy and now a municipal judge in Beaufort, South Carolina, to get a pulse check on what the Carolina papers were reporting. "What's happening? Who's stabbin' me in the back today?" Lee wanted to know what Lee Bandy, head of the Washington bureau for the *State*, was saying. Meanwhile, Sally was serving him breakfast in a bedroom dominated by a NordicTrack treadmill exerciser and a huge-screen TV tuned to the news. Breakfast was like dinner: pork chops or ribs, maybe some fried shrimp or chicken. While Lee ate, watched the news, and made phone calls, Sally pressed his pants and dealt with the *other* children. At six-fifteen his driver arrived to take him to the office.

The calls began the moment Lee stepped into the limo, which had four phone lines — incoming, outgoing, personal, and a portable. Calls to fellow early risers — Mama always, Charlie Black, Ed Rogers. Then on to strike calls for the day, usually stirring recipients out of their sleep and chatting as though, hey, isn't everyone up at this hour? "Did you read the story in the *Post* yet? No?" The paper that Lee had been briefed on the night before was still resting in their doorway. "Page twenty-two. Get back to me."

At six-thirty he was leaning back behind his desk, guitar in lap, looking over a thick news summary prepared by a staffer at five-thirty that morning, sipping Jogger Juice (ordered from a health lab in Colorado) or Jolt (all the sugar, twice the caffeine), and huddling with Brooke. He liked her skills and personality, but beyond that she showed dedication and a willingness to hang in there. Some friends of Lee felt Brooke was keeping them away from him, but Lee was moving on, and most of it was his decision. When her boys had left to live with their dad in North Carolina, Brooke had begun burying herself in work, and now that meant Lee. She arrived each morning at six-fifteen. Every time he left the office, she decluttered his messy desk. Lee wanted her with him at all times. "If you can't talk to Brooke," he told a longtime friend, "you can't talk to me." From a distance, her family — northeastern liberals — had misgivings about the extent to which Brooke was wrapped up in Lee's life, but she knew that if they came face-to-face with Lee, he would win them over.

Other staffers, still damp from five o'clock showers, drove through D.C. darkness to make Lee's staff meeting, which now began at seven sharp in a tiny windowless room. Communications director Goodin, chief of staff Matalin, and press secretary Leslie Goodman smoked, to the discomfort of others, except Lee, who still smoked a pack of Winstons — on Fridays only. The atmosphere was relaxed, a mingling of news, gossip, and Lee's lessons on the political business of life. Briefed on the news, Lee was ready to dispense marching orders. You had to get a counterstory out by ten so that the targeted reporters could develop it and meet their deadlines.

Goodman enumerated less important press requests, which could be voluminous. "Maria Shriver has been calling." In past years, the chairman of the RNC had a hard time getting a cab, never mind requests for face time. Smart reporters weren't interested in hearing the standard propaganda of the party line. Now the story was about this young buck Atwater. "Eric Alterman of the *New York Times* wants to see you." Matalin usually became the intermediary for such sessions. She was glib, funny, not your traditional Republican flak. The press liked her. Ann Devroy of the *Post* was one of her closest friends. For that, Lee liked her.

After Lee gave Alterman the green light, Lee called in John Buckley, who was handling press relations for Ed Rollins in the Republican National Congressional Committee office downstairs. What do you hear about this *Times* guy? Who's he talking to? One day, when Alterman was scheduled to interview Lee at the RNC, several busloads of protesters from Chicago pulled up in front of the building to protest some obscure party action. Alterman was on his way. Matalin and Buckley were dispatched to flag him down so that he wouldn't see the demonstration. Mary succeeded in finding Alterman and turning him around.

With his captive audience, Lee gradually came to use staff meetings to go on about movies, meals, music — you name it. "Last book you've read?" he'd ask around the table. "Discuss."

"You just didn't bring anything up at these meetings," recalled Debbie Messick, deputy communications director. "What was the point? Everyone reported to Mary. I wasn't going to bring up anything that I hadn't cleared with Mary, and she didn't want anything brought up in front of Lee that he might decide to get involved in and step on her turf. He would meddle and complicate matters. Therefore, the meetings became Lee sitting there entertaining us with stories of road trips, or meetings with the president, or candidate encounters. Or some disgustingly stupid chainsaw movie he had seen."

Lee also began to display his temper. He was like a boot-camp drill instructor, tearing down recruits so that he could rebuild them to meet his needs. Initially, Matalin took the brunt of Lee's tirades — about everything from schedule snafus to office supplies. Brooke lived in fear that he would single her out for some misdeed whenever he tried to govern by tirade. Once when a request for furniture went unheeded, Lee became furious. "I'm the chairman of the goddam party and I can't get a couch!" he screamed. Mark Goodin sat there reading news clips. Mary Matalin did her makeup. Lee's aides eventually stole a couch from another office.

Lee was especially grouchy if something prevented him from exercising for an hour every day. He liked to jog the Mall from the RNC to the Lincoln Memorial and back, or to go to the Y, where he put his tapes in the stereo system and everyone listened to the blues while he did the StairMaster. He followed this with calisthenics, push-ups, sit-ups, working himself into a sweat-filled frenzy that left him exhausted and looking as if he had just come out of a shower. But when Lee arrived back at the office, his grouchiness was gone. A tall glass of water and lunch — two hamburger patties, no roll, from the Capitol Hill Club next door — were on his desk. He wolfed the food down, and pushed on through a day of appointments, visits to the White House, fund-raisers across town or even out of town. At the office Lee was a phone fanatic. At the end of the day, all call sheets were reviewed, and if someone failed to return one of the hundreds of calls the office received daily, Lee gave that staffer hell.

• • •

It was unusual for the head of RNC to have an entourage, but Lee had three young advance men — Blake Williams, who traveled with him at all times, and two aides who set things up at the desti-nation. Their job was to get Lee from one location to another, to tell him where to go, whom he was to see, and to provide compan-ionship, because Lee never wanted to be alone. Blake toted a big Halliburton aluminum camera case with Lee's schedule, briefing papers for all stops, a stash of Tabasco sauce with the Bush '88 campaign logo on the label, seven sets of cufflinks and tie bars for the gents, stickpins for the ladies, fifteen RNC or presidential pens, Plato's *Republic* (Cliffs Notes version), Machiavelli's *The Prince*, and Sun-tzu's *The Art of War*, a Wizard with the numbers of anyone Lee might want to reach on short notice (office, home, car, beeper, date of birth, and Social Security number for White House clearance), and three Motorola flip phones. The RNC had bought the phones the first week they came out for $2,000 apiece — not because one might fail, but because Lee conducted several phone calls at once. "One of the most joyous times to be around Lee was when he was 'out of pocket' on a plane," said Mark

Goodin. "It was the saddest moment in my professional life when they put phones on planes." Lee's luggage also included a gym bag containing a Walkman, blues tapes, and jogging gear. And the Strat. Moving Lee from place to place was no easy task. He didn't drive a car, seemed disoriented getting on and off planes, and had to be handled like a big kid.

Lee signed on with the Walker lecture agency, receiving up to $10,000 for a speech, sometimes with two events on the same trip. Sally often accompanied him on such outings, and the easy money pleased her, especially at tax time. Once, when Blake was on vacation, Lee took Leslie Goodman and Brooke Vosburgh with him to Puerto Rico for a speech. When the women decided to stay over for a weekend on the beach, they bade farewell to Lee as he left for the airport with a local escort who dropped him off at the terminal. Lee couldn't make out the directions he had been given on a sheet of paper, didn't know what plane to get on — there was no one there to point him in the right direction. Normally the advance guys would have been there to make sure he reached his seat on the plane. But no, the women were back at the hotel. In fact, they were dozing in the sun. Lee was furious. He went to a phone booth, where passersby could see him jumping up and down and screaming at Brooke for the screwup. Somehow, he made it back to the office, and he was still fuming about the ordeal at the staff meeting the following Monday morning.

On another occasion, Lee had to make an appearance at a function at the "Hinckley Hilton." Blake got Lee to his seat, returned to the car and went for something to eat with driver Mark Mascarenhas. When they returned, Lee was standing at the curb talking to someone he had met at dinner. Blake made the mistake of saying, "Sorry you had to wait on us."

When Lee settled into the backseat, he went into a tirade. "Goddammit, what have you guys been doing?" He kept smacking the back of the front seat while chewing them out. "Jesus Christ, I thought you were supposed to be taking care of me! What the hell do I have you for?" The next morning Blake called Lee's curbside companion to apologize.

"How long were y'all sitting out there?" Blake inquired.

"We'd just walked out." Classic Atwater. If he could make a point and get some future mileage out of a situation, Lee loved to pounce.

The fund-raising circuit was grueling. Lee didn't like to say no. One weekend he flew from D.C. to Dallas to El Paso, back to Dallas, to Upstate New York, then back to Dallas to Nashville, then back to D.C. It was always quick in, quick out, eating on the plane. He went to Hawaii for thirteen hours, Tokyo for thirty-six, and Sally got all excited but had no time to tour.

In reception lines, Lee kept Blake Williams nearby in case someone wanted to talk about something that was — or wasn't — important. He was besieged by favor seekers who would hand him a business card, a résumé. "Here's Blake, my deputy chairman," Lee would say. "Talk to him, and we'll get right to work on it." Williams took notes, feigning outrage, sincerity, special knowledge, or whatever was called for.

Lee liked to be in the know. If he wasn't, he had a cover-up line. Once Lee was greeting donors at a dinner in Illinois when someone expressed regret that a committeewoman couldn't attend. "She's having surgery, you know."

Lee acted surprised, which surprised others who presumed that he already knew. After all, it was in *all* the Illinois Republican papers. "Goddamn it, Blake, why didn't you tell me about that?"

It was his advance man's job to respond, "Sorry, Lee. Forgot to mention it."

Lee remembered faces and names, in that order. When meeting women, it was "Hey, hon," with a kiss on the cheek, especially in the South. If he forgot a name, he could recall a detail and be so personable that an acquaintance didn't realize he had never spoken her name. He liked to have a photographer around so that he could greet someone, make small talk, shoot the picture, then just keep movin'. If the photographer ran out of film, Lee's instructions were to just keep flashing as he gripped, grinned, and kept 'em moving through. But if Lee said, "I'll call you," or "I'll take care of it," he was as good as his word. It was the advance man's responsibility to get word back to the staff for action. At the end of a trip, Lee reviewed business cards for follow-up, even flirtations. "She's cute," meant another number for the travel Wizard. "I definitely want to remember her."

His awareness of the moods of people in the crowd was like radar. If he felt that someone didn't like him, either he would try to curry the person's favor or he would be relentless in making him or her dislike him even more. When Lee spotted congresswoman

Pat Schroeder at a reception, he marched over and tapped her on the shoulder. "Hey, it's me," he said, putting out his hand. "Lee Atwater, the most evil man in America." Choking on her drink, Schroeder managed a hello, then regained enough composure to introduce Lee to her husband, whom Lee talked to for several minutes. Nice fella. Then he worked the room.

Most of the time Lee flew private planes provided by state party or Republican benefactors, and RNC charters when commercial schedules didn't work. At the end of an event, no matter how late, Lee always tried to get back home to read the early-bird edition of the *Post*. While being driven home, Lee would scan the paper and make calls to operatives in the Rockies or on the West Coast, finally arriving at a side street near his house. Then, rather than disturb Sally and the kids, he might have Mark park the car while he sat in the back seat dialing on into the nonexistent night.

By and large politics is devoid of charm, sex appeal, or the talent to amuse, but Lee Atwater added a touch of showbiz sizzle. The Stratocaster was his tool. He lugged it everywhere, to the office, on planes, on presidential trips, where he always managed to find an hour a day to practice. In November, Lee had made the acquaintance of P. J. O'Rourke, the provocative political writer for *Rolling Stone*. Atwater invited him to the Inaugural Gala and the celebration at the restaurant afterward, and when *Rolling Stone* carried a rave review of the festivities — including Lee's performance — it almost brought tears to the closet rock star's eyes. Because *Rolling Stone* had been a counterculture magazine that, incidentally, had gone mainstream, Lee's critics held their tongues as he argued that he was using music to spread the Republican cause. "I firmly believe that I can have fun and do my work at the same time," Atwater insisted, speaking to another journalist. "And merging my musical love and my political career — well, that's been a big unintended bonus."

Lee Atwater was the '60s' favorite kind of hero — a successful rebel. He worked at it so thoroughly that his image became his life. "What he is attempting, by doing little more than acting naturally, is to make it acceptable for anyone of any age and any class to be a Republican, no matter what their race or religious background," wrote journalist Carl Cannon. "He wants to put a little soul into party politics, some mirth and zest, and to put the emphasis of the Grand Old Party on that last word." Lee Atwater became a political showman. To young Republicans he was more than a celebrity. He was a hero.

Life was filled with White House receptions, parties, dinners — Lee barely dropped by his home in the evening. Fundraisers all over the country. Everyone famous calling him on the phone. In his desk he kept a script from Chuck Norris, with Lee's part (a DEA agent) highlighted, if only he could get away for a weekend in the Philippines to shoot the scenes! He was mentioned on *L.A. Law*. Also on *thirtysomething*. He was a question on *Jeopardy!* (Mama's favorite show.) He played with the band on Letterman. Band leader Paul Shaffer thought the bluesman was too intense: "As soon as he learns where to lay out, he'll be cool."

Lee was fascinated by actresses, beautiful women whose lives had been largely shaped by their looks. He could relate to that — his career had been forged largely by how he was perceived by others. And he had massive crushes on movie stars. Cheryl Ladd was wonderful, right up there onstage during the introductions at the Inaugural Gala. At one fund-raiser Raquel Welch was his woman of desire. His mission for the evening was to get to know her (he had the staff research every movie she had ever made). Of course, he ended up sitting next to her, regaling her with details about her film career. At the staff meeting next day, all he talked about was how great Raquel looked. (She sent Lee her workout video.)

At another fund-raiser Lynda Carter was the guest, and Lee told her how wonderful she looked after the birth of her child. She told him that her secret to weight control was to pop an Altoid mint whenever she felt like eating. The strong mint flavor satisfied her taste buds for two hours. Combining weight control and breath hygiene in one little mint — what an idea! As it happened, Lee was obsessive about his breath. Since he was in the business of meeting people up close and personal, he was always brushing his teeth, gargling with Scope before meetings. The advance guys had to carry Certs for him — he sucked two at a time. Now, with typical exuberance, Lee switched to Altoids, which he chomped by the handful.

Lee received letters from teachers and librarians asking him about his reading preferences as a teenager. "I am a great believer in the importance of reading as an educational tool, and pride myself on still being able to read two books every week despite a very busy schedule," he replied. In addition to several of the standard recommendations — Dickens's *David Copperfield*, Twain's *Tom Sawyer* and *Huckleberry Finn*, Maugham's *Of Human Bondage*, and Conrad's *Heart of Darkness* — Lee suggested that high school students read historical books, including *Abraham Lincoln*, by Benjamin Thomas; *George Washington*, by Thomas Flexner; and *The Killer Angels*, by Michael Shaara.

Post reporter Paul Taylor invited Lee to speak to a class he was teaching at Princeton, where Lee explained how he had established early goals for himself in college after reading Plato's *Republic*. He had come away "determined that I was going to spend my years from age twenty to forty being educated," he said. "And if I happened to get anything else — fame, fortune or money — along the way, that would be fine. But I really wasn't going to decide what to do with my life until I was forty. . . . I'm thirty-eight now, so I've still got two more years of the education process. But politics is the best way to get educated, because you need to know something about everything. You need to know about history, statistics, human nature, sociology, current events, political science, and if you're lazy like I was, it keeps you on your toes, because you gotta learn every day. *Root hog or die!* as they say."

Actually, apart from his daily horoscope and the morning news summary, Lee didn't read much anymore. He wore disposable contact lenses, which gave him such discomfort that by the end of the day he liked to remove them. And his schedule left him even *less* time to read the two books a week that he never read in the first place. Researchers read the books that Lee started, carried around, and liked to discuss; he read the tight summaries they prepared on index cards. If a forthcoming book was significant, Lee tried to get his staff supplied with an early reviewer's copy, or even galley proofs. He had staffers call authors, asking them for manuscripts still in production. Then Pinkerton or Gary Maloney would read the book and give Lee a briefing.

Lee's sense of celebrity often took a wayward political path. In March he served as grand marshal at a St. Patrick's Day parade in Columbia, where he was becoming a bona fide cult figure. He waved to the crowds from a convertible with signs on either side: PARDON JAMES BROWN. He visited his idol at the South Carolina penitentiary. In staff meetings Lee would even suggest that freeing the godfather of soul might be a smart thing for Bush to do. Lee's advisers had their doubts about his ability to pull this one off, and about the advisability of getting a wife-beater out of the slammer using Republican pull. The idea faded.

• • •

In Washington the ability to draw attention to yourself is one of the most valuable assets a person can have. But when it comes to dealing with the press, a high profile makes you a target, especially if you're perceived as part of the president's inner circle. Mike Deaver had taken a fall after riding high as Reagan's image maker. He called Lee at home one evening. "Keep your head down," he said. "Take it from one who knows." If politics and showbiz were indeed bedmates, overexposure could be hazardous to career advancement. Still Lee pushed on. He did a gig at Anton's 1201 Club, nearly earning equal billing with the show's star, B. B. King. He took the Red Hot & Blue Band to Carnegie Hall for an appearance with the New York Pops.

Out of control, thought Mark Goodin. In one of their earliest conversations, Lee had told Goodin that when he was young he had wanted to be a rock star; now he was one. Lee was beginning to believe his own hype, was fixating on music and this hipster creation. In March he posed for a picture to appear in a summer issue of *Esquire* magazine with his jogging pants pulled down to his ankles while he saluted the camera. Goodin predicted that Barbara Bush would be unhappy.

"Oh, you're just being an old lady," said Lee.

On the phone one day, John Buckley was discussing the new visibility that Lee had brought to the RNC. "You know the guy's not circumcised," said Buckley's fellow Atwater watcher, " 'cause there's just no end to that prick."

Goodin had done enough time with Strom Thurmond to be unimpressed by Lee's upwardly mobile tendencies. At times he hardly recognized his old buddy. Goodin had been stunned when Lee told him to fire all the research and communications staff during his first week on the job. "Clean house," said Lee. "I want nothing but campaign people at those jobs." Goodin had tried to get Lee to soften, and he'd saved a few spots to maintain some institutional memory, but Lee seemed to owe an abundance of favors. The strain was accentuated several months later when Lee handed Goodin the résumé of a childhood friend who had worked at a radio station in Columbia, saying, "I've got this guy I want you to hire, and I want you to pay him $40,000 a year."

"What's he supposed to do?" asked Goodin.

"Whatever I tell him to."

Goodin paused. "I don't get this," he said. "I just finished laying people off who busted their asses for George Bush — and we are hiring some flak from a radio station in Columbia? For $40,000 I could have kept two researchers at minimum wage!"

"This guy is a good PR man," said Lee. "Just do it."

Goodin fumed as Lee's pal came onboard to drum up publicity and work as a musical advance man — a roadie! — for the chairman of the Republican Party. Must-Hires are a part of life in politics: to the victor go the spoils. But Goodin began to sense that the guy he loved like a political brother was losing interest in the business of politics. Lee's command focus was now on his own blues-driven persona. Goodin wondered whether some of Lee's self-created publicity wasn't affecting his brain. Certainly it was having an effect on the workings of the office.

Brooke eased Lee into shifting the staff meetings to eight o'clock, but these sessions continued to be not for the faint of heart, because Lee grew more angry, vitriolic, even irrational. Except for Goodin, staffers were afraid to cross Lee. Instead of working with Rollins, who had become head of the Republican National Congressional Committee, Lee grew suspicious of him. Here was his old sparring mate with offices in the RNC building, at a salary double Lee's. "Does that fucker know that I'm in charge?" asked Lee. "If he thinks he's going to be in the press all day . . . you know, I could have gotten Bush to head off that job. I sure hope that he understands I am in charge of the RNC!" The friction between Atwater and Rollins didn't lead to an explosion only because Buckley and Matalin kept the peace between offices.

Mary Matalin was quickly becoming one of the boys. A woman who acts like a man seems to understand men, and therefore she's everything a guy could want in a woman, right? She had many of the characteristics that men typically admire in each other — fair play, a sense of duty, and a predilection for lots of goofing around. She rode a bike to work, set out her makeup during the staff meeting — complete with curling iron and mirror — and got herself ready for the day while the meeting went on. Matalin knew her blues music from growing up on the South Side of Chicago. She worked out, went on and off diets, smoked cigars, ate dry cereal from boxes, loved dirty jokes, had gone through two divorces, and liked to conduct business at night, often sitting around her office drinking a bottle of wine. Collectively, these traits said to guys like Lee: Hey, I understand you.

Lee poked fun at Mary, but he also understood that, despite her tough city-kid exterior, she was emotional at the core, took criticism to heart, and always tried to jump higher the next time. "He kept making me grow," she recalled. "He knew the things that terrorized me, and he would force me into them."

In 1989, for the first time in anyone's memory, the Democratic National Committee softball team beat the RNC squad, 9–6, in a hard-fought seven-inning game played on The Ellipse in front of the White House. Mary's fault, absolutely. As athletic Democratic "field office" players rounded the bases, Lee screamed at his chief of staff for not lining up ringers for *his* team. "Why didn't you think of it? Didn't you know?! Anyone who knows about this game has to know we need ringers!!" For Lee, of course, nothing was a game. During the game there was some light taunting between him and opposing chairman Ron Brown. When the game was over, an elated Brown teased Lee as the teams were shaking hands. Lee lunged, and players had to separate the two party chairmen. The next morning, Lee beat on Mary again, scolding her for not being a master manipulator in the world of softball. "Ringers!!"

No man is a hero to his valet, and Lee was certainly no celebrity to his closest staff. If anything, they bristled at the notion. Brooke Vosburgh didn't have time to think of Lee as being famous. She had worked for Donald Regan — the guy who ran Merrill Lynch, served as secretary of the treasury, then ruled the West Wing of the White House as chief of staff to the president. If Brooke called almost anyone in the world and said, "Don Regan wants to meet with you," the person would cancel anything and fly into town. When Lee wanted to meet with some famous person, there were no guarantees that it was going to happen. Lee, to her, was just someone who did well in his segment of the political world. She knew his insecurities, how hard he fought for visibility, and how occasionally he would get little signals that he wasn't as big as he wanted to be — terrible seats at the State of the Union, for instance.

Brooke was beginning to realize that very little of Lee's behavior was spontaneous. Almost everything he said, everything he did was premeditated. He had a gift for establishing intimacy on short notice, yet it was packaged. She saw him use reassuring words to put others at ease with his requests or his quirks of anger. Then he would use the same words with her. When Brooke told Lee that she didn't trust him, he grew angry, then he went through a mood change and assured Brooke that, with *her*, the words were true. He began to delegate very personal aspects of his life to her. At meetings he wanted Brooke to sit, not next to him, no, *right beside* him. Her job was to tell it as she saw it, to summarize what others were thinking, and then to give her view without bias. Ultimately, though, Lee trusted only himself.

One morning Leslie Goodman came into Brooke's office asking if Lee had a brother. A reporter had inquired, and the question was a surprise to the press secretary. Brooke didn't know. Intuitively, she felt she shouldn't approach Lee about it. Shortly afterward, on a trip to Columbia with Lee, Brooke saw a picture of Joe tucked away in the den at the Atwater home. She was already feeling amazed to be in the house where Lee had grown up — it seemed so small for someone who was so much bigger than life. Seeing the picture of Joe also opened a new dimension to Lee for Brooke, to know that he had been walking around with this inside him all along.

• • •

Because in the late '80s the Republican Party was good at winning the presidency, but poor at scoring victories further down the ticket, Lee quickly established an agenda: The GOP would break the Democrats' thirty-five-year hold on the House by targeting twenty to thirty incumbents who appeared vulnerable and recruiting highly qualified Republicans to oppose them each election year. He also wanted to gain control of as many governorships and state legislatures as possible in order to affect the drawing of congressional district lines after the 1990 census. Republicans had received about 48 percent of the composite vote in recent House races, but they controlled only about 40 percent of the seats.

As a flanking action, Lee developed Operation Outreach,

a strategy for recruiting blacks and other minorities, traditionally supporters of the Democratic Party. He thought it imperative for his party to broaden its base. The boomers did not have racial prejudice instilled in them, Lee told colleagues. In fact, they felt guilty for the sins of their forefathers, so racial politics would backfire. Because many younger members of the press were baby boomers, recruiting minorities was also the smart thing to do media-wise. Bush had met with more black leaders before he was inaugurated than Reagan had in two terms as president. On the anniversary of Martin Luther King Jr.'s birthday, three days before he took office as head of the Republican Party, Lee spoke at the Atlanta church where King had preached. Still the *New York Times* took him to task for his part in the Willie Horton TV campaign, adding that he bore "some responsibility for making the Republicans so vulnerable to such racist infiltration."

In an op-ed response, Atwater wrote: "Making black voters welcome in the Republican party is my preeminent goal. . . . If our party is to step out of minority status it must be the party of all Americans. Anything short of that is unacceptable."

Then a setback. David Duke, former grand wizard of the Ku Klux Klan, was elected to the Louisiana state legislature as a Republican. He made noises about running for governor. If Duke got a leg up, he would be the most visible pol in the so-called New Republican Party. How to handle this? Atwater and Mark Goodin set in motion a process for drumming Duke out of the party, using a rule that stated that in the absence of a full national convention, the executive committee of the RNC could pass emergency resolutions. They then drafted an emergency resolution condemning Duke, saying he was not a Republican. Atwater denounced Duke as a "charlatan" and taped a commercial for black radio stations condemning the candidate. In the end, Duke won by a slim margin (about 200 votes), in part because the interference from Washington had created a sympathy vote. "I'm just as Republican as Lee Atwater," Duke said.

"I think the chickens have come home to roost," said Ron Brown. "Lee Atwater has made his own bed. The Republicans have made their own bed. The idea of Republicans reaching out to blacks is absurd." Around the same time Howard University blew up over Lee's being appointed to the board of trustees.

Reality settled in deeper for Lee, Ed Rollins, and the whole GOP when, during a four-month period, there were five special congressional elections, including valuable contests in Florida (Claude Pepper died), Colorado (Dick Cheney moved from House whip to secretary of defense), and Indiana (to fill Dan Quayle's old seat). Republicans assumed that the Atwater magic would bring victories; owing to this smugness the RNC used template strategies in these campaigns and lost four of the five races. "After all these months of paying attention to the minutiae of politics, and after all the secondhand lessons in Sun-tzu — 'Study the territory. A good warrior understands that a change in territory dictates a change in tactics,' etc. — we weren't paying very close attention to the fact that the territory was changing and our tactics weren't," reflected Mark Goodin. There was a growing sense that nobody was watching the store.

As much as any policy wonk, Atwater was tied closely to the task of advancing the Bush presidency. He knew that some in the administration looked at political consultants as necessary evils during a campaign and unwelcome houseguests afterward, but he took enormous pride in what he did. He was not going to be treated as a lesser person because of his profession. He was not intimidated by blustery bigmouths who knew more about policy issues. He never let Sununu browbeat him into doing things that were politically stupid just for the sake of policy. Lee knew he would be open to charges that he was focusing the party apparatus too narrowly on the interests of the White House rather than on the needs of other Republicans. Still the key to Lee Atwater's program for building a Republican majority by the millennium was for George Bush to be a successful president.

Lee kept in close contact with the White House. His pal Ed Rogers arrived there each morning at 5:30 to do intelligence and news reports for Sununu, who came in at 6:45. Bush usually came down at 7:05 and hung out in the Oval Office until the 7:30 staff meeting. Lee, after a briefing by Rogers, liked to drop in at 7:10 for coffee and political updates with the president. For Bush politics was a necessary evil in his life. But Lee loved it, relished being political adviser to the president of the United States.

Making the Bush presidency a political success was a problem for Lee because of all the president's men. Nicholas Brady, for instance, was for a tax increase from day one. Brady, a fourth-generation millionaire with thirty years on Wall Street and an upper-crust New England pedigree, had been one of George Bush's closest friends in government service, which they had both entered from noblesse oblige. Bush had made his old friend secretary of the treasury — a questionable choice in many minds — but in the president's compartmentalized view of the world, Brady was his chief economic adviser. Then Richard Darman, pigeonholed as the budget director and resident guru on spending policies, endorsed the tax increase, though he knew there would be political consequences if the increase was implemented too early. Sununu remained quiet on the topic. Lee hated it.

Eventually Sununu cratered on taxes. He was won over by Darman's argument that all the *smart* people realized this supply-side stuff was nonsense; all the *smart* people knew that you can't grow out of a deficit; all the *smart* people recognized that we are undertaxed in some areas. All of Sununu's life he had been on the outside — he was too ethnic, too short-tempered, too . . . smart. Now here was a smart insider group that *wanted* him. Lee was outflanked and outnumbered.

Lee found himself jockeying for private time with Bush, who had cut back on his jogging — Lee's old access to Bush — from four times a week to maybe twice a month owing to concerns about security and crowd control. As chief of staff, Sununu usually made the final call on how Bush would spend his day. Proximity is power. In meetings sometimes Sununu sat in, sometimes not. Often it was difficult to know where Bush's decisions stopped and Sununu's began. One spring afternoon, Lee and Roger Stone met for a run along the Tow Path. Lee needed a reality check on what was going on in the White House. There was no right or wrong to politics; there was only smart or stupid, and while a tax increase might be the smart thing for the economy, a quick read of Atwater's lips said that politically it was stupid.

Lee and Stone had been at odds since a bitter exchange when Stone went with Kemp in the primaries. Stone viewed the run with Lee as a chance for reconciliation. "Well, you were right about Bush," he said as they jogged along. "I guess I was wrong."

"Don't be so sure," said Atwater. "The guy has no political

instincts whatsoever. Bush and this crowd are going to screw it up. Bush won't get reelected."

• • •

On Friday, June 2, Lee was more wired than usual. He sat in his office surrounded by some of the best minds in the building — Goodin, Pinkerton, Goodman, Matalin — as they fired questions at him to prepare him for his first televised encounter with Ron Brown on *Sunday Morning with David Brinkley*. Atwater stood in particularly stark contrast to Brown, the high-paid lawyer and lobbyist who was chairman of the Democratic Party. Like Atwater, Ron Brown had taken over his party in 1989. He was as outspoken and partisan as his Republican counterpart. Otherwise, they were another odd coupling. Brown had the proper demeanor of a straitlaced Republican; Atwater was a country boy who seemed better suited to playing to the masses. "Who would have thought that the Democrats would have as their chairman a button-down lawyer who went to Middlebury College," said Lee, "and that the Republicans' chairman would be a fella from South Carolina who got through school by playing rock 'n' roll?"

Atwater called these grill sessions "murder boards," because his colleagues pretended they were a bunch of reporters and practically killed him with questions. A thick briefing book with likely questions and recommended answers sat on the table. Lee wanted to be ready because it was a time of tremendous turmoil between the parties. After tottering for months, Democrat Jim Wright had just resigned as Speaker of the House. His successor, majority leader Tom Foley, had become the victim of a smear campaign conducted by disgruntled Wright supporters who thought Foley was a little too anxious for Wright to leave; they were spreading unsubstantiated rumors that Foley was homosexual. The whispering campaign was also abetted by an aide to GOP whip Newt Gingrich. Phil Jones, a CBS News correspondent, was in hot pursuit of the rumor, and it nearly reached the status of story on May 28 when Dan Rather asked House majority whip Tony Coelho of California, "Some of [the Republicans], with a wink I'm told, were passing the word that, 'Listen, the worst of it is not even over yet.' . . . Do you know of anything of an ethical, character nature that would prevent Tom Foley from being the next Speaker?"

Mark Goodin had lunch with Phil Jones that week and was

so taken aback by the rumor that he called Mike McCurry, his counterpart at the DNC, to give him a heads-up. McCurry had already heard it.

During the murder boards, Jim Pinkerton cautioned Lee about being critical of the incoming Speaker, because Foley had the respect of George Bush. "Yeah, OK," said Lee. "No problem."

Lee was also focusing on another big encounter that weekend — the twentieth anniversary reunion of the Flora High Class of '69. He had kept in touch with many high school pals, placed some in political jobs, and conducted a deliberate campaign to include them in his life as he moved up the political ladder. He used the class directory from a previous reunion to send notes, pictures, pens, and political memorabilia to old chums. He loved seeing old friends, though the meetings always happened where he wanted to meet, and lasted for as long as he wanted to meet. On visits to Columbia, Lee liked to make the rounds at Five Points, where the college kids hung out. Then he'd go to play guitar and sing at Bullwinkle's, a tavern run by one of Lee's classmates. The calls would go out: Lee's playing Friday at nine, and he'd like you to come. The place would be filled with big-name politicos drinking longnecks side by side with guys from filling stations . . . all because they knew Lee.

Lee had been looking forward to the Flora reunion for two decades, and even more since he had promised to provide the entertainment. In addition, Howard Fineman, the top political gun from *Newsweek*, was trailing Lee on this trip for a book about the new wave of Republican operatives — and Lee was the leader of the pack! Lee and Sally arrived in Columbia at four o'clock, to be met by Doug Seigler, with whom Lee had bonded in a Dark Horseman slap fight back in the Flora days. Seigler drove them to the Radisson Hotel. That night Lee got together with a couple of new friends he had brought into town: Chuck Jackson and Sam Moore. On Saturday, the festivities began full tilt.

Late Saturday afternoon, Leslie Goodman arrived from D.C. with word that the Brinkley show had been canceled — Tienanmen Square had blown up in China. Lee was delighted. "We will party tonight!" In addition to luring Sam and Chuck, Lee had used his clout to attract Isaac Hayes. Not only was Isaac one of Lee's musical heroes, he was also the A–number one dude who played the Duke of New York in one of Lee's all-time favorite movies, *Escape from New York*. "This will be one reunion they'll never forget!" Lee vowed.

That night many pretenders to the Class of '69 showed up, along with teachers. All available alums from Upsetter's Revue played on and on — culminating in the appearance of the star of the show, the hardest-working man in Columbia: LEE ATWATER!

Lee was still trying to impress his old girlfriend Debbie Carson — like him, married with two kids. Still in love with the spotlight after all these years, he called her over to the photographer he had commandeered for the occasion. "Come have your picture taken with me!" Debbie felt uneasy once again at Lee's showmanship, his desire to please the crowd rather than carry on a genuine conversation. He looked tired, stressed out. She asked if he was happy. "I don't know what you're talking about," said Lee, not making eye contact.

"I'm just concerned about you," said Debbie.

"No, everything's fine," Lee replied. "I love my job, love Washington." Someone else came along for a picture with Lee, and the party rolled on until twelve-thirty, then moved up to Lee's room with former Upsetter's Revue member Joe Sligh and all the Atwater irregulars until four o'clock in the morning. The next day Lee flew into Jackson, Mississippi, for a performance with B. B. King, staying over for a political reception and some press work. Monday morning he flew back to D.C., where another battle was already underway.

As Lee and Sally were flying to Columbia the previous Friday, a "talking points" memo was being sent by the RNC to Republican leaders so that they could "set the record straight" about Tom Foley. "Many in the Democratic Party and the media will be portraying him as the 'darling' of the moderates," wrote Mark Goodin in a cover note. "In fact, Mr. Foley has a long history as a liberal — including a recent 85 percent rating by the ultra-liberal Americans for Democratic Action." Attached, in a different typeface, was a three-page attack memo pointing out that Foley was more liberal than his predecessor, Jim Wright. The memo, written by one of Don Todd's bomb throwers in oppo, went one step further, comparing Foley's voting record with that of "the ultra-liberal representative from Massachusetts, Barney Frank," noting that "Foley voted along with Frank 81 percent of the time." The memo rambled on with three-column charts and stats that made Frank and Wright out to be saintly compared to this incoming devil Tom Foley. It was your basic Republican nuclear bombast, including the charge that "Foley Demeans President Bush" by saying of the '88 campaign, "I've always thought of George Bush as an honorable and upright man, but this is not a campaign he can conduct without blushing." There was only one little twist that separated this memo from a thousand others that Mark Goodin had approved: its cute title — TOM FOLEY: OUT OF THE LIBERAL CLOSET.

The memo's title and the choice of Barney Frank, an openly gay congressman, for comparison created a firestorm in press rooms. "Everyone believed intuitively that Atwater had done it," recalled Ann Devroy of the *Post*, "because it had Atwater written all over it." Or maybe it had happened by osmosis. Certainly, if Lee hadn't done it directly, he had set the tone or atmosphere — like Henry II complaining about Thomas à Becket, so that someone down the line said, Well, I'll sure make the boss's day with this one.

David Rogers of the *Wall Street Journal* called Leslie Goodman on Monday while Lee was flying home. "Where is Atwater?" Goodman passed Rogers along to Goodin, who tried to dampen the fire, but the reporter was persistent. That night Rogers called Lee at home, where he was having a massage. Lee said he would call him back; then he called Goodin at home and told him that Rogers was incensed. There were only five papers in the world that mattered to Lee Atwater, and the *Wall Street Journal* was one of them.

"This may force me to quit," said Goodin.

"Let's not overreact," said Lee. "I'll get them calmed down at the White House." He called Rogers back and sparred with him over the memo and the title. "I don't disapprove of it," he said. "I'm not disavowing it."

Goodin only wished he *could* disavow the whole mess. That night he turned to his wife. "I think I'm history," he said.

Tuesday morning Lee was pleased. The story had run in the AP and the *Post*, but with no emphasis on the sexual innuendo. Though embarrassing to the RNC, it also had the kind of sting that Lee liked. Initially, too, he felt that the story would have a brief arc in the press. A little damage control would handle it. At the staff meeting it was agreed that only Goodin was to talk to the press; he had twenty-four hours to contain the story. But the calls became a torrent. Lee was on the phone constantly, trying to manage the spin. Then Barney Frank, who was being pursued by the *Washington Times* for a story about his driver running a bordello out of his apartment, went into spin control of his own. He told House minority leader Bob Michel that unless he denounced the Foley memo, Frank would "out" some people on the GOP side of the aisle in the Senate. (Regarding Foley, he said, "I never heard anything about Tom.") Doubtless, Frank had read Machiavelli, too.

After Frank unloaded, the AP called Goodin. "Congressman Frank is engaged in wishful thinking and an attempt to smear Lee Atwater," he offered as counterspin. When the story came in on the wire, though, Goodin's heart sank. He circled the story with a blue marker and went up to see Atwater on the fourth floor. Lee was on the phone. Mark made a "time-out" sign to interrupt.

Lee covered the phone. "What is it?"

"You need to see this," said Mark. "It's an AP story that's moving. It's on this Foley memorandum."

Lee grabbed the sheet and read it. "This bumps it into the news cycle," said Goodin.

"Faa-bulous plus!" said Lee, giving Mark a high five.

Goodin relaxed, thinking maybe he had added it up wrong. He went back to his office, where Don Todd was waiting. "This is starting to get play," said Todd.

Initially, the AP had characterized the memo as a document "which some Democrats say calls into question . . ." The frenzy began. The wire's second version called it "a smear memo widely denounced by Republicans." The Barney Frank spin took hold. The final version labeled it "the smear memo which insinuates . . ." And when the *Wall Street Journal* story hit, the House leadership went into a panic. That night Barney Frank was on the evening news. Everyone started to pile on, including Republicans.

Lee went into command focus. His own survival was at stake. He wanted to get out the word that he did not do this thing. His biggest fear was that Sununu was going to call for his resignation, and Bush might buckle. At eight-thirty that night, the tension built as he called Foley and apologized. Foley's attitude was a mixture of graciousness and anxiety. In fact, Foley was so uncomfortable about the situation that Lee began to sense some daylight. "Shit, he has to be guilty," Lee laughed to a staffer after the phone call. "He was so nervous about it, I mean he wants it to go away more than *we* do."

Despite Foley's assurances that Lee would not be blamed, Lee knew there would be a battle ahead. He made a list of all the people who might take him out, and how each of them could be dealt with. First, he called Bush and apologized. He talked to Sununu constantly, always impressing on him how it would be worse for them if he got taken out.

That night, Lee called Goodin in. "This is fucking out of control," he said. Matalin was in the office. "Let me see that goddam thing again." Goodin got the distinct impression that Lee was looking at the memo for the first time. His earlier reaction to reporters was probably based on an index-card summary or a briefing by Mary, not on reading the actual document, Goodin thought. If the media only knew how ridiculous it was to think that Lee had approved this memo in advance — he didn't read *anything* that came out of RNC research or communications.

Back in January Lee's signature had appeared on a fundraising letter that criticized a 50 percent congressional pay raise as exorbitant. Then his staff found out that the pay raise had been proposed by Reagan, and that Bush had endorsed it only a week earlier, calling it "overdue"! Leslie Goodman had sprung into action, saying that Atwater was "not opposed to the pay raise," and that he had ordered changes in the letter, including deletion of the two paragraphs criticizing the pay raise, but certain unnamed RNC staffers had screwed up. Now where were those certain unnamed staffers when Lee needed them?

"Goddam it, this is stupid!" Lee was screaming. "This is fucking stupid!" Mark and Mary huddled afterward. He told her that events were propelling him to resign. All he wanted was her personal reassurance that he would be taken care of financially. He had just bought a house, was struggling with a mortgage, and had three kids. "I don't want to be out on the street," Goodin said. "I'm going to be radioactive for at least a year."

"Oh, it won't come to that," Matalin said.

Wednesday morning Dan Quayle tried to intercede for Goodin. "What's the hubbub? This is nothing. We're going to hand up one of our people for this?" He went in to see Bush, but the president was enraged. Bush viewed the memo as something that could cripple his ability to work with Congress early in his administration. He wanted to nip this in the bud — fast.

Goodin was in Lee's office that morning when John Sununu called. Lee put him on the speaker phone. "You have to do something about this. The president is very upset. This cannot sit," said Sununu.

"No, that's exactly what they want," Atwater argued. "That's the worst thing we can do."

"You know, I don't think either of you understand what the president is saying," said Sununu.

"Oh, I disagree," said Goodin. "I know precisely what he's saying."

"Something must be done about it," said Sununu.

Then Lee and Mark were alone. "There's no doubt in my mind where this is heading," said Mark. "It is only a question of how much blood is going to be on the floor when it happens, and I am not going to sit here and fight the president of the United States. He'll win every time."

"Now, Mark . . . ," said Lee, halfheartedly.

"I'm taking myself out."

They got a bit emotional, looking mostly at the floor. "I'm really sorry, buddy," said Lee.

Goodin said he wanted to tell his family first, and then his staff. He said he would not do interviews. He went down to his office on the second floor, typed his letter of resignation, and left with a year's severance pay.

When Lee read the early-bird edition of the *Post* that night, it featured the story of Mark's resignation, along with a quote from Ron Brown saying that Goodin should not "take the fall" for an operation that was "up to its knees in sewer-style politics." Brown called on the president to remove Atwater and "stop this madness by telling operatives to stop peddling rumors, stop spreading dirt and put away the negative campaign playbook."

On the same page, Ed Rollins struck again. "I think for party partisans to be out spreading any kind of rumor or innuendo is totally irresponsible and I would discourage it," said the deputy chairman of the Republican National Congressional Committee, "and if I found it going on in my own committee I would fire the person doing it."

There is a pattern to most political scandals. Once the story breaks, the chief expresses total shock that any of his staffers could have done such a thing. He volunteers to work with authorities in nabbing the culprits. They usually turn out to be loners, who are ceremoniously fired. Then comes the settlement stage, the nolo contendere plea, and damage control with assurances that problems like this are the exception, not the rule. That systems will be changed so that these mistakes will not occur in the future. How high would this scandal go?

In the wake of Goodin's departure came the conspiracy theories. Who did what? Theory one: After his lunch with Phil Jones, Goodin had told friends in the media that CBS had the goods on Foley being gay. Thus, when the memo came out, Goodin was not credible when he denied that it had something to do with that rumor. Theory two: The memo was approved by one of Goodin's deputies (standard practice for Goodin) and it was already in the mail when Pinkerton gave the heads-up warning during "murder boards." As a cover-up, Goodin had hand-carried the memo to get approval from Matalin while Lee was flying down to Columbia. Mary approved it, not picking up on the sexual innuendo either. Nobody was sure what really had happened.

Regardless, the Democrats were reluctant to let Atwater off the hook — he was the one they wanted to take the fall. Indeed, if people looked at patterns of conduct in order to determine whether a first-time offender should get the maximum sentence, it was generally agreed that Mark Goodin was not a dirty player. He came from years of working with Strom Thurmond, who was a nut about chain of command and control; you didn't put out a thank-you letter without the senator seeing it. Before that, Goodin was at newspapers, where there was always an editor reviewing his copy, asking him questions. But Goodin was also headstrong, growing cockier on the job. He liked to feed Lee's weaknesses, fanning the coals of controversy. On the permanent campaign, he remained a strong advocate of oppo research as a way to knock an opponent down to size. Why didn't Goodin raise the issue during the murder-board session? For Lee, the problem was not Goodin's failure to read the memo with due diligence; rather, it was a failure of judgment. Goodin should have read the explosive political environment. But would his departure be enough?

On Thursday, at a Capitol Hill Club breakfast meeting, Lee

was pummeled with criticism from Republican congressmen who had not read the memo but were reacting to the press hysteria. And that night Bush would be holding his first prime-time presidential press conference. Lee was afraid that after yesterday's exchange with Sununu, he would be fired on national TV. He was on the phone to Ed Rogers throughout the day while Bush prepped for the press. Certain that the Foley memo would come up, Lee and Rogers fashioned a reply for the president, which Rogers had typed on an index card.

As the day wore on, Lee grew more anxious. At six o'clock he went for his usual run, returning to the office in jogging gear and sitting on the floor in front of the television to watch the news. Waiting for the press conference to begin, he started doing sit-ups — 40 . . . 50 . . . He worked himself up to a frenzy . . . 80 . . . 90. . . . "I don't know what they're telling him," he said. At the last minute, Rogers decided against giving the index card to the president . . . 150 . . . 160. . . . He couldn't be sure that Sununu wouldn't turn on him . . . 180 . . . 185. . . . National news for three days, and the worst thing that can happen to a member of the inner circle is to be mentioned in a press conference — the press love to go negative . . . 200 . . . 225 . . . 250. . . . "Goddammit, goddammit," he said. "It's always your friends that fuck ya. I can't believe this." Lee's staff hadn't seen him so worked up since the Jesse Jackson sellout at Howard University.

When the question came up, Bush was ready. "Disgusting," Bush called the memo. "It's against everything that I have tried to stand for in political life." And what about Atwater? Bush said that Lee "looked me right in the eye and said he did not know about it, . . . and so I accept that." Lee Atwater fell back in a joyous pool of sweat. How could he have ever worried about George Bush? Isn't loyalty what politics is all about?

10

THE SPOILS OF WAR

You can tell whether you've gone native if you . . . assume
Lee Atwater is a household name everywhere.
— *Washington Post Magazine*, July 1988

Lee needed to get away from Washington. On Friday he put in a
half-day, then joined Sally, and they drove to the mountain house
they had bought in March. At High Knob they relaxed for the
weekend with old Carolina pals Mike Ussery and Jim McCabe
and spouses. The cabin was near Front Royal, Virginia, a blue-
collar town of twelve thousand that was Lee's type of place. Nobody knew him, and he could blend into the masses. Paul Laxalt
and Ed Rollins also had homes there. Lee's was built into the
side of a steep hill, with four bedrooms, a small kitchen, and
an airy family room with a cathedral ceiling and a deck that
overlooked a wooded ravine. The walls were covered with framed
pictures of the Atwaters with dignitaries, and above the fireplace
hung a large portrait: Lee in a clown outfit with a bulbous red
nose.

The friends talked about the June issue of *Esquire*, with the
provocative photo of Lee that Goodin had been such an old lady
about. It was a feature about how even celebrities put their pants
on one leg at a time. There was nothing risqué about Lee's photo,
but he most definitely looked like someone who had been caught
with his pants down. The significance was not lost at the White
House, where Barbara Bush, on seeing Lee's red running shorts,
"saw a little red herself," reported the *New York Times*.

Bar had been quite vocal about the Foley affair as well. "It was the most outrageous, unattractive, not nice memo," she said, "and I was ashamed of it, as was my husband." Regarding Lee, she added, "I think he is one of the best politicians I know, and someone on his team made a terrible mistake. But they won't make another one, will they?"

When Barbara Bush spoke, Lee Atwater listened. "If you're in my job and the candidate's wife don't like you, you're in a heap of trouble," he said. "No matter how smart and no matter how good you are, she gets the last word." Lee had befriended her boys, and she saw him as a son, but one whose hands had to be slapped once in a while. Lee saw her as an extension of his own mama, someone he admired and whose approval he sought, his bad-boy conduct notwithstanding.

"Mrs. Bush, thanks for your support this week — It has been a most unpleasant one and I hope it is behind us," said Lee in a handwritten note to the First Lady on Friday, June 9. "What I hate the most is that I created a problem for the President — it makes me sick. I'm going to get things cooled down and vow not to ever put him in this kind of situation again."

Whenever his aides wanted Lee to think twice about some unseemly activity, they would say to Lee, "Don't you think this could be trouble if Mrs. Bush finds out?" Yet he continued to flagrantly pick up and date women, often introducing his current companion as "a friend" to colleagues and friends who knew better. This made insiders uncomfortable, and a few senior staffers — who also had to deal with Lee when Sally was by his side — felt that they had become his accomplices by trying to act normal in both situations. Several friends and advisers talked with Lee about the risks his philandering created. There were eyes everywhere. Lee's activity seemed compulsive to staff members. "He just couldn't resist, and there were plenty of opportunities," said one. "I would get Must-Hires, people with no talent that I could see."

Lee's persona changed instantaneously when a female was around, particularly if she was attractive. He had a way of confronting females that was awesome to observe. Once, returning to the RNC from a meeting at the White House, Lee was talking politics in the elevator with several staff members when a trim dark-haired woman stepped into their midst. Most men would be thankful for the three-mirror glimpse elevators usually provide. Not Lee. For him, no one else was in the elevator except Lee and this comely young thing. He started a conversation with her immediately: full eye contact, soft smoky voice, interested in who she was, wondering if there was anything he could do to make her day brighter. By the fourth floor, Lee had the woman's full attention in one corner. The staffers went back to their offices, leaving Lee and his newfound friend to consider more interesting possibilities.

As predatory males went, Lee was certainly the life of the Republican Party. Indeed, the party was full of young, glamorous, smart, trust-funded women who gravitated toward power figures like Lee. Even though he struck some onlookers as doing an act, what he did still translated into sex appeal because a certain kind of woman — often quite intelligent — could recognize the thought and creative energy that it took to create such a character. It was flattering to be in Lee Atwater's company, perhaps even in his employ.

Lee talked with trusted friends about his unhappiness in marriage. He wanted to know all the details of any impending divorce, especially divorces involving children. Not that he was at odds with Sally, who, by most estimates, was not nearly tough enough in dealing with Lee. Rather, Lee was at odds with marriage itself, which he considered a waste of his valuable time. Sally was a mom who had learned to function in many ways as a single parent, though always yielding to the schedule that drove Lee from one crowded day to another. Even when her husband was around, he often had cronies or aides with him. When the couple did communicate, it was usually in a crowd or on the run — sharing a dais, going to Larry King's latest wedding.

Lee often called Sally from the office, the car, the road for a stiff, hurry-up conversation that aides called The Drill: "How are the kids?" Oh, fine. "Put one of them on." Some chatter. "Put your mom back on." Closely followed by, "Gotta go." That was family for the day.

Lee didn't work very hard at his marriage. What began in Union had become a disconnect. Sally was at home with the kids. Lee just happened to sleep there most nights. Did Lee love Sally? After eleven years of shared history, they were *family*, but he was perfunctory in his affections. Lee wasn't good at family nurturing, so he didn't fake it. Sally admired the honesty. "I love her so much," he reflected in a private recording near the end of his life. "But we both are aware something has been missing for many, many years. And I think we both reluctantly agree that although we do love each other, we are going to remain married, and I love the children, there will always be something a little off, a little unorthodox about our marriage." Sally had taken enough psychology in college to theorize that Lee was afraid of getting close to the kids because something might happen to them, a residue of Lee's feelings about the loss of his brother, Joe. Sally behaved like an old-fashioned wife who turned her head the other way when her man was bad. She was a giver, and Lee was one of life's takers. For Lee, fun was central to life, and life got progressively better as his career moved along.

Some saw Sally as soft only on the outside, tough and even calculating from within. She did luncheons with the Senate wives, dinners at the White House. Through her marriage, she gained entrance to the life that she enjoyed, plus kids and a nice house. And Lee came across as a happily married man, for that was the spin. After all, that was his approach to life: there was reality . . . and then there was the Atwater version.

Sara Lee had been born by cesarean section, and the procedure had knocked Sally back for a year. Lee had urged her relentlessly to get back in shape, and she did — partly because she wanted to have another baby. Ashley had been a vaginal birth, with Lee in attendance and amazed — for a while. Then the attending doctor, who had a passing interest in politics, asked about life in D.C. As Lee and the doctor chatted, Sally felt neglected again. Was insensitivity one of those male things? Get me a nurse, thought Sally. Still, she wanted to have a boy. She kept in shape for a third child. Lee was indifferent. Two was fine with him; he had no macho yearnings for a son. But Sally loved mothering, nurturing the needs of an infant in her arms.

Sally never looked better than she did for the trip to Israel with Lee in August, a visit sponsored by AIPAC (the American-Israeli Political Action Committee). Although Lee's press secretary Leslie Goodman and a small entourage accompanied them, Sally and Lee were at last alone and far removed from the urgencies of Republican politics — up to a point, anyway. They toured Jerusalem, visited Bethlehem, Masada, the Dead Sea, spent a night at

a kibbutz. There were meetings with Defense Minister Yitzhak
Rabin and Jerusalem mayor Teddy Kollek, military briefings, a
helicopter tour of the Golan Heights and Lebanese border. When
Lee took a drive in an Israeli tank, he strapped on a helmet and
insisted on posing for a photo that parodied the Dukakis ad of sweet
memory.

The trip conjured up religious sentiments in Sally, things
that Lee never felt comfortable discussing for more than a moment. Is man good or evil? Sally said good. Lee wasn't so sure.
He would taunt Sally about her religious bent sometimes, asking,
"How do you know Jesus was the son of God?"

"You have to do some things on faith alone," Sally responded.

Lee had studied the Bible at Newberry, a Lutheran school,
and to Sally he always seemed to have the debater's advantage. He
just wouldn't buy into the notion of faith. "Jesus Christ was one
of the best politicians ever," Lee said. "He sent twelve men out
and they changed the world." Now that was something he could
appreciate.

At eight-forty-five on the Sunday evening of August 6, when
Lee and Sally Atwater returned from Tel Aviv to their Washington
home, Lee was still an apostate getting ready for a meeting with
Sununu at the White House next morning. Sally was pregnant for
a third time, with the baby due in April 1990.

• • •

To work for Lee meant barely encountering Sally except through
messages, often about the business side of marriage. She paid the
bills, worried about money. He trusted her to do the right thing
for the family — she had bought the house, for instance. Lee was
proud of the fact that he had never lobbied, which was where
the real money was for consultants. Never did, never would. He
made $125,000 as head of the RNC, plus speaking fees that raised
his annual income to about $200,000. He didn't want anyone to
question how much he was spending on videos, tapes, albums. If
Sally brought up the topic, he would scream: "Sally, goddammit,
I don't have time for this shit!"

"Tell him he needs to make more money," Sally once told a
secretary.

"Would you like to speak with him?"

"No, no," said Sally. "Just tell him. He'll get mad at me." In many ways, like Lee, Sally never left South Carolina. When driving to the RNC to join Lee for an evening function, she would worry about where she was going to leave the car, whether she had enough quarters for the meter. She didn't act like someone who could park anywhere, even have someone take care of the car for her. She didn't act like a chairman's wife. But then, Lee didn't necessarily act like a chairman.

Lee had no budget sense whatsoever. He rarely carried money. His driver took care of out-of-pocket needs with $300 from petty cash. Often Lee's face was his identity, at least in D.C. People gave him things: meals, guitars, candy, flowers. A box of cosmetics arrived from a firm owned by an admiring Republican — mousse for everyone! Lee rarely discussed the cost of doing business. The work that went on at the RNC was in response to a higher calling. The RNC was not a government agency, of course, so there were many perks and some blurring of expenses. Lee occasionally liked to say he was going out of town on a business trip when in fact he was holed up in a favorite hotel just across the Potomac for three glorious days and two fun-filled nights with a companion. The hotel bill was paid using an RNC credit card that also earned points toward free airline tickets. Thus staffers in the know referred to Lee's weekend jaunts as his "frequent fucker miles."

At the RNC the annual budget ranged from $35 million to over $100 million, quite a bit of swing depending on fund-raising efforts. If someone needed serious money and he approved of the idea, Lee said, "Talk to Jay Banning," the financial director. "He'll fix it." If Banning thought the numbers were out of line, he told Lee. But Lee didn't like to discuss money, so staffers were careful about bringing up the topic, lest it be seen as insulting.

Once an assistant went to Lee after several months of struggle, saying, "I'm working too many damn hours, and you're killing me."

"How much you making?" said Lee. He had no idea. He upped the salary $5,000 on the spot. When Brooke Vosburgh received a serious job offer from a big-shot CEO, she was seriously considering the change because it represented security, better benefits, and . . . Lee wouldn't hear of it. Instead, he increased her salary by $20,000 overnight and that was that.

Lee loved to run but hated to walk — that's why God invented limousines. Lee averaged over three thousand miles a month in the RNC limo, a dark blue Lincoln Town Car, usually traded in annually. Three thousand is a lot of travel for someone who never took car trips longer than ninety minutes. Lee hated waiting in line, waiting for luggage, waiting for anything. He didn't like the limo he inherited because of the velour seats; he couldn't slide in and out quick enough. Lee wanted leather, which meant the Signature Series with stereo, automatic climate control, dimmers, air suspension, automatic everything. The leather version didn't have a great stereo system, though, so the limo was upgraded again. Then, when compact disc players for cars came along, there was another change — this model had smoked windows, too.

Roger Stone, with his enthusiasm for Eastern medicine, had introduced Atwater to acupuncture years earlier; the forty-five-minute sessions were a wonderful way to relax. On Saturday mornings Lee's driver Mark — who garaged the car at his home thirty-one miles outside the city — picked Lee up at eight-forty-five to drive him to his acupuncturist, three blocks from Lee's home. Mark waited until Lee emerged all loose and happy, then drove him three blocks back home.

Although other chairmen sat up front with the driver, Lee liked sitting in the back, enjoying the status of Republican statesman. The car's plate, which used to be RNC-1, had been changed to something less conspicuous. Better for speeding or making a turn against the light, for there was always some vigilante Democrat in the District ready to call and complain. Better for not being found out, too, for Lee lived in constant fear that he was going to be caught in a scandal.

On more than one occasion, Mark thought they were being followed. Lee suspected that the DNC or Foley or maybe the Democratic Congressional Committee might put a tail on him. On these days, Lee broke his normal patterns, going in and out of the RNC through the parking garage under the building, or even leaving through the Capitol Hill Club by way of the fourth-floor corridor that spans the alley between the two buildings. This enabled him to exit the RNC, go through the club and out its front door, and look down at the RNC like a spectator.

Arthur Andersen, the RNC's auditors, contributed $15,000 annually to the Republican cause, and each year representatives of the firm brought the check to the chairman's office, where it was customary for them to receive a report on politics of the day.

When the Andersenites arrived to see Lee, they received no political insights. Instead, they found the chairman sitting behind his desk, his feet propped up, strumming a guitar. "What do you guys think of this?" he asked, and started singing.

• • •

In the summer of 1989, Fred Vail, a Tennessee political wannabe who had run for Congress a few times, came up with an idea that Lee found irresistible: recording a blues album. Vail owned part of Treasure Isle Recorders in Nashville. He volunteered recording studio time if someone else would handle the other expenses. Enter Mike Curb, a veteran record producer and former lieutenant governor of California who had become Lee's fund-raising buddy on the Republican tour. Vail and sound engineer Jack "Stack-a-Track" Grochmal, known for stacking vocal layers, drove up to D.C., and the deal was done.

Lee wanted to do an album that would pay homage to some of the great R&B singers and performers who for one reason or another didn't have proper exposure. Good music, and not bad politics either — an album appealing to a demographic that the Republican Party never appealed to before. Of course, this was an opportunity to advance Lee's own image among young rock 'n' roll Republicans. There was some squabbling over contracts, but eventually the musicians Lee wanted came aboard. When Lee negotiated, he had an aura that convinced them this was a good thing, even if it wouldn't make much money. Hey, we're gonna have one hell of a good time! And of course everyone knew that Lee had power beyond what he could pull off onstage. Who knew what other doors he might open? The exploitation was mutual.

Musically, the album was a sound track from Lee's growing-up years. "I always have a song in my head," he often said. Although he declared himself a blues man, Lee really liked a cross-over of blues with Memphis-style R&B — the Stax sound from the '60s and early '70s. His favorite jogging song was "Rescue Me," by Fontella Bass, for instance. For the album Lee invited Chuck Jackson, a South Carolinian who had sung two of his favorites, "I Don't Want to Cry" and "Any Day Now." He called Sam Moore, from Sam and Dave. Isaac Hayes, before turning his "Theme from Shaft" into a black anthem of the '70s, had backed up Otis Redding and written most of Sam and Dave's megahits; Lee called him the

King. Add to the mix Billy Preston, the Memphis Horns, Arletta Nightingale, Carla Thomas — top that with B. B. King — and it's a big tent.

Lee enlisted Wendell Moore, manager of the Red Hot & Blue restaurant, to help him select songs. The album consumed him. Day-to-day politics was increasingly handled by RNC political director Norm Cummings, new communications director B. Jay Cooper, and Mary Matalin. Brooke Vosburgh kept Lee's personal schedule meshing with the office. If the president called, Lee was there. Otherwise, Lee's mind was elsewhere. He practiced more, spoke with old friends about the album, discussed little else during the morning staff meetings. One hot summer day he took off for the mountain house with his beloved Strat and two South Carolina buddies to work up another song list for the album. En route, they got lost and found themselves at a small river. They got out of the car and started walking along the water. Lee began to undress. Even musicians get a break, you know. The trio went skinny dipping, sitting in cool water away from all the heat and worries of being chairman of the Republican National Committee.

Lee negotiated with artists, managers, irate spouses; brought albums to the office; taped tunes he wanted to do; arrived at songs with the deliberation of a youngster making a Christmas list. One afternoon while on a presidential trip, Lee called Wendell Moore at the restaurant. "Little Ed and the Blues Imperials are appearing at a theater right across the street from our hotel!" he shouted. "I'm going tonight!"

In 1969, the year Lee graduated from high school, B. B. King was opening for the Rolling Stones. Now he was about to cut some tunes with Lee Atwater. "How does that saying go?" King reflected to a reporter. "Dancers want to be singers, and singers want to be dancers. We all try something different from time to time."

To offset any criticism of Lee's priorities, most of the recording dates were scheduled for weekends. B. B. was only available on Wednesday, September 6, however. Lee arrived at the Treasure Isle studio at noon for what was more like a jam session than a recording date. He wasn't sure he could keep up with the master. He and B. B. just kept jamming until something acquired musical unity, and they went with it. They did a howling instrumental version of "The Thrill Is Gone," B. B.'s signature song. Lee showed respectable licks as backup to B. B.'s solos. "You came a hell of a long way," said King. "I can tell you that right now. That was all right with me."

Finally, after three false starts, they moved into an instrumental shuffle with dueling guitars and a backbeat that everyone liked. They had been sitting there for two hours now, but when they listened to it on playback, there was satisfaction. "That's a fine groove," said Atwater.

B. B. agreed: "It feels real good." The song, augmented with horns and some light choral touches a few weeks later when the Bad Girls were in the studio, would become "Red Hot & Blue," the title track for the album.

Lee knew practically every blues song ever recorded, including the B sides. While tuning their instruments, he asked B. B., "Do you know 'Knock on Wood'?" Atwater was astonished to learn that B. B. — his hero, his main man — didn't know this soul standard.

"I remember the tune," said B. B., "but, to be honest, the terrible thing about a guy like me is the only tunes I played all these years is my own catalog. So I wind up being a complete dummy — I don't know no tunes at all!"

"A lot of us wish we were dummies!" hollered Atwater. The sessions with B. B. King went smoothly, though Lee was limited on guitar. He tended to use the same guitar licks over and over. His voice, too, lacked power, and he got tired as sessions wore on. Lee came back later to overdub some guitar solos and vocals.

"He was respected by B. B. for what he did," said coproducer David Shipley. "And as a singer he had a lot of soul. I guess you would say for a politician he was pretty good."

The rhythm section was jamming one weekend, and Lee went into gyrations. The blues do that — you can't just absorb this music with your mind; you need to embrace it with your emotions. "Is the tape still going?" Lee yelled. Somebody said yeah, and he said, "Let's do one in E." Though Lee didn't have a singing voice, he could create the sense that the song was coming directly from somewhere within his soul. The band moved into "Bad Boy," an old Eddie Taylor song with lyrics that Lee had updated to suit his own hard-charging image: "I'm a bad bad boy, from way down in Washington, D.C."

Although Lee had never recorded anything anywhere, he was soon in control. Jack Grochmal, the sound engineer, left after

Lee started barking orders on the morning of the second session. David Shipley took over in the booth. After several takes of the Lee Dorsey hit "Ya Ya," Lee was even coaching Chuck Jackson. "Now Chuck, here's one way we can do it," he said. "You sing the second verse, just sing the same thing that I sing. Then there's a piano, then there's an interlude; then you sing, then there's my guitar, another interlude, and then we come back and I will sing, and then we jump in and just vamp out."

They did the take, which featured a raunchy guitar solo redolent of Lee's old Duane Eddy records. "Play it, Lee," said Jackson, having fun. "I'm so lonely!"

Afterward, Lee, unhappy with his guitar part, said, "Forget that one. That was a dud." They went into another take, which he abandoned after a few bars. "Whoa, stop it, stop it!" he said. "Let's do it again."

"See how I got a man elected president?" said Lee to the musicians. "Let's do it quick, quick, *quick*! This is going to be one hell of a thing to do live in the White House."

"I love the way you think!" said Jackson. "I'll be right there with you."

"We can do it at the White House if you want to," said Lee. "A Fourth of July thing or something."

Jackson laughed. "You know, one of the most exciting things I ever saw was when we were onstage and Lee looked down at the president when he went into his James Brown thing. The president just looked up at Lee, and he didn't know whether to shit or go blind. I'm standing there looking at him, and Mrs. Bush is right there with it, clapping her hands."

They did a final take. Perfect.

Lee wanted to record "Te-Ni-Nee-Ni-Nu," which Shipley thought was a bubblegum song. They had put it aside, recorded other songs, but Lee kept coming back to it. Eventually, they recorded eighteen songs, all of them long takes. There was only room for twelve on the album. "Let's negotiate," said Lee, dropping songs they had worked on for hours.

"OK, I give up," said Shipley. "Te-Ni-Nee-Ni-Nu" became the first song on the album.

At the final session they recorded "People Get Ready," the Curtis Mayfield pop spiritual, a good ensemble song that the group sang as a finale. Late that night, Lee and Wendell Moore went back to the hotel. The album would be released in the spring, maybe April. Meantime, Wendell would start planning a Red Hot & Blue Revue — a tour for Lee and the restaurant's band that would kick off in Columbia. In the spring, Wendell would come aboard the RNC as Lee's personal road manager to coincide with the album's release. Lee stretched out on his bed atop the covers. He loved talking with Wendell about the blues. In fact, they were probably two of the few white guys who had seen every black exploitation film of the '70s — from *Super Fly* to *Shaft Goes to Africa*. The sound tracks, man! Lee asked Wendell, "You having fuunnn?"

"Man, this is like a dream come true for me!" said Moore, who had grown up in a little town in west Tennessee. He told Lee how he had actually worn out a copy of *Isaac Hayes Live at the Sahara Tahoe*, a gift from his grandmother on his fifteenth birthday. Lee looked at him with that grin.

"Well, how do you think *I* feel?" he said. His leg was shaking now like a backbeat to the pleasures of the day. The movement seemed to be consuming his entire body. "I'm actually *playing* with him."

• • •

For a year now Lee had endured headaches, a limp in his left leg, and heartburn. He had been consuming aspirin and Tums, waiting for what a doctor called a "stress fracture" in his foot to heal so that he could run full speed. Still, he ran. In December Lee had a premonition that something awful was going to happen to him. He told Sally about his dreams, and she said she felt the same aura. At a fund-raiser, she would be watching Lee give an inspiring speech, and a feeling of danger would come over her afterward. Their premonition was so strong, it reminded Toddy Atwater of that time thirty-five years earlier when she and Harvey sensed that something was going to happen to little Joe. Because of his busy schedule, Lee had canceled several medical appointments. One day at his desk, his left arm went numb.

"I don't feel my arm!" he shouted to Brooke. "Call the doctor, I think I'm having a heart attack!" They rushed Lee to a doctor, who gave him a complete physical, including a stress test. Except for some heartburn — "Lay off the Tabasco" — he was in great shape. He called his mother, ecstatic. "Mama, I got a clean bill o' health," he said. "I feel wonderful."

"You are overdoing it," she said, unconvinced. "Lee, you can't live long, staying up late, abusing your body." Still, if something was going to happen to Lee, it would show up in the test results, wouldn't it?

In late autumn of 1989, Lee called several senior staffers into his office. He leaned back in his chair, strumming the unplugged guitar as usual, seemingly relaxed. "We think the *Post* has something that's a problem for me," he said. "A story about me being supposedly involved with someone at the White House, and they have pictures." The pictures showed Lee entering or leaving an apartment building where the White House staffer lived. "It's not good," he said. "What do I do about it?"

"Well, is it true?"

Atwater stopped strumming and looked the inquisitor in the eye for at least thirty seconds.

"Yeah, it's true," he said.

They went through the details of the story point by point. Lee had visions of a page-one story with a photo that would embarrass the president and Mrs. Bush yet again. At some point even presidents have to do things they don't necessarily want to do.

"Well, does Sally know what's going on?" someone asked.

"Yeah, she knows," said Lee, implying that they had a kind of understanding.

While going through the story, breaking it down, they came to the conclusion that Lee could really lean on the reporter. After all, Lee wasn't a cabinet member, wasn't an elected official. He was still entitled to a private life, and, if the reporter went with the story, innocent bystanders would be hurt. For Lee and the staffers, it was a defining event. Several had cautioned him about the risks his womanizing posed for himself, and, by extension, them. Perhaps this would end a most dangerous game.

After the strategy session, Lee called the reporter to challenge the merits of the story. It never ran. He also made a few changes in his modus operandi. Clearly, the front entrance meant risk. From now on, he would wear a baseball cap and casual clothes, go around to the back of the apartment building, and climb through a window into his lover's ground-floor quarters.

In the office Lee's mood swings became extreme, his rages out of scale. For the holiday season he decided to send a personally inscribed 1989 Presidential Inaugural book, from a warehouse of unsold copies, "to every Republican in North America." This project consumed several hours daily as books were brought in for his loopy scrawl, then carted off to the mailroom. Even Mark Goodin got a copy: "I know it's been a tough year," scribbled Lee, "but I want you to know that in my judgment it has been a good year for our friendship. You handled yourself well and I'll never forget." One night Lee came back to sign books, but someone had failed to bring up a supply from storage. He was furious. He called Mary Matalin on her beeper, which made *her* furious. She was there to help run the RNC, not to get involved in Lee's Christmas card list. Find the advance guys *now*, he insisted. Have books delivered to me *now*, and have everyone back in the office at six in the morning, when he would be ready to sign more books.

On Friday, December 15, the RNC threw a huge party. In political terms it hadn't been a very good year: Howard University, David Duke, the Foley memo, some lost elections, and growing concern about Lee's priorities on the job. Financially, it had not been a very good year either. Atwater was the greatest fund-raiser of his Republican generation, but that money went to state reps and candidates; back at the RNC funds were tight. The party was more about image, a celebration of Lee, capped by a blues show led by "the bad boy," as he introduced himself, and the stars on his album. For a self-invented man, this was what success looked like. There was grumbling among staffers when the customary Christmas bonus — a week's salary — was slashed. Instead, they got the party — and a personally signed copy of the Presidential Inaugural book. During the show, Lee paused before one number. "This is dedicated to the audience," he said, "if you know what I mean." The song was "Steal Away."

• • •

Lee was looking ahead to a big year in 1990 — who knew how big? Matalin and Pinkerton both kidded Lee about prepping for a second career as a talk-radio celebrity or a TV commentator. One afternoon, Pinkerton was visiting Atwater at home in his bedroom, where Lee was lying on the bed idly watching TV. "Jim, what do you think my name ID is?" Pinkerton guessed 20 percent. "Forty-one," said Atwater. "Forty-one percent of the people know who I am."

Even before he was a Name, Lee used to kid with Ann Stone,

Roger's first wife, about the casting for his life story. Michael J. Fox, said Ann. Lee liked that thinking. "Michael J. Fox — *with an edge!*"

After introducing the president at a "Hinckley Hilton" reception on the evening of January 18, 1990, Lee was being driven away for an evening on the town when Mark said, "Boss, I think we're being followed." Lee was furious. They drove up Connecticut Avenue, past the Chinese embassy, and onto the Taft Bridge, where Lee shouted, "Stop the car!" Mark hit the brakes in the middle of the bridge. The cars behind him did likewise, leaving the shadows in a tight squeeze. "I'm gonna find out who they are!" said Lee, jumping out of the limo. Blake Williams, riding shotgun, ran after Lee, but he wasn't quick enough.

"You boys seem to know where I'm going," said Lee to the followers. "Why don't you give me a ride home?" He climbed into the backseat of their car, and off it roared. Mark and Blake gunned the limo and followed that car — to the Atwater residence.

The boys turned out to be two reporters from *Spy* magazine who were tailing Atwater around Washington to see if they could dig up some dirt on the chairman. Lee welcomed them into his home. They all ended up in the basement den, where he played a demo tape from his sessions with B. B. King. "*I'm bad, I'm bad, I'm the worst you ever had,*" he sang, flailing away on Strato air guitar. They spent the evening playing music and chatting in front of the TV. The news featured a special report on Mayor Marion Barry, who had been busted at 8:27 that night as he put a piece of crack into a pipe and lit it in room 727 of the Vista Hotel.

"That's our hotel!" said the *Spy* guys. "We're staying there — on the seventh floor!"

Lee roared. "I can't believe it," he said. "You two bozos have the story of the century in the room right next to you, and you're chasing boring ol' me around!"

Lee had always said he would never run for office, but a political virus had invaded his body and was threatening to take over. "Once you are in this business, you are halfway there," observed Mark Goodin. "It doesn't corrupt you, but it co-opts your spirit. It co-opted Lee. The ramshackle, long-haired, guitar-playing nomad had come to ultimate glory — sitting in the backseat of a limousine being driven around as leader of a national political party. Pretty heady stuff. When your brain gets fixed on that, it tends to tune out a lot of what is going on around you."

Even Carroll Campbell noticed that Lee had gotten to be a bit full of himself. They talked, but not as often, and they didn't have long conversations like they used to have. "He was operating in a different arena," he said. "It was a different Lee."

But Lee's big plans weren't all about himself. Pinkerton ran into Lee at the Y, and they went to Old Ebbitt Grill at Fifteenth and H Streets for lunch. There Lee told Pink he was trying to make a change in the Republican platform on abortion in 1992. Pinkerton was skeptical. Sununu had dictated that policy. "I'm going to spend the next two years traveling around the country saying, 'Listen, as a matter of loyalty to me, I want you to help work to change this platform to make it a big tent platform.' Loyalty will overcome ideology in this case." Lee Atwater's "big tent" concept of the Republican Party would soften some of the edges sought by the conservative faithful. Big Tent. The concept had been kicking around for a while. LBJ used the term. It was so simple it seemed stupid. All it required was a little bit of high political acting. But with Phyllis Schlafly and all the others against it, how was Lee going to turn things around?

"What you don't understand," he told Pink, "is I have a bigger following in the party than Schlafly does." Atwater wanted to tap into the bipartisan yearning for a candidate above politics. Lee was not looking for uniformity among diverse elements, but unity of purpose. He knew that even among Christians there was infighting; Pentecostals at odds with evangelicals, and so on. Years earlier, while traversing the back roads of Georgia, he had talked to the older Reaganites about the necessity of compromise, of tolerance, of giving a little to get a lot rather than risk total defeat. Now there was a need to tear down walls. Didn't Jesus pray in the Bible "that they all may be one" (John 17:21)? How could he get these groups to seek the highest common good rather than the lowest common denominator? Atwater didn't expect people to change their minds, but he was confident he could convince them to give in for the party's long-term benefit.

• • •

For two weeks in early '90 Connie Chung's *Eye to Eye* camera crew followed Lee around — in his office, at home, on the road. Now, in Columbia, they were setting up at Bullwinkle's, where Lee was scheduled to play with his local band. Lee wanted this profile to be perfect. It was his first appearance on TV as a bluesman. "We want to start out in high gear," Lee told drummer and advance man Rick Peterson. "I want everything in a frenzy!"

Lee, wearing blue jeans and a Hawaiian shirt, was being driven to the bar in a truck. By radio, he told Peterson when he would arrive, right down to the minute. Peterson had wired Lee with an FM portable microphone. The band played a loose blues shuffle that Lee knew, so that when the truck pulled up — with Connie's film crew at the front door — he burst out, wailing on his guitar, then pranced through the crowd as it went wild. He leaped onto the stage and sang a nasty version of, you got it, "Bad Boy." The video cameras whirred on and on.

On Wednesday, February 21, the bad boy was seated in front of three cameras in his office with Connie Chung. As the crew ran a light check, Connie tried to put Lee at ease. He was in a state of high anxiety. The interview would be shot in four twenty-minute segments, snippets of which would be used in Chung's profile. "I want you to be real relaxed, but also be up and funny, and — you know what I mean? — the way you *are*, really," she said. "You know what I mean?"

Lee laughed. Connie was putting Lee at ease, and Lee was stroking Connie's ego. Lee talked about W. C. Fields and the Three Stooges, whose movies he saw as parables of class warfare. "If you look at a good Three Stooges, it's always pie fights. Who's in the pie fights? Upper brow and upper-crust elitists. They poke fun at the existing baloney in society back in the forties. I think it's great satire, great lowbrow humor. And I love it." Of course, not everyone was like-minded. "There's a big gender gap on the Stooges," Lee said. "Women don't like them. They always say, 'They make me nervous.'"

"Oh, no, no," said Connie.

"Yeah, but you're different," said Lee, laying on the charm. While the cameras were synchronized, Lee left the room briefly to tell staffers that he had disarmed the enemy.

As the interview got underway, however, Connie's gentle, nonthreatening style made Lee reflective. "I think my whole generation went through a period in which we lost sight of a lot of things," he said. "Now, as we get toward middle age, we are reevaluating things. I certainly am. I have in the last three or four years. That's what life is all about. You live it, and then, from time to time, you sit down and reevaluate it. My career was *waaay* more important to me ten years ago than it is now."

"That's very strange," said Connie, "because you are at the pinnacle. You have reached one of your biggest goals, to be chairman of your party, right?"

"My biggest goal has always been to get my career goals behind me before I was forty. I think that career goals are too selfish. My goal in life, from the time I was twenty, was to become wise. I wanted to get traditional career goals behind me by the time I was forty so I could spend the rest of my life going out and doing things I want to do because they are selfless. What I ultimately want to become is a college professor because I think nothing is more important than teaching."

Connie asked about the Tom Turnipseed episode, and Lee revised the script. What had been a strategic attack on his part, when describing the incident to journalists in '81, was now a *counter*attack, with perhaps a bit of youthful indiscretion added in as well. "I was about twenty-six years old, and this fella Turnipseed started attacking me. And so, in my response, I was thoughtless in my wording and I attacked him back. And I apologized. It didn't ruin him," said Lee. "As a matter of fact, the only way he can get on TV anymore is by attacking me. And he does, all the time." (Over the years, Turnipseed had become something of a character around Columbia, appearing in TV ads for Turnipseed & Associates, his law firm specializing in injury claims, and handing out little packets of turnip seed with the phone number 800-833-HURT.)

"The Willie Horton issue became your baggage," said Connie. "You became handcuffed to Willie Horton. George Bush came out clean, and James Baker came out clean, even Roger Ailes came out clean. It became your baggage. You don't mind? Don't you feel *used?*"

"Well, I can survive that. No, I don't feel used. You know, politics is politics." Then Lee regrouped. "George Bush did not run a racial campaign. I think if George Bush or Lee Atwater ran a racial campaign, George Bush's approval rating among black voters in this country would not be 67 percent. It's as simple as that."

"Is it fair to say that you used to bask in the glory of being a little dirty trickster?"

"I don't think I've ever basked in any kind of glory. It is fair to say this: I'm the same guy I've always been. I haven't changed one whit, and I'm not *gonna* change one whit. I'll be the same guy when I walk out of this that I was when I walked in, because to me, ever since I've been conscious, all that's mattered to me is being who I am and what I am on my own terms. That's very important to me, and that's what I do now. A lot of people don't like that, particularly a lot of people in politics. They say, 'Well, look at this image.' *There's no image. I'm real. I'm absolutely real!*"

"There is an image, though. Describe yourself for me, OK?"

Lee seemed nonplussed. "I'm not gonna describe myself for you," he said. "That would appear . . . that would . . . that wouldn't . . . be, uh, proper . . . for me to describe myself."

"You know who you are," said Connie. "You just said you're . . ."

"I know *exactly* who I am. And anybody who wants to spend about ten minutes talking to me will know, too. So I'm not gonna sit around and describe it." He laughed uneasily.

"Why? What's wrong with it? You know that you have a certain reputation as a politician. Tell me what that is."

"Effective."

• • •

In March Atwater used his effectiveness and broke precedent by taking a strong hand in several big-state gubernatorial races. He talked Robert Taft II into running for secretary of state in Ohio so that George Voinovich could run unchallenged for governor. He got Miami mayor Xavier Suarez to drop plans to run in a primary against Governor Bob Martinez. He got the president to schedule two trips to California for Pete Wilson's campaign. And in Illinois Atwater flatly endorsed Governor Jim Edgar against a pro-life primary challenger.

In Florida, at a fund-raiser, Lee was introduced by Jeb Bush, the president's son. It was a large boisterous crowd. Waiters were still serving and folks were still talking as Lee approached the podium. Accustomed to having the full attention of a room, Lee stood there while the drone continued. "Well, I'll just stop now and let you all finish your conversations," he said softly. Like a teacher waiting for his noisy class to settle down, he stepped back from the microphone. A minute went by. Then another. He just stood there. Gradually, the group of fifteen hundred stopped talking, and Lee gave his standard stump speech, which had them on their feet applauding. People rushed the stage to see him — a response that Lee usually relished — but he broke away and said to Blake Williams, "Let's get out of here." He had a fearful look in his eye. "Let's just go anywhere." Williams led him to a hallway near the hotel kitchen where busboys were working. Lee sat down on the floor, looking as though he had just run six miles. Blake talked to him for ten minutes, until he calmed down enough to go back in and work some tables.

Sally was looking forward to their trip to Puerto Rico together in March. They both loved the Cerromar Hotel in San Juan. The hotel featured a long water slide that bathers use to float down into the pool. On their last visit, Lee had swum against the current *up* the slide. Perhaps this time he could relax at last. He would also give a speech to the National Second Mortgage Association for $8,000, which would come in handy since the new baby was due in a month. By now Sally was huge. For the past two months, in order to sleep she had been sitting in a chair through the night.

On Friday, March 2, Lee and Sally got up at 5:00 to catch an 8:07 flight from Dulles to San Juan. After checking into the hotel, Lee went for a run with Blake Williams. Usually, they ran six miles, occasionally more. After half a mile, though, Lee stopped. "My leg just feels like rubber," he said, kicking his left foot for emphasis. They turned around and walked back to the hotel. Blake was astounded. In all of their years together, this was the first time *ever* that Lee had stopped exercising. That night, after the speech, Lee couldn't sleep. He didn't use the pool, couldn't seem to relax. Saturday night, again no sleep. Sally thought it was his adrenaline as usual.

When they returned from Puerto Rico on Sunday, Lee went to bed at six, exhausted. The next morning, Sally watched him come down the stairs holding both rails, limping. That left leg seemed worse than ever. He walked like an old man, thought Sally. If he's like this at thirty-nine, what's he going to be like at sixty?

At the office, he looked at a speech he was to deliver the next day at the Simon Weisenthal Center. It struck the big tent chord, emphasizing that there was no room for racism in the party. With Louis Farrakhan and David Duke in the news, Lee practiced a sound bite: "I don't care if he's a bigot in a bow tie, or

a bigot that's been blown dry — we've got to end bigotry and racism in America." Then he went to a fund-raising breakfast at the
Ramada Renaissance for Senator Phil Gramm. Lee had a special
fondness for party switchers, and Gramm was gutsier than most.
Other switchers moved their camps under cover of darkness, but
Gramm had resigned from the House as a Democrat and run for
reelection as a Republican.

When Lee arrived, Bob Dole had just finished speaking.
Gramm introduced Lee, who went into autopilot with his stump
speech again. The press was not invited to this closed-door function, yet the doors were open as the hotel staff prepared a buf-
fet outside in the hallway. Blake Williams ate some fruit along
with advance man John Schmidt and Lee's driver Mark. The
speech was so canned that they were lip-synching Lee's best lines.
Suddenly, Lee stopped.

He was telling the group how the campaign picture of
Dukakis in a tank had made the candidate look like Rocky the Flying Squirrel — a line that usually got a roar — when he felt his left
foot start to shake uncontrollably. Lee stared at his leg as everyone
in the room looked at him in silence. Instantly, the twitch moved
into his leg and up the left side of his body. Lee clutched the right
side of the lectern, shook his head violently, and an involuntary
scream came out of him, *Yaaahhhhh!* Blake and John looked at
each other, thinking for a moment that it might be a cowboy yell
for effect. By the time they realized it was pain, Lee had collapsed.
"Help me! Somebody help me!"

John Schmidt cleared the room. Lee finally came to. "God,
what was that?" he said. Lee wanted to get up. Within minutes
he was on a stretcher, heading toward an ambulance. "Hell of
a way to get attention," Lee said to Bob Dole, but no one was
laughing.

In the ambulance, Lee had a vision. He saw a stage with a
banner across it that said, THIS IS A TEST, like a TV program interrupted for the emergency broadcasting system. Lee couldn't figure
out his vision. What *was* the test?

At the George Washington University Hospital emergency
room, Brooke and Sally arrived shortly before Lee had a second
seizure. "What's going on? What's happening to me?" he asked.
Dr. Burton Lee, the president's physician, observed the seizure
and called Sally aside.

"Your husband has a brain tumor," he said. "He's got about a year to live."

"How do you know?" she asked, stunned as much by the physician's cold, blunt delivery as by the harsh diagnosis. "How can you say that?"

"It's just my business," said Dr. Lee. He was an oncologist.

"Call Mama," Lee said to Brooke. To her he looked like a little boy, lying flat with his shirt and tie, putting out his hand to hold. Here he was in an old hospital, its physical plant somewhat dilapidated but its reputation sterling. When Ronald Reagan was shot at the Capitol Hilton, he was brought to GW. If you're going to have a seizure on short notice, this was where you wanted to be. Brooke filled out the forms to admit Lee.

From the RNC, Mary Matalin kept calling Brooke's pager, frantic. "What's going on? How are we gonna handle the press?" The doctors were wondering what to say. "Tell them to say nothing," said Matalin. "We'll handle it from here."

Brooke phoned Toddy, who took the call in the principal's office at A. C. Flora High. When Toddy hung up, she knew exactly what the tumor meant. "I'm about to lose another son," she said to the principal.

Later that night, Lee called from the hospital. "They say I've got a tumor the size of a hen's egg," he said. He wanted Toddy and Harvey to come up next day. "Mama, regardless of what happens, we want this thing to be upbeat. No tears. Nothing sad. We're going to face it, and that's the way it's going to be."

"Of course," said Toddy. "You're not going to see me cry." Later, in private, she wept.

CHAPTER

11

THE FINAL CAMPAIGN

[Lee] told me a number of really rotten things he
had done to me that I never knew about. He just
had to get them off his chest, and he asked me to
forgive him, and I did. Was the transformation real,
or was it a desperate grasp? "I'm gonna die, so just to
be sure, get me a crucifix, a yarmulke,
and a witch doctor!"
— Roger Stone

A brain tumor is a horrifying diagnosis for anyone, but for a man who was mostly wits and brain power, it was a perverse act of God. "My nine-month headache," Lee called it. Until confronted with the diagnosis, Lee thought that cancer happened to other people. Two older cousins had died from brain tumors — Pete Page, on his mother's side, at forty-five in 1978; and Charles Atwater at forty-two in 1982. Charles had called on Toddy and Harvey once in Columbia while Lee and Sally were visiting. Everyone had greeted him graciously, but it was painful to view his swollen face and bald head. Lee had quickly excused himself.

Lee didn't like to be around anyone who was ill, couldn't handle the raw emotion. In 1988 he had arranged for his childhood pal David Yon to take a job at Commerce, where his former aide Craig Helsing was chief of staff. Suddenly, doctors discovered a tumor between Yon's heart and spine. The job was canceled, and Yon went into surgery. Lee barely acknowledged his buddy's ordeal. He kept too busy with transition work.

Now Lee was facing serious illness, and it was like a visit to a foreign land. "Diagnosis: cerebrum (right parietal lobe), astrocytoma, grade 3," noted the George Washington University Medical Center Surgical Pathology Report on March 6. "The tumor is high grade displaying markedly atypical glial cells and scattered bizarre multinucleate forms."

Tumors are graded from 1 to 4; the higher the number, the more severe and aggressive the tumor, and the lower the expectation for a good outcome. Even within a grade level, the degree of malignancy can vary from mild to aggressive. Another complication is whether growth is localized or multifocal. Dr. Charles Rogers, the director of radiation and oncology at GW, examined the scans and thought Lee's tumor was somewhere between the size of a golf ball and an egg. But that image is misleading. An astrocytoma is not clearly delineated, ready to be scooped out. It is like clouds in the sky, with a dense center and vaporous margins. You have to assume that it's considerably more extensive than you can see on a scan.

In Western medicine, cancer is battled with the "slash, burn, and poison" approach of surgery, radiation, and chemotherapy. At GW, once Lee's doctors had diagnosed the astrocytoma, they thought it needed treatment with an external radiation beam. Radiation would be safer than surgery because no foreign bodies would be forced into his brain, and the radiation would treat other cancerous cells in Lee's brain as well. Brain cancer differs from other types of cancer in that the cancer cells don't metastasize to other parts of the body through the blood or lymph streams. But cells migrate rapidly within the brain; therefore, even if a brain tumor is localized, another one can develop.

Lee's seizure made him feel vulnerable, both personally and publicly. The first thing he wanted was to control the story in the press, lest the media write him off as a lost cause. His worst fear was that he would go from being the center of George Bush's political concerns to being an outsider. While Lee rode in an ambulance to Holy Cross Hospital in Maryland for an MRI (magnetic resonance imaging) scan at the end of his first day at GW, he and Mary Matalin gamed out the specifics of spin control.

State reporter Lee Bandy got stiffed. After the initial brain scan, Mary Matalin told him, "The first battery of tests show nothing." There were reports that Atwater had been on a liquid diet,

Bandy said. Could his collapse be linked to that? "We all were taking that stupid powder stuff," said Matalin. "We stopped on Valentine's Day." In fact, she confessed to Bandy that she and Lee "would lock our doors and sneak chicken wings." Bandy filed an optimistic story under the headline ATWATER'S DOCTORS SEE NO DIFFICULTY FROM BRAIN TUMOR for Carolina consumption in the *State* on Wednesday.

Dan Balz and Ann Devroy led the spin brigade at the *Post* with a story titled, NONMALIGNANT TUMOR FOUND IN ATWATER'S BRAIN. Dr. Edward R. Laws, head of the neurosurgery at GW, said, "Lee Atwater completed tests this morning which revealed a small, nonmalignant growth in the right side of his head. No surgery is planned, and we expect no difficulty with follow-up treatments." Tumors are either benign or malignant. What did *nonmalignant* mean?

Ann Devroy had Mary Matalin on the phone. "Mary, I want the truth," she said. "This is not what you say it is. There's something real bad happening here."

Mary burst into tears. "No, he'll be out of the hospital in a couple of days," she said. Friends don't spin friends, do they?

● ● ●

Sally was at a loss. She was too pregnant, too fatigued, too far adrift from Lee's life to step in now. Over the years, as Lee's career demanded more and more, Sally had become simply another member of his support team. That was how she viewed marriage. "Wives kind of learn to do what's needed," she said. "That's what marriage kind of is, that support thing. I always just kind of *did* it."

Sally spent that first night with Lee in the hospital. She worried about his ability to cope with a medical ordeal. She remembered how impatient Lee had become the time that Sara Lee had an earache. Sally had taught children with handicaps, even in wheelchairs; had been in mental institutions where patients were strapped to chairs; had seen the underside of life as an aide to a caseworker in college, calling on welfare cases, visiting cancer wards. Her training had taught her always to be calm and clearheaded. To others this looked like indifference, or even a glazed quality. Inside, she was heartsick for Lee, but — as Lee often said — you've got to just keep movin'.

Sally felt blessed because Lee had a wonderful staff — Brooke to coordinate office matters and Blake Williams and John Schmidt to run interference. Mary Matalin would run the RNC, with Charlie Black, Ed Rogers, and others on call for advice. You never know where your positives are going to come from, thought Sally. The next day Lee signed over power of attorney to her.

Meanwhile Lee was getting to know people at the hospital. "Hi, I'm Lee Atwater, who are you? Call me Lee." He looked everyone in the eye, made everyone feel important. After a few days, the doctors were his best friends, and he was introducing them to visitors, who were also his best friends. Thousands of phone calls, cards, notes, gifts arrived from well-wishers. Richard Nixon himself brought in a copy of *In the Arena* inscribed: "I can think of no one I'd rather have in the arena with me." Arnold Schwarzenegger sent flowers: "From one terminator to another."

Lee Atwater was a VIP patient, someone whose condition was treated almost as though it were classified information. This gave him leverage that ordinary patients aren't able to exercise, for better or for worse. GW had loved the Ronald Reagan experience. There were still posters on bulletin boards about "the *Saving* of the President." Lee had the same Oval Office aura and was catered to accordingly. Physicians themselves are skeptical of the VIP treatment. Many say they would prefer *not* to be treated as a VIP because it does not necessarily bring out caretakers' best skills. "If I get a serious problem, I'm going to check myself into a hospital five states away under an assumed name and let them take care of me," said one GW practitioner.

On Thursday afternoon, Lee checked out wearing a sport jacket over a Three Stooges T-shirt that read JUST SAY MOE!! "One of my intellectual heroes," he explained, hugging nurses and bantering with the press. "This proves to my legions of critics once and for all that I do have something in my brain."

Later that day Brooke drove her white Jetta to Lee's home, where he called her up to the bedroom. She felt awkward. Toddy seemed to give her the cold shoulder, busying herself with fruit baskets downstairs, but Sally gave Brooke a big hello. Lee was stretched out on the bed watching a big-screen TV. "Close the door," he said. Brooke sat on the edge of the bed as Lee told her he'd spoken with Sally and with Mama, explaining that Brooke was central to his life now. No matter how much or how little time he had left, he wasn't going to waste any of it, and he knew absolutely that Brooke had to be there. Lee said that he loved her, and there would be a place for the two of them together when this was over. Brooke was dazed.

For over a year now, Brooke had been Lee's secret sharer. When he wanted everyone out of the room, she stayed. Her only job was to take care of him, and no one had ever been as good at it as she was. Brooke knew when Lee was tired or hungry; she knew he wouldn't eat the bread on the hamburger. She had worked with him for eighteen hours a day for nearly eighteen months now. Lee trusted Brooke, yet, as a student of people, he often said he couldn't figure her out. He spent a lot of time trying to understand her, and this attention gave her a sense of self-validation that she hadn't experienced with a man before.

Brooke and Lee embraced for the first time, and Brooke felt something stirring within her that she had never given voice to, something that she had started wondering about in the fall of '89 on a campaign trip to Oklahoma, when Lee insisted that she ac-company him — not because he needed her; he just wanted her companionship. Brooke had seen the women come and go in Lee's extracurricular world — at times, he couldn't even remem-ber their names. Yet she knew Lee was a bright, interesting guy, and he was worth the effort. Brooke found herself leaving the bed-room, walking down the steps toward the little white Jetta, think-ing, with Toddy so annoyed, what chance did she stand of making Lee happy?

Serious depression hit Lee on Saturday. Lying in bed, he tried to play the guitar and couldn't coordinate the chords. He went downstairs, where Brooke and Mary were waiting to visit. They all took a small walk to a neighbor's house, and Lee was so fatigued by the effort that he was unable to climb back up the stairs to his home without assistance. Mary and Brooke looked at each other. This guy who used to run six miles a day, absolutely exhausted?

On Monday, March 12, he met with the president and Sununu in the Oval Office at ten-thirty. They had already been briefed by Dr. Burton Lee and knew far more than Atwater was prepared to acknowledge. Lee, desperate for normalcy, said it was a lesion, and if you *had* to have one, this was eminently treatable.

There were a lot of prayers around the White House, but not a lot of hope.

• • •

The potential spread of cancerous cells to other parts of the brain is the critical issue in managing a brain tumor; it also explains why surgery alone doesn't work. You can only take out what you can see on an X ray or computerized tomography (CT) scan. In the '50s and '60s, when radiological techniques were not as sophisticated as they are today, surgeons were quite aggressive, removing as much as half the brain and producing patients who were nonfunctional and didn't live too much longer. Microsurgery advances in the last twenty years have allowed for safer removal of tumors so that other therapies — radiation and chemotherapy — have a chance to work.

"I don't want to be a professional cancer patient," Lee told the doctors initially. He didn't want to grab at every straw. So at GW they commenced with a program of radiation. One day Lee asked Dr. Rogers how he was going to measure success.

"Months go by before we can measure the benefit of this treatment," Rogers explained.

"Well, what do I do now?" Lee asked.

Rogers sensed that Lee was uncomfortable with radiation therapy because it was not dramatic. One day, following a discussion of Civil War strategies, Rogers told Lee he was like the reincarnation of a Confederate general who wanted to get on his horse, pull out his saber, and run off in one direction or another. He added: "That is the antithesis of the way our specialty is practiced."

Rogers was treating Lee with external-beam radiation therapy, which made the environment around the tumor hostile. But the tumor was still there, waiting. For Lee, the treatment was too passive. Rogers arranged for Lee to visit with a patient who had a similar tumor and had survived more than five years with radiation therapy. "Do you consider yourself cured?" Lee asked. "Does it ever trouble you that this might come back?"

In politics, some operatives wait for a reporter to do a story that they hope will turn out positive for their candidate. Lee talked to reporters, gave them glimpses of the story until he found one who was willing to tell it *his* way. Now Lee was looking for a physician who would tell him what he wanted to hear.

With the radiation treatments underway, Lee returned to the

RNC, where he was greeted with a banner over the doorway and staffers hanging out the windows, cheering. The heavy doses of medication had no effect on his office wit. "Don't bother me," he told Bobby Holt, the Republican fund-raiser who wanted to crash a lunch at the White House. "I've got a tumor." At a staff meeting on Wednesday, March 14, he was in great spirits, signing notes to hundreds of well-wishers. For many months only the chairman's personal staff would know how serious his diagnosis was.

Lee placed his full command focus on the battle to beat brain cancer. As always, he looked to control a hostile environment through knowledge, so he began his campaign with oppo research. Pinkerton was reading medical books. Faxes were coming in from doctors all over the world. Lee assigned Mary to do a report on experimental acupuncture treatments in Russia. But Lee's campaign had a flaw that he should have recognized immediately considering his political experience: heightened expectations.

After a meeting on March 21, Lee left at eleven-thirty for an appointment with an acupuncturist in Bethesda. In the waiting room Brooke received a call from GW. A report had arrived from Dr. Gerald Posner, a neurologist at Sloan-Kettering whom Dr. Burton Lee had asked to look at Lee's tests. Posner was pessimistic. Lee had a grade-three gleoblastoma astrocytoma, he said, which meant that he had a fifty-fifty chance of living two or three years with the course of radiation underway. Brooke broke the news at the Tow Path, Lee's favorite place for jogging and thinking through issues.

Lee took Posner's report calmly. Gleoblastoma. Both his cousins had had the same death sentence: gleoblastoma multiform astrocytoma. The tumor in his brain could double in size in seven days. George Gershwin died from this particular form of cancer at age thirty-eight; Bob Marley at thirty-six. Suddenly, Lee wanted to get home. He asked Mama and Sally to come up to his room, where Brooke relayed the information again.

They suggested that Lee talk to John Bunch, an emergency-room physician friend from South Carolina who was now in Front Royal, near the mountain house. Bunch knew Barry Smith, a doctor who knew Paul Kornblith from their days together at the National Institutes of Health. Kornblith, a doctor specializing in interstitial surgery for brain tumors, was now at Montefiore Hospital in New York City. Within hours, Lee was calling Kornblith's office. The next day he spent forty minutes on the phone with the doctor. Lee then met with Dr. Laws at GW, who reiterated that Lee was receiving the right treatment. The doctor told Lee that Kornblith's surgery was risky to quality of life and offered no better long-term results. "Once you choose an aggressive route, you become part of the hospital environment," warned Laws. Still, he encouraged Lee to meet Kornblith and make his own decision. Lee had already scheduled an appointment in New York.

Paul Kornblith, a neurosurgical oncologist, was head of a department that used several protocols to deliver more targeted, focused radiation using "seeds" implanted in the tumor, in combination with standard radiation, chemotherapy, and surgery. The outside world considered this protocol on the cutting edge, but for Kornblith it was fairly conventional. As far back as the '30s, radioactive seeds had been placed in tumors, but because they often shifted, controlling the radiation was difficult. The approach was discarded in the '50s, but around 1975 Dr. Phil Gutin in San Francisco, among others, developed techniques whereby radioactive seeds could be placed and *held* in position. Lee had sent Gutin his X rays for review. Gutin called back, saying that in many ways he agreed with Dr. Laws — given the time frame, and the risk to quality of life, he did not think his procedure would be worthwhile.

For Kornblith, however, the key to success was Lee — a patient who was young and in good shape, with the right attitude, support team, and a tumor that Kornblith considered relatively localized. Kornblith noticed how Lee had marched into the office on Monday, full of enthusiasm. "Let's go after this damn thing, do something about it!"

Kornblith was politically independent, and indifferent. In 1988 he hadn't even voted in the presidential election, but politics had nothing to do with that. He was just too busy. As chairman of the department, he played a role in every procedure: thirteen hundred cases a year. Kornblith had operated on members of families of senators and congressmen while at NIH from 1978 to 1986. Although nothing would help his Montefiore program more in terms of visibility and funding than to do well with a public figure, Kornblith feared there might be more negatives than positives in treating a celebrity — more time spent on staffers, telephone lines, security, reporters, prominent visitors. A VIP usually has questions,

questions, questions; in Lee's case, it was like being part of an
interrogatory.

Kornblith consulted with Harry Zimmerman, a tough, no-
nonsense pathologist who had practiced since 1925 and was considered the dean of the field. He had worked with Dr. Harvey
Cushing, the pioneer who described the different tumor types,
and, when Cushing died, Zimmerman did the autopsy. He also
performed the autopsy on Einstein's brain. Lee stared the old
man in the eye. "You have a very aggressive, malignant tumor,"
Zimmerman told Lee, eyeball to eyeball. Then the world's most
famous neuropathologist said: "This is grade 4."

Lee was sure he could get at least five good years, and Dr.
Kornblith was reassuring in the early days. "You never kill opti-
mism, never squelch the spirit — but only 5 percent beat the odds,"
recalled the physician. Kornblith told him they couldn't be sure
how the tumor would behave until they dealt with it. They *could*
be sure what would happen if they *didn't* do anything — he was a
dead man. If they were going to do the interstitial procedure, they
had to do it now, before the tumor grew.

Lee asked his mother, "What do you think?"

Toddy answered, "What have you got to lose at this point? If
you want to do it, I'm with you. Go ahead." After Lee left the room,
Toddy stayed behind. She had seen Lee's two cousins die terrible
deaths after brain operations. She wasn't taken in by the razzle-
dazzle in Lee's world. "If this procedure works, that's fine," she said
to the doctors. "But if it doesn't, please don't torture him to death."

•   •   •

One side effect of the cancer was a kinder, gentler version of Lee
Atwater. The shift was almost instantaneous. On his way to the
hospital for a radiation treatment the second week, Atwater called
Lee Bandy on the limo phone. "I can't imagine me getting back
in a fighting mood," he said. "I don't see how I'm ever going to be
mean."

Each year on Christmas Eve, Lee would tag along with Sally
and the girls to a Methodist church service, but he made no pre-
tense of believing in institutionalized religion. He studied television evangelists the same way he used to observe barkers at the
carnivals of his youth, fascinated by their fund-raising techniques.
Sally took the kids to church and to Sunday school, but for Lee

Sunday was another workday. Few people were more astonished than Sally, therefore, when her husband took a sudden interest in things spiritual. "I mean, here you are looking at a man, chairman of his party, thirty-nine years old — did he need God?" asked Sally rhetorically. "And then he got sick."

Lee tried a little of everything. There was an alliance of born-again pols — Chuck Colson, Mike Deaver, Harry Dent. Lee called them all, looking for a spirituality he could comprehend. He rented *The Ten Commandments*, and began a search for a good religious movie that would explain it all. When Charlie Black gave him a Bible, skeptical friends were reminded of a story told about Lee's old celluloid hero W. C. Fields, who was caught thumbing through the Bible on his deathbed. "Bill, what are you doing?" asked a visitor. "Looking for loopholes," replied the showman.

On Friday, March 16, after a White House breakfast with Junior, Lee struck up a conversation with the president's secretary Patty Presock. She suggested he call Doug Coe, a low-key religious leader who worked with members of Congress on a National Prayer Breakfast. If religion and politics ever met at a river, this was the spiritual Tow Path for Lee.

On March 27, one day after returning from the Kornblith encounter, Lee arrived at The Cedars, a Virginia mansion overlooking the Potomac that served as headquarters for Doug Coe's Fellowship Foundation. The well-groomed beauty of the grounds reminded visitors of a southern plantation. Lee, using a cane, walked into the main house and sized up the sixty-year-old luncheon host. "I've been in this city for many years now, and I never heard of you," he said. "Who *are* you, anyhow?"

"Well, we have many mutual friends all over the city," said Coe. "I've heard about you for a long time."

"What have you heard?" asked Lee.

"I've heard you're a real son of a bitch," said Coe with a smile. And so that dialogue began.

At five o'clock the following afternoon, Gary Maloney arrived at Lee and Sally's home with a Catholic priest. Maloney, a research aide to Pinkerton and a devout Catholic, sat on the stairway while Lee was baptized. The priest also heard his confession, administered last rites, and left rosary beads, which Lee wore as a lucky charm. Everyone was serious about it, except Lee.

"Mama, am I Catholic now?" he asked Toddy the next day.

"Of course not!" she snapped. She didn't care about Lee's choice of denomination — if she thought he had made a thoughtful decision. But with her boy all drugged up and grasping at religious straws, this was like a spiritual hijacking. "The priest was supposed to have heard Lee's confessions," Toddy confided lightly to a friend afterward, "but I don't think he could have stayed long enough to hear all of those."

• • •

On Tuesday morning, April 3, as copies of *Red Hot & Blue* were being shipped to record stores, Lee was readied for the interstitial radiation surgery at Montefiore Hospital. To minimize media attention, he had registered as Stonewall Jackson. Attendants put his legs in elastic stockings to prevent an embolism and gave him Valium. The whole team showed up around seven-forty-five. They quickly sedated him and bolted the metal crown that would hold his head stationary, leaving four indentations that would be visible in his scalp for the rest of his life. When they wheeled him out, he was in a twilight sleep. Lee was slid into a CT scanner, which produced a clear image of the brain, the tumor, and the metal frame. Using coordinates, the team plotted the paths their probes would take through Atwater's brain.

In the Montefiore procedure, as in many neurosurgeries, the patient is awake; the brain feels no pain, and it is necessary for doctors to talk with the patient in order to check the accuracy of their probes. The right frontal lobe, where Lee's tumor was located, is the cognitive center, controlling memory, speech, and other intellectual functions, as well as emotions and personality. A nearby area controls motor functions such as the use of arms and legs.

Lee was heavily sedated but still conscious when the attendants wheeled him into the operating room. The operation, which took five hours, was eerily straightforward. Dr. Kornblith was present, but he was not scrubbed in, not an operator. Lawrence W. Davis was radiation oncologist. Alan D. Hirschfeld was the stereotactic surgeon. Dr. Charles Rogers of GW was by Lee's side, holding his hand; he had come along to ensure continuity of care and to minimize the embarrassment of a patient abandoning treatment at the hospital that had, after all, saved the president. Using a hand drill, Dr. Hirschfeld made ten small holes in the skull.

The team inserted thin, flexible closed-tip plastic tubes containing rigid metal rods through the holes and into the tumor. Later Larry Davis and his team would remove the metal rods from the tubes and insert plastic filaments containing "seeds" with 8,000 rads worth of radioactive isotope into the tubes.

During one probe, Lee felt something go wrong. "Hey, guys, I just lost my left side," he said. Rogers felt Lee's hand go limp.

When Lee returned to his eighth-floor room at one-thirty, the crown was off, his head was partially shaved, and he wore a turbanlike bandage with a catheter sticking out. The implants made Lee a hazardous zone. A lead shield was placed around his bed. RADIOACTIVE signs went up in his room. The tubes containing the seeds would be left in place for four days. No one knew if Lee would regain use of his left arm — maybe when the swelling went down. His left arm was in a sling, and he wore high-top sneakers to support his ankles.

The president called early. All the GOP members of Congress sent a card. Marilyn Quayle visited the hospital and seemed to lift Lee's spirits. Donald Trump called, as did Tom Brokaw and Secretaries Brady and Mosbacher. Flowers and fruit baskets rolled in. Lee was winning over the whole crowd on the eighth floor. Everyone was listening to *Red Hot & Blue* and asking for autographs. Dr. Hirschfeld's wife made cookies for him. The doctors got Sally and Toddy to go to a polo match to benefit the hospital. One doctor approached Lee to see if the president might attend a fund-raiser for his temple. Only Jesse Jackson was turned away. "I didn't want to be part of another Jesse Jackson photo opportunity," said Lee.

The day after surgery Lee was so exhausted Brooke had to spoon-feed him lunch. Lee felt a cramp in his left leg, different from a seizure. Ultrasound confirmed that he had a blood clot, one of many side effects that would follow. Lee was put on Heparin, a blood-thinning drug that created its own side effects. On Friday night at eleven-fifteen, Drs. Hirschfeld and Davis removed the catheters from Lee's skull, gave him Demerol, and stitched him up. The day ended with the RADIATION signs coming off the door. "If I'd ever known how bad it was," Lee told David Yon, "I wouldn't have been brave enough to go through with it."

On Saturday night, April 7, Mama, Brooke, and Barry Smith sat with Lee to watch the twelve-minute segment by Connie

Chung. The profile had been aired to coincide with the release of
Red Hot & Blue. Now the album was out, and he was on his back
in a hospital room. "I'm the same guy I've always been," the Lee
from February told Connie. "I haven't changed one whit, and I'm
not *gonna* change one whit."

• • •

Back home, Lee and Sally continued to lead a kind of split-level
life. Downstairs was Sally, the kitchen, and the little kids, most
of the time. Upstairs was Lee, his operation, his team. Sally had
almost no involvement in Lee's care or decision making. Once,
when George Bush was visiting, she excused herself and went
to the kitchen, as though the men were going to discuss state
business.

Brooke, under Lee's spell, thought they might have five
more years, which they could stretch to ten. OK, there would
be a limp, perhaps — but there would also be a future together.
She interacted with the doctors and anyone Lee wanted to see,
including Sally and his staff. If this were Brooke's husband, however, and if she were pregnant and had small children under-
foot, she would have locked the door and said, "Stay away. We
need to be alone. We'll let you know if there's anything you can
do." Sally went along with Brooke's presence — Lee needed an
intermediary, and Sally couldn't stay with him night and day.
She viewed Brooke's devotion as yet another example of Lee's
incredible ability to talk anyone into anything. If he could have,
she thought, he would have talked somebody into dying for
him.

Both Toddy and Sally were concerned that Brooke and Lee
would become part of the Washington gossip mill. Sally also lived
in fear that the kids would wonder what was going on. Brooke
usually arrived early, stayed late, and went home to her condo,
but occasionally she spent the night on a couch, or Lee beckoned
her to lie beside him. There was great tenderness and intimacy
in their relationship — Brooke bathed Lee, cared for him like a
loving spouse — but no one could determine whether they were
in fact lovers. An aide came into the bedroom one night and
found Lee and Brooke fast asleep, but saw an innocence to the
scene. He tiptoed out and got the third degree from Toddy the
next day.

Everyone pretended to act normal — or what passed for normal under bunkerlike conditions. Sally knew all about political wives, the wives who came to D.C. with their husbands and the ones who replaced them. She had sat in many meetings over the years, trying to put together a PAC for women candidates — with the first wives sitting on one side of the table and the current wives on the other. "It's just a wild situation up here," she said. "People ought to know it when they come into it."

Perhaps the old maxim was true — southern women are soft on the outside, but hard within; northern women are hard on the outside, but with a soft underside. On Brooke's part, Lee's declaration of love had caught her totally by surprise. If someone had asked her if she loved Lee before his seizure, her response would have been, "What, are you kidding? I *hate* him." Yes, he was only her entire life, but she never intended for this to happen.

Lee drew the circle tighter and tighter around the bunker. Brooke became the person you dealt with to get to Lee. Leslie Goodman, the RNC press secretary, was almost out of the loop. Mary Matalin, who was experiencing flashbacks of her mother's death from cancer at an early age, found it hard to be around Lee for extended visits. To find out what was happening, she'd call Brooke, then share the update with reporters as though she were at his side daily. Mary told Lee that if he wanted to get religious over this ordeal, he should consider Brooke a gift from God.

Within weeks after the surgery, Lee lost most of the left side of his body — even that leg stopped shaking after thirty-nine years of uninterrupted fidgeting. The right leg picked up the beat. Moving Lee from bed to wheelchair took two people. Steve Allman, a college student built along linebacker lines, was hired as an aide. House doors were widened, the upstairs carpeting was removed, and an electrical lift was installed on the stairs (the kids loved to play with it).

Seizures stalked him. When Lee felt one coming on, his body stiffened. "Oh no!" he moaned, eyes wide, everything shaking. Some were over in a minute; others were violent, causing Lee's head to crash back into the pillow over and over for twenty minutes. Then he lay exhausted and scared. One Monday in April he experienced nine seizures. In a six-week period, he was admitted to the hospital five times, once leaving the hospital at noon only to have a seizure at home that afternoon. One evening at the Palm restaurant with Sig Rogich and some friends, Lee felt a seizure coming on. His aides surrounded him in the wheelchair, as if they were conducting a business huddle. The seizure, a small one, worked its way through, and no one in the restaurant realized what happened.

At eight o'clock on Monday, April 16, Sally went to the hospital, where her labor was induced. At three-forty-five that afternoon, with her mother, Theodosia, in attendance, she gave birth to Sally Theodosia, 9 pounds and 3 ounces.

Shortly afterward, Ron Brown sent over a little stuffed donkey with a note. "I just wanted to make sure that little Sally has a well-balanced upbringing," said the chairman of the Democratic Party. "Please make sure that this donkey stays by her side at all times (smile)." Lee was floored by the gesture. Whenever Lee had bumped into Ron on the social scene, he had always shaken hands and moved on. Ron was too likable, and Lee wanted to hate him for purely political reasons. "How can this guy be my enemy now?" Lee asked. "How can I be effective?" It wasn't fair.

Lee, unable to attend the birth of his third daughter, wanted to surprise Sally by accompanying her home. But on Thursday, April 19, he had a serious seizure. Sally and the baby arrived at eleven-thirty as Lee was preparing to leave by ambulance for GW. Diagnosis: blood clot in the left leg again.

Potentially lethal blood clots are common in patients who have had brain surgery. The brain is rich in thromboplastins, which clot any bleeding inside the skull; they do damage control. When the brain is assaulted by surgery, radiation, and chemotherapy, however, thromboplastins can enter the body's peripheral blood and create blood clots elsewhere. One of Lee's doctors, who happened to be on a golf course, phoned in his opinion that Lee had to go on Heparin intravenously for ten days, or have a filter implanted in his vena cava, one of the large veins leading to the heart, so that clots could not reach his heart and lungs. Treatment was put off when the doctors at Montefiore and GW disagreed about the best course. The clot moved from Lee's left leg to his right while they were deciding what to do.

The dean of the GW medical school huddled with Dr. Paul Ebin whom Kornblith had sent from Montefiore to assess the situation. They agreed that Lee was in danger of suffering from the celebrity syndrome: Everyone wanted to be part of the act. And so it was that Dr. Ebin called a friend in D.C., who gave him the name of a friend, who wasn't in town, but whose associate — an oncologist named Phil Cohen — came over to see Lee. In the midst of all the confusion over specialists pulling the star political patient in different directions, Cohen said, "Lee, you need a doctor."

Cohen called in Michael A. Newman, a good listener, a big-picture thinker, and a patient advocate who was not intimidated by anyone. Newman drove to the Atwater home on a rare Sunday afternoon when he wasn't on call. He recalled watching the news when Atwater was originally hospitalized. He had told his fourteen-year-old daughter, Sarah, that he doubted the early prognosis that the RNC chairman would be fine. Lee's face looked slightly more rounded than in those news clips, but he had the same sharp questioning eyes. Newman thought that although Kornblith was a good physician, the interstitial radial therapy was not a good treatment. Certainly, if he had Lee's tumor, he would take Decadron and travel to places he had always dreamed of — he wouldn't surrender precious time for a few additional months of medical ordeal. To tell Lee this, though, would be to deliver a death sentence. In medicine, as in politics, candor can kill.

Newman quickly ascertained that as far as Lee Atwater was concerned, the interstitial procedure was the *only* thing he could do. It was an action-oriented treatment with a nuclear quality that resonated with Lee. "Lee's illness was like a Rubik's Cube — colors and patterns that he had to keep twisting to get into place," recalled Newman. "Lee never doubted that if he kept twisting, twisting . . . he'd get it."

In Michael Newman, Lee Atwater found someone who in many ways was a doppelganger. In a profession that stresses conformity, Newman was an independent spirit. Though bald and ten years older than Lee, he remained trim, riding his bike to and from the office. He was up at five-forty-five each morning and read the *Post* and the *New York Times* before leaving the house to make his hospital rounds. In college he was a history major, a military buff; he had spent some time in China, and even knew Sun-tzu. He enjoyed B. B. King, and he shared Lee's indifference to money as an end in itself. Unbeknownst to Lee, Newman's list of patients included two other political celebrities: James Brady and Ed Rollins.

Lee said, "You know, we don't disagree on many things, do we?"

No, said Newman.

"That's why the Republican Party can be the party of the majority." Lee suggested putting Newman on retainer. "Is $4,000 a month OK?"

"That's too much," said Newman. Atwater was taken aback. They discussed it further, finally agreeing on $2,500 a month, to be paid by a well-heeled Republican wheeler who did a lot of military contracting.

Newman revealed that in '88 he had given $200 to the Dukakis campaign, and his daughter Sarah was a Dukakis volunteer. Lee laughed. Most of his doctors were Jewish Democrats. They talked about fraternities: they were both ATOs — with a difference. At Stanford, Newman's chapter got a scolding letter from the national fraternity because they were pledging Jews. So the chapter withdrew from the national association, and Newman never really learned the secret handshake. "Oh, they were assholes," said Lee, extending his hand and showing his doctor the ATO grip.

Newman wanted to be in charge. Lee wasn't used to this. He still wanted to keep his options open, explore other medical treatments. Newman gave him six weeks. Then he wanted Lee's full command focus.

After learning of Norman Cousin's book about self-healing through laughter, Atwater spent nights watching videotapes: *The Andy Griffith Show, The Complete Three Stooges, Car 54, Where Are You?* He tried massage therapists, dream therapists, guided-imagery tapes of waterfalls, audiotapes of organ music and waves crashing on the shore, and acupuncture. He went to a psychiatrist, taking both Brooke and Sally. (As a standard test for mental alertness, the psychiatrist asked Lee to list the presidents in order backward; Lee got to Chester A. Arthur before the doctor said that was sufficient.) When a healer told Lee to get rid of his black T-shirts and start wearing red underwear, he did. Tibetan monks visited, studied Lee's urine, recommended creams and vitamin therapy; even Sally spoke up against that approach.

While giving Lee an acupuncture treatment at home, Bob Shapero took note of the mantralike list on the wall of the bedroom: Faith, Superior Attitude, Courage, Strength, Purpose, Determination. They were all *attitude* expressions. Shapero recommended that Lee meet Susan Trout, a spiritual counselor who helped people to grow, even in the process of dying. Trout, a fiftyish woman who directed the Institute for Attitudinal Studies, met Lee on June 8 for a hello that grew into two hours.

Lee said his greatest fear was facing death. He opened up with Trout, discussing Joe's death, its effect on his mother's faith, the pain it brought him. "Do you know how horrible that was? Can you imagine what it was like to hear your father crying? To have your mother not able to deal with this at all?" Trout described Lee's terror as being analogous to falling into a black hole with nothing to stand on, nothing to hold onto, no way out.

"Where did I go wrong?" Lee asked.

"I think your head and your heart are out of alignment," said Trout. He had used his head to control, manipulate others throughout his life, she said, and he had set his heart aside. He had no instrument to determine whether his actions were for the highest good — and he knew it. Lee was a disconnected man. With his family, he was thinking about work; at the office, he was thinking of end-of-the-day activities.

"God, you're perceptive!" said Lee. Christianity counsels us to forgive those who trespass against us, and Buddhism says our enemies are our best friends because they challenge us to transcend ourselves. But politics argues that we must punish our enemies. Lee had made it his lifework to understand his enemies, but not to the extent that he could empathize with them, because then he couldn't do what needed to be done. Now Trout was telling him he had to realign his life and look for the highest good. Lee told Trout about his vision in the ambulance, the sign saying THIS IS A TEST. To change so dramatically in such a short time — could he do it? Now, *that* would be a test.

"It takes a lot of work and healing," she said.

Toddy called in the middle of the session. Harvey had just come from surgery for bladder cancer, and they weren't sure he was out of the woods. Lee was shaken. Trout watched how he tried to suppress his feelings and change the subject. She told him to be honest with his emotions. Feel them. Talk about them. When she left, Lee cried. She had stirred things up, but he liked the feeling afterward. By the end of the month, they had met seven times.

Even in his search for spirituality, Lee was a pragmatist in a field of ideologues. "What is your technical plan?" Lee asked Trout one day. She had no real plan, but she sensed terror and wanted to help Lee reduce his fear. The first thing was to make a "List of Regrets," events and relationships that needed healing. Top of the list for Lee was the death of Joe, which he could barely discuss. Next was his relationship with his father. Sensing his work ethic, Trout asked him to make a list of "unfinished business." To a guy who always took care of business, that had enormous appeal.

• • •

On the sunny Wednesday morning of June 13, three old Reagan operatives met at the Tow Path: Lee, Lyn Nofziger, and Ed Rollins. They sat on beach chairs, ate hot dogs, and talked about the old days. Lyn and Ed had both survived medical ordeals and political defeats. Lyn survived, in part, when Lee had broken his "no consultants" vow and put him on retainer at the RNC. Rollins, on the other hand, had survived in spite of the efforts Lee started to chronicle. It was like hearing confession, thought Rollins, but everything sounded petty. Rollins had always envisioned Lee becoming an eighty-five-year-old guru spinning war stories on a southern porch. Now he could see that Lee wasn't going to make it.

In order to get her dad's attention one night in late June, Sara Lee wore makeup and one of her mother's dresses and imitated a news anchor interviewing Lee. The ten-year-old asked Mr. Atwater questions about his illness and, of course, his job. This Lee could relate to. Beneath the humor of the situation, he felt guilty about the time he had wasted talking to the press, to doctors, to everyone but his children. He always took pride in his efficiency, but now he felt he had apportioned his time to tasks that, on balance, really didn't matter.

Lee began a series of "forgiveness letters" and "forgiveness calls." He wrote to his date the infamous night he was Brother of the Month back at Newberry. He wrote to David Yon, asking forgiveness for being so insensitive when his friend was ill the year before. "Very seldom does a man get a friend like you, and when he does there is no amount of gold, no amount of stereo equipment or free liquor that would allow him to hamper such a friendship."

Lee wrote to Pug Ravenel. "I really truly have gotten what I've wanted out of life thus far, but I have been ham-handed and a braggadocio," he said. "The way I've dealt with you and past campaigns isn't becoming of me, and it has not been helpful for you, particularly since I have nothing but respect for you, and it has bothered me for quite sometime." He told Ravenel that he learned mightily from the '78 campaign. "If I could, frankly, defeat you . . . from a purely selfish standpoint I felt that it would help my career, put me on the political map. . . . I love Strom Thurmond . . . and I frankly thought you were threatening him and it scared me. As a matter of fact it was that fear that led to some of my more zealous (and as the media says) 'ruthless' actions involving your campaign. But not one time during that campaign did I lose my respect for you." Lee said he felt guilty about making speeches afterward "in effect bragging about 'what I did to you.' . . . I'm not proud of that fact today," he added, "but I'm not asking for forgiveness, and I'm not asking for acknowledgment of this letter. I swear to you no one alive knows this is being written other than myself and Brooke, who will type it." He added a postscript by hand: "Please take this in absolute *sincerity*."

Lee wrote to Tom Turnipseed with similar sentiments. "Nothing is confidential in politics," Lee said, "but as I lay here and write this letter, I want you to know that that is my intention. . . . Out of everything that has happened in my career, one of the low points remains the so-called 'jumper cable' episode. As both of us know, it has never been fully or truthfully explained, and it has been rehashed so many times that we have both been hurt from it. I've been under the weather lately, and it's my hope that you'll grant a sick man a favor and try to forget it. Please understand that for the last few years I have tried not to talk about it, and I've tried to rectify it, but it goes on and on due to the 4th estate. . . . While I don't anticipate that we will become political allies or that either of us will change our philosophy or our outlook, I do want you to know that I would be one happy guy if we could put some of this bullshit behind us. . . . I made a mistake. I don't want to sit down and rehash it, but part of the mistake was being 25 years old, acting cute, and bragging about it in a way that distorted the whole story."

• • •

Lee Bandy, who had covered Atwater since the college days, was
intent on getting the real story. He had been in the lobby at
Montefiore the day of Lee's surgery. He kept hearing rumors, kept
pestering for an interview. Finally one day Lee called: "Come see
me. Everything off the record."

Although the chemotherapy was fairly benign, Lee's medication was beginning to take its toll. The seizure medication Dilan-
tin also made him sleepy. Decadron, a steroid that controls brain
swelling and maintains alertness, caused devastating changes in
body fat: Lee, who always prided himself on having a flat stomach, now had a puffy abdomen and a buffalo hump across his
back. He also developed striae — red areas caused by an increase
in blood vessels and a pulling apart of skin by fat. Another side
effect of Decadron was osteoporosis, a thinning of the bone that
would eventually cause collapse of the spine. Lee couldn't twist
or even move without pain. Eventually he would need a brace.
Furthermore, as the brain tumor shrank in size, Lee's head actually grew larger, because dead brain cells retain liquid. The
shrunken tumor was forced up against the lobe that affected his
motor coordination.

For the Bandy visit, Lee was groomed and rested. He even
got up and took a few steps with a cane to show Bandy that he
was strong. They chatted for a while, with Lee feigning amaze-
ment at Bandy's report that Pat Robertson had come by the hospital to pray for him. "How'd you get that?" Lee asked, wondering
if there were spies in his camp. No, Bandy had got it from a
source on the Robertson side. The interview was brief — Lee had
to take a pseudocall from the president; he was sure Bandy would
understand. When Bandy left, Lee collapsed from the fatigue of
it all.

On Wednesday, June 27, Lee felt a burst of energy and told
Ed Rogers to call a meeting at the RNC. Lee came up the elevator. Only a few staffers saw him go into his office. He called Mary
Matalin and asked her to join the meeting. She walked in, saw
him in the wheelchair, and burst into tears, and that choked Lee
up. Then he got a grip and ran a good forty-minute meeting with
Rogers, Newt Gingrich, Ed Rollins, B. Jay Cooper, Leslie Goodman, and Jeanie Austin. Afterward Lee cried on the drive home.

Dr. Newman called Brooke about a memo Lee was preparing for Sununu to prove that he was still a player. He was concerned about its clarity. He had also seen incontinence, anxiety,
and the loss of strength on Lee's left side. Brooke's instincts had
told her that something was different: Lee appeared to be "wound
tight," but she had attributed it to his lack of sleep and the decreas-
ing efficacy of Valium. Newman thought there was more to it,
and he planned some tests. On June 29, Lee underwent another
MRI to compare with similar scans in March. The report noted,
"Overall size of the edema and enhancing tumor mass has clearly
increased, having a much more lobulated configuration at this
time." Also "more problematic is an oval, 1-cm area of enhance-
ment posteriorly to the right of the fourth ventricle. This was not
identified on the earlier studies."

"Well, Doc, what do you think?" Lee asked Newman.

"I think this thing is gonna get you," said Newman. He felt
like the campaign manager who had to tell his candidate he was
going to lose. "But we don't know when."

Newman had long talks with Lee, Sally, and Brooke — together and individually — about what to expect. He told Lee to
enjoy every moment of every day with his family. Brooke called
Charlie Black and Mary Matalin, who were shocked by the
news. Sally, concerned about health insurance and benefits, felt
strongly that Lee should remain chairman of the party. All agreed
that Charlie should take over as RNC spokesman but leave the
chairmanship to Lee. Newman suggested a living will.

On the Saturday night of June 30, Lee Atwater was feeling
quite vulnerable. "Today is the first day of the rest of your life," he
whispered into a minicassette recorder he used to dictate letters
and reflections. "That was one of the great posters of the late '60s.
I think all of us remember it from our college days. Even then it
sounded a bit trite and silly. But on June 30, 1990, I had to face
up to a startling fact. Today *was* the first day of the rest of my life,
and it didn't seem that there would be much *of* it."

Lee recounted lying in a small cylinder for eighty-five minutes that day for a CT scan that confirmed there had been some
growth in his tumor. "Right now I'm taking it in stride, but that's
not natural for anybody, and it's certainly not natural for me. . . .
So I decided to try to write a book." Lee took a long pause. "My gut
tells me that if I can truly get absorbed, truly get lost, truly think

of nothing but the book, that would add a few more months and leave a message here after I left the planet." Another pause. "Who knows? This might be the only time I even do this [dictation]." His voice became choked.

"By this time tomorrow . . .

"I might be so depressed . . .

"That I can't do anything."

He clicked off the recorder.

Dr. Edward Laws came to the house to look at Lee's scans. He thought that the tumor had grown, but it was mostly dead tissue. He felt that Lee needed debulking surgery: they could go in and take out that necrosis, get what tumor they could, and implant chemo seeds. Lee could buy years of quality life out of all this. Dr. David O. Davis, who read scans for a living, met Lee at GW. He agreed that the tumor had not crossed the center line, and that the tumor was larger because of increasing necrosis. Lee still needed surgery, but not until the necrotizing had finished. The one area of concern was the spot in the lower back of the brain, which showed up white on the scan. "We can't do anything but watch it," Davis said.

Those conversations lifted an enormous cloud. Lee called Newman, who spoke with Davis and then came over and said that Lee had gotten a reprieve. He could prepare to live rather than die. Lee was like the guy in the casket who hears the eulogy and gets up to see whom they are talking about.

Still, illness had taken its toll. Because of his enlarged head, Lee needed bigger sweats and wore a jacket that snapped up the front. He wore elastic kneesocks, a brace on his left leg, and oversized jogging shoes that aides had to work his feet into. Getting Lee dressed and in his chair was becoming increasingly difficult. At times he would gripe about the transition from runner to wheelchair occupant, but mostly he just kept movin'. When a hospital bed was installed at home, he tried all night to move the bed up and down and forced himself to go through the pain of some of the positions, believing he was doing himself some good. It took an orthopedic surgeon to convince Lee that he couldn't speed up recovery by pushing things.

One of Lee's ongoing ordeals was constipation, a side effect from the pain medication he took in such abundance. In the hospital one evening, Lee was given a viscous Gatorade-like solution called Go Litely to loosen things up enough for a physician to clear out the blockage with a colonoscope. Newman stood nearby as Lee looked at the drink container warily, his leg swollen, his abdomen distended, feeling weak all over. "I have no dignity left whatsoever," Lee announced.

"You have to drink a gallon of this stuff," said Newman.

"You gotta be shittin'," Lee said.

Newman laughed. "That's the idea!"

On the Fourth of July, the day that Lee had once scheduled for playing blues with Chuck Jackson at the White House, he took a drive with Blake, John Schmidt, and Brooke through Old Town in Alexandria. They stopped at the Video Vault, Lee's favorite spot for B-movie rentals, owned by his old college roommate Jim McCabe. Then they drove along the parkway and back home as Lee looked out the window at everyday people enjoying the simple fun of the Fourth. "I don't have a life," said Lee. "I have nothing."

• • •

"I've got to do what I think is right," said George Bush in July 1990 as he conceded a need for new revenue. Suddenly those lips were saying "taxes." Lee was distressed. When Bush broke his vow, he broke one of Atwater's commandments for politicians — you are only as good as your word. Democrats crowed, and the conservative wing of the GOP rumbled.

On Monday, July 9, Lee poured all of his energy into a conference call to RNC committee members gathered in Chicago. Atwater wanted to head off a battle within the party, which would tear them apart just as the Democrats were showing signs of unity. "For the first time in two years they had a meeting with three different big news stories, and not a single one of them said they were in disarray," said Lee. "Ron Brown is finally showing some leadership and getting the party together. . . . So we cannot come out of *our* meeting with the story being that the Republicans are pissed off about taxes. . . .

"Taxes, as long as it's not personal income taxes, we can survive that too, I'm convinced of it. I think it probably hurts, but it won't hurt but a month or so, and it won't hurt going into the election. It's too abstract." The key consideration, he added, was expectations. "They're getting up slightly too high, and we've got to get them back down again because this is gonna be a tough year, and if we're out there whipping up expectations, we're gonna get our ass handed to us."

Matalin discussed the tax pledge a bit more. Then Lee broke in: "Hey, gang, I gotta run over to the hospital to do my physical training. Mary, the meeting's back in your hands. Thank you for everything. I love ya all."

As Lee fell back in his bed, exhausted, voices trickled through the speaker phone in his room. "Good to hear you, Lee. . . . Good luck . . . take care of yourself. . . . Doesn't he sound *great*?!"

As Lee's physical stamina began to fade, Brooke's resolve that he must not give in grew stronger. Lee had trained her too well. When he wanted to skip physical therapy, she pushed him on. During therapy one day she left the room for a few minutes. When she came back, the therapist and Lee were both staring at his legs, waiting for a seizure that Lee felt coming on. "I'd have a seizure, too, if you stared at me like that," said Brooke. "Lee, you need to get up, keep moving!" The seizure began.

Brooke was concerned about Lee's behavior toward others. He could be irate with his staff, whose occasional bickering he did not find worthy of his command focus. "You need to show some interest and consideration in them as people," Brooke said one afternoon. He talked so much about the lessons he'd learned, from faith to love and human relationships, she told him. Wasn't it time for practical application? "It's so unfair," she said. And she wept.

Lee had never been able to respond to raw emotion. "This fairness thing is bugging me to death," he said in his prayers one evening. "Sure, nothing's fair. But to watch somebody cry two or three times a day because things 'aren't fair' drains me. You know it does, Lord, and you know why it drains me."

Brooke was also haunted by the fear of being perceived as Lee's mistress. Even in the hospital, Lee was keeping up with old lovers. One afternoon, when several old Carolina buddies were visiting, Lee asked Brooke to leave them alone for an hour. He was expecting a visit from the woman he had been visiting when pictures of him pursuing extracurricular activities nearly made the *Washington Post*. Brooke, upset, waited in the hospital lobby and watched the woman stride in — tall, slender, with long dark hair flowing — and sweep into the elevator. Later, when Brooke returned, Lee asked the guys to leave. "This is how I feel good about myself," Lee explained. "These are the same guys who knew me when I was the unathletic guy. I had to show them, as sick as I am, as bad as I look, I can still get the girl."

The two began to quarrel. Initially, Lee liked the give-and-take of these sessions. "Brooke, you gave me positive reinforcing criticism, and I need it desperately," he said. But Brooke's lament about fairness struck Lee as a negative. One summer night Lee collected his thoughts and spoke into his minirecorder. "What I'm asking of you is not fair," he said to Brooke. "Life is not fair. The world's not fair. But we both have to accept that. It's not fair, and there's not a single thing that's going to happen that's going to make it fair. . . ."

Lee heard someone coming up the stairs. His voice dropped to a whisper.

"One day I can look you in the eye and promise you I'll more than make up for it if it's the last thing I do. I can't tell you exactly how, I can't tell you exactly when, but I'll spend my entire life letting you know my appreciation. But until then, for the next few months, I'll need ultimate sacrifices." He clicked off the recorder and dealt with the visitor. Later that night he returned to his tape recorder in a deep, plaintive whisper. "Let's make the number one goal getting out alive. Obviously, I'm the one who's got the brain tumor; it's gonna be a little tougher on me. It may be tougher on you from an emotional standpoint, because you're the one being treated unfairly. But at this point, let's get through it alive, and then figure out what we do from there. We can do so much. We can be one of the most unique couples ever. And I mean of a big, big magnitude. Napoleon and Josephine. I know it sounds corny, but we can't do anything if I can't be alive, and you're the person I need more than anybody else to help me keep alive."

The Atwater Trust was established to offset Lee's medical bills and provide for the family. Calls and letters went out, coordinated by Bobby Holt, Bush's master fund-raiser. Checks came in, many in thousand-dollar multiples. Armand Hammer, in Mexico receiving experimental cancer treatment himself, sent $10,000. Lee's limo became a traveling office where he made follow-up calls of thanks along with small talk about the new baby and Washington politics.

"It is very gratifying and humbling to know that in less than a month a half million dollars could be raised on my behalf," said Lee, thanking the Lord in late July. "I just love people, and I love humanity, and I've got to learn to be a giver. . . . And I'm not gonna tune into you just to ask for things. I'm really not. Because you've given, given, given to me, and I don't deserve it after forty years of being callused, high agnostic at best, probably even an atheist, cynical, using your name in vain — which I still do, but you know I keep catching myself — and then all of a sudden I have a giant problem and you fix it overnight. I don't expect that. I'll take it, but I don't expect it."

Occasionally, while driving about, Lee saw old friends. He no longer hid behind the smoked windows. Instead, he lowered them, enjoyed talking to strangers — for to many, as the steroids made his face puffy, he was now a stranger. Once he saw Larry King walking along M Street in Georgetown. In addition to appearing on Larry's radio and TV programs over the years, Lee had attended the broadcaster's most recent wedding. King couldn't believe it was Lee, he had changed so much. They talked about the latest breakup in King's marital career. "You know that time you came to the hospital to see me with Julie," said Lee. "I knew there was trouble in paradise. But I didn't want to say anything." Lee saw shock in King's face. As the limo pulled away, he acknowledged, "This is one bitch of a thing."

Lee called Kornblith at nine o'clock on July 20 to go over the doctors' decision to put off a debulking operation one more time. The doctor reminded Lee that he had grilled the team throughout the day and was now calling at home on a Friday night. Kornblith said that pressing doctors could cause a hurried or wrong decision. Both Kornblith and Newman had told Lee he would never be pain-free again, but he had to concentrate on living, that he had to be a role model, not only for other people, but for himself.

That night Lee prayed. "Let this be the first day in the new Lee Atwater, the thoughtful Lee Atwater who is going to enjoy every sweet, sweet, sweet breath you give me here on earth," he vowed. "I want Brooke to know that this is the week I'm really gonna try. I want her to be proud of me. I want Sally to be proud of me. I want everybody to be proud of me because I've got to show that Lee Atwater really is Lee Atwater and that I am an honest, decent guy with no hidden agenda, with no selfish agenda. . . . These are the things I've got to do for you, Lord. I'm not doing them for myself. I'm going to do them for you, and in the process I'll prove them to myself."

• • •

In trying to mend a political fence with his letter to Pug Ravenel in June, Lee caught his old nemesis by surprise. In mid-July Ravenel replied, "Lee, if you can do one thing that would benefit yourself and the whole political process, you might consider this: find a way and lead us away from negative campaigning and toward campaigning on positive values." The politics of hope was being displaced by the politics of fear: "Fear of taxes, fear of social security cuts, fear of communism, fear of crime, fear of blacks or Jews, fear of less wealth. . . . Can we not inspire people to look forward and up instead of over their shoulders and around every corner?"

Ravenel's query caught Lee's fancy. He dictated a reply that grew over several days, finally sending a six-page single-spaced response on July 30. Lee said he agreed with Pug "in terms of trying to make politics more positive." Lee had originated his tactics in an era when going negative was necessary to defeat Democrats in the South. "The most salient issue in politics is hypocrisy," Lee liked to say. By pointing out the dichotomy between what a candidate says and what a candidate does, Republicans could get that 60–65 percent of the white vote they needed to offset the usual monolithic black vote for the Democrats. But that world was changing. A negative campaign wasn't what it used to be because both sides were slinging mud from the get-go. This led Lee to another theory.

"Not to be flip," he wrote to Ravenel, "but let me spend a minute telling you about the Atwater Bullshit Theory. If you look at one trend the last ten or fifteen years in this country, it has been that people have solidly and steadily lost faith in all American institutions. Ask them about lawyers. They'll tell you they're full of bullshit. Ask them about politicians. Full of bullshit. Ask them about the media. Full of bullshit. Ask them about organized religion. Full of bullshit. Ask them about S&L. It's all bullshit. I hate to be this cynical, but I think it just happens to be true. There is so much bullshit permeating our society, it has created an unprecedented number of what I call negative or populist voters. They think they are getting it from both ends. They think that government is working on behalf of the welfare crowd and on behalf of the rich, and they are getting soaked right in the middle. It is this populist voter that I have focused on in more than forty elections. I think it will be very tough to change their attitude. What I do think we can do is move negative campaigning off a personal level and on to an issue level. But I still think that so-called negative themes and negative messages are going to be part of it for the next few years."

Out of the bullshit, however, Lee saw "a new consensus developing, and in my judgment it is positive." Fostered mostly by the baby-boom generation, "It consists of issues that are no longer on the traditional liberal/conservative continuum. When I got into politics, environment was a liberal issue. It is now a total consensus issue with all age groups. When I got into politics, day care was a liberal issue. It is now a consensus issue. Education is a consensus issue. Health care is a gargantuan issue for the '90s. With the Atwater Bullshit Theory in mind . . . those who do not make promises, do not bullshit, but just make rational explanations of the changes that are going on around the world and in our society will do very well. . . .

"Pug, I believe there is an invisible hand in the American electorate that will not let negative campaigning go but so far. I have total faith and confidence in it," Lee wrote, turning his sickbed into a soapbox. "Although I do not see an early end to populist — what many call negative — campaigning, I do think that we can end strident personality campaigning, and that we can change the nature of American politics and make it geometrically more positive than it has been the last few years simply by cutting a lot of the bullshit, getting sincere, honest solutions to critical problems, and not insulting the American electorate."

• • •

In mid-July George Bush came to the Atwater home with his son George W. The president held three-month-old Sally T in his arms. Lee's anxieties about his boss fell away. That night, he thanked God: "You know, I really thought that I might have an insecure relationship with President Bush, and I was always worried about it. But look, Lord, you made sure that that was one of the strongest relationships I had. And what a way to find out." Immediately Lee channeled his raised spirits into the political arena. "I want to make August my rally month," he prayed. "We got little more than a month this summer, and all of a sudden it's September and we're into a general election. I've made a conscious decision that I want to be a player in this election."

As August grew near, Lee delivered long, meandering midnight-of-the-soul meditations, reflecting on problems with

Sally, with Brooke, with staffers; with medication and side effects; and always anxiety about what the next test might reveal. He drifted in and out of sleep as organ music played on the boombox in his bedroom. Lee prayed with more fear than fervor, like a politician trying to make a deal with God before an uncertain election. "Let's face it, I'm starting to believe, which is what's got to happen: believe . . . be*lieve* . . . be*lieve* . . . be*lieve.* Come hold my hand and help me cross that last little threshold to believe. Every minute and every second I'm trying to cross the threshold, and I *will* because I already sense it. I do sense it. I *do* sense it."

At night Sally heard Lee's cries of pain. This was more than a test, she thought. This was the final exam.

Sally, continued to focus on the three children. She was breast-feeding Sally T. As the baby grew, Lee faded. Sally was struck by the sad juxtaposition. She reflected on how Sally T had come home from the hospital just as Lee was leaving home for the hospital — a defining event, Sally concluded. She began to take things one day at a time. She started to read her daily horoscope; it always had an up side for her (a Taurus, born April 29). One night she felt scared, but then the feeling passed as quickly as it had arrived. Afterward, Sally felt sure that God would be there for the Atwater family.

One August day Lee asked Doug Coe to come to the hospital. An emergency. "I've about had it up to here, Doug," Lee said. When Coe arrived, Lee looked at him with his best piercing glare. "This Jesus business. Is he God or isn't he God? Tell me. Some say he's God, some say he's man."

"This is something you've got to decide for yourself," said Coe. "I'll just tell you a little story." Lee gave Coe his full command focus.

"You're big on the golden rule," said Coe. "Now, let's say that you were the most powerful figure in the universe, and you could say 'Let there be a star or a planet,' and — boom! — it exists. Or you wanted to create elephants, and — boom! — there were elephants, or cows or human beings. Anything you wanted, you have all the power, right?

"So you're sitting up on a cloud somewhere looking down on earth, and you see these cows grazing in a field, and you decide that you want to be a real companion to those cows — now what would you do?"

That picture of God becoming man had the clarity of an

index-card summary. "I got it! I got it!" Lee shouted. "Don't tell me any more, don't tell me any more. It's very clear, I see it precisely!"

On the Thursday morning of August 2, as Iraqis swept into Kuwait, Lee met with Roger Stone and Pat Haas, an editor who did major public-figure books for Scribner's, to discuss writing his memoirs. Ever since Newman had told him things looked black, Lee had been looking for a project to focus on. "I've got to get obsessed," he told himself. He believed his obsessive qualities "helped lead to my entire health breakdown, but they have served me exceptionally well in my career, and I might as well use them this last year to try to make some kind of statement."

Later that day, Lee checked into GW. Lee's August hopes turned into despair. The tumor, like crabgrass, had begun to seed itself, taking hold in the spinal column. He lost all strength in his left hand. When Lee tried to move, the pain was as bad as pain gets. He was comfortable only in bed on morphine, supplemented with Halcion and Valium. Mike Ussery called from Morocco, where he was ambassador. "If I could get a gun right now, I'd pull the trigger!" said Lee in a high-pitched voice.

That Saturday Brooke couldn't wake him. Newman and a steady stream of other doctors ran tests. They yelled right into his face, every twenty minutes, "Lee, can you hear me? Lee, wake up!" During the sleep Lee would respond to questions, knew people by name, but couldn't awaken. A total of twenty-five hours of sleep with assorted stages of delirium. He asked Brooke to track down the phone number for Wild Eyes Cody. Finally, when Lee surfaced, he ate like a bear coming out of hibernation — cheeseburgers, grilled cheese, frozen yogurt, bananas, a Popsicle.

On Thursday, August 16, Dan Quayle visited Lee in the hospital. Most of the regulars were there. As Quayle was giving a summary of political races and White House events, Lee looked at the VP intensely through a morphine mist. "Dan?" he said.

"Yes, Lee?"

"Could you get me a Q-Tip?"

Quayle looked around in disbelief. "Yeah, sure," he said.

"One of the good ol' timey Q-Tips," said Lee.

"What are ol' timey Q-Tips?" asked the vice president.

"Wood," said Lee. "Not plastic."

Dan Quayle handed an ol' timey Q-Tip to Lee Atwater.

Lee still wanted to play the Stratocaster. Because his left arm was useless, he called Ron Wood, who coached Lee by phone on how to use a slide; John Schmidt ran a butter knife up and down the neck of the guitar as Lee plucked out notes with his right hand. Late one night, Steve Allman carried Lee down the back stairs of GW and propped him up in the backseat of the limo. They drove to a lot behind a restaurant where Lee, using a pellet gun poked out the rear window, shot rats going in and out of a Dumpster.

Word reached the far-flung corners of Atwater's world — death wasn't just inevitable; it was imminent. Old nemesis Rich Bond sent a letter from Europe. "Did I ever tell you that you're my hero?" Bond wrote. "I learned more from you than anyone else in my life. When you were well, you were an inspiration to me. Now that you're ill, your courage, dignity, and spirituality is an even greater inspiration to me."

Because Brooke was with Lee every day, she didn't see the deterioration. To her he looked the same, even though she could see the alarm in visitors' eyes. One day orderlies were moving Lee, hooked up to a catheter and IVs, from his room to another floor. Distracted, Brooke got far ahead of the stretcher. Looking back, she saw an entourage moving a patient who was all strung up on support systems. Oh, that poor guy, she thought. He's close to death. Then a chilling realization swept over her: It was Lee.

• • •

"Ladies and gentlemen, this is Lee Atwater, broadcasting to you on Friday, September 7, from my new home, the George Washington Hospital," said the emerging author, dictating his memoirs. "I am now an intellectual. I have never before claimed to be an intellectual, and as a matter of fact there is a big part of me that is *anti-intellectual*." Lee took to the book project with vigor, dictating by day and giving the tapes for transcription to Linda Guell, the assistant to Strom Thurmond who had given Lee his first glimpse of the Senate back in 1971. "I can write anything that I want. I can have a ball with this damn thing if I play it right. I can have more fun as a writer than I ever thought of having as a politician. . . . I'm still Lee Atwater. I can still kick ass."

In rambling recollections from his hospital bed, Atwater conceded that he'd had his "ups and downs" while managing the '88 Bush campaign, but "I'm very proud of the fact that as far as I know,

I'm the only guy who successfully completed managing an entire four-year presidential campaign." What separated Lee from other operatives was his view of the electorate: "I think American culture and lifestyle have more to do with how voters vote on issues. In other words, I think the kind of food a voter likes, the kind of movie a voter goes to, what a voter does with his free time, where he goes, where he takes his family — these things are a lot more important than how he stands on Nicaragua."

Lee wanted to include a chapter on baby-boomer politics. "It's the biggest demographic group in the history of any society," he said. "They're never going to be totally monolithic, but there are startling trends among them, including a spiritual regrowth, an art renaissance, a participation in local government, and new consumer trends. . . . This group is going to be the center of the universe really for the next twenty years."

He wanted a chapter on the Sun-tzu factor in politics, spinning a tale about how he got the idea to hot-wire Bush's '88 firewall by moving the South Carolina primary up to the Saturday in front of Super Tuesday, for instance. "My plane was about three hours late, and I went to a movie called *The Color of Money* — it was about shooting pool. I had been having trouble thinking of the best way to utilize 'one move,' . . . the oldest Sun-tzu axiom going. I was sitting there, and when that first cue broke, I had it — leverage — one ball smashes into others, and you've got a shot to run the table. So I figured why not take a shot and see if we can't run the table; win every state and every delegate on Super Tuesday. That cue ball has to be South Carolina. So how do we maximize South Carolina as a cue ball? Well, we make sure it's on a Saturday, with no corresponding Democratic primary." That drought of news ensured "maximum media coverage."

In fact, the South Carolina Republican primary, established by Carroll Campbell & Co. in 1980, had *always* been on the Saturday preceding other southern primaries, because that was the easiest day to use schools as polling stations. Like some of his cohorts in the press, Lee didn't like to let the facts get in the way of a good story.

Lee also wanted to include "a large chapter about what some people call negative politics. I want to clear that up and call it comparative politics, and I want to straighten out all of this criminal furlough stuff. Dukakis was stupid on it. He was wrong, and I want to try to square that away." And he wanted a chapter on the golden rule. He didn't want to get into any heavy religious thinking, but, hey, this was politically smart. "Do unto others as you would have them do unto you. What religion could be against that?"

Lee wanted a chapter in his book entitled "Brooke," because "Brooke Vosburgh, a woman who has worked for me — that some people would call a secretary — has become more vital than an executive assistant. She has become, among other things, a friend and best pal and the most vital political functionary in my life." He felt that the chapter on Brooke "would help women in America to know that if they get into politics, they don't have to be secretaries, they can be partners and players. That to me is very important."

Oh, yes. One more thing. "There must be a chapter on the Atwater Bullshit Theory," he said. "We can elaborate on that later."

Atwater sent a copy of the book outline and excerpts to the president, who took them to Camp David to review in the midst of doing battle with budgets and Iraq. George Bush arose early on the Saturday morning of September 15 to read the pages from his old consigliere. "I was touched by the excerpt on Bar and me," he said in a note he typed himself. "Your credibility may be challenged because of that generous assessment, however." Then he added, "I loved your comments on Brooke. I have long known that she is a very special person, but you put it in the best perspective ever. Give her my love."

Lee's favorite spot at GW was the chapel, where he often went for a morning visit in his wheelchair to pray aloud. One day in late summer, when Brooke arrived at the hospital, Lee announced that they were going to be married. Aides wheeled him down to the chapel, where the couple improvised a wedding ceremony, with bent paper clips in lieu of wedding bands. When Lee told close friends, they couldn't determine whether it was an act of tenderness or one more scene in a sad little comedy.

• • •

Many dismissed Lee's relationship with Brooke Vosburgh as a boss-secretary fixation or the patient-nurse syndrome. Others thought it unseemly and even cheap. Brooke held Lee's hand as he went through the MRIs, exposing herself to radiation. Did Lee love Brooke in return? He said he did, and doubtless he loved and respected and admired her loyalty. But most of Lee's confidants thought that Brooke believed in the power of love, while for Lee this was yet another manifestation of his love of power.

By mid-September, Lee had been in the hospital for six weeks, and Brooke began to take charge of his life. They started to argue over treatment, medication, what he should be eating, how he should exercise — things that spouses quarrel about. In the old office days, Brooke had found it necessary to hold her ground because Lee was so manipulative with others. Now, she wondered, how much of his illness was real, and how much was an extension of his prankishness? Brooke's toughness did not soften even as Lee grew softer. He had trained her to meet his own standards of performance, yet when he finally had the focused, keep-movin' lieutenant he could trust — even love — he no longer had the stamina to keep up. "You think you're my boss!" he yelled. The nearly-weds were heading for a bitter breakup.

Lee called in Doug Coe, ostensibly to talk about the commandments. At the Sixth Commandment, Lee started ruminating about his relationships. He told Coe that since he had found God, he had taken a personal vow not to commit adultery. Then he started talking about his love for Brooke, asking Doug if the relationship was right or wrong. "And don't give me any bullshit here," said Lee. "I don't have a lot of time, Doug. Is it or isn't it right?"

Coe demurred, but Lee persisted. Finally Coe said, "Jesus was right on that. That's something you shouldn't do."

Lee cried for twenty minutes. Then he got hold of himself, pushed the button by his bed, and called for Brooke. The three of them talked openly. Lee tried to negotiate a deal with Doug. He said he could honor his commitment to Sally, but he wanted Brooke to be with him every day, and many nights, with the understanding that he wouldn't break the adultery rule.

Lee had no concept of what he was asking, thought Coe. When he left, the couple quarreled. Lee said that if Brooke left him, she would be breaking a commitment. His heart didn't seem to be in the argument, however. Brooke said that he was using Doug to release himself from an emotional bond he had made with her. At last she was beginning to understand. Lee needed her out of his life so that he could start to right his wrongs. Brooke left, saying that she loved him and would pray for him.

Lee called in Blake Williams. Several months earlier, Lee

had broken a rib when Blake fainted while holding Lee in the bathroom. Blake wasn't as strong as some of Lee's other aides, but he was absolutely trustworthy and never talked back. "Brooke's gone," he said. "You're in charge."

• • •

On Friday, October 26, Lee Atwater returned to Columbia, South Carolina, for the first time since his two-month hospitalization. More than four hundred people paid $25 apiece to attend a barbecue on the banks of Lake Murray to help defray Lee's medical bills, which were approaching $750,000. Friends warned others that he looked different. His staff tried to keep photographers away. Lee's face was swollen from steroids, and he was paralyzed in a wheelchair. His hair had turned curly and was falling out in clumps. Someone suggested a wig. "No," he said. "This is it. What you see is what you get."

Still, when he had to put on a show, Lee was right on. An aide wheeled him into the hall as a band vamped and old friends applauded. From his wheelchair he sang one more soulful version of "Bad Boy." Reporters asked questions, and he fired back at the same old pace, reminiscing about his youth and attending political rallies at the lakeside resort. "I've eaten so much barbecue out here I could puke just thinking about it!" He talked about his spiritual transformation, his "Jesus Christ experience," calling it "the greatest thing that has happened to me . . . I hope every one of you will find tonight what I've found," he said. Then he excused himself for a brief private meeting with Governor Campbell and his family.

Lee Bandy started to piece together a story about Lee's spiritual change. One source was Doug Coe, a longtime friend who went to same church, the Fourth Presbyterian in Bethesda. Lee Bandy also knew that Harry Dent had visited Lee and had steered political evangelist and *Born Again* author Chuck Colson, as well as private evangelist Susan Baker to Lee's side. Susan, in turn, had urged her husband James to make a ministry of Lee's ordeal, and the secretary of state had become a frequent visitor. All Bandy needed was Lee to confirm the story, give him a few quotes to plug in, and he could file it.

On Halloween, Lee's favorite holiday, Bandy called Lee at home. "I have found Jesus Christ," he confirmed. "It's that

simple . . . It's just no point in fighting and feuding." He said
he had adopted as his life's credo the golden rule, "Do unto
others as you would have them do unto you. I wish more people
would spend more time thinking about the golden rule. I wish I
had."

Lee's born-again experience, with timely coverage just before the fall election, struck some onlookers as good ol' Lee using the media as usual. Bandy saw a different story. "Aside from
a new inner peace and joy," he wrote, "Atwater has experienced
what doctors said is a remarkable rally from his bout with a life-
threatening brain tumor." Bandy quoted Ed Rogers, Lee's associate
spinmeister, as saying, "I use the word 'miracle.' " Bandy's report,
titled STRICKEN ATWATER REORGANIZES LIFE, PRIORITIES, ran in the
State then went out on the wires. The *Chicago Tribune* picked
it up, giving the story a page-one headline: GOP BAD BOY: I HAVE
FOUND JESUS CHRIST!

Harry Dent was pleased. He had received word that Lee,
under pressure from some RNC members not to engage in Jesus
talk, would probably be relieved of his duties as chairman soon
after the fall election, so his media shelf life was limited. Dent
explained his take on the article in a memo he wrote to a colleague at the Campus Crusade ministry three days after the article
came out: "It was decided to break the story with the right perspective rather than the wrong perspective since pagan reporters
were beginning to inquire about what was happening to Lee
Atwater." Because Coe was "a universalist," engaging in "that 'Jesus isn't that necessary' stuff," Dent liked the Jesus spin on Bandy's
article.

One of the so-called pagan reporters in pursuit of Lee's story
was Todd Brewster, a writer for *Life* magazine. Leslie Goodman
had heard the same pitch from *People*, the *Post*, NBC — everyone wanted to do "Whatever Happened to Lee Atwater?" She and
Mary were looking for a nice writer to feed the story to; they weren't
sure how the religious thing would play if Lee couldn't control his
own spin. Meantime Pat Haas at Scribner's was still looking for a
writer to work on Lee's memoirs, and a magazine story could serve
as a test run. Haas and Brewster met with Roger Stone, then Lee's
agent Julian Bach, and a deal was done. The contract with *Life*
called for two thousand to five thousand words on Lee's "recent
political and personal experiences," due by December 7. Payment

was $7,500 for Lee; Brewster would be working on a day rate for the magazine. It was a fairly standard contract with one clause inserted for Lee: "*Life* affirms its commitment to publish photographs that present you with dignity."

Though Lee had wanted to get his story told, by the time Todd Brewster arrived in November, the tumor had had a huge effect on his personality, creating bouts of depression and confusion. The radiation had also caused damage, killing millions of brain cells, creating swelling. The medications, too — especially the steroids — affected Lee's moods and awareness. Most of Lee's quick wit and intelligence had drained away.

Todd moved quickly, doing preliminary interviews with Sally, Jim Pinkerton, Roger Stone, Michael Newman, Ed Rogers, and others. Getting Lee to open up was difficult, however. Brewster went through the meandering memoirs that Lee had dictated as background information. One name kept coming up: Brooke Vosburgh.

Brooke was still on the RNC payroll. She had traveled to San Diego as part of a site-selection group working on the Republican convention. She spent several days with Mary Matalin touring the city, ending up at Sea World where they sat watching Shamu, drinking beer, laughing and talking about their wacky boss. He was increasingly erratic, said Mary, calling her countless times every day, inevitably asking about Brooke. If Mary said they hadn't talked, Lee didn't believe her; he thought they were conspiring. He also called Brooke regularly, but if she wasn't in, he would leave a message saying, "Don't call back."

One evening Todd Brewster phoned Brooke and said, "I've been given permission to speak to you." Brooke was brought back to help Lee with the interviews. On the morning of November 15, Lee, Brooke, and Todd decided to talk in the limo. Mark drove, with Blake in the front seat, as Lee, Brooke, and Todd — at six foot three inches — scrunched in the back. In sharp contrast to Lee's drawl, Todd was a rapid-fire interviewer with a deep voice reminiscent of a low man in a barbershop quartet. "When you first started facing the cancer," said Brewster, "did you say to yourself, 'I've had tough battles before, and this is like a campaign'?"

"Well, to be honest with you, I really didn't do that," said Lee. "I'd be lying to you if I told you I did."

"Now, Lee, this is an instance that you handled something

medical very campaignlike," said Brooke. "You called in John Bunch and Barry Smith and sat around your conference table and laid out all the facts. You had Mary Matalin there, and I was there. . . ."

"We got any Tylenol?" said Lee. "Yeah, you're right about that, Brooke."

Then Todd asked, "Was there a point early in this, Lee, when you faced a worst-case scenario with the cancer? Did you think what cancer means about life and death?"

"Sure, and I still do. It comes and goes. I try to subjugate it, and I can for long periods of time. But it always comes back. You can't ever stop it, Todd. It always comes back."

"But you must develop in some way. With each new time of thinking about it and talking to people about it, you probably come more to grips with what life and death mean."

"You'd think you would, but you really don't," said Lee.

Lee's short answers weren't giving Brewster the stuff that good interviews are made of. He changed direction. Others had told him about alternative therapies that Lee had tried. "What things did you try that failed, what did you try that succeeded?"

"I got a couple of holistic people," said Lee.

"Tell me about the holistic people."

"Masseurs, mainly."

"What did they do?"

"Give you massages and little lectures."

"Massages and lectures?"

"I don't want to get into that," said Lee.

Brooke tried to pick it up. "Not even the Tibetan?" she asked.

Todd said, "I think we're going to have to get into a lot of that, Lee, to get people to understand what you've been battling."

Lee turned it over to Brooke. "Tell him the Tibetan thing," he said.

And so they beat on, with Todd asking questions, Lee diverting all depth and details to Brooke, with time out for small talk and errands. They stopped at a drugstore to get candy fireballs, which Lee put in both cheeks. They stopped so that Lee could take some medication. Then they headed toward home. Todd asked, "Lee, do you want to talk about what the message would be?"

"The message needs to be me talking about faith, strength,

courage, brotherhood, and all that overcoming this stuff. That's what the message needs to be. Human relationships."

"Overcoming what?"

"Cancer. It's still not over, but nevertheless I had so much courage that I got up there and fought it like a real man."

For five days, Lee drifted in and out of moods and medical distractions, trying to talk with Brooke and Todd as they drove around the city. While Todd dug for the truth, Lee tried to gloss over events. Lee couldn't read, couldn't keep his contact lenses in. Still Todd bought it when Lee said that in the last year he had read *All I Really Need to Know I Learned in Kindergarten, Two Thousand Insults for All Occasions,* and *In Pursuit of Reason: The Life of Thomas Jefferson.* He even said that he loved Jesse Jackson.

Todd grilled Lee about the incoming head of the RNC. Sununu had been looking for someone quietly since June. Charlie Black had turned down the job. William J. Bennett was Sununu's ultimate choice — not Bush's choice, not Lee's. Lee hadn't followed the press speculation and was surprised. Bennett, a one-time liberal Democrat, had been education secretary, then drug czar; though blunt and combative in demeanor, Bennett knew nothing about the nuts and bolts of running campaigns.

Lee spun the writer about Bennett, as though all was well, but inside he was hurt and unsettled. He would become chairman emeritus. Lee went to Bennett to make sure that his position would have clout, not just be honorary. Bennett seemed surprised at Lee's insecurity, that Lee would even suggest that it might be a question. In the reshuffling, Lee was keeping five RNC employees — Brooke, aides Blake Williams, John Schmidt, Steve Allman, and driver Mark Mascarenhas.

• • •

Since Brooke had left the scene, Lee had used private donations to hire his old pal Linda Reed, now Linda O'Meara. After working for Lee during the South Carolina campaign for Reagan in 1980, Linda too had ended up in Washington, as a clerk. During Lee's early years in the White House, when Sally lived in South Carolina, Linda often cooked for Lee and served as a hostess when he wanted to entertain guests at home. Later her daughters would baby-sit for the Atwaters. Her first husband died, and she later

remarried. As Lee moved up, so too did Linda. She had been director of administration for Reagan/Bush '84 — a job that placed her
in charge of Brooke Vosburgh. After the campaign, when Brooke
was about to take her job with Donald Regan, a friend cautioned
Brooke that he was difficult; "After Linda Reed," she replied,
"anyone's a piece of cake."

Linda Reed O'Meara became a key player in the Atwater
household after Brooke had left. She came in part because she had
grown more religious, but mostly because she felt she owed Lee
an enormous debt. Sally had viewed Brooke as a wedge between
Lee and herself. Linda could read the Bible, cook southern-style
meals, oversee volunteers, work from six-thirty in the morning till
nine-thirty at night, go home and tend to a husband and children,
then come back the next day for more.

Lee told Brooke he had talked to Sally, saying he needed
Brooke around him to keep movin'. Sally replied that she was
deeply hurt. If something was happening between them, she
thought one of them should be an adult and say, this is wrong.
That stopped Lee in his manipulative tracks. After all their years
together, he was still trying to put something over on the mother
of his children. There *had* to be something between them, but he
had difficulty saying anything so direct to Sally. Instead he sent her
a telegram reassuring her of his love. Hey, if you can't say it, *send*
it. For Sally, it was enough.

And so Lee and Sally started to rekindle their relationship.
"I know you've got a lot more days for me on earth," Lee told the
Lord. "I don't know how many it is, but every single one I want to
relish and enjoy, show my love to you, show my love to Sally, show
my love to everybody else. . . . Not only do I have a good wife; I've
got a good adviser. Sally always gives me good advice. She doesn't
realize it, but 99 percent of the time I take it. I particularly have
to rely on her judgment now, because I am not objective, and I
don't know when I'll be totally objective again."

With Linda around, Lee had the daily support he needed
without the emotional overload he faced with Brooke. When Lee
described to Brooke how hurt Sally was, she could see that their
future was dying. Brooke told Lee that she accepted that he was
never going to leave Sally. Regardless, her job was to keep movin'
on the *Life* project.

On Wednesday morning, November 21, Linda called

Brooke to say that Lee was too tired to do the interview scheduled for ten o'clock. Brooke said that Lee had plenty of time to rest, and that she wasn't going to take no for an answer. Sally and the kids had driven to South Carolina for Thanksgiving, so Lee was home alone. It was a perfect day for a session with Todd. Brooke drove her little VW to the house, taking in Washington's autumn beauty.

Brooke went up to the bedroom, which was totally black despite the roaring sun outside. The shades were drawn, and Lee was propped up in bed, wide awake, with soft music playing. In the corner sat Linda, reading from a stack of catalogs. Lee seemed happy to see Brooke. "Are you going to meet Todd?" she asked. "You need to get up. You've made this obligation to Todd. You told me you'd take this seriously. . . ."

Linda began to back Brooke out of the room. "You need to be more gentle with him," she said. If Brooke didn't calm down, they would get someone else to work with Lee on the book.

Lee said, "Linda, leave the room. Leave me alone in here with Brooke." Linda left, and Brooke locked the door. Lee asked her to lie down beside him. "You don't have to be mean," he said.

"It's not meanness," said Brooke. "It's wanting you to live up to your potential." Everyone was walking on eggshells, she said. Brooke reminded Lee of Stuart Barnwell, his roomie from the early days who had recently died of cancer. Lee was upset because no one had told him how seriously ill Stuart was. People were afraid to tell him even if it was raining outside because they feared his reaction. "You can also be mean," Brooke said.

"We deserve each other," Lee agreed.

When Brooke tried to get him moving, Lee started to cry. Linda began to pound on the door. "Let me in!" she shouted.

"Leave us alone!" Brooke shouted back.

O'Meara found a key and opened the door. "Get out!"

Brooke went downstairs while Linda calmed Lee. Brooke sat on the front steps of the house, trying to calm down herself. Later Steve Allman brought Lee into the kitchen for lunch. Lee asked Linda to ask Brooke to come in. He told her, "I'm not going to do it. I just can't do it. I'm so sorry."

"That's fine, Lee," said Brooke. "That's up to you. Have a wonderful Thanksgiving. I'll talk to you when you come back."

In Columbia later that day, Lee tried to have dinner with

friends at his parents' new condo, but he was too ill. Harvey was battling cancer as well, and the outlook was not good. Lee returned to his hotel room, equipped with a hospital bed, and tried to rest up for his never-missed visit to the town of Salley for the Chitlin' Strut on the Saturday after Thanksgiving. He watched television as friends dropped by. Saturday came and went. Lee didn't make it to the Strut.

After returning to Washington on Sunday, Lee told Dr. Newman that he couldn't handle the emotional turmoil in his life. He was upset about the Bennett appointment, his father's illness, and Brooke. The pain and drugs intensified everything. Newman called Charlie Black, enumerating Lee's problems. Charlie said that he could handle at least one of them: Brooke. The ultimate political handler was now in the hands of his own handlers.

When Brooke arrived at ten o'clock Monday morning, Charlie was huddling with Sally, Linda, Todd, and Mary Matalin in the living room. Charlie said that Lee needed to be let off the hook for a week, and that Todd Brewster would have to do interviews with others. Brooke was to continue working with Todd, but she would report to Mary hereafter. Brooke stood up. "There's no reason for me to stay here now," she said. "I'll just leave."

Mary followed her out, filled the front passenger seat of the little Jetta with her long frame, and started screaming. "What's going on? What is the story? Sally said you are never to walk in her house again!"

Brooke couldn't figure out whom Mary was mad at — Lee, Charlie, or herself. She told Mary about finding Lee in the dark. "They're letting him die," she said, "and I can't let him go."

"You have to let him go," said Mary. "He wants to die."

• • •

Lee left a message on Brooke's answering machine. He had made a commitment to Sally, he said.

Brooke called Charlie, saying she was being jerked around. "You are," said Charlie, "and if you want to designate me as the jerk, that's fine." Brooke turned off her beeper. In early December she joined the presidential entourage for a ten-day swing through South America.

Pat Haas backed away from the book deal, but the *Life* story was still on. On Wednesday, December 12, Brewster met with Lee and Mary Matalin to go through his fourteen-page draft. He read it slowly and deliberately, making sure it was sinking in. Mary sat on the opposite side of the bed. Looking at Lee struggle to shift from one coherent thought to another, she worried that Brewster was taking advantage of him. Mary didn't think the piece would ever see the light of day; she viewed the writer as just another medication, someone creating busy work for Lee in his final days. After an hour of listening to Brewster's deep baritone, Lee approved the reading. Mary said nothing. Downstairs, Leslie Goodman read the manuscript as they all talked. Then Brewster caught a plane back to New York, where he joined longtime friends at Avery Fisher Hall for a sing-along of Handel's *Messiah*.

William Bennett visited the RNC. Morale was low among those close to Lee, who knew how sick he was, and among the workers in the rest of the building, who by this time knew that the truth had been kept from them. The staff was in disarray, many preparing their résumés or already gone. Operation Outreach was down to one survivor. Bennett saw a lot of work here, and not enough money. Just before Christmas, to the embarrassment of all concerned, he pulled out.

• • •

The realization that this would be Lee's last Christmas made the holidays haunting. With Brooke gone, Sally was around more. She even tried to learn some of the medical procedures. At High Knob one day, on the deck of their home, Lee felt the need to confess every indiscretion. He launched into a litany of all the affairs he could remember in front of Sally and a couple of longtime friends who had dropped by for what they thought would be an easygoing visit. "How can we be so foolish?" Lee wondered aloud. Everyone felt excruciatingly uncomfortable.

At another time Lee, falling apart but still weight conscious, snapped to Sally, "What is this blimpo mode you are in?" Sally had taken to wearing sweatsuits most of the time. She was still trying to lose the weight from her third pregnancy, but mostly the sweats made it easier to care for Lee and the kids. She could sleep anywhere in the house: a couch, the kids' rooms, even in a chair in the family room.

Sally excused most of Lee's lack of consideration as "a man thing" she had endured for years. "I should have been tougher on him," she told a friend. Or perhaps on herself. Sally had married Lee without talking about Joe. If Lee insisted that his wife not enter that part of his life, how much was he going to let her into the rest? "If I was the one with a brain tumor, I'm not so sure Lee would have been there for me," Sally told Toddy one evening.

Toddy's wry response: "Sally, he would have *hired* somebody."

Sally's religion gave her a stronger sense of acceptance. She would never have fought death like Lee had; she would put herself in God's hands and know she was safe. God answers all our prayers, but sometimes the answer is just plain no, so she believed. Sally couldn't talk with Lee about this, though. Once when she tried to ask him how he wanted her to raise the kids, if something should happen, he shooed her away. Lee had spent all of his life in the public eye, hating to lose, and he was still fighting to win, to stay alive. He was losing everything. Sally had spent her life in Lee's shadow; now she was ready to see, before he did, that shadow was fading.

Lee and Sally went to the White House for one of the multiple Christmas parties the Bushes had for staff. At home Linda arranged a series of holiday potlucks and open-house gatherings. With Sally T on his lap, Lee sat in his wheelchair near the Christmas tree, teary-eyed, telling old political pals that he loved them. "This is what life is all about," he said to Gail Jones, his favorite nurse, whom he had hired away from GW. "Christ, Gail, all the steroids have turned me into a sappy old woman!"

A brain scan after Christmas indicated that Lee's tumor was 20 percent larger, mostly owing to necrosis, but there appeared to be live growth at the rim, a grim indicator. His doctors also suspected another tumor. Lee's headaches grew worse, as did his mental status. Surgery to remove a large mass of dead tissue near the tumor, to prevent the swelling from pushing the brain stem down into the vertebrae, was set for Monday, January 14. Two days before entering the hospital, Lee received word that "Red, Hot & Blue," the album track that he wrote and performed with B. B. King, had been nominated for a Grammy: best contemporary blues recording of 1990.

In the hospital, Lee bantered with Newman. "Doc, you ain't doing shit for me."

"Jeez, Lee, I've been bustin' my ass," said Newman. "I think I've been doing a *hell* of a job. What do you have in mind?"

They stared at each other for a moment, neither man blinking.

"How 'bout tradin' places?" Lee said softly.

In the recovery room after the surgery, Lee called out, "Joe, come home! Joe! Joe!"

Matalin and Goodman spun the press, which duly reported that there was "no active tumor tissue in the mass that was removed, and the procedure was deemed 'very successful' by surgeon Edward Laws." The next day, however, *Life* magazine hit the newsstands featuring "Lee Atwater's Last Campaign." The subhead explained, "Battling an inoperable brain tumor, the bad boy of Republican politics discovers the power of love — and a dream for America." The story was a shocker, with text and photos that were shots heard 'round the political world.

Photographer Lynn Johnson's pictures told more than the text. Alongside file photos that showed Lee jogging and playing the guitar, the new shots showed Lee bloated and in a wheelchair. Clearly he was on drugs and in pain. Was it right to quote someone in Atwater's condition, whether he agreed to it or not?

Atwater's "deathbed confession" remains controversial to this day. Many interpreted it as a renunciation of the decade he had helped make possible. "Long before I was struck with cancer, I felt something stirring in American society," he said. "It was a sense among the people of the country — Republicans and Democrats alike — that something was missing from their lives, something crucial. I was trying to position the Republican Party to take advantage of it. But I wasn't exactly sure what 'it' was. My illness helped me to see that what was missing in society is what was missing in me: a little heart, a lot of brotherhood."

For many readers, there was a little credibility problem here. He's been a bastard all his professional life, said his critics, and now we're supposed to believe him when he says he really loves us? Which was the real Atwater? Was it the old version, which no longer worked because he had fallen mortally wounded on the battlefield, or the new, some inner self that had finally struggled to the surface?

Make no mistake about it: Lee still believed in the power of negative campaigning. "I prefer to call [it] comparative campaigning," he said. "Negative makes it sound as if you're beating up on the guy for no reason, which is different from choosing symbolic platforms, like the Pledge of Allegiance or the furlough program in Massachusetts, upon which to make compelling comparisons between candidates." No, Lee wasn't apologizing for that. "In 1988, fighting Dukakis, I said that I 'would strip the bark off the little bastard' and 'make Willie Horton his running mate.' I am sorry for both statements: the first for its naked cruelty, the second because it makes me sound racist, which I am not. . . . Mostly I am sorry for the way I thought of other people. Like a good general, I had treated everyone who wasn't with me as against me."

Was that an apology? For a mere $7,500 Lee had decided to plead his case in the court of public opinion. The outcome to this day is a hung jury. For one thing, Lee was apologizing to Dukakis for what he had said — but disowning how others had taken it. He apologized for the "naked cruelty" of his statement about Dukakis, and for *sounding* — not acting — racist in his use of Willie Horton. While conceding that he felt sad that he had brought pain to anyone, he only acted as a "good general" must in order to win the war. With Lee Atwater, it's better to think of his apology as emotional damage control. Hey, let's get on with life, he seemed to say in *Life*, even as he was getting on with death. In most cases, a grudge is worse than the slight that gave rise to it. Morally, Lee was taking what he always sought in the political battlefield: the high ground.

The media picked up the story and ran with it, erasing the subtlety of what Lee said in the interviews. The regrets of a dying man are delicate — easily turned with post-event spin. Lee's new "gentler, kinder" persona, linked with his apology to Turnipseed (which Turnipseed had released to *Harper's*) and his regrets about his treatment of Dukakis, represented a bigger act than his enemies were ready for. Instead of accepting the regrets of a dying man, they used his apologies as a rationale for continuing their grudges — as though to say, "See, we were right all along." At that point Lee was deteriorating so rapidly, he had neither time nor strength nor inclination to defend himself against the spin of his political enemies.

Lee resigned from the RNC, which paid tribute to its fallen leader at the semiannual meeting in late January. A videotape introduced by Charlie Black chronicled Lee's career. It was a montage of happier, healthier days — Lee Atwater as everyone wanted to remember him. Afterward the committee granted Lee the title of general chairman and confirmed Bush's new choice of Agriculture Secretary Clayton Yeutter as party chairman. Yeutter had a strong sense of loyalty, certainly, but the closest thing to political involvement in his résumé was his experience heading Farmers for Nixon in 1972.

• • •

The pain continued, "worse than bone cancer," said Newman. Lee regulated his own dosage of morphine with a red button on the IV, the accumulated effects of which were streaks of delirium and paranoia. He thought that everybody was out to kill him. Lee insisted that visitors, including longtime staffers, be frisked. As extra security, he asked one of his aides to "pack heat": a short-barreled Smith & Wesson .357 magnum with hollow-point bullets.

A psychiatrist who visited Lee on January 23 noted "marked cognitive deficits." Lee told him that "in 1943 Curley of the Three Stooges had farted in the very same bed that he was now occupying." Lee also expressed fear that the Sterling Club, one of the Flora High rivals, was trying to poison him. He wouldn't eat unless Linda O'Meara cooked the food and tasted it in front of him.

On the Thursday morning of January 31, Lee summoned what strength remained in his body and attended the National Prayer Breakfast, led by Doug Coe. His speech for this final public appearance was short: "I love Christ!"

He returned to the hospital, where a psychiatrist noted that Lee had no idea of the month or year, but he knew he was at GW. "He then perseverated on the theme of having committed some sins in the past of a sexual nature and for which he is being punished, and repeatedly asked me for help in getting rid of these sins." One week later, psychiatric notes indicate that Lee knew Bush was president, but could not recall who had preceded him.

One afternoon Mary Matalin biked over to the hospital where Lee was talking with Doug Coe. She watched him try to focus on the conversation, then caught his eye. For the first time she saw a forlorn look that said it was over. Mary backed out the door, walked down the hall, and leaned against the wall. She slid to the floor and melted in a pool of tears.

The pictures in *Life* scared nearly all but the faithful visitors away. Linda put out an appeal for help, for covered dishes, for volunteers to write thank-you notes. "Lee got tons of people jobs, and you would have thought that tons of people out there would have offered to help," she said. Some members of the South Carolina crowd whom Lee had been so kind to in the early days at the White House came through. But the bureaucrats, the legions in Atwater's Army, were nowhere to be seen. "Lee couldn't do anything for people anymore," said Linda. "It was Washington politics at its purest. This is the meanest town in America."

The RNC sent someone to inventory the computer, the fax, the phones that used to link Lee with some of the most powerful people in the world. Linda suggested that the items be given to Sally as a gift. No, they would have to be returned.

At three o'clock one morning in late February, Lee could not remember Brooke's number or last name, so he called the White House and asked for help. There an operator figured out who Brooke was and how to find her. A few days earlier, Brooke had asked Newman if she could "just go into his room at midnight and sit there for a while. No one would ever have to know." Lee told Newman no, he had promised Sally that he would never see or talk with Brooke again. Now, at three A.M., Lee was on the phone apologizing for not seeing her. He felt torn and guilty, and he wanted Brooke to know that he would always love her.

Brooke was actually being spared. The last time she had seen Lee, he was gravely ill, but he was still Lee. Now he could only move his right hand. For Brooke, Lee's call was a painful but comforting closure, like sun coming through a cloudy day along the Tow Path.

Lee Atwater had once told a writer that he wouldn't worry about the future until he turned forty. On February 27, President George Bush met with senior advisers in the Oval Office and accepted the advice of Chairman of the Joint Chiefs of Staff Colin Powell to halt the Persian Gulf War. That same day a small display ad appeared in the *State* featuring a picture of Lee at age five atop a pony. "Lordy, Lordy," was the caption, "Look Who's Forty!" Lee was at home worrying about his future in a wheelchair, his face swollen from steroids, his body useless and in pain.

"It was a campaign he couldn't have fought harder, and couldn't have won," said Sally. "Lee always said that forty was going to be the different year. And it was."

Mary Matalin called Lee to wish him happy birthday. They

talked politics, of course. Lee said that Bush and Sununu were going to face a bad economy in '92 and wouldn't know how to handle it. And for Mary he offered one bit of advice: "Quit dating Democrats."

On March 5 Lee entered GW at 3:18 P.M. — exactly one year after his initial seizure, one year after Dr. Burton Lee had said he had a year to live. Dr. Charles Rogers was on the case again. Scans showed that the tumor had spread along his spinal cord. During the past year, Lee had spent 160 days in the hospital, and scores of additional days in physical therapy or in labs for scans, tests, and medication. The cure was worse than the cancer. "If this is a test, as I thought riding along in the ambulance that long-ago March day," Lee had told Todd Brewster, "then I'm not sure if you pass it by displaying the determination to live or the courage to die."

One week after being admitted, Lee was near death. The right leg stopped twitching, then the foot, finally the toes. His neck and chest were flecked with the purple marks of radiation. He coughed and gurgled, unable to clear the phlegm in his throat. A catheter carried fluids from his body. No sensations. No control. Still the blue eyes retained their piercing quality. Sitting up in the hospital bed, he looked at Newman with a mixture of "bewilderment and understanding," the doctor would record in his notes. "Like some animal caught in a net exhausted but not subdued, struggling to affect events." He wanted watermelon juice, not easy to find in March. His juice couldn't come from a blender, either. Had to be squeezed by hand.

"Mama," Lee's voice said on the phone. "I don't think I'll ever see you again. Can you come up here?"

Toddy was tending to Harvey in Columbia. "I'll be up there in two hours," she said. In Washington, she took a motel room, but Lee insisted she sleep in his hospital room.

"I want to die," he told Toddy. "Just get a gun and shoot me, Mama. You're the only person who can do it."

"I'm the only person who can *not* do it, Lee," she replied. "I gave you life. I surely can't take it away from you."

Throughout his life Lee was sustained by the single-minded love of Toddy, but she also represented another side of the dilemma that drove him. Toddy was in the room when Joe pulled the boiling oil on himself; she was the link to the trauma that engulfed Lee. Lee had never put himself through the torturous exercise of figuring out how Joe's death affected his life. He chose to submerge it. In that sense, he was very much like his mother, an heir to a crusty dysfunctionalism that might be called southern gothic. Joe's death had bonded a mother who felt it was her fault to a son who couldn't forgive himself for surviving.

"Lee, I spent all of your life making you feel guilty," said Toddy.

"Mama," said Lee, "what if you *hadn't*?" If not for her, he probably would have done even *worse* things.

Toddy wished she could turn back time. She and Harvey should have talked about Joe to Lee, but they just *couldn't*. Now she was feeling guilty for every little thing, even denying Lee that extra five dollars on the class trip to Washington.

"Mama, after Joe died, I remember you read a lot and tried to find meaning to all of that," said Lee. "Did you ever find it?"

"No, I didn't," she replied. "But I made up my mind about my own religious convictions, and I have always tried to live by the golden rule. That runs through all religion in one way or another. If you do that, you can't go wrong."

"Mama, what was the *real* impact of Joe's death on me?" Lee asked.

Toddy couldn't answer. Lee had done so much, so quickly, to her it seemed as if he had been living for the two of them.

"Mama, wasn't Joe lucky?" Lee whispered. "Wasn't Joe lucky?"

In Room 2136 at GW on Thursday, March 28, Lee Atwater struggled to remain conscious. Ed Rogers held Lee's hand and shouted; Lee squeezed back. Steve Allman thumb-wrestled one final round with Lee's right hand. Nancy and Ronald Reagan came by for a visit. Jim Baker came. The secretary of state's first wife had died of cancer, and he had been through the same vigil with a cot in the room. Baker could see that Lee's eyes were becoming fixed. The infamous Atwater stare now beheld death.

That night Lee had a seizure. His temperature shot up. A nurse put a cold sheet beneath him. "This bed is cold as kraut!" said Lee. Something got Sally up at five-thirty, and she went back to Lee's bed, where Toddy was on vigil. Sally thought that she wouldn't want to be in the room when her husband took his last breath, but a new strength had displaced that fear. Hot with fever, Lee cried out, asking her to take the blanket off. Even on oxygen, his breathing was labored. Gradually, softly it eased off. Sally and Toddy stood beside the bed as Lee took his last breath at 6:12. A nurse kept his stethoscope on Lee's chest as the runner's heart beat on for twelve more minutes. Then the race was over. Sally and Toddy kissed him, and as a gentle rain began to fall on the city, Lee Atwater was pronounced dead at 6:24 A.M. on Friday, March 29, at the age of forty years, one month, and three days.

Sally walked down the hallway to where a little office had been set up. Linda was there, and they embraced. Linda had a list of people she was going to call. "We gotta do one thing first," said Sally, "because Lee would have wanted it. You gotta call Lee Bandy and give him the scoop."

Many of the obits got it wrong, quoting from the *Life* piece, making Lee seem rueful about being such a hard-nosed campaigner. Mike Dukakis helped the spin along, expressing his condolences for the family, then adding, "At least he had the decency to apologize." News segments on ABC and NBC included images from the Willie Horton ad that Atwater *didn't* create as backdrops to their commentary. Lee was being spun in his grave. At the funeral in Columbia, one of Lee's political beneficiaries, Dan Quayle, spun back, wryly suggesting in the glow of the Republican-led victory over Iraq that "today the world spins in new directions — and Lee Atwater played a vital part in the making of all that history." At the Democratic National Committee, Ron Brown ordered that the flag be flown at half-mast.

• • •

Can someone who had so many flaws be considered great in the final analysis? The answer to that is another question: Is there any *other* kind of great man? Lee's life had been forged in reaction to a deeply painful experience as a child, one that led him to impressive achievements — often at others' expense. Had he wronged so many others because he felt so deeply wronged himself?

Lee often used the word *existential* to explain himself. "This is sort of an existential situation," he liked to say when he called for action. For Lee, *existential* meant finding your own meaning in a random, godless universe that was not meant to be particularly just or fair or kind — or anything. "Here we are," Lee said, "surrounded by idiots on all sides. This is all bullshit around us. This is *us*. People understand what has to happen." Any meaning to be found comes from you and what you *do*. "Yes, I'm a doer," he would say. "I'm here to make a difference." And he did.

Lee Atwater was the first of an already disappearing breed, still at the top of his game when he died. Only when you look at the Republican Party during his lifetime do you realize how much of his history is woven into the history of the party. His imitators, not having picked up on the traits key to his success, often come off as desperate and methodical. They have depersonalized the art of political handling. It was the human aspect of politics that always interested Lee Atwater. That, combined with wit, intelligence, and a love for the game, made him the best political campaign manager who ever lived. Lee, master of the managed persona, tried to make himself bigger than life, bigger than the lowly job many of his candidates and colleagues thought he held. And he succeeded: Lee Atwater's most memorable creation was Lee Atwater.

In the confusion that followed his death, someone took Lee's beloved Stratocaster from the basement in his home. It has not been seen since.

ATWATER
H. LEE
1951 — 1991
TEACHER, LEADER, HUSBAND
FATHER, SON
I DO NOT CHOOSE TO BE A COMMON MAN.
IT IS MY RIGHT TO BE UNCOMMON.
I PREFER THE CHALLENGES
OF LIFE TO GUARANTEED SECURITY,
THE THRILL OF FULFILLMENT TO THE
STATE CALM OF UTOPIA.
I WILL NEVER COWER BEFORE ANY MASTER,
SAVE MY GOD.
REPUBLICAN CREED

Under the Republican Creed: At the end of his life's campaign, more than anything else Lee Atwater considered himself a teacher.

Sources and Acknowledgments

Among those who provided me with interviews were Warren
Abernathy, Robert Adams, Larry Addison, Wick Allison, Steve
Allman, Anne Atwater, Sally Atwater, Toddy Atwater, Lee Bandy,
Jay Banning, Haley Barbour, Scott Berkowitz, Robert J. Bidinotto,
Charles Black, Susan Bolotin, Todd Brewster, David Broder,
Floyd Brown, John Buckley, Reid Buckley, Rick Burt, President
George Bush, Governor Carroll Campbell, Andrew Card, Bill
Carrick, Debbie Carson, Dick Cheney, Marvin Chernoff, Doug
Coe, Chuck Conconi, B. Jay Cooper, John Courson, Rhonda
Culpepper, Norm Cummings, Mike Curb, Allison Dalton, Jim
Davis, Michele Davis, Michael Deaver, Ken DeCell, Wade Delk,
Harry Dent, Ann Devroy, Howard Dickman, Frank Donatelli,
Governor Michael Dukakis, Theo Dunbar, Bill Edens, Thomas
Edsall, Mickey Edwards, Henry Eichel, John Ellis, John
Ellsworth, Tucker Eskew, Susan Estrich, Benny Ferrell, Don
Fierce, Howard Fineman, Margaret Fiore, Eugene Gatlin, Ken
Gilmore, Ben Ginsberg, Vic Gold, Mark Goodin, Leslie Good-
man, Rudi Gresham, Jack Grochmal, Anne Groer, Linda Catoe
Guell, Eddie Gunn, Pat Haas, Joyce Hearn, Craig Helsing, Chris
Henick, Dr. Alan D. Hirschfeld, Mickey Page Hogarth, Rick
Hohlt, Margaret Holliman, Chuck Jackson, Bette Jamison, Lynn
Johnson, Gail Jones, Ron Kaufman, David Keene, Geoff Kelly,
Anna Belle Kibler, Larry King, Eric Knudson, Dr. Paul Kornblith,
Warren Kraft, William Kreml, Dr. Edward Laws, Gary Maloney,
Mark Mascarenhas, Mary Matalin, Jane McCabe, Jim McCabe,
Larry McCarthy, Pam McQuay, Debbie Messick, Wendell Moore,

Dr. Michael Newman, Lyn Nofziger, Daniel Okrent, Linda
Reed O'Meara, Steve Pastorkovich, Rick Peterson, Bill Phillips,
James Pinkerton, Henry Price, Richard Quinn, Charles Ravenel,
David Remnick, James Robertson, Dr. Charles Rogers, Ed Rogers,
Sig Rogich, Ed Rollins, Lois Romano, Larry Sabato, John Sasso,
John Schmidt, Doug Seigler, Jim Shahin, William Shand III,
Bob Shapero, Rick Shelby, David Shipley, Craig Shirley, Rick
Silver, Kelly Sinclair, Scott Sinkler, Betty Sisk, Ray Sisk, Joe
Sligh, Dr. Barry Smith, Dale Smoak, Randy Snow, Stu Spencer,
Don Sprouse, Mark Stencel, Stuart Stevens, T. E. Stivers, Roger
Stone, Ann Stone, Charles Strickland, Jan Collins Stucker, Paul
Sullivan, Governor John Sununu, Paul Taylor, Sam Tenenbaum,
Bob Thompson, Senator Strom Thurmond, Don Todd, Warren
Tompkins, Susan Trout, Beegie Truesdale, Ned Tupper, Tom
Turnipseed, Margaret Tutwiler, Craig Unger, Mike Ussery, Fred
Vail, Brooke Vosburgh, Barbara Walsh, Dan Warner, Dolly Wells,
General William Westmoreland, Linda White, Jim E. White-
head, Ralph Whitworth, Blake Williams, Rich Williamson, Joe
Wilson, David Yon, and Michael Zoovas.

While most of the information in this book was derived from
interviews, I did obtain material from print sources, including the
following:

Chapter 1, Defining Events: "I think I learned pretty early that in
the end it's only you," Lee told journalist David Remnick for "Why
Is Lee Atwater So Hungry?", *Esquire*, December 1986. All subsequent references to Lee's conversations with Remnick, whom I
interviewed, are related to this pivotal magazine profile of Lee on
the ascendancy. Facts about Lee's youth and genealogy are based
upon interviews, school yearbooks, and *Atwater History & Genealogy*, Francis Atwater, 4 vols. 1901–1927. Quotes are also taken
from Lee's childhood scrapbook, which he titled "The Public Life
of Lee Atwater (Through Age Twenty)." Quotes from Lee's correspondence are taken from his letters written to his mother from
Fork Union. Excerpts from the poetry of Steve Sisk are taken from
Come on Down: Writings by Steve Sisk (Columbia, S.C.: The State
Printing Company, 1970).

Chapter 2, Life of the Party: In this chapter and elsewhere I have
quoted from journalist Jan Collins Stucker's "What Lee Atwater

Knows About Winning," *Southern Magazine*, April 1989. The
Karl Rove episode is chronicled by John Saar, "GOP Probes Official as Teacher of 'Tricks.' " *Washington Post*, August 10, 1973.
Some details of Lee's first date with Sally on George Bush's boat
are taken from William Greider's interview with Lee, "The Power
of Negative Thinking," *Rolling Stone*, January 12, 1989. One
source for my commentary on the changing nature of the South
is the essay by Roy Blount, Jr., "Bad Guys and Good Ol' Boys:
The Changing Face of Dixie Virility," *Men's Journal*, December
1994–January 1995.

Chapter 3, The Education of a Consultant: Lee chronicles
the Carroll Campbell campaign of 1976 in the sixty-two-page work
project he submitted in partial fulfillment of the requirements
for the master's degree in mass communication in the College
of Journalism, University of South Carolina, May 1977: Harvey
L. Atwater, *A Campaign: The 1976 State Senate Campaign of
Carroll A. Campbell, Jr.* Information on the Finkelstein poll used
in the '78 campaign is taken from Phil Gailey, "Bigotry Issue in
Carolina Campaign," *New York Times*, September 24, 1986. Tom
Turnipseed's early work with the Wallace presidential campaign is
described in Stephen Lesher's *George Wallace: American Populist*
(Reading, Mass.: Addison-Wesley, 1994).

Chapter 4, Lee Atwater's Office, Can You Hold?: Peggy
Noonan is quoted from her book about the Reagan years, *What I
Saw at the Revolution: Political Life in the Reagan Era* (New York:
Random House, 1990).

Chapter 5, The Permanent Campaign: Resources include
The Power Game: How Washington Works, by Hedrick Smith (New
York: Random House, 1988); Henry Eason, "A Southerner in
Reagan's Court," *Atlanta Weekly Sunday Magazine*, Atlanta Con-
stitution, September 13, 1981; Rusty Lang, "Bush Might Cam-
paign for State GOP, White House Aide Says," and "Air Tragedy
Came Close," *Tulsa World*, January 17, 1982; and Lou Can-
non's canonization of Ed Rollins, "President's Chief Political Aide
Emerges as a Tough 'Enforcer,' " *Washington Post*, April 21, 1982.

Chapter 6, The Odd Coupling: Some background information on the new breed of political consultant is taken from *The
New Kingmakers*, by David Chagall (New York: Harcourt Brace

Jovanovich, 1981). The "Thirteen Keys to the Presidency" that influenced Lee can be found in Allan J. Lichtman, "How to Bet in '84: The Only Presidential Election Guide You'll Ever Need," *The Washingtonian*, April 1982. This was published in book form: Allan J. Lichtman and Ken DeCell, *The 13 Keys to the Presidency* (Lanham, Md.: Madison Books, 1990). Some information about the Camp David meeting is from Ann Grimes, *Running Mates: The Making of a First Lady*, (New York: William Morrow, 1990). Quotes from "Memorandum to the Vice President" are taken from the memo to George Bush dated December 19, 1984. Lee's full text on the baby-boom phenomenon can be found in *Left, Right & Babyboom: America's New Politics*, edited by David Boaz (Washington, D.C.: Cato Institute Publications, 1986). Since Lee's death, the number of journalists permanently stationed in Washington has increased to 17,000; for a fuller discussion of the care and spinning of the "national press," see John Taylor, "Take Journalism," *New York* magazine, April 26, 1993. Quotes regarding Clark Clifford are taken from Lee Atwater's incomplete doctoral thesis, *The Campaign to Re-Elect the President, 1981–84*, draft dated December 1, 1984. And for readers who have forgotten the solution to the "nine-dot" challenge, here it is:

Chapter 7, The Hazards of Duke: Quotes attributed to Dayton Duncan in this and subsequent chapters are from his essay "The Miscovered Campaign," *Boston Globe Magazine*, June 11, 1989. Quotes from Pug Ravenel's letter to the Dukakis campaign are taken from *All by Myself*, by Tom Oliphant and Christine Black (Chester, Conn.: Globe Pequot Press, 1989). Robert J. Bidinotto's often-referenced "Getting Away with Murder" is from the July 1988 issue of *Reader's Digest*. Quotes from campaign coverage are taken from three articles in the *Gannett Center Journal*, Fall 1988: Sam Donaldson's "On the Dukakis Campaign Trail: A Journal of the Campaign from Labor Day to Election Day"; David Hoffman's "On the Bush Campaign Trail"; and Larry McCarthy's

"The Selling of the President: An Interview with Roger Ailes." Lee's spin quote to Marilyn Rauber is taken from "Atwater, Carrick Flying High after New Hampshire Primary," *Greenville News*, February 21, 1988.

Chapter 8, The Tar Baby: Quotes from the debate at Harvard's Kennedy School are taken from *Campaign for President: The Managers Look at '88*, ed. David R. Runkel (Westport, Conn.: Auburn House Publications, 1989). Lee told Eric Alterman, "As a white southerner, I have always known I had to go the extra mile to avoid being tagged a racist by liberal northerners," in "G.O.P. Chairman Lee Atwater: Playing Hardball," *New York Times Magazine*, April 30, 1989. The origins of the campaign against Atwater at Howard University are taken from Steve Piacente, "Atwater Rocks National Politics," *Sunday Post-Courier* (Charleston, S.C.), March 19, 1989. Quotes from correspondence between the Bush campaign and NSPAC are taken from three complaints on file at the Federal Election Commission, 999 E. Street N.W., Washington, DC: MUR (Matters Under Review) #2638 (June 28, 1988) complainant George Bush for President Committee Inc., respondent NSPAC, 520 pages; MUR #3069 (May 25, 1990) complainant Ohio Democratic Party, respondent NSPAC, 742 pages; MUR #3556 (July 14, 1992), complainant Bush/Quayle Primary Committee Inc., respondents NSPAC and Floyd Brown, 171 pages. Lance Morrow is quoted from his essay "The Cure for Racism," *Time*, December 5, 1994. Quotes regarding the outcome of the '88 election are from Allan J. Lichtman and Ken DeCell, *The 13 Keys to the Presidency* (Lanham, Md.: Madison Books, 1990).

Chapter 9, Top of the World: Lee's observation to Carl Cannon is taken from "The People's Republican," *Washington Dossier*, June 1989. Lee's comments at Princeton are taken from Paul Taylor's *See How They Run: Electing the President in an Age of Mediaocracy* (New York: Alfred A. Knopf, 1990).

Chapter 10, The Spoils of War: The infamous photo of Lee Atwater with his pants down (used as the image for the cover of this book) was taken by Lou Salvatori for an *Esquire* photo feature story called "One Leg at a Time!" June 1989 issue. Quotes from the recording session at Treasure Island Recorders, *Red Hot & Blue* session tapes, September 6, 16, 17; October 20, 21, 28,

1989, courtesy Mike Curb of Curb Records, with special thanks to coproducer David Shipley. The *Spy* magazine episode is based upon my interviews with witnesses, as well as quotes from Joe Queenan's *Imperial Caddy: The Rise of Dan Quayle in America and the Decline and Fall of Practically Everything Else* (New York: Hyperion Books, 1992). Quotes from Lee's interview with Connie Chung, his last major interview before the brain seizure, are taken from a transcript of Lee's private audiotape of the interview; the broadcast version was considerably shorter.

Chapter 11, The Final Campaign: All quotes are from interviews or from medical records at George Washington University Hospital. Quotes from Lee's conversation with Todd Brewster are taken from Lee's private audiotape of their meetings. "Lee Atwater's Last Campaign," by Lee Atwater with Todd Brewster, appeared in the February 1991 issue of *Life* magazine. My special thanks to journalist Jim Shahin for giving me access to interviews he conducted with members of Lee's family and entourage after the funeral in Columbia, April 1991.

Other books that provided a backdrop to research on Lee and his campaigns include

Cramer, Richard Ben. *What It Takes: The Way to the White House*. New York: Random House, 1992.

Edsall, Thomas Byrne, and Mary D. Edsall. *Chain Reaction: The Impact of Race, Rights, and Taxes on American Politics*. New York: W.W. Norton & Co., 1991.

Germond, Jack W., and Jules Witcover. *Wake Us When It's Over*. New York: Macmillan, 1985.

Germond, Jack, and Jules Witcover. *Whose Broad Stripes and Bright Stars?: The Trivial Pursuit of the Presidency, 1988*. New York: Warner Books, 1989.

Goldman, Peter, and Tom Mathews. *The Quest for the Presidency 1988*. New York: Simon & Schuster, 1989.

Hagstrom, Jerry. *Beyond Reagan: The New Landscape of American Politics*. New York: W.W. Norton, 1988.

Matalin, Mary, and James Carville. *All's Fair: Love, War and Running for President*. New York: Random House, 1994.

Rollins, Ed. *Bare Knuckles and Back Rooms: My Life in American Politics*. New York: Broadway Books, 1996.

Sabato, Larry J. *Feeding Frenzy: How Attack Journalism Has Transformed American Politics.* New York: The Free Press, 1991.

• • •

I am indebted to the following people and institutions for providing answers, opening doors and easing the way for my research:

Larry Beinhart, Sidney Blumenthal, Lilia F. Brady, Pilar Carpenter, John Christie, Caroline Critchfield, Douglas Dinsmoore, Maureen Dowd, Katherine Dudley Hoehn, Sandra M. Hughes, Milo Moran, James Morgan, Tricia Moseley, David Moniz, Peter Guralnick, Jack Limpert, David McClintick, Holly Richardson, Jim Ritz, Ric Ross, Boots Thompson, Linton Weeks, and Marjorie Williams.

My thanks to Jane D'Alessandro of the Melrose Public Library for assisting with numerous inquiries; to Kate Broughton for listening to me and to Lee's music, and for helping to craft the proposal (complete with audio cassette); to Christopher Hartman for chasing down numerous details; to James DeButts for research assistance in South Carolina; to the Health Information Management Department at George Washington University Hospital for retrieving records on their way to microfilm; to Lou Salvatori for a photographic defining event; to Lynn Johnson for insightful images of the final campaign; to Greg Paul, my longtime partner in the publishing wars, for sideline support these past three years; to Leon Taylor for editorial assistance in the early rounds; to Linda Parent Spikol for insight at the final bell; to Nadine Krasnow for proofing the pages; and to Alyce Blaisell for loving patience all the way.

Finally, this book would not have been possible without the support, drive, and insistence of my agent Helen Rees; the fortitude of editorial director Bill Patrick at Addison-Wesley; the careful copy editing of Maggie Carr; the gentle steering of production editor Beth Burleigh Fuller; the wise counsel of Bob Dancy; and the meticulous just-keep-movin' style of my editor John Bell.

John Brady
Boston
October 1996

Index

Readers can obtain a complete index to *Bad Boy* in the following ways:

- On the World Wide Web at

`http://www.awl.com/gb/authors/brady/badboy.html`

- By electronic mail. Send a message to:

`badboy@aw.com`

In the message's subject line, type the following:

`send index`

Within a day the index will be transmitted to the electronic mailbox from which you sent that message.

- By regular mail. Please send a self-addressed, stamped, business-size envelope to the following address:

Bad Boy Index
General Books Editorial Department
Addison Wesley Longman
One Jacob Way
Reading, MA 01867-3999

About the Author

John Brady is a journalist and consultant to magazine publishers, having served as editor of *Boston* and *Writer's Digest* magazines and founding editor of *The Artist's Magazine*. His previous books include *The Craft of Interviewing*, which has become a standard primer for journalists, and *The Craft of the Screenwriter*. A registered independent from Massachusetts, he is currently teaching as the Hearst Visiting Professor at the University of Missouri School of Journalism.